City & Guilds

NVQ/SVQ
Technical Certificate

Professional Cookery

Level 2

2nd edition

Series Editor: **Pam Rabone**

Holly Bamunuge • Trevor Eeles • Mark Furr
Shyam Patiar • Dereick Rushton

Heinemann

Part of Pearson

Heinemann Educational Publishers
Halley Court, Jordan Hill, Oxford OX2 8EJ
Part of Harcourt Education Limited

Heinemann is the registered trademark of Harcourt Education Limited

Heinemann is an imprint of Pearson Education Limited, a company incorporated in England and Wales, having its registered office at
Edinburgh Gate, Harlow, Essex, CM20 2JE. Registered company number: 872828

First edition © Harcourt Education Ltd 2006
Additional material © Pearson Education Limited 2010

First published 2006; this edition 2010

12 11 10
10 9 8 7 6 5 4 3 2 1

British Library Cataloguing in Publication Data is available
from the British Library on request.

ISBN: 978 0 435027 16 2

Edited by Eleanor Barber, Sue Harmes, Maggie Rumble
Designed by Kamae Design
New edition typeset by Phoenix Photosetting
Illustrated by Asa Andersson, Ron Dixon, Steiner Lund, Mark Turner and Kamae Design
Original illustrations © Harcourt Education Limited, 2006
Cover design by Georgia Styring
Printed in Italy by Rotolito
Cover photo: © City & Guilds
Picture research by Emma Baddeley, Kay Altweg and Caitlin Swain
Original photographs by Jules Selmes and Adam Giles

Acknowledgements

The publisher would like to thank Phil Dobson, Leighton Anderson, Adam Pickett, Richard Brocklesby, Rod Burton, Colin Cooper, David
Hunter, Ian Monger, Tony Perry and Anthony Wright of the Birmingham College of Food, Tourism and Creative Studies, Iain Baillie, Gerry
Shurman, Rob Zahra and Ben Ross of South Downs College; and Andreas Hein of Farnborough College, and Stanley Bamunuge for their
invaluable help.

Thanks are also due to Marcus Wareing for providing the Foreword and 'Marcus says' tips; and Judi Strain for the Functional Skills mapping.

The authors and publishers would like to thank the following individuals and organisations for permission to reproduce photographs:
p.40: WoodyStock/Alamy; pp.131, 133, 134, 135 top, 136–41, 147, 150, 179r–87, 189–92, 216, 217, 221–4, 226, 230, 242–52,
269–73, 276, 324–6, 331–3, 338 lower, 356, 358, 366–8, 388, 392, 393, 395–7, 426, 445: Harcourt/Jules Selmes; pp.151, 156, 160,
188, 207, 209, 210, 233, 238, 262, 301, 311, 315, 319, 328, 337, 374, 375, 378, 380, 390, 398, 400, 411, 412, 415, 417, 419, 425,
431, 432, 433, 438, 447, 448, 463, 466: Shutterstock; p.135 lower: G. Tomsich/SPL; pp.152, 164: Roddy Paine/foodanddrinkphotos.
com; p.153: Graham Kirk/Anthony Blake Photo Library; pp.163, 236: Joff Lee/Anthony Blake Photo Library; pp.172–3, 176, 178: Meat
and Livestock Marketing Services; p.198: Martin Brigdale/Anthony Blake Photo Library; pp.204, 436: Tim Hill/Anthony Blake Photo Library;
pp.206; 458: Sian Irvine/Anthony Blake Photo Library; p.229: Hilary Moore/Anthony Blake Photo Library; pp.258, 278, 289, 464: Food
Features; pp.275, 279: Lori Alden; p.299: Profimedia.CZ s.r.o./Alamy; p.343: Philip Wilkins/Anthony Blake Photo Library; pp.344, 408:
foodfolio/Alamy; p.424 left: Maximilian Stock Ltd/Anthony Blake Photo Library; p.424 right: Studio Adna/Anthony Blake Photo Library;
p.437: David Marsden/Anthony Blake Photo Library; p.450: George Hunter/Superstock; p.472: Andreas von Einsiedel/Alamy.

The authors and publishers are grateful to those who have given permission to reproduce material. Every effort has been made to
contact copyright holders of material reproduced in this book. Any omissions will be rectified in subsequent printings if notice is given to
the publishers.
Nash, C. (1998) *Food Safety: First Principles*, Chartered Institute of Environmental Health. Reproduced by permission of CIEH – pages
37 and 41

Crown copyright material is reproduced with the permission of the Controller of HMSO and the Queen's Printer for Scotland.

Steiner Lund would like to thank: Catering Department, East Leigh College, Hampshire; Eugene Hood, The Royal Society for the Protection of
Birds (RSPB); John Robinson, Family Butcher, Stockbridge, Hampshire; David H Batch, Lockerley Hall Farm, Lockerley, Hampshire.

Websites

There are links to relevant websites in this book. In order to ensure that the links are up to date, that the links work, and that the sites
are not inadvertently linked to sites that could be considered offensive, we have made the links available on the Heinemann website at
www.pearsonhotlinks.com. When you access the site, the express code is 7162P.

Contents

Foreword

Congratulations! As a trainee chef you have embarked on one of the most rewarding and challenging careers there is. Going to college and working for a City & Guilds qualification is the best start you can get. But don't think the learning ends when you get your certificate.

My career with food started when I was 16, when I went to college. More than 20 years later I am just as passionate about food and still learning and adding to my basic training from all those years ago.

Food has always been part of my life – my father ran a fruit and vegetable business supplying schools and local restaurants and my brother trained as a chef, inspiring me to follow. On day one at Southport Technical College I just knew I had made the right choice, everything just dropped into place and I had found something I truly loved.

I continue to be inspired but now it's more about the individual ingredients, what is available today and how can I bring out the best flavour, what I should pair it with. At the restaurant we never stand still, we are constantly trying new dishes, testing and tweaking until we reach perfection.

Since I started cooking, the world of catering has changed. Chefs are better known, there are more cooking shows on TV and diners have greater knowledge about food than ever before. It can only get better - what a fabulous time to be joining the world of cooking and hospitality, with so many opportunities throughout the industry.

Food alone is no longer enough. Successful restaurateurs need the whole package, which means understanding the consumer, learning to manage a team, handling finances, but most of all its about hospitality and the whole experience from the moment the guest books a table.

Hospitality is a great industry to work in. It doesn't matter where you start from, if you have determination and ability, if you are prepared to work hard and grab every opportunity to learn, the future will be bright for you.

This City and Guilds course is the foundation to your future – my advice, listen to your mentors, keep your head down and work hard, the sky is the limit!

Marcus Wareing
Marcus Wareing Restaurants Ltd
Marcus Wareing at The Berkeley
London

Introduction

This book has been designed with you in mind. Its purpose is to provide:

○ the knowledge requirements of the key units for Level 2 S/NVQ Diploma in Professional Cookery (7132)

○ the knowledge requirements for the Level 2 Technical Certificate in Hospitality and Catering Principles (Professional Cookery 7091)

○ a reference book for you to use while working towards your qualification and after you have qualified.

The catering and hospitality industry

The catering and hospitality industry is large. There are many roles to choose from and different types of businesses in which to work. The skills and knowledge you will develop while working towards your NVQ will be put to good use in the industry.

Your job title and tasks will be defined by which part of the industry you are working in. The table below shows various job roles which you could undertake with a Level 2 S/NVQ Diploma qualification and the sort of functions or tasks you will undertake.

Sector	Job title	Role	Core functions
Traditional brigade (fine dining)	Commis chef	To prepare, cook and present food (covering all sections of the kitchen)	Prepare, cook and finish basic dishes; ensure quality; manage portion control; participate in stock control; minimise waste
Mainstream	Line/section chef	To process, cook and present food	Process, cook and finish dishes; manage portion control; participate in stock control; minimise waste
School catering	Cook	To prepare, cook and present food	Prepare, cook and finish dishes; manage portion control; minimise waste

Figure i.1 Job title and tasks at entry level

When deciding which part of the industry you would like to work in you need to take into account the different roles and functions as well as the hours of work and terms and conditions.

What is an S/NVQ (Scottish/National Vocational Qualification)?

An NVQ assesses a person's technical competence to perform a job. It can also form part of an Apprenticeship. The assessment is continual but you will only be assessed when you are competent at a task. NVQs are divided into units. In order to pass a unit you need to fulfil various requirements.

Each unit has a

Unit aim

This explains what the unit is all about and relates the unit content to typical tasks you may carry out.

Learning outcomes

Each unit is then divided into learning outcomes. These outcomes are either about practical skills (tasks) that you need to be able to perform or the knowledge needed to carry out the tasks within your job role.

What you must cover

This details the range of situations/tasks and/or commodities that you need to demonstrate you can cover.

Evidence requirements

This details how much needs to be assessed by observation and how much can be covered by other methods of assessment.

How do I gain an NVQ?

The flowchart below summarises the process of gaining an NVQ. Each stage is discussed in more detail on the next page.

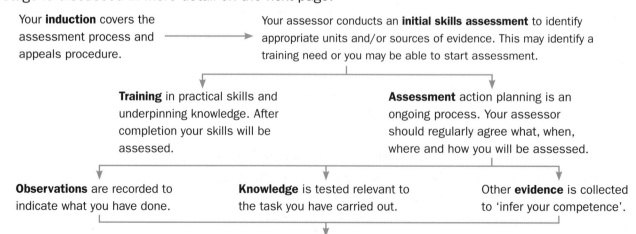

Your **induction** covers the assessment process and appeals procedure.

Your assessor conducts an **initial skills assessment** to identify appropriate units and/or sources of evidence. This may identify a training need or you may be able to start assessment.

Training in practical skills and underpinning knowledge. After completion your skills will be assessed.

Assessment action planning is an ongoing process. Your assessor should regularly agree what, when, where and how you will be assessed.

Observations are recorded to indicate what you have done.

Knowledge is tested relevant to the task you have carried out.

Other **evidence** is collected to 'infer your competence'.

Figure i.2 How to gain an NVQ

Quality assurance – is undertaken by an internal verifier who checks the quality of the assessment you have received by regularly sampling your assessor's work.

Induction

You should receive an induction as soon as you start your NVQ. This should include an overview of the assessment process and a detailed explanation of the appeals procedure which you must follow if you meet a problem.

Initial assessment

When you start your qualification you should have an initial assessment. Together with your assessor you will work through the units you have selected to do in order to identify how much knowledge and/or skills you may already have. Your assessor may have a special form to record an action plan so that you are very clear about what needs to happen next.

Training

If your initial assessment identified a training need you will receive training in practical skills and underpinning knowledge before your skills and knowledge are assessed.

Assessment

Your assessment will be ongoing with your assessor. You should receive assessment plans outlining what you have achieved and what you have to do next.

Observation

Your assessor will observe you carrying out tasks. The outcomes will be recorded in your portfolio.

Knowledge testing

You will be required to answer questions to prove you have the knowledge that underpins your performance.

Other evidence

It may also be possible to collect other evidence including:

○ witness testimonies – from colleagues or managers at your place of work
○ assessment of prior learning or experience – evidence that you may already have some of the skills or experience required by the qualification, e.g. a food safety certificate
○ work product (naturally occurring evidence) – e.g. menus, recipes, temperature check charts, photographs of dishes you have prepared.

Expert witness

May be used where additional support relating to the assessment of technical competence is required. The expert witness will need to provide evidence of their own competence and be able to demonstrate through relevant qualifications, practical experience and knowledge about your performance.

Professional discussion

Professional discussion is a really good way of providing additional evidence to confirm your competence. It can be used at the start of the qualification to identify your daily tasks or throughout your assessments to fill gaps in your evidence.

Your assessor will work with you to decide on the best method of collecting evidence for each unit.

Your portfolio

All evidence should be placed into your portfolio and will need to be referenced to the NVQ standards. You may be given a paper logbook showing these standards. There are different styles of logbooks depending upon which awarding organisation you are registered with. Alternatively you may be using an e-portfolio such as the ProActive e-portfolio which is linked to the qualification. Your assessor will advise you on whether you will use a logbook or the ProActive e-portfolio.

Who checks my portfolio?

Your assessor will make decisions on your competence and work with you to help you build your portfolio of evidence.

In order to ensure fairness and to monitor the quality of the assessment an internal verifier (quality assurance person) will check the assessor's work regularly. This may be by observing them assessing you or by sampling evidence already collected and logged in your portfolio.

Shortly after you start your NVQ you will be registered with an awarding organisation, e.g. City & Guilds. It is responsible for checking the quality of the assessment and internal verification. The awarding organisation appoints an external verifier to carry out checks on the assessor and internal verifier.

Apprenticeships & Technical Certificates

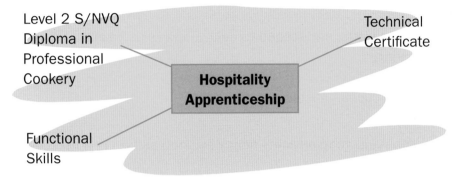

Figure i.3 Qualifications that make up the Hospitality and Catering Apprenticeship

Technical Certificate in Hospitality and Catering Apprenticeship framework

Some of the chapters in this book provide knowledge towards your Technical Certificate. This is a qualification that you will take as part of your Hospitality and Catering Apprenticeship programme. As you work through the units in your Technical Certificate you will have the opportunity to learn, develop and practise the knowledge and skills for employment/or career progression in the Hospitality and Catering sector. The Technical Certificate contributes knowledge and understanding towards your S/NVQ Level 2 qualification in Professional Cookery whilst containing additional skills and knowledge which go beyond the scope of the S/NVQ.

How this book can help you

Each chapter covers the requirements for one or more NVQ units, and relevant Technical Certificate units, so you can use the book to:
- develop your knowledge
- identify the tools, equipment and ingredients for the practical activities undertaken in the 'what you must cover' and the practical outcomes 'be able to'.

Throughout the book there are useful tips and activities that you can use as well as key recipes to help you work towards your qualification. Photographs identify ingredients and the sequence of complex practical tasks. Clear illustrations identify the equipment and tools that you will need.

Key features

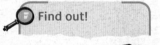

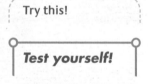

Marcus says	Practical ideas and tips from top chef Marcus Wareing.
Definition	All important technical words are defined to help you develop your underpinning knowledge.
Did you know?	Interesting and useful culinary facts.
Chef's tip	Useful practical ideas and good advice – nearly as good as having a real chef to help you!
Healthy eating	Ideas for healthy alternative ingredients and methods.
In the kitchen	These short real-life case studies tell you about the experiences of other people working in the catering industry.
Remember!	Important points to promote good practice in the kitchen and reminders about safe working practices.
Find out!	These independent research activities help you explore new areas and extend your knowledge.
Video presentation	When you see this feature you will know that there is a related video clip at http://www.proactive-online.co.uk.
Try this!	Short practical activities for you to try in the classroom. Sometimes they may provide evidence for your portfolio.
Test yourself!	At the end of each chapter there is a set of questions to check your knowledge.

Preparation	4
Cooking skills	2
Finishing	2

Skill levels for recipes indicate how easy or difficult the recipe is.

E-learning

The ProActive Catering e-learning site can be accessed at http://www.proactive-online.co.uk. If your centre has a licence then you will be given a login and password.

There are various types of electronic resources available on the site for independent learning:

○ Video clips clearly demonstrate skills, e.g. how to cut a chicken for sauté.
○ Interactive tutorials teach you about a specific topic, e.g. food safety. At the end of the tutorial there is a short multiple-choice test which checks your understanding.
○ You can print off recipes, menus and worksheets as directed by your assessor.

1 Health and safety

This chapter covers skills and knowledge in the following units:

o 7132 Unit 101 (1Gen1) Maintain a safe, hygienic and secure working environment

o 7132 Unit 102 (1Gen7) Maintain, handle and clean knives

o 7091 Unit 151 Safe, hygienic and secure working environments in hospitality

Working through this chapter could also provide the opportunity to practise the following Functional Skills:
Functional English – Reading Level 1
Functional Maths Analysing at Level 2 – Recognise 2D representations of 3D objects; find area, perimeter and volume of common shapes

In this chapter you will:

Know how and be able to maintain personal health and hygiene	7132 – 101.1,2	7091 – 151.2
Know how and be able to maintain a hygienic, safe and secure workplace	7132 – 101.3,4	7091 – 151.3
Know how and be able to maintain, handle and clean knives	7132 – 102.1,2	
Know employee's responsibilities under the Health and Safety at Work Act		7091 – 151.1

Health and safety regulations

Working in a safe manner

It is important that all workers are able to carry out their tasks without causing any accident or injury to themselves or others (e.g. work colleagues or members of the public). Many years ago injuries at work were quite common, but since the Health and Safety at Work Act 1974 was brought in, most people take much greater care to work in a safe manner. This means there are fewer accidents in the workplace.

Figure 1.1 All chefs need to know the laws on health and safety

The Health and Safety at Work Act gives everyone certain responsibilities. While at work you must:
- take reasonable care of your own safety and the safety of others
- work in the manner laid down by your employer, especially regarding safety
- tell your supervisor if you see anything that you think may be unsafe and could cause an accident.

Try this!

Try to remember an accident that you saw or one that happened to you.

- ○ *What happened?*
- ○ *How many people did it involve?*
- ○ *What pieces of equipment (if any) were involved?*
- ○ *Did it involve any of the 'fabric' of the building (e.g. the floor)?*
- ○ *How was it dealt with?*
- ○ *Who dealt with it (the manager or Head Chef)?*
- ○ *What did they do?*
- ○ *Did the accident result in any changes in the area afterwards, e.g. a change in the position of some equipment or a different floor surface being laid?*

Figure 1.2 What is the cause of this accident?

In the kitchen

A student visiting a fast-food restaurant was electrocuted when she accidentally touched a live wire sticking out of a hand dryer which had been vandalised. The dryer had been damaged at least ten days prior to the accident but had not been repaired.

Figure 1.3 Negligence can result in serious consequences in the workplace

The Health and Safety at Work Act makes sure that employers do not put their staff in dangerous situations where they could hurt themselves or others. Under this Act, employers must:

- ○ keep all their staff safe while working
- ○ provide safe equipment, tools and surroundings in which to work
- ○ train staff how to work, clean and maintain equipment they use
- ○ produce a policy document telling everyone how to behave safely
- ○ provide first-aid equipment and help
- ○ keep an accident book and use it correctly.

Did you know?

During the past ten years over 2,000 workers in the catering industry have had to take more than three days off work to recover from an accident in the workplace. Over 800 of these people suffered a major injury.

Did you know?

The most common dangerous occurrences in the catering industry which break the Health and Safety at Work Act are:

- o missing guards on food slicing machines
- o trailing cables
- o insecure wiring on plugs
- o faulty microwave seals
- o broken or worn steps
- o poor lighting of work areas.

In the kitchen

A waiter refilling **flambé** lamps turned into a human fireball when the vapour given off from the fuel ignited around him. The flammable liquid had not been stored properly, the waiter had not been trained properly in this procedure and there were no suitable fire extinguishers to use nearby.

Figure 1.4 Training is essential in preventing disaster

Laws relating to working safely

The Health and Safety at Work Act is an 'umbrella' act. This means that it includes other important regulations which relate to health and safety. The table below discusses some of these regulations.

Regulation	Example
Control of Substances Hazardous to Health (COSHH) Regulations 2002 Identifies dangerous chemicals, e.g. cleaning agents. Chemicals must be labelled accurately. They must only be used after suitable training has been given. The correct protective clothing, e.g. gloves and goggles, must also be used.	A kitchen porter was provided with a very effective oven cleaning chemical. He kept it in a spray container under the pot wash sink. The kitchen porter had been trained how to apply the chemical and given a mask and gloves to wear. He kept this protective clothing in his locker. While the kitchen porter was on holiday the trainee chef was told to clean the oven. He tried to use the same chemical, although he had not been shown what to do. This was against the Regulations as he had not been trained how to use the chemical and he had no access to the protective equipment supplied. The chemical should have been kept in a locked cupboard when not in use. 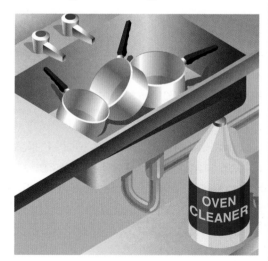

Reporting of Injuries, Diseases and Dangerous Occurrences Regulations (RIDDOR) 1995 Concerns the reporting of major or fatal injuries to any person in an accident connected with the business where you work. The report must usually be made to the Environmental Health Department of the local council.	A chef slipped over on a greasy kitchen floor while carrying a pan of hot water. She sustained serious burns and had to go to hospital. The accident was recorded in the company's accident book. To comply with RIDDOR the local council was informed. This resulted in a Health and Safety Inspector visiting the premises to carry out an investigation of how the accident happened. 
Manual Handling Operations Regulations 1992 Aims to reduce the number of accidents caused by people moving heavy and awkwardly shaped items while at work. Adequate training must be given and equipment provided to help move items safely. See page 29, Safe working practices.	A dinner for 500 guests was going to be held in the exhibition hall of a large conference centre. All the equipment and prepared food needed to be transported from the kitchen to the hall which was several hundred yards away. The last time this type of function was held, the staff had to carry all the items on trays and in large containers. Some items were so heavy that two people had to share the load. After the event had taken place, one of the chefs had to have time off work with a strained back. This time trolleys were provided to move the equipment, and all the staff had received training in lifting heavy items safely to satisfy the Manual Handling Operations Regulations. 
Provision and Use of Work Equipment Regulations 1998 Used together with the Prescribed Dangerous Machines Order to make sure people are not injured when they are using machines and other equipment while at work. Before using any type of machinery or equipment the member of staff must be trained in the correct procedures. If the machine is listed under the Prescribed Dangerous Machines Order then no one under the age of 18 may clean, lubricate or adjust it.	A young chef was asked to clean the meat slicing machine after use. He had not yet been trained how to do this but thought it should be easy enough. He dismantled the machine as much as he could but then cut his hand on the sharp blade he had exposed. The chef should not have attempted to clean the machine without first being trained to do so safely. This could have resulted in an offence under the Prescribed Dangerous Machines Order. 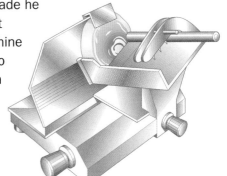

Fire Precautions Workplace Regulations 1997 Ensures there are suitable measures in place to protect staff and keep them safe in the event of a fire. There should be appropriate fire extinguishers supplied and a rehearsed evacuation procedure. See page 24, Fire in the workplace.	Some hot fat fell onto the solid stove top in a busy kitchen during service. The fat caught fire and spread over the cooker. The chef at the stove turned off the equipment and looked for a fire blanket to put over the flames. The case on the wall nearby where the fire blanket should have been was empty. By the time the chef had located a foam fire extinguisher the flames had spread up the wall of the kitchen. The fire brigade had to be called to put the fire out. The employer could have been prosecuted under these Regulations because they had failed to maintain the appropriate equipment to extinguish fires. 

Figure 1.5 The different regulations that form part of the Health and Safety at Work Act

Where to find information

It is very important to work in a safe and hygienic way for several reasons:

- It avoids injuring yourself or others.
- It is usually quicker and easier.
- It is more professional.

There should be a Health and Safety representative at your workplace. You should follow any guidelines they give you about safe working practices. If health and safety regulations are not met you or your employer could be fined and your workplace may be closed down until safety improvements have been made. The fine for not following health and safety law is unlimited. You could also be sent to prison for an unlimited length of time! This means that a serious health and safety problem, e.g. a major accident, could be very expensive and also give the person responsible a criminal record.

In due course you will need to know more about health and safety in your workplace. You can:

- ask your supervisor
- ask your Health and Safety representative
- ask your Human Resources Manager
- look on the staff notice board.

Find out!

- What year was the Health and Safety at Work Act introduced?
- If there is a safety problem at work what is the name of the government organisation which will become involved?

Find out!

Which of these prescribed dangerous machines can be found in your kitchen?

○ Worm-type mincing machines
○ Rotary knife bowl-type chopping machines
○ Dough brakes
○ Dough mixers
○ Food-mixing machines (when used with various attachments)
○ Pie- and tart-making machines
○ Vegetable-slicing machines
○ Potato-chipping machines
○ Circular knife-slicing machines
○ Machines with circular saw blades
○ Machines with a saw in the form of a continuous blade or strip
○ Wrapping and packing machines.

Test yourself!

1 Complete the sentences.
The _____ and _____ at Work Act requires all staff to work safely in the kitchen.
All _____ are responsible for the safety of themselves and others.
Staff can find out more information about these Regulations by asking their _____ and looking at the _____ .

2 What do these initials stand for?
a HACCP
_____
b COSSH
_____
c RIDDOR.
_____

3 Name two common dangerous occurrences which break the Health and Safety at Work Act.

4 How old must a person be in order to clean a machine listed under the Prescribed Machines Order?

5 Complete the sentence.
The Manual Handling Operations Regulations aim to _____ the number of _____ caused by people moving _____ and _____ shaped items while at _____ .

Personal safety and hygiene

To avoid accidents you must be alert and able to see ahead to notice any possible danger. The safety of you and your colleagues in a catering kitchen may be affected by:

○ being short of sleep
○ being under the influence of alcohol or drugs
○ having long hair which is not tied back correctly
○ wearing jewellery.

Long hair or jewellery could get caught in machinery or cause hygiene problems by falling into food which is being prepared.

Figure 1.6 Proper attire and behaviour is not just about being professional – it is about safety too

Personal hygiene

Personal hygiene is very important when working in a catering environment. You need to be pleasant to work with (no body odour!) and feel comfortable in the kitchen. Make sure you wash your hair – if it feels sticky and heavy it will not be pleasant to work in a hot kitchen. Clean your teeth regularly – your colleagues will not want to work near you if you have bad breath! Keep your hands and nails clean and in good condition when working directly with food. See page 46 for more information.

Figure 1.7 Would you want to eat at this chef's restaurant?

Clothing, footwear and headgear

Your uniform should fit correctly and be comfortable to wear. If your shoes are too tight and make your feet hurt, for example, you will not be able to concentrate properly. This could cause an accident if you are using dangerous equipment, e.g. knives or mixers.

It is important to wear the correct clothing in the kitchen, not only for health and safety but also to create a professional image. Customers, visitors and other members of staff are impressed by kitchen staff who are dressed in a clean, smart uniform. Kitchens may have 'house rules' regarding correct dress but it will be a version of the traditional chef's whites.

Did you know?
The traditional chef's hat is called a toque and is tall to allow air to circulate and keep the top of the head cool. This was supposed to help to prevent baldness! However, with people growing taller and extraction canopies having to be fitted over stoves, a growing number of chefs wear the flat skull cap style.

Hat This should be close-fitting and clean. It should be made of an absorbent material and washable or disposable. A hair net should be worn underneath if your hair reaches below the collar.

Necktie This should be made of cotton, correctly tied and clean.

Jacket This should be made of an absorbent, thick but cool material (usually cotton mix). It should be double-breasted, so it can be fastened either way to give a double layer of material across the chest, and long-sleeved for protection.

Apron This should be made of white cotton with long strings to tie in front. It may be bibbed. It should cover you from the waist to below the knee for protection, but should not be any longer as this would be a safety risk.

Trousers These should be cotton mix and loose-fitting for comfort. They should not be too long as this is a safety risk.

Shoes These should be comfortable, strong, and solid with protected toes. Clogs may be acceptable; trainers are not. Footwear must have non-slip soles and non-absorbent uppers. Socks (or tights) must be worn.

Figure 1.8 The correct clothing

What to do if you injure yourself

Despite wearing the correct uniform and working as safely as possible, it is quite likely you will injure yourself at some time while working in a professional kitchen. The most common injuries are slight cuts and burns.

A small cut may be self-treated if appropriate. Wash it, dry it with a clean, disposable cloth or tissue and then cover it with a waterproof blue plaster. Occasionally the cut may need protecting with a **finger stall** over the dressing. If self-treatment is not possible, call a first-aider.

A small burn may also be self-treated if appropriate. Immediately plunge it under cold running water and hold it there until all the pain has gone. Do not put any type of cream on a burn. A burn should not normally be covered. If it blisters seek the advice of a first-aider.

Report all injuries to your supervisor and make an entry in the accident book. See page 19, Reporting accidents.

Definition

Finger stall: a plastic tube that fits over a dressing (bandage or plaster) on an injured finger to protect it. It is secured by an elastic strap around the wrist.

Did you know?

A first-aider is someone who has successfully studied a first aid course run by the British Red Cross, St John Ambulance Association or the St Andrew's Ambulance Association. This qualification lasts for three years. After this the course needs to be retaken.

Reporting illnesses and infections

Report any illnesses or infections to your supervisor. An illness may prevent you from working until you are better, on health and safety grounds; even if you feel quite well you may be very infectious and risk passing the illness on to your fellow workers or customers.

Illness may be brought on by activities at work, e.g. a new cleaning chemical may react with your skin and make it sore, itchy or cause a rash. If this happens your employer may provide you with gloves to wear when you use this chemical in the future.

Figure 1.9 Wearing appropriate gloves for a task may help prevent skin problems

Test yourself!

1 What is the best material from which a kitchen uniform should be made?
   a Nylon
   b Plastic
   c Cotton
   d Rubber.

2 What is the correct length at which an apron should be worn?
   a Just above the ankle
   b Just above the knee
   c Just below the hips
   d Just below the knee.

3 What is the purpose of wearing a necktie?
   a It looks smart
   b It absorbs sweat
   c It indicates your job
   d It supports your neck.

4 What should you do if you feel very tired after work?
   a Go to bed early
   b Eat a large meal
   c Go out with your friends
   d Watch more television.

5 What four things should you do if you accidentally cut yourself slightly while at work?

6 What should you do if you burn yourself and a blister forms on the burnt area?

7 What should you do if the skin on your hands becomes itchy and flaky?

8 How often must a first-aid qualification be retaken?

9 Which of these organisations run first-aid courses?
   a Red Arrows
   b Red Cross
   c Red Square
   d Red Aid.

10 Complete this sentence
   All injuries must be reported to _____ _____ and an entry made in the _____ _____.

Hazards in the workplace

Types of hazard

Think of a catering kitchen – what types of **hazard** exist there?
Look at the picture below. How many accidents can you see waiting
to happen?

Figure 1.10 Spot the hazards in this kitchen

From the picture you can see there are several types of hazard.
They can be grouped according to their causes:

○ Hazardous substances
○ Hazardous equipment
○ Hazardous work methods
○ Hazardous work area.

Definition
Hazard: something which
could be dangerous.

Hazardous substances

Any substance that is not in the appropriate place or is not being used correctly may become a hazard. In catering, the types of substances that may become hazardous include:

- Cooking oil, which may:
  - overheat and catch fire
  - get spilt on a floor and make it very slippery.
- Cleaning chemicals, which may:
  - be used incorrectly, e.g. not **diluted** sufficiently
  - not be used with the appropriate protective equipment, e.g. goggles and gloves
  - be mixed together and give off dangerous fumes
  - be decanted from a large, labelled container into a smaller, unlabelled container and mistaken for another liquid.

COSHH

The COSHH Regulations form part of the Health and Safety at Work Act. They are rules which control substances which are considered hazardous to health. The COSHH Regulations state that:

- chemicals that may be dangerous to people must be clearly identified
- those chemicals must be stored, issued and used safely
- training must be given in the use of these chemicals
- suitable protective clothing must be provided when using the chemicals.

When using any type of chemical:

- always follow the manufacturer's instructions carefully
- never mix one chemical with another
- never move any chemical from its original container into an alternative one which is incorrectly labelled or has no label at all
- never use food containers to store a cleaning chemical
- always store chemicals in the correct place.

> **Definition**
> **Dilute:** to add extra liquid (usually water) to make the solution weaker.

> **Did you know?**
> Using a cleaning chemical, e.g. bleach, in a stronger concentration than necessary does not kill more germs or get the job done more quickly. Instead it:
> o wastes the cleaning chemical (which can cost quite a lot of money)
> o might damage the surface on which it is being used
> o will need more rinsing off after use (which makes the job take longer in the end!).

> **Definition**
> **Caustic:** a substance that will stick to a surface and burn chemically. It is used for heavy-duty cleaning.

In the kitchen

A pub kept some beer pipe cleaning fluid in an unlabelled, clear glass bottle on the floor. It was placed near the beer pipes ready to use. A new member of staff who was very thirsty opened the bottle and drank from it. The liquid was clear and looked like lemonade but in fact was an extremely strong, **caustic** chemical. The member of staff suffered extensive burning of mouth, throat and stomach and can no longer eat normally.

Figure 1.11 Never pour a liquid into an unlabelled container

Hazardous equipment

Hazardous equipment can be manual or electrical. Training must be given in the operation of equipment and the equipment must be checked regularly.

Types of manual equipment include:
○ knives and choppers
○ mandolins.

Cleaning and sharpening knives

Chefs who use knives should be responsible for cleaning and maintaining them. Keep both the handle and blade clean. This prevents your hand slipping and bacteria spreading. Wash knives thoroughly between tasks, using detergent sanitiser, and rinse well in very hot water. Dry on a clean, disposable towel.

A blunt knife means that you have to apply more pressure and so the knife is more likely to slip. You must know how to sharpen your knives using a wet stone or steel. Incorrect use can be dangerous. You may need to take very blunt knives to a butcher who will use a grinding stone. Knives should always be thoroughly cleaned after sharpening as there may be metal fillings on the blade.

Knife care and safety

Poor knife techniques and untidy work methods are often a cause of accidents in the kitchen. Follow the rules below:

○ Store knives and choppers in a specially designed area when not in use, e.g. in a box, wallet or on a magnetic rack. Storing loose knives in a drawer can damage the blades and cause injury.
○ When moving knives, transport them in the appropriate box or case.
○ When carrying a knife, always point it down and hold it close to your side. Work colleagues can be unintentionally stabbed if this rule is not followed!
○ If passing a knife to a colleague always offer it to them handle first.
○ Never leave a knife on a work surface with the blade upwards.
○ Never leave a knife hanging over the edge of a work surface.
○ Never try to catch a falling knife – let it come to rest on the ground before you pick it up.
○ Never use a knife as a can opener or screwdriver.
○ Do not use a knife or chopper which is blunt or has a greasy, loose or damaged handle. A knife in any of these conditions can easily slip and cause a serious cut. Report any damages to knives to your supervisor.

Figure 1.12 A mandolin

Chef's tip
A good way to test whether a knife is sharp enough is to slice a tomato.

Chef's tip
See the Appendix on page 473 for more on types of knives and sharpening.

Video presentation
Watch *Choosing the right knife* and *Sharpening a knife* for safety tips.

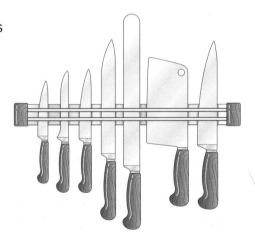

Figure 1.13 A set of chef's knives. Always take care when handling these

- It is recommended that you use colour-coded knives to prevent cross-contamination or allergenic reactions amongst customers. See Chapter 2.
- Only use a knife on a chopping board which has a damp cloth underneath to prevent slippage. If using a chopper, clear the area before use.
- When wiping a knife clean after use, wipe from the blade base to the tip with the sharp edge facing away from your body.
- Never leave a knife in a sink. Wash and remove it immediately.

Electrical equipment

Hazardous electrical equipment includes:

- slicing machines
- mixers
- mincers
- blenders.

These are known as **prescribed dangerous machines** and have special regulations relating to their use. See the table on page 5.

Rules for operating machinery

- Always follow the manufacturer's instructions.
- Never operate machinery if the safety guards are not in place. Many machines will not work unless correctly and fully assembled. However, some older models may work without the safety equipment being fitted (be very careful with these).
- If the machine will not work properly seek help from your supervisor.
- Ensure that the correct attachments are being used on the equipment for the task to be carried out.
- Never push food against a cutting blade with your hands – use a proper plunger or the handle supplied. (Many chefs have lost fingers by not following this rule!)
- If using a spoon do not let it touch any moving parts. If it does the spoon and the machine will be damaged.
- Do not use faulty machinery. Label it 'out of order' and unplug it or partly dismantle it so it cannot be used. Report the problem to your supervisor so a repair can be arranged.
- Do not overload electrical sockets. This may cause a fire or cause fuses to blow and could affect everybody working in the building.
- Do not operate electrical equipment with wet hands or near sinks or any other sources of water. An electric shock could result from this action.

Chef's tip
See pages 147, 183, 220 and 249 for more about selecting the right knife for the task.

Remember!
Take great care when operating machinery. No one under the age of 18 may clean, lubricate or adjust a machine if they will be at risk of injury from a moving part.

Remember!
Before using any type of machinery or equipment the member of staff must be trained in the correct procedures. They must be fully instructed about any danger which may arise and be supervised adequately by someone with knowledge and experience of the machine.

- Keep your hands away from sharp blades. Wait for them to stop rotating after switching the machine off before starting any other activity, e.g. cleaning.
- Make sure the power is disconnected before starting to clean electrical machinery.
- Do not use machinery if the plug or flex is damaged in any way.

Hazardous work methods

Many accidents are caused by poor work methods. Before starting work consider these points:

- When a range of tasks have to be completed they should be carried out in order.
- Finish one task before starting the next.
- Assemble all the equipment necessary before starting the task.
- Allow sufficient time and space to carry out the task involved.
- Follow a logical sequence. The flow of work should move one way e.g. left to right.
- Make sure there are no spillages on the floor. They will make the floor slippery and could cause an accident.

Hazardous work area

Some areas of the kitchen may not be the most appropriate to work in, for example:

- A larder area might be very cold. It is difficult to prepare food with very cold hands.
- The kitchen may be very crowded if there are several staff on duty. It is easy to collide with other people in a small space. This could be very dangerous if you are carrying a pot of hot liquid.
- Floors can get greasy and wet if spillages are not cleared up quickly and thoroughly. Staff walking from the kitchen into a walk-in cold room and out again may make the floors slippery.

Figure 1.14 An untidy work area showing hazardous work methods

Figure 1.15 How a work area should be organised for safety

Did you know?

If a floor is getting slippery during service, you should throw several generous handfuls of salt over the surface. This is a quick, temporary remedy as the salt absorbs the liquid or grease. The floor can then be cleaned properly when there is time.

Reporting hazards

If you see a hazard in your work area which could cause an accident you should do one of two things:

1 Make the hazard safe, as long as you can do so without risking your own safety.
2 Report the hazard to your supervisor as soon as you can, making sure no one enters the area without being aware of the danger.

Two good ways in which you can warn other people about hazards are:

○ block the route past the hazard
○ use a sign.

A sign is usually the best way. Temporary signs may be handwritten if there is no alternative. Many signs involve visual symbols which are best in case people passing the hazard cannot read English. Where signs are in frequent use, e.g. fire exits, they are produced in colours that can be seen by colour-blind people.

Some hazards are temporary so the sign relating to them should also be temporary, e.g. a wet floor sign. Others are there because of the nature of the building, e.g. a low beam may have a permanent sign nearby warning everyone to mind their head.

> **Did you know?**
> To warn others in the kitchen that a hot saucepan had just come out of the oven it was traditional to sprinkle flour on the handle or cover the handle with a cloth.

Commonly used hazard warning signs

The colours of the signs indicate the type of hazard involved:

○ A black and yellow sign is used with a triangular symbol where there is a risk of danger, e.g. 'Mind your head'.
○ A red circle with a line through it tells you something you must not do in the area, e.g. 'No smoking'.
○ A solid blue circle with a white picture or

writing gives a reminder of something you must do, e.g. 'Shut the door'.

○ A green sign with a white picture or writing is

indicates fire-fighting information.

When using chemicals that could harm you the

an emergency sign for escape or first aid.

○ A red sign with white symbols or writing

following signs may be displayed on the container:

○ Corrosive – could burn your skin.

○ Poison – may kill you if swallowed.

○ Irritant – may cause itching or a rash if in contact with

skin.

Find out!

What type of chemicals used in your workplace have these symbols?

What type of protective equipment should you wear when using them?

18

Reporting accidents

All accidents should be reported to your supervisor in order to prevent further similar accidents and identify potential problem areas, and also to comply with legislation. Each accident is recorded in an accident book which must be provided in every business.

The key information that has to be recorded about an accident is the:

○ date and time of the incident

○ full name and occupation of the person involved

○ type of injury

○ location of the accident and what happened

○ names of any witnesses to the accident

○ name and job title of the person completing the report

○ time and date the report was made.

Accident report

Details of person involved
Name: _John Smith_____ Occupation: _Chef_____
Type of injury: _Serious burn_____

Incident details
Location: _Kitchen_____
Date: _20/11/06_____ Time: _19.45_____
Details of witness: _Bob Jones, Samantha Rice, Faye Lemon____
_____
_____

Description of what happenend:

While handling a heavy pot of boiliing stock the chef slipped and spilt the contents on his arm. He sustained heavy burns and was sent to hospital.

Report completed by: _Sarah Jane Smith_____
Job title: _Chef_____
Date and time of report: _20/11/06 20.30_____

Figure 1.16 An accident report form

A serious accident has to be reported to the Environmental Health Officer of the local council. This may be done by phone at first and then followed up in writing. A serious accident means: broken bones, loss of a limb or eyesight, electric shock, or any other circumstance which involves the person being kept in hospital for more than 24 hours.

Try this!

Worksheet 2

Complete a blank accident form describing the following incident.

Beryl Smith, who worked in the pot wash, came into work on Monday morning as usual. She had just returned from her mid-morning break when she slipped on some grease. This had dripped onto the floor from a saucepan left on her table which had tipped onto its side. She fell down, banged her head on the leg of the table and cut her ear. Mr Newman, the chef who is a first-aider, treated the cut, which soon stopped bleeding. He made Beryl sit in the office for a while to make sure she had no ill-effects from banging her head. After about 15 minutes Beryl felt able to carry on with her work. The grease on the floor was cleared up by the kitchen porter while Beryl was being looked after.

Test yourself!

1 Write down four safety points about using electrical equipment.

2 Write down four safety points about knives.

3 What action should you take if you notice each of the following situations:

a The handle of a floor mop has fallen across the corridor, blocking the way. It had been left leaning against the wall.

b Some boxes stacked up on a high shelf are leaning to one side and looking as if they will soon fall down.

c A corner of vinyl flooring has come unstuck and is likely to cause someone to trip over it.

4 Match the signs to the written warnings.
   a Danger _____
   b No entry – restricted area _____
   c Now wash your hands _____
   d Emergency exit _____

i   ii   iii   iv

5 Complete these important safety points which you must follow when using any type of chemical.
   a Always follow the m_____ i_____ carefully.
   b Never m_____ one chemical with another.
   c Never m_____ any chemical from its o_____ container into an alternative which is i_____ labelled or has no l_____ at all.
   d Never use f_____ c_____ to store a cleaning chemical.
   e Always s_____ chemicals in the correct p_____.

6 There are 12 rules for operating machinery. Write down 4 of them.

7 Why might it be difficult to work in the following places?
   a A larder
   b A crowded kitchen.

Emergencies in the workplace

Types of emergency

Several types of emergency can happen at work. They include:

- a sudden serious accident or illness of staff or customers
- the outbreak of a fire which cannot be safely put out
- a security alert in the building, e.g. a bomb scare
- the failure of a major system in a building, e.g. power, drainage.

Each of these needs to be dealt with in a different way. The management of the organisation should have systems in place to deal with each of them. Some of these systems may involve certain members of staff being trained in particular skills, e.g. first aid or fire fighting. Other procedures may mean that all staff need to carry out special tasks when a particular type of emergency happens. These procedures need practising every so often and this is why routine building evacuations take place and alarms are tested regularly.

The main types of emergency can be dealt with in the following ways:

- **Illness:** Trained first-aiders on duty to help with staff or customers who are taken ill or have an accident. Security/door staff trained in calling an ambulance or doctor and escorting them to the medical emergency smoothly, e.g. by holding lifts ready for them and having information about the person concerned available.
- **Fire:** A thoroughly rehearsed fire evacuation procedure which can take place quickly and without panic, allowing for all people in the building to be accounted for to make sure they are safe.
- **Security:** A fully rehearsed emergency procedure to prevent unnecessary disruption to the normal running of the building, but allowing a full evacuation if necessary. Special training of security staff and telephonists in how to deal with suspicious packages or telephone calls threatening explosions.
- **Supply failure:** Depending upon the system that has failed, the building may have a back-up system, e.g. a generator which can take over automatically with very little disruption. Some services, e.g. the water supply failing or a gas leak, may mean the building has to close until the problem can be put right. Sometimes the area around the building can be affected as well.

First aid

Special courses are run for people who wish to learn how to treat minor injuries and apply techniques which may help to save the life of someone who has been involved in a serious accident or who has become very ill. It is always useful to know what to do in the event of a medical emergency, and if you become a first-aider it gives you skills which you can use at any time. Find out more by visiting the St John Ambulance website. A link is available at www.heinemann.co.uk/hotlinks – just enter the express code 7162P.

Even if you are not a first-aider there are some basic techniques which it is helpful to know about in case there is no one else around to treat someone who has had an accident.

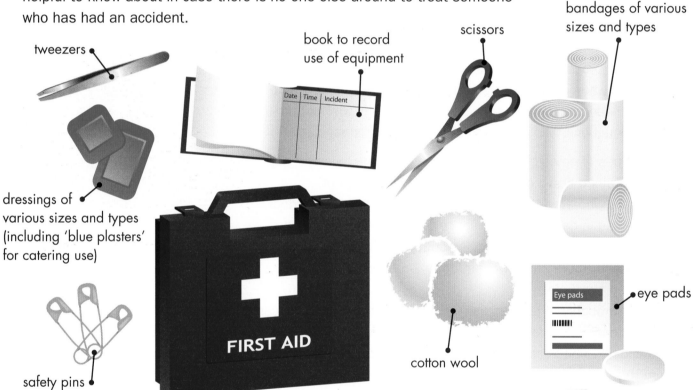

tweezers

book to record use of equipment

scissors

bandages of various sizes and types

dressings of various sizes and types (including 'blue plasters' for catering use)

cotton wool

eye pads

safety pins

Figure 1.17 Contents of a first-aid box

first aid guidance card

What to do in the event of an accident

- Visually make sure the injured person is in no further danger. Do not touch them.
- If there is any machinery involved immediately turn off the power at the plug or the main switch. This is very important if you think the person may have been electrocuted. Otherwise if you touch them you will get electrocuted too.
- Contact your supervisor and get the help of a first-aider.

- If this is not possible:
  - Telephone 999 (free call – even from a locked phone).
  - Ask for the ambulance service.
  - Give your telephone number so you can be called back.
  - Give the location of the accident.
  - Describe what has happened and give details of the injuries as clearly as you can.
  - Follow any instructions given over the phone. This may be giving some first aid, getting information from the injured person or going to a meeting point to wait for an ambulance.

How to treat a casualty while waiting for help

- Talk to the person and reassure them. If you do not know them, find out their name and where they live. Be kind and considerate.
- Tell them that help is on the way.
- If they feel cold, cover them with a blanket or any available clothing. Try not to cover a major burn.
- Do not move the person unless they are in danger of further injury.

See how to treat a minor cut or a burn on page 10.

Figure 1.18 Reassure the casualty

Emergency procedures and how to follow them

When there is an emergency it is important that everybody does exactly as they are told and follows the rehearsed procedure. The immediate result of most emergencies is evacuation of the building.

Evacuation procedure

If you have to leave the kitchen as the result of an emergency, remember to do the following:

- Turn off all the power supplies (gas and electricity). This may mean hitting the red button in a modern kitchen or turning off all the appliances individually.
- Close all the windows and doors in the area.
- Never stop to gather personal possessions.
- Leave the building by the nearest emergency exit (do not use a lift).
- Assemble in the designated area away from the building.
- Answer a roll-call of names so that everyone knows you have left the building safely.

External emergency procedure

If there is an emergency, e.g. a bomb alert outside the building, you may have to stop working and take shelter inside. Staff should rehearse for this type of emergency as well as the evacuation procedure. This external emergency procedure should include the following instructions:

- Turn off all power supplies in the kitchen.
- Close all the windows and doors in the area.
- Do not stop to gather personal possessions.
- Gather in a designated safe area. This is usually in central stairwells or corridors away from windows and as close to the middle of the building as possible.
- Stay in this area until told to leave by an emergency official.
- Answer a roll-call of names to make sure no one is missing.

A modern kitchen has a red button that turns off power supplies in an emergency.

Fire in the workplace

Fire is very dangerous and can easily become life-threatening. It is very important that you know what to do in the event of a fire. Respect fire and treat it with the utmost caution.

Did you know?

Many fires on catering premises have been started by a spark from the stove being sucked up the extraction canopy. When that canopy is dirty and coated with a layer of grease a fire can easily start. Because the smoke gets sucked up through the extraction system, no one may be aware there is a fire until it has spread to a dangerous level. Some commercial insurance companies will not insure catering premises unless the kitchen canopy is professionally cleaned very regularly.

Causes of fire in the workplace

Fires can quite easily be started in kitchens. There are hot stoves which are left on for long periods of time and hot fat in fryers which can overheat and catch fire. There is a large amount of electrical equipment which can develop a fault and start a fire. Over 28 per cent of fires on catering premises start in the kitchen and are caused by cooking procedures.

Figure 1.19 A fire can start when a spark from the stove is sucked into a dirty extraction canopy

How to minimise the risk of fire

Careful work practices and being observant are the main ways of reducing the risk of fire. These good practices include:

○ keeping hot work areas clean of fat and grease
○ never overfilling fryers and frying pans
○ keeping walls and canopies around stoves clean
○ not allowing cloths to dangle over stoves
○ not overloading electrical sockets
○ never leaving electrical appliances on unattended
○ ensuring that staff and public areas are free of debris.

In the kitchen

A **smouldering** oven cloth nearly caused a serious fire in a London hotel. One Sunday afternoon a young chef was very keen to leave work after lunch service. He changed into his outdoor clothes as quickly as he could. Then he threw his chef's whites and cloths into his locker. He did not realise that his oven cloth was smouldering. After a while the fire alarm in the hotel sounded. The sensor board indicated the problem was in the male changing rooms.

On investigation the room was found to be full of smoke with a fire building up inside the young chef's locker. It was put out promptly, which was a good thing as the changing room was located next to the fuel store where tanks of oil were kept.

Definition

Smoulder: to burn slowly with a small red glow and little smoke.

Understand how a fire can start

Fire needs three things to burn. As soon as one is removed, the fire will go out.

Fuel: fire has to be fed and will use any substance that will burn, e.g. gas, electricity, cloth, oil or wood. Once the fuel has been used up the fire will go out.

Oxygen: fire requires oxygen to keep going. If the source of air is removed the fire will go out. This is why a fire blanket can put out a fire.

Heat: fire creates heat. If the heat of the fire is removed the fire will go out. This is how many fire extinguishers work.

A fire can be put out by:

○ **starving** it of fuel
○ **smothering** it by removing air
○ **cooling** it by taking away the heat.

Figure 1.20 The three components that fire needs

The significance of fire alarms

Fire alarms are required in all businesses over a certain size. They save lives and are essential in large buildings. They are required in all businesses that need to have a fire certificate to operate. See Fire safety laws on page 28.

Fire alarms work by fitting smoke and heat sensors in various parts of the building. When any of these sensors are activated an alarm sounds. The sensor that has been activated shows up on the control panel and the area it covers has to be investigated immediately.

Sometimes a sensor may sound the alarm even though there is no apparent reason. This may be due to the system developing a fault. The area covered by the sensor must always be checked, even if nothing is found. A false alarm must never be assumed. If a false alarm continues to occur then an engineer will be called in to check the system.

Testing fire alarms

To ensure the alarm system is working correctly it should be tested regularly. Most businesses check their systems at the same time every week. This involves:
○ all staff being told when the test takes place so they know they do not have to evacuate the building
○ the alarm bells ringing on and off for a few minutes.

If the alarm sounds at any other time, all members of staff should follow the procedure they have been taught. This usually means leaving the building and assembling in a particular area outside. At the assembly point there is a roll-call (a type of register) to make sure that everyone has left the building and is safe.

Some alarms have two stages:

Figure 1.21 Taking a roll-call

Stage 1: The smoke or fire sensor will set off the first alarm, which sounds briefly. Trained members of staff will then investigate the area. If they can deal with the cause of the alarm, or if it is a false alarm, no further action is taken.

Stage 2: Should there be a fire or other emergency, the second stage of the alarm will be activated. This means the alarm will sound continuously and the building will be evacuated. The fire brigade will also be called.

How to deal with a fire

A fire can easily start in a kitchen, so it is important to know what to do if it happens. Sometimes a drop of grease will catch fire on the stove and go out by itself almost at once. This is not an emergency. However if it does not go out and gets bigger it could become dangerous.

If you are going to try to put out a small fire, you need to know which extinguisher to use for which type of fire. If you use the wrong one by mistake it could make the fire much worse.

Once you have used a fire extinguisher you must let your supervisor know as it has to be refilled as soon as possible. Extinguishers must be checked each year to make sure they are full and work properly.

In some situations it may be appropriate to try to put out a fire that has just started, but you must act speedily!

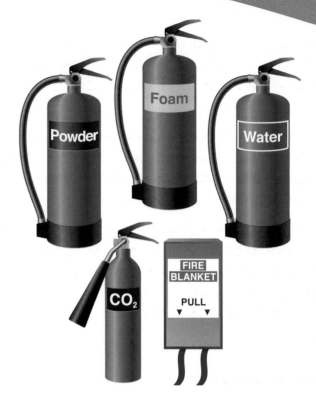

Figure 1.22 Types of fire extinguisher

Situation	Response
A person's clothes catch fire	Quickly wrap them in a fire blanket or wet tablecloth (or similar) and lay them on the floor. This excludes air and heat from the fire so it should go out. Do not take off the blanket or tablecloth. Call for a first-aider to attend the scene.
A pan of fat catches fire	Turn off the gas or electricity and quickly cover the pan with a lid or fire blanket and leave it where it is. Use an oven cloth if possible to protect your hands. The fire should go out by itself after a few minutes as the air has been removed. **Do not** try to move the pan. **Do not** put water on this type of fire as it will make it much worse immediately.
An electrical appliance, e.g. a mixer, catches fire	Turn off the electricity at the plug and use a carbon dioxide extinguisher. This gas cools the fire and removes the oxygen. It does not conduct electricity and is safe to use on electrical machinery. **Do not** use any other type of extinguisher in this situation.

Figure 1.23 Action to take to put out a fire

If a fire starts that cannot be put out easily:
- raise the alarm by operating the nearest fire alarm or shouting 'Fire!'
- follow the procedure as rehearsed in your company fire training.

27

Worksheet 3

Try this!

Imagine a fire were to break out now.

○ **Where is the nearest fire extinguisher?**

○ **Where is the nearest emergency exit point?**

○ **Where do you have to assemble outside?**

Without asking for help, see if you can answer these questions explaining the procedure your company wants you to carry out in the event of a fire.

Afterwards, answer them again with the help of someone who knows the correct answer. Were you right?

Fire safety laws

The main fire safety law is the Regulatory Reform (Fire Safety) Order 2005. The Health and Safety at Work Act also contains specific regulations concerning fire precautions at workplaces and there is also European law relating to fire precautions. Fire safety checks may be carried out by an inspector from the Local Authority.

All businesses over a certain size have to have a fire safety risk assessment completed by the owner. The assessment should be reviewed regularly.

The assessment should cover the following:

○ The total number of people allowed in the building at any one time (one reason why a nightclub has to restrict how many people can enter).

○ The use of the premises.

○ The provision of:
  – fire exits
  – fire doors
  – extinguishers
  – alarm systems
  – emergency lighting
  – signage.

Remember!
The thick, toxic smoke that a fire gives off kills and injures people more than the flames. It is very important to keep fire doors closed to stop smoke spreading. Thick smoke can make escape from a burning building impossible.

Remember!
Emergency escape routes must always be kept clear and unlocked. Never leave anything in front of an emergency exit. Most deaths in fires occur because people cannot get out of the building.

Test yourself!

What type of extinguisher would you use for each type of fire?

a Paper in a waste bin.

b A frying pan of burning oil on a stove.

c An electrical food mixer smoking and starting to burn.

Safe working practices

It is very important that everyone at work tries to work in a safe manner. Many accidents can be avoided if you remember:

- that any spillages should be cleaned up immediately
- that any slippery surfaces should have warning notices nearby
- that no items should be placed in corridors and walkways, for any reason
- to take care when lifting and carrying items
- to use a trolley or sack truck whenever possible to transport large or awkward items
- to get help if you cannot manage to move or clear away an item easily
- to keep your work area clean and well organised
- to plan the movement of all items in advance
- not to rush around the kitchen
- to consider others working around you.

Safe lifting and handling techniques

It is very easy to hurt yourself if you do not know how to lift and move items safely. It is not just heavy items that can cause problems when moving them about.

- Be very careful moving pots containing hot liquids. Do not have them too full.
- When taking items out of ovens be careful not to burn someone who may be passing by.
- Do not overload trolleys or trucks.
- Always make sure you can see where you are going.
- Stack heavier items at the bottom and lighter items at the top of a pile.
- Do not stack shelves too high.
- Use steps with great care. Have someone hold them at the bottom if possible.

Figure 1.24 Careless handling and lifting can lead to problems

Lifting a heavy object

To lift a heavy object safely needs correct training. A few guidelines follow:

○ Keep your muscles relaxed: tense muscles strain easily.

○ Plan what is to be carried to where.

○ Check the route is clear, doors open, ramps in position, lights on.

○ Get help if the object is likely to be heavier than you can easily handle.

○ Position your feet carefully at either side of the object to keep your balance.

○ Use one hand to support the weight of the item, the other to pull the item towards you. This way your body can take part of the weight. Use your whole hand to lift, not just the tips of your fingers.

○ Do not twist to change direction as you are lifting or carrying. Move your feet in plenty of small steps.

Figure 1.25 Lifting a heavy object safely

Try this!
Try lifting a medium-sized, empty box following the guidelines above to avoid straining yourself.

Test yourself!

Correct the following phrases:

a Spillages should be cleaned up when convenient.

b Newly delivered boxes can be left in corridors.

c When moving a lot of items put as much as you can on the trolley to save time.

d Get out all the equipment for the day at once and keep it on your work station.

e Decide where you are going to put the items you are carrying when you get to your destination.

Security procedures

Security procedures on catering premises are important for a variety of reasons:

○ To protect staff, visitors and customers on the premises.
○ To reduce theft and pilferage.
○ To help to keep a workplace safe and secure.

Some businesses have designated security staff with specific responsibilities, e.g. a night porter in a hotel.

Keeping the workplace secure

Situation	Procedure
Key control	○ Always follow the correct procedure for issuing and returning keys. ○ Never leave keys in locks – replace them in the correct place after use. ○ Never lend keys to someone else – make them sign for them as you have done. ○ Never leave secure areas unlocked and unattended.
Personal possessions	○ Do not take anything valuable to work. If you have to, keep it locked in your locker. ○ Respect workplace rules regarding personal possessions. ○ Do not take personal bags into your work area – you could be suspected of theft. ○ You may be asked by your employer to agree to the right to be searched at random to deter theft.
Visitors and customers	○ Challenge politely anyone who is in your area who you do not recognise. 'Can I help you?' is the best way to start. ○ If the person says they are waiting for a member of staff, check the name and position of the person they are waiting for. Try to contact that person, while keeping an eye on the stranger to make sure they do not wander off. ○ Escort anyone who appears to be lost to the nearest supervisor or manager.
Closedown procedures	○ Make sure you check all doors and windows are closed. ○ Check that all cooking and preparation equipment is turned off and/or put away. ○ Check that all storage areas – fridges, freezers, dry stores and cupboards – are secure.
General observation	○ If you see someone behaving suspiciously, tell your supervisor as soon as you can. ○ Try to remember what any suspicious person looks like as well as what they were doing. ○ If you see an unattended package and you do not know what it is, **do not touch it**. Inform your supervisor as quickly as possible. ○ Some companies put signs up to remind staff to be aware of security.

Figure 1.26: How to keep the workplace safe and secure

Property

Lost property

Your workplace should have a procedure for dealing with **lost property**. It will involve you giving the item to your supervisor and telling them:

○ where the item was found

○ the date and time the item was found.

If the item you found is not claimed by the owner after a certain period of time, it may be given back to you. Some businesses put unclaimed lost property into a charity box or sell it and put the money into a staff fund.

Security when dealing with customers' property

If you have to handle customers' property you must be very careful. You have a duty to keep the property of others safe and secure. Make sure you record:

○ a description of the item

○ to whom it belongs

○ the date and time it was left with you

○ where it was kept

○ the date and time it was returned to the customer or passed to your supervisor.

This information should help you if there is any query in respect of the property.

Definition

Lost property: an item left behind by someone else.

Find out!

What procedure does your establishment have for dealing with lost property?

Reporting incidents

It is very important that you report anything happening that is out of the ordinary or that you feel is not 'right'. It does not matter if it turns out not to be of concern on this occasion – it could be a very helpful observation for your manager or the police next time.

When you report an incident you must try to remember as much detail as you can. You may be asked to complete an Incident Form with details of:

○ date of the incident

○ time of the incident

○ place of the incident

- who was involved
- what they looked like
- who saw the incident
- a description of what happened
- how long the incident lasted
- whether anybody was hurt
- whether there was any damage to property
- whether the emergency services were called.

You would then be asked to sign and date the form.

Try this!

Study the picture below for three minutes. Close this book and write down all the details that would be needed on an Incident Form.

Figure 1.27 Can you describe what happened here?

Test yourself!

Give one security procedure for each of the following issues:

a Key control

b Personal possessions

c Visitors and customers

d Closedown procedures

e General observation.

Further information

Useful organisations

○ St John Ambulance
○ Health and Safety Executive
○ Royal Society for the Prevention of Accidents
○ Hotel and Catering International Management Association.

You can find out more about these organisations by visiting their websites. Links have been made available at www.heinemann.co.uk/hotlinks – just enter the express code 7162P.

2

Food safety

This chapter covers skills and knowledge in the following units:

- 7132 Unit 203 (2Gen3) Maintain food safety when storing, preparing and cooking food
- 7091 Unit 252 Food safety in catering
- 7091 Unit 265 (part) Kitchen administration in the hospitality industry

Working through this chapter could also provide the opportunity to practise the following Functional Skills:
Functional English – Reading at Level 1
Functional ICT Developing, presenting and communicating information at Level 2 – apply a range of editing, formatting and layout techniques to meet needs, including text, tables, graphics, charts, graphs or other digital content

In this chapter you will:

Know how and be able to keep yourself clean and hygienic	7132 – 203.1,2	7091 – 252.1,2
Know how and be able to keep working area clean and hygienic	7132 – 203.3,4	7091 – 252.3
Know how and be able to store food safely	7132 – 203.5,6	7091 – 252.4
Know how and be able to prepare, cook and hold food safely	7132 – 203.7,9	7091 – 252.4
Know how to maintain food safety	7132 – 203.8	7091 – 252.4

Food safety hazards

What is a food safety hazard?

If food is not prepared, stored or cooked correctly it becomes a **hazard** and those who consume it may become very ill or even die. This is why there are many laws and regulations controlling the provision of food. In the catering industry this puts a great responsibility on all employees whose job involves food preparation.

The main hazards that can affect food are:

o bacteria
o chemicals
o viruses
o moulds
o physical contaminants.

To be able to control these hazards you need to know how they can affect food.

Bacteria

Bacteria are **micro-organisms**. They cannot be seen with the naked eye and cannot be tasted or smelt if they are on food. Not all types of bacteria are harmful – indeed some are very helpful to us. However, some bacteria cause illness; they are known as **pathogenic** bacteria and can cause food poisoning.

Bacteria multiply by splitting into two. They can do this every 20 minutes. This means that after a few hours one bacterium can have multiplied to over one million. When there are about one million pathogenic bacteria per gram of a portion of food eaten, food poisoning can occur.

> **Definition**
> **Hazard:** something which could be dangerous.

> **Did you know?**
> The Basic Food Hygiene test makes sure food handlers know the main principles of food safety. Some food handlers take the Intermediate Food Hygiene examination. Supervisors may take the Advanced Food Hygiene qualification.

> **Definition**
> **Bacterium**: a single bacteria, which is a single-celled organism.
> **Micro-organism:** a very small life form which cannot be seen without a microscope.
> **Organism:** any living animal or plant.
> **Pathogen:** an organism that causes disease.

Figure 2.1 Bacteria can multiply very quickly

Bacteria multiply when they have ideal conditions to grow. These are:

o **Food**: Bacteria multiply on food, particularly protein-based food, e.g. meat, fish and dairy items.

o **Moisture**: Bacteria thrive in moisture, but cannot survive in food preserved by drying, salting or adding sugar.

o **Warmth**: Bacteria prefer body temperature but they are also happy at room temperature. In the fridge or freezer they do not die but become **dormant**, so they do not multiply. High temperatures of over 70°C for more than three minutes will kill most bacteria.

o **Time**: In the best conditions the fastest time in which a bacterium can multiply is ten minutes. The average time for most bacteria is 20 minutes.

o **Oxygen**: Some bacteria need oxygen to multiply, and others prefer no oxygen. There are also types of bacteria that multiply regardless of whether there is oxygen or not.

Some bacteria can form **spores**. These form a protective coating in which the bacteria can survive being cooked, dried and treated with cleaning chemicals. They cannot multiply when in this state, but when the conditions become more suitable, they start multiplying again.

Definition

Dormant: not active or growing.

Did you know?

Certain types of bacteria are very useful to us. We use some types of bacteria to:
o grow crops
o digest food
o treat sewage
o create medicines
o manufacture cleaning products
o make food, e.g. yoghurt and cheese.

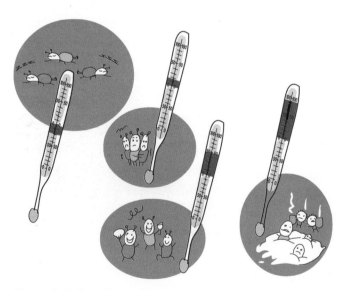

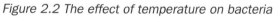

Figure 2.2 The effect of temperature on bacteria

*Figure 2.3 Some bacteria can form protective **spores***

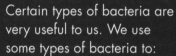

Definition

Spores: cells produced by bacteria and fungi.

The types of bacteria that cause food poisoning are called pathogenic bacteria. The table below shows common types of pathogenic bacteria.

Pathogenic bacteria	Where they come from
Salmonella	Raw meat and poultry, eggs and milk, pets, insects, sewage
Staphylococcus aureus	Human body (skin, nose, mouth, cuts, boils), milk
Clostridium perfringens	Human and animal **excrement**, soil, dust, insects, raw meat
Clostridium botulinum	Soil, raw meat, raw, smoked and canned fish
Bacillus cereus	Cereals (especially rice), soil, dust

Figure 2.4 Types of pathogenic bacteria

Food-borne diseases are caused by micro-organisms which are found in food and water but do not depend upon them to survive. This makes them different to bacteria. Only a small number of these micro-organisms are needed to cause illness.

The table below shows where food-borne diseases come from.

Micro-organism	Where they come from
Campylobacter	Raw meat and poultry, milk, animals
E. coli 0157	Human and animal gut, sewage, water, raw meat
Listeria	Soft cheese, **unpasteurised** milk products, salad, pâté
Shigella	Water, milk, salad, vegetables

Figure 2.5 Sources of food-borne diseases

High-risk foods

As the tables above show, there are several types of food that can harbour the dangerous bacteria that can cause food poisoning. These are known as high-risk foods for these reasons:

○ They are mainly ready-to-eat foods which will not be cooked further (cooking can make food safe to eat).

○ They involve mixing and processing several ingredients. This increases the preparation time at room temperature. Time and temperature are needed by bacteria to multiply.

○ Some dishes involve breaking down and mixing surface tissue with internal muscle. This happens with minced meat, poultry and fish. Few bacteria are found within the muscle and when this is cooked in a large piece, e.g. chicken breast, the bacteria on

Definition

Excrement: solid waste matter passed out through the bowel.

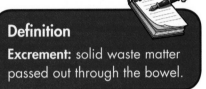

MORE TAKEN ILL IN E. COLI OUTBREAK

CAMPYLOBACTER BUG ON THE RISE

FOOD POISONING SHUTS SCHOOL

Girl, 5, struck down by E. coli

Figure 2.6 Food-borne diseases are widely reported

Definition

Pasteurised: has been heat treated.
Unpasteurised: has not been heat treated.

the outside surface are killed quickly. If the meat is minced, the outside surfaces – which contain more bacteria – are mixed in with the muscle areas.

○ Some ingredients are sourced from high-risk areas, e.g. seafood from contaminated water.

○ Some food is poisonous if it is not cooked correctly. Red kidney beans can make people ill if they have not been boiled for at least ten minutes. (Tinned red kidney beans are safe as they have been thoroughly cooked as part of the canning process.)

○ **Toxins** forming in poorly stored oily fish, e.g. tuna, sardines and salmon, can cause severe illness.

○ Shellfish, e.g. mussels, may become poisonous if they have fed on toxic **plankton**. This particular plankton only occurs at certain times of year in specific areas and so fishing is restricted during this season.

> **Definition**
> **Plankton:** a layer of tiny plants and animals living just below the surface of the sea.
> **Toxin:** a poison produced by bacteria.

The most common high-risk food categories:

○ Cooked meats and poultry, plus pâtés and spreads made from these ingredients.

○ Meat stews, gravy and meat-stock-based soups and sauces.

○ Milk, cream and eggs – particularly items that involve raw or lightly cooked ingredients. Artificial creams and custards are included here.

○ Shellfish and seafood including prawns, mussels, oysters both raw and cooked.

○ Cooked rice that is not used immediately.

Chemicals

Poisoning from chemicals is rare in the UK but it does happen occasionally. Some chemicals can get into food accidentally and can cause poisoning. These are examples:

○ **Cleaning chemicals** can cause poisoning if surfaces and equipment have not been rinsed properly. When the surfaces and equipment are used, the chemical residue can contaminate food.

○ **Pesticides** may be present from harvesting crops which have recently been sprayed with chemicals. In this case, poisoning can occur if the food is not peeled or washed properly.

○ **Metallic poisoning** can occur if food is poorly stored (e.g. leaving food in unlined tin cans in the fridge), or if food is cooked in unlined copper or aluminium pans, particularly acidic foods, e.g. fruit.

Figure 2.7 Metallic poisoning can occur from poor storage

Viruses

A virus is a germ which causes disease. Viruses are even smaller than bacteria. Viruses multiply once eaten so only a few of these tiny micro-organisms are needed to cause illness. The most common food that can cause viral poisoning is shellfish, which may have been grown in contaminated water and not been correctly cleaned before consumption. Viruses can be also passed from person to person via poor personal hygiene, e.g. not washing your hands after using the toilet.

Moulds

Moulds are multi-cellular organisms which will grow on food of all types – sweet, salty, acid or **alkaline**. They grow fastest at a temperature of 20–30°C, but can also grow slowly at temperatures as low as –10°C. Mould spores survive in the air, so even if they are destroyed by cooking it is virtually impossible to prevent them existing on food. Some moulds produce toxins which cause food poisoning symptoms and also may cause cancer. Moulds present on cereals, nuts, herbs, spices and milk can produce toxins in this way (see Food spoilage on page 66).

Figure 2.8 Mould

Definition

Alkaline: a chemical substance that is not acidic.

Did you know?

Some moulds are very useful to us. Particular moulds are produced to ripen cheese, e.g. Danish Blue and Roquefort.

Did you know?

Procedures for handling food safely have existed for centuries. Some religious laws mirror basic food hygiene rules.
o Many people from other parts of the world eat with their hands. In these countries you should only eat with your right hand. This is because when going to the toilet, you should wash your bottom with your left hand.
o Jewish people separate the preparation and consumption of milk and meat products. Sometimes these items are prepared in different kitchens so that no equipment comes in contact with the wrong food type.

Figure 2.9 Eating with your right hand

Physical contaminants

Any item which is discovered in food when it is not supposed to be is a foreign body. Foreign bodies found in food include:

- pieces of glass, plastic and metal, and flakes of paint
- mouse and rat droppings
- gemstones and settings of jewellery
- blue and natural-coloured plasters
- strands of hair
- flies, caterpillars and other insects
- pen tops, drawing pins, paper clips
- screws, nuts and bolts.

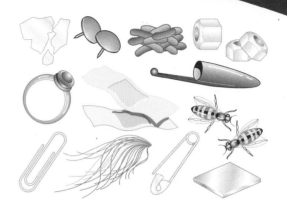

Figure 2.10 Foreign bodies that have been found in food

If such an item is found in food it is extremely unpleasant and upsetting for the consumer and embarrassing and inconvenient for the business. It is very probable that the presence of the foreign body breaks the law – either the Food Safety Act 1990 or HACCP procedures (see page 52). If this happens, the catering organisation will have to look very carefully into its food safety system to find out where it failed.

How can these hazards be controlled?

To control food safety hazards:

- handle food hygienically (see page 44, Personal cleanliness and hygiene)
- prepare food carefully
- store food in the correct manner
- keep all food preparation areas clean
- avoid cross-contamination (see page 70, Controlling food safety hazards)
- cook all food thoroughly.

Why is it so important to control these hazards?

If these hazards are not controlled there is a real danger that you could make yourself ill or be responsible for making your colleagues and/or customers severely ill. People who are weakened through illness or age are more likely to die from a severe bout of food poisoning. You would not like to be the person responsible for this happening. Particularly vulnerable people are:

- elderly
- children
- ill or recovering from an illness
- pregnant women.

Remember!

Always:

- keep yourself and your workplace clean at all times
- wear suitable, clean, washable protective clothing
- protect food from contamination at all times
- minimise the time that high-risk foods are left at room temperature
- keep hot food really hot at 63°C or above
- keep cold food in the fridge at below 5°C
- tell your supervisor your symptoms if you are ill
- take responsibility for working safely and hygienically
- follow all instructions and rules at work
- report all potential hazards.

Fortunately, most outbreaks of food poisoning are not so serious. However, any confirmed outbreak of a food-related illness causes severe problems for a business. Reports in newspapers and on the television and radio will stop many people from visiting a restaurant or take-away outlet. Many catering firms who have had an outbreak of food poisoning have had to close down, so the staff lost their jobs.

Symptoms of food poisoning

The main symptoms are:

o abdominal pain

o diarrhoea

o vomiting (being sick)

o fever.

Other symptoms that may occur are:

o abdominal cramp

o difficulty in breathing

o nausea (feeling sick)

o flu-like symptoms

o rashes

o convulsions (fits).

The time between consuming the food and experiencing the symptoms can be as little as one hour or as long as 70 days!

If you are suffering from food poisoning, the doctor will want to know what your symptoms are and how much time passed from the consumption of any suspect food to the symptoms appearing. This information often gives the first indication of the type of bacteria responsible for the outbreak. To find out the exact cause of food poisoning a **faeces** sample will have to be taken and sent to a laboratory for analysis.

Figure 2.11 The symptoms of food poisoning can be very unpleasant

Definition

Faeces: solid waste substance from the body.

Allergies

An allergy is an intolerance some people have to certain substances, some of which may be types of food. An increasing number of people now suffer from allergic reactions to a range of foods including:

o dairy products (e.g. milk and cheese)

o gluten (e.g. bread and biscuits)

o nuts, especially peanuts

o fish/shellfish

o plants/fungi

o green sprouting potatoes.

Some symptoms of an allergic reaction can be very similar to those of a food-borne illness. It is important that they are not confused. An allergic reaction will only concern one person and usually occurs within a very short time of consumption. An incidence of food poisoning can affect a large number of people at the same time.

Symptoms of food allergies include:

- vomiting
- difficulty in breathing
- diarrhoea
- collapse
- headache
- rash.

The most dramatic reactions tend to occur in response to peanuts and shellfish. Some allergic reactions are very severe, come on very quickly and can be fatal. This is why it is extremely important to inform customers of the precise ingredients in any dish they ask about.

Test yourself!

1 Which of the following is not a pathogenic bacterium?
   a Penicillin
   b Salmonella
   c Staphylococcus aureus
   d Bacillus cereus.

2 Which of the following describes the conditions necessary for most bacteria to reproduce?
   a Warmth, oxygen, food, moisture
   b Cool, oxygen, food, moisture
   c Warmth, carbon dioxide, food, dryness
   d Cool, carbon dioxide, food, dryness.

3 Which of the following is not a symptom of food poisoning?
   a Rash
   b Nausea
   c Sneezing
   d Abdominal pain.

4 Which Regulation concerns the safe system of food production?
   a COSHH
   b RIDDOR
   c HASAWA
   d HACCP.

5 Which of the following statements is true?
   a All pathogens cause illness
   b All moulds cause illness
   c All bacteria cause illness
   d All foreign bodies cause illness.

Personal cleanliness and hygiene

Everyone who works in a job that requires them to handle food must:

- be in good health
- have hygienic personal habits
- wear the correct, clean, protective clothing
- be aware of the potential danger of poor hygiene practice.

A high standard of personal hygiene is a requirement under the Food Hygiene (England) (No 2) Regulations 2005.

General health

Some aspects of health have already been mentioned with regard to safe working practices (see page 29). It is important to remember that working in a catering kitchen can involve:

- standing up for long periods of time
- working in a hot, noisy atmosphere
- having to concentrate and multi-task for long periods of time
- starting work early in the morning
- finishing work late at night.

Bearing these points in mind make sure you:

- have sufficient sleep and relaxation during your time off
- eat regular, balanced meals – this is essential as it is too easy to 'pick' which is not good for your digestion in the long term
- drink plenty of water during your shift at work, otherwise your concentration may be affected
- remember that healthy eating applies to staff just as much as to customers, see Chapter 4.

Personal hygiene practice

Hair: Wash your hair regularly and keep it under a hat. Longer hair should be tied back securely or contained in a net. This reduces the danger of flakes of skin or strands of hair falling into food. Beards and moustaches should also be covered. Do not touch your hair while working. When you have your hair cut, make sure you wash it again before you go to work.

Ears: Do not put your fingers into your ears while working in a kitchen. Earwax and bacteria can be transferred to food and work surfaces and equipment this way.

Nose: The pathogenic bacteria *Staphylococcus aureus* (see page 36) is found in many adult noses and mouths. Sneezes and coughs can spread this bacteria over a wide area. This means that work surfaces, food and equipment can be contaminated very easily. A disposable handkerchief should always be used to catch a sneeze or blow your nose. Always wash your hands thoroughly after using a tissue. Nose picking is an extremely unhygienic activity as is wiping your nose on your sleeve, and neither should ever be carried out in a kitchen (or elsewhere!)

Mouth: Tasting food is essential but you must use a clean spoon each time. A spoon used for one taste should not be put back into the food for any reason without being thoroughly washed first. Spitting is extremely unhygienic – never do this. It is not acceptable to eat sweets or chew gum in the kitchen. Do not lick your finger and then use it to open bags, pick up small, light items or separate sheets of paper. All these activities can spread bacteria easily.

Neck: Do not wear strong perfume or aftershaves, deodorant or cosmetics as they can taint food.

Underarms: Daily bathing or showering removes the bacteria that causes body odour. Perspiration smells can be avoided by using a non-perfumed deodorant.

Hands: The most common method of contaminating food is by having dirty hands. Do not use your fingers for tasting. Keep your nails short and clean. Do not use nail varnish. Watches and rings (other than a plain wedding ring) are not allowed as bacteria can live in the food particles caught under them. Gemstones in jewellery may fall out and become foreign bodies in food. It is impractical to wear a watch because of the frequent use of water in the kitchen.

Remember!
Do not touch any part of any glassware, crockery or cutlery that may make contact with someone's mouth. You would not like to drink out of a cup that someone's fingers had touched around the rim, would you?

How to wash your hands properly

1 Wet your hands with a non-hand-operated warm-water spray or fill the wash hand basin with hand-hot water and wet your hands.

2 Use a non-perfumed antibacterial liquid soap or gel to provide a good lather over the top and palms of your hands, between your fingers, around your wrists and lower forearms.

3 Only use a nailbrush to clean under your fingernails if it is disinfected regularly or is disposable.

4 Rinse your hands thoroughly with clean water.

5 Dry your hands well, preferably with disposable paper towels; hot-air dryers take longer and roller towels must be clean to be safe.

Clothing

It is important to remember the following aspects of good clothing practice:

o Clean, comfortable underwear is just as important as a clean uniform.

o Do not enter the kitchen in outdoor clothing; it will be contaminated.

o Do not wear your kitchen uniform outdoors for the same reason.

o Press studs or Velcro fastenings are more hygienic and easier to use than buttons.

o Change your uniform as soon as it gets dirty. This is usually every day for aprons and jackets. Trousers should be changed two or more times a week.

You may need to wear gloves while at work. Types of gloves include:

o thin rubber or latex gloves for fine work with high-risk foods

o non-latex or vinyl gloves if the food handler has an allergic condition.

See Chapter 1 for more information.

> **Remember!**
> Always wash your hands:
> o when entering the kitchen
> o after using the toilet
> o between each task
> o between handling raw and cooked food
> o after touching your face or hair
> o after coughing, sneezing or blowing your nose into a handkerchief
> o after any cleaning activity
> o after eating, drinking or smoking during a break
> o after dealing with food waste or rubbish.

> **Did you know?**
> There are three items used in hand washing which can contaminate hands rather than clean them! They are:
> o a dirty bar of soap used by many different people
> o a non-disposable nail brush which is not disinfected very regularly
> o a roller towel which is not changed very regularly.

> **Did you know?**
> The most hygienic way of putting on your kitchen uniform is to put your hat on first to stop loose hairs falling onto your whites. When taking off your uniform, your hat should be removed last.

Figure 2.12 The correct order to put on your kitchen uniform

Keep your hair clean and tied back, wear a hat.

Do not touch your ears, do not wear earrings other than sleepers (maybe!)

Taste food with a clean spoon each time.

Use a tissue to blow your nose and wash your hands afterwards.

Wash your underarms regularly, apply unscented deodorant.

Do not wear strong perfume, cosmetics or jewellery.

Cover cuts, burns and sores with a blue plaster dressing.

Keep your nails short and clean, wash your hands frequently.

Change your underwear regularly.

Keep your feet clean and dry, wear clean, cotton socks.

Figure 2.13 Rules for good personal hygiene

Wounds, illness and infection

Working in a kitchen with hot items, knives and dangerous equipment means it is likely that you will suffer a slight injury occasionally. See page 10 for how to treat small cuts and burns and page 22 for more serious accidents.

From a hygiene point of view it is essential that all wounds are covered. This is to:
○ prevent blood and bacteria from the injury contaminating any food
○ prevent bacteria from raw food infecting the wound.

Using a coloured waterproof dressing (blue plaster) keeps the injury clean and protects it. Blue is the best colour for a dressing in food areas as it is easily spotted if it falls off. Very few foods are blue!

Remember!
Always tell your supervisor straightaway if you are wearing a waterproof blue plaster dressing and it goes missing in food!

Spots, blisters and boils are unpleasant skin conditions which can cause problems in food-handling areas because they will be infected with the pathogenic bacteria *Staphylococcus aureus* (see page 36). If you have blemishes on your hands or an allergic condition such as contact dermatitis, work in suitable gloves. If there are blemishes on your face you must be very careful to avoid touching them with your hands while working. In severe cases your supervisor may give you non-food-handling tasks to carry out until the condition has cleared up.

If you are ill and suffer any symptoms that could be from a food-borne illness you must let your supervisor know as soon as possible. The symptoms concerned include:

- diarrhoea
- vomiting
- nausea
- discharges from ear, eye and nose.

You should not work as a food handler while you display any of these symptoms. It is likely you will have to seek medical help if you suffer severe bouts of these illnesses. You may need clearance from your doctor before you can resume work as a food handler.

Your supervisor also needs to know about any similar symptoms suffered by the people with whom you live. This is because you may be a carrier of an infection without displaying any symptoms. If you are a carrier it means you can transmit the infection to others.

Certain illnesses legally need to be reported to the local health authority. Many of them are identified by the symptoms listed on page 43. Your supervisor or doctor should arrange for this to be done if necessary.

Remember!
Many people pick up 'tummy bugs' while on holiday abroad. If you do so, you need to tell your supervisor before you return to work.

Test yourself!

1 How often should you have a bath or shower during a working week?

2 How many occasions are there when you should wash your hands before resuming work?

3 What is a 'carrier' of a food-borne disease?

4 When changing ready to start work, which item of kitchen uniform should you put on first?

Cleanliness and hygiene in your working area

Cleaning is an essential process of removing dirt. It is vital to the safe operation of food businesses. Cleaning staff are employed in many establishments but it is the responsibility of all employees to make sure:

○ all equipment and work areas remain clean

○ the environment they work in is clean and safe.

Why clean?

Cleaning is essential in an area where food is handled for the following reasons:

○ To reduce the danger of contamination of food from:
  – bacteria, by removing particles of food upon which they can feed
  – pests
  – foreign bodies.

○ To create a good impression for:
  – customers
  – other staff and visitors
  – inspectors.

○ To reduce the risk of:
  – accidents
  – equipment breakdown.

Marcus says

Look after your kitchen and the equipment in it. Regular and thorough cleaning will not only extend the life of the kitchen but more importantly will reduce the risk of food contamination.

The main principles of cleaning in a kitchen environment

Methods of cleaning

Cleaning has to be carried out in all areas of the kitchen. These include:

○ **surfaces**: floors and worktops

○ **equipment**: manual or electrical machinery

○ **utensils**: hand-held kitchen tools

○ **touch points**: e.g. door handles.

The main stages of thorough cleaning apply to each area:

1 Switch off and unplug electrical machinery.
2 Pre-clean to remove any loose dirt and heavy soiling, e.g. soak a saucepan, sweep the floor, wipe down a mixer.
3 Clean by washing the item with hot water and detergent. Use a suitable cloth or brush to remove grease and dirt.
4 Rinse with hot water only to remove the detergent and any remaining dirt particles.
5 Disinfect with extremely hot water (82°C) or steam in a controlled area, e.g. in a dishwasher or a second sink. Where this process is not safe or practical use a chemical disinfectant. Apply it to the appropriate surface and leave it for the length of time stated on the instructions.
6 Final rinse to remove all cleaning chemical residue.
7 Dry–air drying is the most hygienic; otherwise use paper towels or clean, dry cloths.

Figure 2.14 Cleaning a slicing machine

Types of cleaning agent

○ **Water** is the most effective cleaning agent. It can be used hot or cold and also under pressure. When used in the form of steam it can also disinfect. Water leaves no residue and is very environmentally friendly. It is also used for rinsing.
○ **Soap** is made from fat and caustic soda. Soap can leave a scum on surfaces, so it is not suitable for kitchen cleaning. Disinfectants are sometimes added to soap for hand washing.
○ **Detergents** are chemicals manufactured from petroleum. They break dirt up into fine particles and coat them so they are easy to remove. Detergents can be in the form of powder, liquid, foam or gel. They usually need mixing with water before use.
○ **Disinfectants** are chemicals that will kill bacteria if left in contact with the surface for a sufficient amount of time. It is better to apply them with a spray rather than a cloth. Their efficiency is affected if the surface that is being treated is not clean.
○ **Sanitiser** is a chemical which can clean and disinfect. It is often used in sprays for hard surface cleaning. It needs to be left in contact with the surface to be cleaned for a sufficient amount of time to be effective.

What to disinfect	Example	When to disinfect
Food contact surfaces	Chopping boards, containers, mixers	Before and after each use
Hand contact surfaces	Refrigerator handles, taps, switches	At least once per shift
Contamination hazards	Cloths and mops, waste bins and lids	At least once per shift, cloths and mops after each main use

Figure 2.15 Disinfection frequency table

Find out!   Worksheet 5

Some materials will be damaged by usual cleaning methods and therefore, need special attention. Find out how the following materials should be cleaned:

o cast iron
o copper
o aluminium.

Find out!

How does your establishment colour-code small cleaning equipment?

Types of cleaning equipment

To clean effectively you need suitable equipment. This is likely to include:

o small equipment, e.g. cloths, brushes, mops and buckets
o large equipment, e.g. dishwashers, jet washers, wet and dry vacuum cleaners.

Small equipment should be colour-coded so that it is only used in the correct areas and for the correct job. Red equipment could be used in raw food preparation areas, and yellow in cooked food preparation areas for example. A blue set of equipment could be reserved for cleaning changing-room areas and this should be stored separately.

Cloths frequently spread more bacteria than they clean away. All reusable cloths should be changed every few hours in a shift as they will contain constantly increasing numbers of bacteria at room temperature. Reusable cloths should be washed and disinfected thoroughly before being dried ready to use again. It is more expensive but much more hygienic to use disposable cloths. These are available in a range of colours to help with coding and controlling where they are used.

Figure 2.16 Colour-coded kitchen equipment

Remember!

Never use a cloth that has been used on a floor or in a toilet area to wipe a work surface.

Cleaning schedules

A cleaning schedule forms part of the HACCP procedures and may be used together with checklists to ensure a thorough job is done.

A cleaning schedule is a written plan that tells everyone in the kitchen:

- what items and surfaces are to be cleaned
- who is to carry out these tasks
- how often the cleaning is to be carried out
- when the cleaning should be done
- how long it should take to clean correctly
- what chemicals and equipment are needed to clean it
- what safety precautions should be taken when cleaning, e.g. wearing goggles and gloves, putting out warning signs
- the method of cleaning that should be used.

Frequently used items and work areas may have to be cleaned after each task in preparation for the next. It is the responsibility of all food handlers to carry out this clean-as-you-go system correctly. It is particularly important when you are preparing raw foods. You must disinfect the work area thoroughly once you have cleaned it, to prevent cross-contamination.

> **Remember!**
>
> Hazard Analysis and Critical Control Point (HACCP) is used to describe an internationally recognised way of managing food safety and protecting consumers.

> **Find out!** Worksheet 6
>
> How frequently are the following cleaning tasks carried out at your workplace?
> - Cleaning the ovens
> - Washing down the walls
> - Cleaning out the refrigerators
> - Cleaning the bin area.

Cleaning schedule and checklist

Area/item of	Frequency	Responsiblity	Cleaning materials	H&S precautions	Method of cleaning	Checked by
Walls	Daily	Kitchen porter & 2nd chef	Detergent & cloth	Ladder to be used to reach areas above shoulder height	1) Pre-clean 2) Clean, apply detergent with hand-held spray, leave for 2 mins 3) Rinse 4) Air dry	
Floors	Daily	Kitchen porter	Detergent & mop & bucket	Hazard notices to be put out in entrances to the area being cleaned	1) Pre-clean 2) Clean, apply detergent with mop 3) Rinse 4) Air dry	
Work surface	Daily	Chefs	Sanitiser & cloth	None required	1) Pre-clean 2) Apply sanitiser with trigger spray, leave for 2 mins 3) Wipe over 4) Air dry	
Oven	Weekly	Kitchen porter	Oven cleaner	Rubber gloves, overall, mask & goggles	1) Ensure oven is turned off & cool 2) Pre-clean 3) Clean, apply oven cleaner, leave for 30 mins 3) Rinse 4) Air dry	
Fridges	Weekly	Kitchen porter & 2nd chef	Hot water & detergent	None required	1) Pre-clean 2) Clean, apply detergent with hand-held spray, leave for 2 mins 3) Rinse 4) Air dry	
Bins	Weekly	Kitchen porter & 2nd chef	Hot water & detergent	Gloves	1) Pre-clean 2) Clean, apply detergent with hand-held spray, leave for 2 mins 3) Rinse 4) Air dry	
Windows	Monthly	Kitchen porter	Hot water & detergent	Ladder to be used to reach areas above shoulder height	1) Pre-clean 2) Rinse 3) Air dry	
Ceiling	Monthly	Kitchen porter	Detergent & cloth	Ladder	1) Pre-clean 2) Clean, apply detergent with hand-held spray, leave for 2 mins 3) Rinse 4) Air dry	
Freezer	Monthly	Kitchen porter & 2nd chef	Hot water & detergent	Gloves	1) Pre-clean 2) Clean, apply detergent with hand-held spray, leave for 2 mins 3) Rinse 4) Air dry	

Figure 2.17 Example cleaning schedule and checklist

Hazards associated with cleaning procedures

The COSHH Regulations cover cleaning because there are several
potential hazards which could occur. These are some of the hazards:

o Using dirty cloths to clean, which spreads bacterial contamination.

o Using the same cleaning equipment to clean raw food
  preparation areas as well as those for preparing cooked food
  and causing cross-contamination (see page 73).

o When cleaning has been carried out very poorly and
  contamination remains.

o When there is no separate cleaning equipment for cleaning
  toilet and changing room areas and the kitchen so cross-
  contamination is likely.

o Using cleaning chemicals incorrectly, leaving a residue over food
  preparation areas, which will cause chemical contamination (see
  Chemical contaminants on page 39).

o Storing cleaning materials and equipment near to food, or
  storing chemicals in food containers, which could result in
  contamination.

o Pest infestation (see page 55).

Waste disposal

Every catering establishment wants to reduce waste for several
reasons:

o All food thrown away represents lost income to the business.

o All businesses have to pay to have their waste removed, so large
  amounts of waste can increase this cost.

o Reducing the amount of waste produced helps the environment.

o Waste can attract pests which can be a food
  safety hazard.

In every kitchen there should be sufficient waste
bins provided at suitable points. The bins should:

o have tight-fitting lids

o be lined with a polythene disposable
  sack (if appropriate)

o not be overfilled

o be emptied regularly

o be cleaned regularly

o not smell

o not be left in the kitchen overnight.

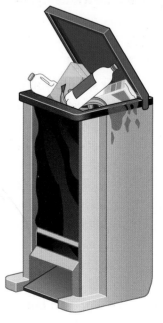

Remember!

Some waste can be
dangerous, e.g.

o broken glass can cause injury

o fat and oil can leak out of
  containers and make floors
  slippery.

Figure 2.18 Kitchen waste bins should be emptied regularly

The bagged waste from kitchen bins should be transferred to a large lidded bin in the outside refuse area as soon as necessary. The bags should be tied securely to prevent any spillages. This will help to reduce the hazard of pest infestation. The outside refuse area should be kept clean for the same reason. Spoiled food may be kept apart from general food waste. Individual bins should be provided for recycling paper, cardboard, glass and plastic. In large businesses this type of waste may be crushed by compactor machines to take up less space before binning.

Figure 2.19 A well-organised outside bin area

Hazardous surfaces and equipment

For reasons of health and safety and to follow the HACCP procedures, it is important to act when you notice any damage to surfaces or equipment in the kitchen.

Remember!

Waste oil should **never** be poured down drains. It should be put in a suitable container (often the drum in which it was delivered). Waste oil may be collected separately from the main rubbish collection as it can be recycled. Eventually it may be used as fuel for cars!

Figure 2.20 Used oil can be poured into a suitable container ready for recycling

Try this!

What should you do in the following situations?

1 You notice a piece of equipment has lost an attachment necessary for it to work safely. Should you:
   o put an out of order notice on the machine?
   o tell your supervisor straight away?
   o look for the missing attachment if you have time?

2 You have heard the motor of a refrigerator struggling. The unit is positioned opposite a kitchen window catching the full morning sun. The motor has to work very hard to keep the inside of the fridge cold. Should you:
   o tell your supervisor about the situation?
   o suggest a better position for the refrigerator if you can think of one?

You should inform your supervisor if you see:

o broken floor or wall tiles

o damaged doors or handles of refrigerators, ovens, cupboards or drawers

o loose handles on saucepans

o light bulbs that have failed inside equipment, e.g. microwaves and refrigerators

o the electric fly catcher becoming ineffective

o gas equipment that becomes difficult to light or goes off during use

o blades on machinery that have become blunt or damaged

o paint flaking from the ceiling and falling on the work surface

o the chopping boards in use being very scratched and pitted

o dripping hot or cold water taps which cannot be turned off

o any blockages, e.g. in preparation sinks or wash hand basins.

There will be many more potential hazards depending upon the size and type of kitchen that you work in.

Try this!   Worksheet 7

Look around your workplace and make a list of all the fittings and equipment that could become a hazard and need attention. The problem could relate to health and safety or food safety. You may be surprised how long the list can be, even in a small kitchen!

Pest control hazards

Pests are responsible for the majority of closures of food establishments by the Environmental Health Officer. Pests are also responsible for large amounts of food being wasted by infestation or contamination. Staff and customers become very upset if they find any type of pest on the premises. Under the HACCP procedures a catering business is expected to have effective pest control methods in place.

Pests live in or near catering premises because they provide:

o **food** in store rooms, waste areas, poorly cleaned production areas

o **moisture** from dripping taps, outside drains, **condensation** droplets

o **warmth** from heating systems and equipment motors, e.g. refrigerators

o **shelter** in undisturbed areas, e.g. the back of store cupboards, behind large equipment.

By removing as many of these conditions as possible, pests may be put off living in the area and look elsewhere.

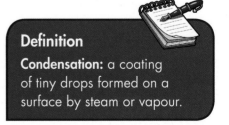

Definition
Condensation: a coating of tiny drops formed on a surface by steam or vapour.

Signs of infestation

How can you tell if there is a pest infestation in your workplace?
Look for:

o dead bodies of insects, rodents and birds
o droppings, smear marks
o eggs, larvae, feathers, nesting material
o paw or claw prints
o unusual smells
o scratching, pecking or gnawing sounds
o gnawed pipes, fittings or boxes
o torn or damaged sacks or packaging.

Pests cause hazards in the following ways:

o Bacterial contamination from pathogenic bacteria found:
  – on the surface of the pest's skin
  – in pest droppings.
o Physical contamination from fur, eggs, droppings, urine, saliva, dead bodies, nest material.
o Chemical contamination from using strong chemicals to kill the pests which then gets into food.
o Cross-contamination which occurs when a pest transfers pathogenic bacteria from one area to another, e.g. a fly landing on raw meat and then moving on to a cooked chicken.

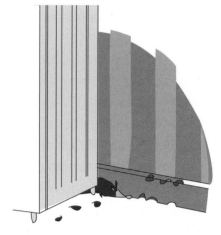

Figure 2.21 Evidence of infestation

Types of pests

Insects

Flies are one of the most common insect pests. They are usually found in places which have not been cleaned thoroughly and where rubbish is allowed to gather. A female housefly can lay up to 600 eggs in her life. An egg takes about two weeks to go through the maggot stage and become a fully grown fly.

Cockroaches are one of the oldest types of insects, said to date from prehistoric times. They do not usually fly and only come out when it is dark. Their eggs take around two months to hatch. They can live for up to a year. Cockroaches can be detected by their droppings or their unpleasant smell.

Weevils are very tiny insects that live in dry goods, e.g. flour, cereals and nuts. They can only be seen with the naked eye if they are moving. It is possible to spot an infestation if there is tunnelling or speckling in the commodity.

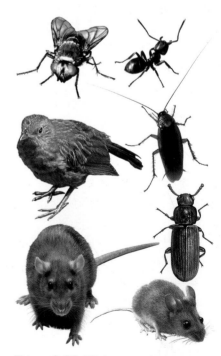

Figure 2.22 Kitchen pests

Ants are attracted by sweet items which have not been stored securely. They usually nest outdoors, and follow set paths to food sources.

Rodents

Rats commonly get into buildings through drains or holes but they also burrow under walls. Rats are a particular hazard as they can transmit Weil's disease, and a worm-type parasite as well as food poisoning bacteria. They also bite. The Norway rat is the most common in the UK. It usually lives outside.

House mice are the main problem in buildings. They can climb very well and cause considerable damage by gnawing to keep their teeth short. Like rats, their teeth grow throughout their lives and unless they wear them down, their teeth will pierce through their heads! Mice dribble urine nearly all the time and leave droppings at frequent intervals. They breed very quickly – a pair of mice can have 2,000 offspring in one year!

Birds

Pigeons, starlings and seagulls can be a problem in outside waste areas where bins are allowed to overflow and are not kept covered. Once in the area, birds may then get into a building through doors and windows and will often try to nest in roof spaces. As well as contaminating food with feathers and droppings, birds can block gutters with nests and spread insect infestation.

Domestic pets and wild animals

Domestic pets (e.g. cats and dogs) and also wild animals (e.g. foxes) can be a problem in outside waste areas if bins are allowed to overflow.

Preventing pest infestation

It is almost impossible to prevent pests entering a building. It is possible, however, to discourage them from staying! There are some ways of preventing pests:

○ Regular thorough cleaning of areas, e.g. changing rooms and food stores, particularly in corners where pests may be able to hide unnoticed.

○ Clearing up any spillages thoroughly and promptly.

○ Not allowing waste to build up and keeping bins covered at all times.

Did you know?

This is what happens when a fly lands on your food: flies can't eat solid food so to soften it up they vomit on it. Then they stamp the vomit in until it's a liquid, usually including several bacteria for good measure. When it's good and runny they suck it all back in again, probably dropping some excrement at the same time. And then, when they've finished eating, it's your turn.

- Keeping doors and windows closed or using insect screens across openings.
- Moving cupboards and equipment as far as possible to clean behind and under them regularly (see Safe lifting techniques on page 29).
- Removing any unused equipment and materials from the area.
- Ensuring food storage containers are properly closed when not in use.
- Checking all deliveries – of all items, not just food – for signs of infestation.
- Storing and rotating stock correctly.

What does a pest control contractor do?

A pest control contractor will inspect premises looking for evidence of infestation by any type of pest. They will then deal with any pests they discover. Finally, they will complete a report describing what action they have taken. A copy of the report is left on the premises.

A pest control contractor may:

- lay bait and set baited traps
- use sticky boards
- install electric ultraviolet insect killers
- spray an insecticide chemical over an area.

The contractor will leave instructions regarding the treatments used. It is important not to touch or move any items that have been left to catch pests. Any sprayed areas must be left untouched for the instructed period of time.

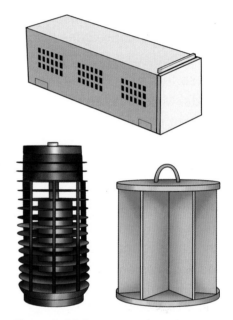

Figure 2.23 Pest control equipment

Test yourself!

1 What is the most important reason for cleaning?
   a To make a good impression on customers
   b To keep the work area pleasant
   c To reduce the danger of contamination
   d To prolong the life of equipment.

2 Which is the correct order for the cleaning process?
   a Pre-clean, clean, rinse, disinfect, rinse, dry
   b Pre-clean, rinse, clean, disinfect, rinse, dry
   c Pre-clean, disinfect, rinse, clean, rinse, dry
   d Pre-clean, rinse, clean, rinse, disinfect, dry.

3 Which cleaning agent kills bacteria?
   a Detergent
   b Disinfectant
   c Soap
   d Warm water.

4 Where might you find an infestation of weevils?
   a Flour
   b Fish
   c Fruit
   d Fennel.

Storing food safely

A considerable range of ingredients is used in the average catering kitchen. If you were to list all the food items used in your workplace it could run into hundreds! Some of these commodities can be stored for very long periods of time before use, e.g. dried fruit. Other food items will only remain safe to prepare and eat for a very short time, e.g. fresh mussels need to be used within a couple of hours of delivery if they cannot be stored in a refrigerator.

Correct delivery and storage of all foods is required under the HACCP procedures and appropriate records should be kept. Efficient stock control and ordering are essential for a well-run catering business, for both food safety and commercial reasons.

Food deliveries

If you receive a food delivery at your workplace you need to check the following.

The **vehicle** delivering the items:

- Is it suitable?
- Is it clean inside?
- Is it refrigerated for the delivery of chilled items?

The **temperature** of the delivered items:

- Are chilled items below 5°C?
- Is frozen produce kept below −10°C?
- Use a temperature probe to check if necessary. If the temperature is too high reject the goods.

The **packaging**:

- Is it clean and undamaged?
- Is there any sign of mould or other spoilage?
- Are any containers dented, bulging or leaking?
- Are the items labelled with:
  - the name of the company?
  - description of the food?
  - product code?
  - ingredient list?
  - use by date?
  - weight?
- Is the 'best before' or 'use by date' still several days in the future?

Figure 2.24 Accepting a delivery of food items

○ Do the items delivered match the delivery note provided in terms of:
- amounts of each item? (e.g. 1 x 25kg bag)
- specification of each item? (e.g. King Edward potatoes)

If you have to reject a delivery make sure:

○ The delivery person has agreed to return the item to the supplier.
○ The item being returned is recorded on either the delivery note or a separate return slip.
○ The delivery person signs the delivery note or return slip, as you may do if requested.
○ You give your copy of the delivery note or return slip to your supervisor as soon as possible. You need to make sure that your employer does not pay for goods that have been rejected and returned.

Preparing food for storage

A delivery must be put into the appropriate storage as soon as possible after arrival – preferably within 15 minutes.

Frozen and **chilled** items must be put away first. Prompt storage is necessary because:

○ frozen items must not be left in warm conditions where they could start defrosting
○ chilled items must not be allowed to warm to an unsafe temperature at which bacteria could grow. This is especially important with ready-to-eat items, e.g. salads.

Packaged items should have storage instructions included on the label. These should be followed exactly.

Fresh items must be put into cool storage to preserve their quality ready for preparation.

Dry goods should be taken to the stores area where they should be entered on to the stock record to prevent theft.

Your employer may have a system for date coding all items delivered. A date sticker may have to be attached to the items as they are put away. As you put new stock away, move the old stock to a position where it will be used first. This is called stock rotation. See page 65 for more information. Handle all items carefully. Do not attempt to lift heavy items on your own (see page 29).

Some items may need to be removed from the original external packaging before storage, e.g. if a cardboard box is breaking or there is

Figure 2.25 Date code deliveries

not enough space to store an item in its full packaging. Care must be taken to transfer any important information, e.g. use by dates, onto the replacement container. Your workplace should have a system for this.

Storing food correctly

There are three main areas where food is stored in the kitchen:

- dry stores
- refrigerator
- freezer.

These may be free-standing or walk-in units.

Follow these general food storage rules:

- Always protect food from contamination by keeping it in suitable containers.
- Store all food items off the floor on shelves or pallets.
- Do not overload shelves.
- Leave space between items for air to circulate.
- Keep storage areas clean, dry and free from debris at all times.
- Rotate stock correctly (see page 65).
- Tell your supervisor about any signs of pest infestation (see page 56).

Dry store rules

- The store should be cool and well-ventilated.
- Flours and cereals may be stored in wheeled bins to protect them from pests. The bin must be fully emptied and cleaned before new stock is added.
- Shelves should not be overfilled and old stock must always be put in front of new.
- Move items from flimsy bags or unsuitable containers, make sure the description label with the 'use by' date is transferred.
- Cleaning products should not be stored with food; they should be in a separate area.

> **Try this!**
> Imagine you have been asked to put away a delivery of fresh, whole chickens. The box they have been delivered in is very weak and flimsy. Describe exactly what you would do to make sure the chickens were stored safely.

> **Did you know?**
> One way of remembering stock rotation is to think 'FIFO'. **F**irst **I**n **F**irst **O**ut – food that is put into storage first should be used first.

Figure 2.26 A well-organised dry stores area

Keep the following items in the dry store:

o Dry foods, e.g. flour, sugar and dried herbs.

o Canned and bottled items (unless the label specifies they need to be refrigerated).

You still need to remember to rotate the goods so that the oldest goods are used first. Although goods in the dry stores last a long time they do gradually deteriorate in quality.

Storage of fruit and vegetables

o Fresh fruit and vegetables should be stored in a cool, dry place.

o Root vegetables store best in a dark area.

o Loose soil around fresh vegetables should not be taken into the kitchen.

o Fresh fruit and vegetables are often stored in a refrigerator if there is space, in a safe position.

Refrigerators

High-risk foods and those which will spoil quickly need to be stored in a refrigerator. This is because most pathogenic and food spoilage bacteria multiply very slowly or not at all between 0°C and 5°C – the temperature of a refrigerator.

How to clean a refrigerator

Points to remember when cleaning either a free-standing or walk-in refrigerator include:

o Carry out cleaning regularly – daily in some kitchens, weekly in others.

o Use a sanitiser (see page 50), rinse it off and dry the surface thoroughly with disposable paper towels or clean cloths.

o Give the door seals special attention but treat them gently to avoid damage.

o Empty and clean drip trays underneath the equipment.

o Thoroughly dry the floor of a walk-in refrigerator to avoid slips.

o Clean the handles and both sides of the doors.

o Clean up any spillages straight away.

o Transfer the contents of the refrigerator to an alternative unit if possible, or at least put them somewhere cool, while cleaning is taking place. Replace them as soon as cleaning has finished and the temperature of the refrigerator is back to what it should be.

All industrial refrigerators should defrost automatically. If ice is allowed to build up inside the unit it will reduce the efficiency of the machine.

Did you know?

A blown tin has both ends bulging as the contents have spoiled and gases have been produced in the process. The contents of these tins are not safe to eat and must be discarded. Be careful! The pressure built up inside the tin from the gases may cause the tin to explode.

Remember!

Even if you are in a hurry do not add new goods to a container already holding old goods.

Storing food inside a refrigerator

When separate refrigerators are not available for raw and high-risk foods then these items have to be positioned carefully in one unit. Raw food should **always** be stored below other food so that no blood or juices can drip down and contaminate items on the lower shelf.

Take care with strong-smelling foods (e.g. strong cheese and fish), as they can taint more delicate items (e.g. milk and eggs) and make them taste very strange. All items in a refrigerator should be covered, e.g. in a container with a fitted lid or covered with waxed paper, cling film, greaseproof paper or foil. Do not put food directly in front of the cooling unit if possible as this can affect how efficiently the refrigerator operates.

The following food should be refrigerated:
o raw meat, poultry, fish and seafood
o cooked meat, poultry, fish and seafood
o meat, poultry and fish products, e.g. pies and pâtés
o the contents of any opened cans in suitable containers
o milk, cream, cheese and eggs, and any products containing them (e.g. a flan)
o prepared salads
o fruit juice
o spreads and sauces
o any other item labelled for refrigeration.

Chilled display cabinets

Food in these units is on display for sale but is being kept cold as if it were in a refrigerator. This is achieved by cold air being circulated over the food. The highest temperature permitted for these units is 8°C. The temperature of these units can be affected by:
o draughts which can alter the air flow
o lighting which can increase the temperature
o sunlight which can also increase the temperature.

Under the HACCP procedures this type of refrigeration should be monitored very regularly.

Figure 2.27 A chilled display cabinet

Remember!
Never put hot food into a refrigerator.
Never leave the refrigerator door open longer than necessary.
Both practices will cause the temperature inside the refrigerator to rise.

Did you know?
Opened cans of food should never be left in a refrigerator. As well as the danger of a cut from the sharp, exposed lid of the tin, if the juices inside the tin are acid (e.g. as with tinned fruit) they can react with the lining of the tin once exposed to the oxygen in air. This reaction can taint the food and give it a metallic flavour which is unacceptable. Some tins now have a plastic coating on the inside to stop this. It is still best to change the container of opened tinned items to be stored in the fridge.

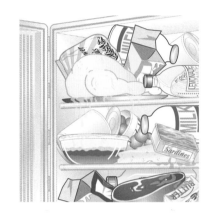

Freezers

Food is frozen to make it last longer without spoiling. It also keeps it safely, as pathogenic bacteria cannot multiply in temperatures below −18°C. However as soon as the temperature rises bacteria may start reproducing. Food that has been allowed to thaw should not be refrozen. This is in case the number of bacteria present have been able to reach a dangerous level and cause food poisoning. If a thawed item has been cooked it may be refrozen. This is because the cooking process will have killed any pathogenic bacteria present.

Storing foods inside a freezer

When loading a freezer with frozen food remember to:

○ make sure all items are well wrapped
○ label items clearly and include the date
○ stack items close together to maintain the temperature
○ place raw food below high-risk foods
○ put stock with the shortest shelf life at the front.

Hot holding of food

Hot cupboards and counter service equipment are designed to store food for a few hours at a safe hot temperature. The heating elements in this equipment are not sufficiently powerful to raise the temperature of the food quickly. This could mean that pathogenic bacteria could survive and reproduce to a dangerous level during the slow heating process.

Did you know?

Unwrapped food in the freezer may suffer from 'freezer burn', i.e. the surface will be damaged as if it has been burnt. When thawed, the quality of the surface of the food will be poor and it may not be usable.

Remember!

If a fridge or freezer breaks down:
○ call the service engineer to come and repair it
○ do not open the door if at all possible.
Most freezers are fitted with alarms that will sound if there is a malfunction.

Remember!

If food has been cooked, cooled and reheated it should never be cooled and reheated a second time. It should always be thrown away.

The following rules apply when using hot holding equipment:

o Always preheat the equipment before use.

o Do not use the equipment to reheat food.

o Check the equipment regularly if hot water is used; if it needs topping up use hot water (not cold).

o If heated lights are used, keep the food fully in the lit areas.

Stock control

Stock control is about maintaining minimum levels of stock to meet requirements for food production. Each commodity should have a minimum stock level set for it. As something is taken out of stores it should be logged. When a commodity reaches its minimum level an order should be generated. Sometimes if there is a large function, for example, additional stock may need to be ordered to meet this need.

Stock checks need to be done at regular intervals to identify ordering requirements and monitor stock shrinkage. A stock taking sheet should be completed. These days stock control is often managed using an Electronic Stock Control system. In this case, minimum stock levels are held in the system and an order is automatically generated when stock reaches that level.

Figure 2.28 A bain-marie, one type of hot holding equipment

Stock ordering process

This begins with the stock taking sheets or the printout from the Electronic Stock Control system. Once a need for an order is identified, it is important to ensure the correct specification which means the quantity required and the quality. Quality agreements with suppliers may include agreed delivery dates e.g. same day, or next day. Many organizations keep a list of preferred suppliers on which this information will be kept. The person drawing up the order may need to get a signature from someone more senior to authorize it. Sometimes a large organization may have different departments and stock may be requisitioned from one department to another using an internal requisition form.

Once the food has been delivered an invoice will follow. When received it should be checked against the order and the delivery note.

Stock rotation

It is very important to use ingredients in the same order that they have been delivered. This is because:

- food loses quality the longer it is kept
- food will have to be wasted if it is not used by the 'best before date'
- food thrown away is money wasted for the business.

Storage systems must ensure that stock is used in the correct rotation. When putting food away it is very important that:

- older stock of the same item is moved to the front so that it is used first
- new stock is never mixed up with old stock on shelves or in containers.

Food spoilage

As soon as fruit and vegetables are picked, animals slaughtered and fish caught the process of decomposition starts. Eventually the food will become unfit to eat. This is known as spoilage. Food decomposition is caused by:

- the action of natural chemicals already inside the food (called enzymes)
- the action of bacteria, moulds and yeasts that are present on the surface of food.

The speed of decomposition can be reduced by:

- preservation, e.g. freezing, canning, drying and salting
- keeping the food at low temperatures, e.g. in the refrigerator.

Decomposition of food can be speeded up by:

- storage in unsuitable conditions, e.g. warm, damp conditions
- contamination by pests
- careless handling causing damage, e.g. the bruising of fruit.

Identification of spoiled food

Food that is no longer suitable to eat may:

- be discoloured at the edges or in patches throughout
- show mould growing on the surface
- have a different, often unpleasant smell
- feel different in texture, e.g. soft, pulpy, dry, cracked and wrinkled
- taste different, e.g. bitter, sour, with an aftertaste.

Many of the conditions that allow food to spoil also allow pathogenic bacteria to multiply (see page 37). This means that spoiled food is often unsafe to eat and may cause food poisoning.

Did you know?

In many countries it is now the law to label food with a date after which it is not assured of being safe to eat. It is an offence to change this date without re-treating or processing the food appropriately. Highly perishable foods (those that spoil quickly) must be marked with a 'use by' date. Less perishable items (which are preserved in some way) are marked with a 'best before' date. These dates indicate that the food will be in its best condition before this date. If consumed after this date it may have deteriorated in quality but it will not be a health risk.

You should not use any such food and report it to your supervisor. The spoiled food should be clearly labelled 'not for human consumption'.

Ways of preventing spoilage

All the methods of keeping food safe from contamination reduce the speed at which spoilage occurs. These include keeping food:

o covered
o cool (refrigerated in most cases)
o dry
o free from contamination.

An alternative way of stopping spoilage is to preserve the food. There are several methods of preservation that can delay the process or prevent it altogether. These include:

o **Heat treatment** by cooking, canning, bottling, sterilising, pasteurising and ultra-heat treatment (UHT). The amount of heat and the length of heat treatment will increase the storage time. UHT products will keep for several months, canned goods will keep for several years.

o **Low temperatures** used in the chilling or freezing of food.

o **Dehydration**, i.e. the drying of fish, meat, fruit, vegetables, soups, stocks and beverages. This process excludes water. Dehydrated items stored in airtight containers will last a considerable period of time.

o **Chemical preservation** by salting, pickling and curing (using sodium nitrate and nitrite salts). This method also alters the flavour of the item. It is often combined with the canning or bottling processes.

o **Vacuum packing**, also known as 'sous vide', is used mainly for meat, fish and poultry. This process removes oxygen from around the food and greatly extends the shelf life. The items should remain in chilled storage.

o **Smoking**, used particularly for fish, poultry and meat including ham and sausages. This process imparts a strong flavour to the food. Smoked items last longer than non-smoked items but still have to be kept in the refrigerator.

o **Irradiation** is a process that kills pathogenic bacteria and spoilage organisms. It works by subjecting the food to a low amount of radiation. It does not kill spores and toxins.

Figure 2.29 Fruit that is canned or frozen lasts much longer than fresh fruit

Did you know?
Some tinned foods have been opened after hundreds of years and the contents have still been edible (although not very nice to eat!)

Remember!
If a tin has been badly dented, damaged or is 'blown' the contents will not be safe to eat.

Test yourself!

1 What is the maximum acceptable temperature for a chilled food delivery?
  a 3°C
  b 5°C
  c 7°C
  d 9°C.

2 What is the correct order in which the following delivered goods should be put away?
  a Frozen, chilled, fresh, tinned
  b Chilled, fresh, tinned, frozen
  c Fresh, tinned, frozen, chilled
  d Tinned, frozen, chilled, fresh.

3 Which part of the refrigerator should be cleaned very carefully?
  a Door seals   **b** Shelves
  c Walls   **d** Floor.

4 What is the term describing damaged unwrapped frozen food?
  a Contaminate   **b** Spoil
  c Burn   **d** Waste.

5 Rewrite these dry store rules correctly.
  a The store should be warm.
  b Flours and cereals may be stored in cardboard boxes.
  c Shelves should be as full as possible.
  d Old stock should be pushed to the back.
  e Store cleaning products in the same area.

6 What does 'FIFO' stand for?
  F_____
  I_____
  F_____
  O_____

7 What is the maximum acceptable temperature for a chilled display cabinet?
  a 5°C
  b 6°C
  c 7°C
  d 8°C.

8 There are three things which can affect temperature of a chilled display cabinet. Write down two of them.

Preparing and cooking food safely

Great care should be taken when preparing and cooking food.

Defrosting food safely

Some food can be cooked straight after being removed from the freezer. If this is the case there will be appropriate instructions on the packet. Otherwise the item must be allowed to thaw before cooking. This is especially important with raw meat and poultry.

The rules for thawing food:

o Always keep thawing raw meat items well away from other food.

o Thaw items in a cool room, thawing cabinet or in the bottom of a refrigerator.

o Always thaw items on a tray where the defrosting juices can collect safely.

o Once the item is thawed keep it in the refrigerator and cook it within 24 hours.

o If using a microwave oven to defrost an item be aware of cool spots where it may remain frozen.

o Never refreeze an item that has been thawed.

Chilling or freezing food not for immediate consumption

If food has been cooked and is not for immediate consumption it should be cooled as quickly as possible. Ideally this should be carried out in a blast chiller (see page 72). Large production kitchens may operate a large cook-chill operation producing hundreds of chilled meals every day. Some cook-chill systems also use the 'sous vide' method for preservation of food in vacuum packs (see page 67). This type of production involves specialist equipment. See page 63.

If food is to be frozen rapidly, specialist equipment is needed to carry out this procedure safely. Blast freezers cool food down to −20°C in 90 minutes.

Did you know?

Be careful with Christmas dinner! Thawing large frozen turkeys has to be carried out very carefully to avoid outbreaks of food poisoning. A 9kg turkey will take several days to thaw. Great care has to be taken to make sure the inside of the bird is defrosted. If not it will not cook to a safe temperature and bacteria will continue to reproduce.

Figure 2.30 Is your Christmas turkey safe?

Did you know?

Some ingredients in dishes do not freeze well. Sauces which are to be frozen should not be made with wheat flour because once defrosted they will separate if not used within a few weeks. Sauce recipes should be adapted to use modified starch instead.

If freezing food you must remember to:

o reduce the temperature as quickly as possible
o keep the thickness of the food to be frozen as even and thin as possible
o wrap the food thoroughly
o label the food clearly.

See page 64 for more information.

> **Try this!**
> If an item is frozen in a standard freezer it will take much longer to freeze and the ice crystals that form within the item will be much larger. This will cause the texture of the item to be poor. Freeze a strawberry in a domestic freezer and then let it thaw! What happens to the strawberry?

Controlling food safety hazards

Methods of controlling food safety hazards

There are four main areas in the production of food where the risk of contamination by those employed in the kitchen is highest. These are:

o cooking
o chilling
o cleaning
o cross-contamination prevention.

Cooking

There are many different methods of cookery. No matter which method is used, it is important to cook food thoroughly. The choice of method should suit the food to be cooked, e.g. you cannot grill an egg. The time and temperature at which the food is cooked must ensure that all the harmful bacteria that may be present are destroyed. This must be achieved without spoiling the quality of the item that is to be served to the customer. Overcooked food may be very safe but may also be **inedible**!

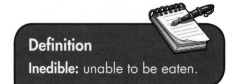

Definition
Inedible: unable to be eaten.

Temperature probe

Some food may reach the required temperature on the outside but still be cooler in the middle. This is where a temperature probe is needed to check that the internal temperature has reached the necessary level.

A temperature probe is a type of thermometer on a long stick that is used to take the core temperature from the middle of food. It is particularly useful when:

o reheating a tray of cottage pie ready to serve on a counter

o testing to see if the inside of a whole chicken is cooked

o measuring the temperature of a joint of meat which is being roasted in the oven.

Temperature probes are usually digital and can be battery operated. It is important to keep them very clean. They should always be sterilised before and after each use, otherwise they could transfer dangerous bacteria from one food to another.

Temperature probes are also useful to check whether food has cooled down to the required temperature before being put into the refrigerator or freezer.

Temperature probes need to be checked regularly to make sure they are working correctly. If they are not accurate they should not be used until they have been repaired or replaced.

To make cooking as safe as possible, remember these points:

o Heat items as quickly as possible to reduce the time spent in the temperature danger zone when bacteria will reproduce quickly.

o Cut large joints of meat and poultry into smaller portions where possible to ensure even cooking all the way through.

o Cook stuffings separately (they often do not reach the required temperature quickly enough and have caused many outbreaks of food poisoning in the past).

o Stir stews and casseroles regularly during cooking to keep the temperature even throughout the pan.

Remember!

Hot food should be held at 63°C prior to and during service. Cold food should be held below 8°C.

Did you know?

To ensure that all heat-resistant spores are destroyed by cooking, a temperature of 75°C must be reached for 30 seconds minimum. In Scotland it must reach 82°C. It is also possible to destroy spores by heating food at a lower temperature for a longer period of time. Such intense heat may damage the quality of the food, e.g. fish tastes best when it is only just cooked. If over-cooked it becomes tough and dry. Meat also becomes dry if cooked too much, and some people prefer to eat meat such as steak rare, which means it is undercooked.

Remember!

Ideally food should be cooled to below 8°C in under 1½ hours. Only a blast chiller will be able to achieve this. Even this equipment cannot cool a large joint of meat within this time. That is why the law states that food should be cooled 'as quickly as possible'.

Chilling

Cooling cooked food is a very high-risk procedure. Unlike cooking, when high temperatures will be achieved to kill bacteria, if there are bacteria alive in the food they will reproduce as it cools.

Harmful bacteria may be present in cooked food as a result of spores not being destroyed in the cooking process. They may also have been transferred onto the cooked food from another source, e.g. dirty equipment. Bacteria will then remain in the food either reproducing at room temperature or dormant in the refrigerator or freezer.

Many catering premises now use blast chillers to reduce the temperature of cooked food as quickly as possible to make it safe.

Cooked food must not be cooled in a refrigerator or freezer where other food is being stored. If a hot item is put into this environment to cool down quickly it will raise the temperature of the surrounding air. This will result in the other chilled food becoming warm. Bacteria may then start reproducing in the food being stored. The warmth may also cause frozen food to start defrosting. Condensation may then occur and drip liquid onto food and contaminate it.

When cooling cooked food remember:
○ The smaller the size of the food item, the more quickly it will cool.
○ Shallow, flat containers have a greater surface area to allow faster cooling.
○ The greater the difference in temperature, the faster cooling will take place.

Cleaning

A high standard of cleanliness is essential to keep the risk of food safety hazards low. Cleaning can reduce the risk of food safety hazards because it:
○ removes food particles upon which bacteria can feed
○ reduces the risk of contamination of food which is being prepared or stored
○ reduces the danger of pests, e.g. insects, rats and mice, coming into the kitchen
○ helps to prevent accidents by providing a clean work area
○ encourages safe working methods
○ helps keep the area pleasant to work in.

See page 49 for more information.

Figure 2.31 A blast chiller

Remember!
Frequent opening and closing of the door of a refrigerator will cause the temperature inside to keep rising and falling.

Figure 2.32 A shallow, flat container allows faster cooling

Cross-contamination prevention

Bacteria cannot move by themselves and so are only able to contaminate food by being transferred onto it by something or someone else. This is known as cross-contamination and is one of the main factors in outbreaks of food poisoning. The main sources of cross-contamination include:

- Hands of staff working in food production areas.
- Cloths and equipment used by staff in these areas.
- Infestation of pests in the kitchen (see page 55).
- Poor storage of food.

Hands: if hands are not washed thoroughly in between one job and another then cross-contamination can occur very easily (see Personal hygiene on page 45). There is a particular risk in the following situations:

- If raw food is prepared, followed by cooked food.
- If food preparation is resumed directly after a visit to the toilet or a smoking break.

Cloths and equipment: if cloths are not changed or cleaned regularly then cross-contamination can occur. Cloths can carry large amounts of bacteria and have been known to spread more over a surface than were present in the first place!

Equipment: this must be cleaned thoroughly after each use and checked for cleanliness before being used again. Some pieces of equipment may only be used for specific types of foods or in certain areas of the kitchen. Large catering operations may have completely separate preparation areas for certain food, e.g. a meat kitchen, a vegetable kitchen and so on. Most establishments have a separate pastry area.

Infestation of pests: Cross-contamination can occur by an insect or animal touching the surface of a raw food product and then one that has been cooked, thus transferring bacteria from one to the other. Pests can also transfer bacteria by leaving fur or droppings on food. (Further information on pests can be found on page 55.)

Poor storage of food: this can result in cross-contamination. If food is not put into suitably sized containers and covered, spillages may result. This could involve amounts of one item falling into another. Apart from being very messy and wasteful, this can become a food safety hazard, e.g. if an uncooked chicken defrosting on the

Remember!

Chopping boards may be colour coded to reduce the risk of cross-contamination. The following code is commonly used in the industry:

- red – raw meat
- brown – vegetables
- blue – raw fish
- white – bakery, dairy
- yellow – cooked meat
- green – salad, fruit

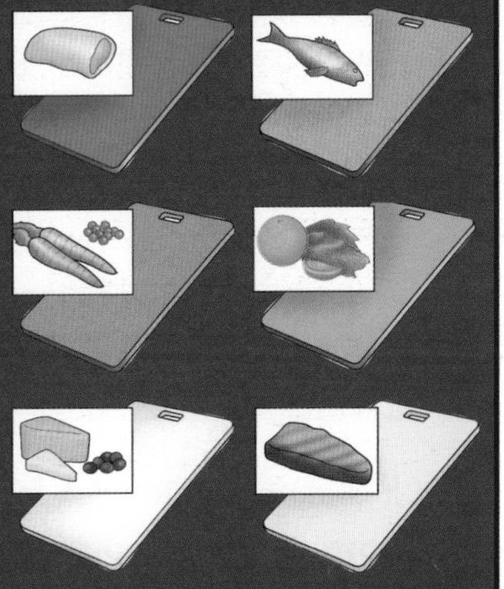

Figure 2.33 Colour-coded chopping boards

Definition

Cross-contamination: Contamination of food by the transfer of bacteria from one item to another.

top shelf of a refrigerator drips liquid onto an uncovered trifle on the shelf below, it is highly likely that salmonella bacteria will be transferred from the chicken to the trifle. (Food storage is covered in more detail on page 59.)

Test yourself!

1 Complete the following statements:

a The transfer of bacteria from raw to cooked food is called _____ _____ .

b The person authorised to enter food premises to inspect them for food safety is called an _____ _____ _____ .

c The main law controlling the hygienic supply, preparation and service of food is called the _____ _____ _____ .

d To make it safe, all raw food should be heated to _____ °C for _____ minutes.

e To find out if food being heated is the correct temperature all the way through a _____ _____ needs to be used.

f The _____ of bacteria may survive high temperatures.

2 It is important to cook food as safely as possible. Why should you do each of the following?
   a Heat items as quickly as possible.
   b Cut large joints of meat into smaller ones.
   c Cook stuffings separately.
   d Regularly stir stews.

3 When would you use a blast chiller?

4 Complete the table with the correct use for each colour-coded chopping board.

Chopping board	Use
Red	
Yellow	
White	
Blue	
Green	
Brown	

Monitoring and reporting

Records have to be kept on a day-to-day basis in a catering kitchen.

The process of monitoring

Monitoring is defined as 'regularly checking condition and progress'. To be able to check condition, it has to be measured against a standard that has already been set. For example, if your speed of work was being monitored, it would be measured against an average that had been worked out in advance. This would be obtained by watching and timing a range of people all carrying out the same task.

In a catering kitchen there are many types of monitoring that take place:

○ The Head Chef monitors the standard and amount of work produced by the kitchen staff.

○ Refrigerator and freezer temperatures are monitored and recorded several times each day.

○ Cleaning is monitored daily by supervisors to make sure standards of hygiene are being maintained.

○ Contractors regularly monitor a range of equipment in the kitchen including:
  – pest control equipment
  – alarm systems
  – fire-fighting equipment
  – microwave ovens and other cooking equipment, e.g. steamers
  – refrigerators and freezers
  – dishwashers
  – extraction systems.

○ Deliveries are checked for quality, temperature, best before dates and correct weight.

○ Rotation of stock is monitored frequently to make sure the oldest products are used first.

○ The amount of wasted food thrown away may be checked very regularly in some kitchens.

○ The presentation standard of the food produced is monitored, often by checking against prepared photographs.

Fridge temperatures

Week commencing: _____

	Time	Signed	Time	Signed	Time	Signed
MON	Temp		Temp		Temp	
TUE	Time	Signed	Time	Signed	Time	Signed
	Temp		Temp		Temp	
WED	Time	Signed	Time	Signed	Time	Signed
	Temp		Temp		Temp	
THURS	Time	Signed	Time	Signed	Time	Signed
	Temp		Temp		Temp	
FRI	Time	Signed	Time	Signed	Time	Signed
	Temp		Temp		Temp	
SAT	Time	Signed	Time	Signed	Time	Signed
	Temp		Temp		Temp	
SUN	Time	Signed	Time	Signed	Time	Signed
	Temp		Temp		Temp	

Comments
_____
_____
_____

Figure 2.34 Temperature control record sheet

The process of monitoring can take several forms, including:

- completing a checklist
- recording specific information on a chart
- filling in particular sections on a schedule
- carrying out spot checks
- questioning staff and contractors
- observing work practices and work areas
- taking samples – of food or **swabs** of work surfaces and equipment
- weighing items
- checking temperatures.

> ### Definition
> **Swab:** a sterile piece of cotton used to take a sample for chemical analysis.

Figure 2.35 Completing a checklist

Try this! **Worksheet 8**

Which monitoring processes would you use for the following situations?

- *Keeping the results of refrigerator temperature checks.*
- *Making sure all areas of the staff changing room have been cleaned thoroughly.*
- *Checking that a meat delivery is correct.*
- *Finding out if there is any evidence of mice in the dry stores area.*

Action to take when monitoring reveals a problem

The purpose of monitoring and checking is to spot a potential problem or risk before it becomes a serious hazard. If checking is carried out regularly then any difference in results should show up very quickly.

The action taken depends on the type of problem. Urgent action is necessary if the problem concerns a possible food safety hazard.

Figure 2.36 What should you do when plated food items do not look like the prepared photograph?

The table below shows the type of action that may be necessary to prevent food becoming a hazard.

Problem	Possible action to be taken
Poor standard of work produced by kitchen staff	Retraining and closer supervision by Head Chef.
Refrigerator temperature rises significantly	Check that the refrigerator is not defrosting automatically. If this is not the case: ○ move items to another refrigerator with the correct temperature ○ unplug the refrigerator if possible ○ put an 'out of order' notice on it ○ tell your supervisor as soon as possible.
A mouse is spotted in the corner of the kitchen	○ Tell your supervisor as soon as possible. ○ The pest control contractor will be called out immediately. ○ Kitchen staff will need to look out for evidence of mouse infestation. ○ Make sure that no food crumbs are left around or any food left uncovered in kitchen and stores areas.
Microwave does not heat the food properly	○ Check the portion of food is the correct size for the time allowed. ○ Test the microwave by heating a cup of water. ○ If it does not perform as it should, unplug the equipment so it cannot be used. ○ Put an 'out of order' sign on the machine. ○ Tell your supervisor. ○ An engineer should attend to rectify the problem.
Chilled produce is delivered in a van that is not refrigerated	○ Check the temperature of the delivered items. If over the safe limit of 8°C, refuse the delivery. ○ Tell your supervisor, as this may have been a problem before and the supplier may be changed.
Out-of-date salad items are found at the back of the refrigerator during a stock take	○ Throw the out-of-date items away. ○ Tell your supervisor, as stock figures will be affected.
A large amount of raw vegetable waste is found in the bin	Head Chef to retrain staff in efficient preparation methods.
A large amount of cooked waste is found in the bin	Head Chef will investigate and take action. Possible reasons: ○ portions served too large. ○ quality of food poor.
The plated food items do not look like the prepared photographs	Head Chef will investigate and take action. Possible reasons: ○ poor quality food used. ○ staff not trained correctly.

Figure 2.37 Action to take when monitoring reveals a problem

The role of record keeping

Under the HACCP procedures it is important to record readings and actions taken while preparing food. These procedures provide protection for the catering business and its employees in the event of a food safety issue.

The Environmental Health Officer visits all catering businesses regularly to check that food is being prepared according to the Regulations. The Officer will expect to see evidence of how food safety is being maintained. They will expect to see records of a variety of monitoring procedures, including:

o temperature records of all refrigerators and freezers

o pest control reports

o probe temperature records of reheated foods and those held at hot temperatures

o cleaning checklists and schedules.

If there was an outbreak of food poisoning in a restaurant, the manager should be able to prove that all the food safety procedures have been carried out correctly. This process is known as showing '**due diligence**'. The Environmental Health Officer may decide that the blame for the outbreak is not with the restaurant and investigate other possible causes, e.g. the food suppliers.

> **Definition**
>
> **Due diligence**: that every possible precaution has been taken by the business to avoid a food safety problem.

The relative importance of different hazards

It is important to be able to identify which situations require urgent action and which problems can be solved a little later on.

All circumstances which put any person in danger should be dealt with immediately. These include any:

o fire or security alert

o accident to any person in the area

o foreign body found in food

o equipment found in a dangerous condition

o floor surface found in a dangerous condition

o food left in an unsafe condition

o food stored in an unsafe condition.

Try this!

Put the following incidents in the order you would deal with them if they all happened together. Then state the action you would take in respect of each hazard.

- *A carton of cream is past its 'use by' date in the refrigerator.*
- *There is a pool of water around the door of an upright freezer and the contents are thawing.*
- *A chef cuts their finger and needs a plaster.*
- *A fly falls in a pan of soup on the stove.*
- *A frying pan overheats and catches fire on the stove.*

Figure 2.38 Can you spot all the things that have gone wrong?

Reporting food safety hazards

It is very important to report all possible hazards to your supervisor.
The situation may result in:

- a serious safety hazard (food or health and safety)
- a high level of wastage leading to shortages and inaccurate stock records
- a repair or service call-out to fix or maintain a piece of equipment or to maintain the hygiene of the premises
- the identification of a need for staff training.

Food safety management systems

In every business that produces, serves or sells food it is vital that there is an organised system to reduce all risk of food safety hazards.

The HACCP procedures require there to be a **documented** system highlighting all areas where special attention should be paid to food safety. The system should cover all food used on the premises and follow the route from the delivery of the raw materials through to the consumption, service or sale of the items.

> **Definition**
> **Documented:** making a detailed record of information.

> **Did you know?**
> The HACCP procedures were first developed in the 1960s to ensure that astronauts going up in space had food to eat that was absolutely safe.

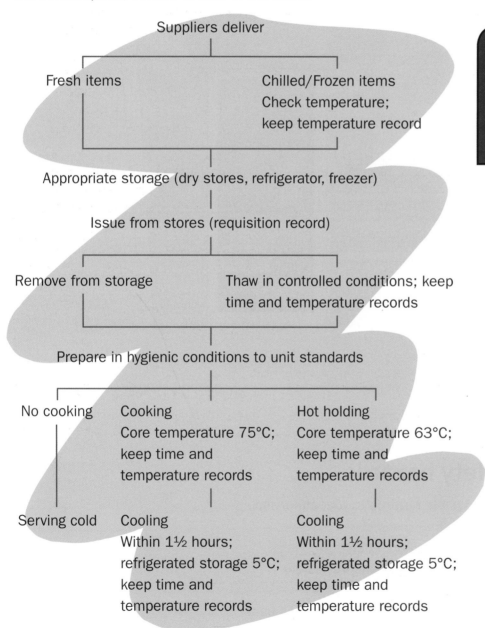

Suppliers deliver

Fresh items

Chilled/Frozen items
Check temperature;
keep temperature record

Appropriate storage (dry stores, refrigerator, freezer)

Issue from stores (requisition record)

Remove from storage

Thaw in controlled conditions; keep time and temperature records

Prepare in hygienic conditions to unit standards

No cooking

Cooking
Core temperature 75°C;
keep time and
temperature records

Hot holding
Core temperature 63°C;
keep time and
temperature records

Serving cold

Cooling
Within 1½ hours;
refrigerated storage 5°C;
keep time and
temperature records

Cooling
Within 1½ hours;
refrigerated storage 5°C;
keep time and
temperature records

Figure 2.39 Example of isolation of critical control points in a kitchen

Step	Hazard	Action
1 Purchase	High-risk (ready-to-eat) foods contaminated with food-poisoning bacteria or toxins.	Buy from reputable supplier only. Specify maximum temperature at delivery.
2 Receipt of food	High-risk (ready-to-eat) foods contaminated with food-poisoning bacteria or toxins.	Check it looks, smells and feels right. Check the temperature is right.
3 Storage	Growth of food poisoning bacteria, toxins on high-risk (ready-to-eat) foods. Further contamination.	High-risk foods stored at safe temperature. Store them wrapped. Label high-risk food with the correct 'sell by' date. Rotate stock and used by recommended date.
4 Preparation	Contamination of high-risk (ready-to-eat) foods. Growth of food-poisoning bacteria.	Wash your hands before handling food. Limit any exposure to room temperatures during preparation. Prepare with clean equipment and use this for high-risk (ready-to-eat) food only. Separate cooked foods from any raw foods.
5 Cooking	Survival of food-poisoning bacteria.	Cooked rolled joints, chicken, and re-formed meats e.g. burgers, so that the thickest part reaches at least 75°C. Sear the outside of other, solid meat cuts (e.g. joints of beef, steaks) before cooking.
6 Cooling	Growth of food-poisoning bacteria. Production of poisons by bacteria. Contamination with food-poisoning bacteria.	Cool foods as quickly as possible. Don't leave out at room temperatures to cool, unless the cooling period is short, e.g. place any stews or rice, etc, in shallow trays and cool to chill temperatures quickly.
7 Hot-holding	Growth of food-poisoning bacteria. Production of poisons by bacteria.	Keep food hot, above 63°C.
8 Reheating	Survival of food-poisoning bacteria.	Reheat to above 75°C.
9 Chilled storage	Growth of food-poisoning bacteria.	Keep temperatures at right level. Label high-risk ready-to-eat foods with correct date code.
10 Serving	Growth of disease-causing bacteria. Production of poisons by bacteria. Contamination.	COLD SERVICE FOODS – serve high-risk foods as soon as possible after removing from refrigerated storage to avoid them getting warm. HOT FOODS – serve high-risk foods quickly to avoid them cooling down.

Figure 2.40 Critical control points – Department of Health.

The stages a food safety management system should cover are:
- quality, packaging and temperature of the food at delivery
- packaging, temperature, location and method of storage
- method of preparation
- type and length of storage between preparation and cooking
- method of holding hot food after cooking

o method of cooling and storing after cooking

o method of reheating cooked food

o method of serving.

Identify types of food safety hazard

Food safety hazards can come from the most unlikely sources – some of them quite unexpected. When trying to identify possible food safety hazards you need to be very open-minded.

The table below shows the questions you need to ask when trying to identify food safety hazards:

Question	Possible answers
Where could harmful bacteria be found in the workplace?	o Poor cleaning of equipment. o Insect or rodent infestation. o Poor hygiene practices of staff – not washing hands sufficiently, staff being ill and still coming to work.
What can cause cross-contamination?	o By using the same chopping boards for raw and cooked foods. o By storing raw food above cooked food in the refrigerator. o By food handlers not washing their hands thoroughly in between dealing with raw and cooked foods.
What other possible ways are there for food to be contaminated in the workplace?	o Cleaning chemicals getting into food from poor storage or not rinsing properly. o 'Foreign bodies' getting into food from breakages not being cleared away carefully.
Which high-risk foods come into the kitchen in an uncooked state?	o Chicken o Eggs o Meat o Vegetables o Rice. These are high-risk due to the food poisoning bacteria or toxins that may be found in them in their raw state.
Is it possible for harmful bacteria to be able to multiply to a dangerous level?	o Is any food cooked and then left out at room temperature for a long time before being put in the refrigerator? Is there a better procedure that can be used? o Is any high-risk raw food left out for a long time at room temperature? Can this be avoided? o Is there ever a significant delay between cooking food, keeping it hot and it being served? Is there an alternative to this practice?
Is a probe used correctly to ensure thorough cooking and reheating of food?	If no, what happens instead?

Is food ever served before it has been reheated properly?	If yes, why and how can this be avoided next time?
Is frozen food sometimes not defrosted in time?	If yes, what happens?
Does the correct equipment exist in the kitchen for certain processes? Is it used when it should be (e.g. a blast chiller used to chill food quickly)?	If the equipment is not available, what happens?
What happens when demand is unpredictable? How is extra food provided at short notice?	Is there a stock of stand-by items kept in a freezer? How long does it take to get this ready for service?
What happens when food has to travel some distance between preparation and service? Does this happen when the food is hot or cold?	Is specialist equipment provided? If not, how is the food kept free from contamination and at the correct temperature?

Figure 2.41 Identifying food safety hazards

Try this!

Look at the table above. Now think about your workplace. Make a similar list that identifies risk areas that exist with present work practices. This is the first stage of the HACCP procedures for creating a food safety management system.

Test yourself!

1 Which of the following is an example of monitoring food safety?
   a Taking fridge temperatures
   b Writing weekly menus
   c Washing the kitchen floor
   d Calculating food cost.

2 What is the process of collecting information to prove food safety called?
   a Assessing hygiene methods
   b Monitoring bad practice
   c Copying clear records
   d Demonstrating due diligence.

3 What is the principle involved in stock rotation?
   a First in last out
   b Last in last out
   c First in first out
   d Last in first out.

4 Which of the following is not an example of a HACCP record?
   a Staff rota
   b Temperature chart
   c Cleaning schedule
   d Equipment checklist.

3

Teamwork

This chapter covers skills and knowledge in the following units:

- 7132 Unit 104 (1Gen4) Work effectively as part of a hospitality team

- 7091 Unit 152 Effective teamwork

Working through this chapter could also provide the opportunity to practise the following Functional Skills:
Functional English Speaking and listening – consider complex information and give a relevant, cogent response in appropriate language; present information and ideas clearly and persuasively to others

In this chapter you will:

Know how and be able to plan and organise own work	7132 – 104.1,4	7091 – 152.1
Know how and be able to work effectively with team members	7132 – 104.2,5	7091 – 152.1
Know how and be able to develop own skills	7132 – 104.3,6	7091 – 152.1
Know how to support the work of a team		7091 – 152.2

Effective teamwork

Effective teamwork is vital in the hospitality industry. A good standard of service and production cannot be provided by individuals working alone. A successful meal service depends upon all the staff in the kitchen and restaurant working together to ensure:

o correct timing
o smooth service
o high standard of production
o food served at the correct temperature.

The perfect team will consist of members who:

o are committed to the task in hand
o work together towards a common aim
o are well-organised
o communicate openly.

The benefits of working as a team mean that:

o a higher output of work can be achieved for less effort
o people are usually happier working in a group
o responsibility for work and decisions is shared
o team members are loyal to each other
o the workforce is more creative.

Marcus says

This is vital and there is no room for a 'them and us' relationship between front of house and the kitchen. Everyone is striving towards the same goal and is merely a piece in the whole picture.

In the kitchen

Pat was the manager of a school meals kitchen. Each member of staff was responsible for producing one of the dishes on the menu every day. Her staff often complained about their colleagues' speed of work. They had to wait for each other on many occasions when using the same pieces of equipment such as mixers and ovens. Some staff worked more quickly than others and did not want to be held up. Some staff criticised the quality and flavour of the dishes that others had made.

Figure 3.1 Staff complaining

Pat decided to restructure the organisation of the kitchen. She put her staff to work in teams, each responsible for a group of dishes. She also moved the teams around so that they did not make the same dishes all the time. This meant that the staff had to work together and help each other much more. They organised their use of the equipment better and they stopped criticising each other's dishes. They started to share the recipes they used and found they had more time to get their jobs done.

Figure 3.2 Staff working in a team

Working as a team member also has advantages, such as:

○ feeling more valued at work
○ being able to learn from others
○ being able to show others what you can do
○ greater job satisfaction
○ having the support of others
○ benefitting from any team 'perks' – such as a productivity bonus.

In the kitchen

Jim used to work alone in a small sandwich bar. He was often lonely and struggled to keep pace with demand at lunchtimes when it was busy. He found he had to start work really early in the morning to make sure everything was ready. If he wanted a break or to finish early he had to work even harder to make up for the lost time.

Figure 3.3 Jim was unhappy working alone

Jim moved to work at a larger sandwich shop. He was much happier straight away. There were other people to talk to while he worked and he enjoyed having a laugh and a joke with them. If he wanted a break, others would cover his job so he did not fall behind. He liked being able to help the others if they needed it. As a team, far more sandwiches were being produced than if each of them worked separately. The group liked to try to invent a different sandwich filling each week. Jim enjoyed the challenge of thinking of new combinations of ingredients. The customers liked several of the new sandwiches and sales rose. The owner of the business was very pleased and gave the whole team a bonus payment.

Figure 3.4 Jim enjoyed being part of a team

Types of team

There are two main types of team that work in the kitchen of any food production business:

○ **Formal**: a team that is led by the Head Chef with a deputy and staff running all the areas within the kitchen.
○ **Informal**: a team that is put together at short notice but may not normally work together.

Formal teams have:

○ an appointed leader
○ specific tasks to achieve
○ clear channels of communication
○ clear lines of authority and responsibility.

The diagram below shows how a formal team works in a small kitchen: a 40-seater restaurant.

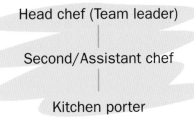

Head chef (Team leader)
|
Second/Assistant chef
|
Kitchen porter

Figure 3.5 A small team in the kitchen of a 40-seater restaurant

A very small catering business will only have a very small team. The members of small teams will work very closely together and eventually be able to help and deputise for each other in all areas.

Below is a diagram showing the organisation of a formal team in a large kitchen: a conference centre catering for up to 1,000 customers at a time. You can see that the large operation has the kitchen split into a number of teams. Each team has a different responsibility.

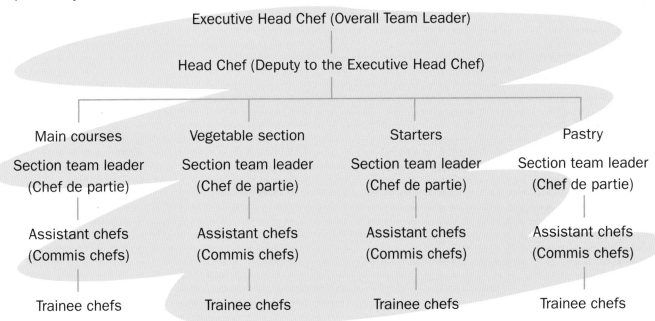

Executive Head Chef (Overall Team Leader)
|
Head Chef (Deputy to the Executive Head Chef)

Main courses	Vegetable section	Starters	Pastry
Section team leader (Chef de partie)	Section team leader (Chef de partie)	Section team leader (Chef de partie)	Section team leader (Chef de partie)
Assistant chefs (Commis chefs)	Assistant chefs (Commis chefs)	Assistant chefs (Commis chefs)	Assistant chefs (Commis chefs)
Trainee chefs	Trainee chefs	Trainee chefs	Trainee chefs

Figure 3.6 A large team in the kitchen of a conference centre

Try this!

Draw a diagram of the organisation of your kitchen. Compare it with diagrams of people who work in other types of kitchen. The charts are likely to be quite different because:

o **some kitchens, such as a small fast-food takeaway, will be very small and employ only a few staff**

o **some kitchens, such as an international exhibition centre with conference and banqueting facilities, will be very large and employ many staff.**

In your diagram, is there one team or several small teams?

Think about if and when any informal teams are used in your workplace. What are they used for?

Are you involved in any informal teams outside the workplace?

The organisation of an informal team cannot be shown in the same way. An informal team:

o develops from a particular need

o exists for a short period of time

o may have a flexible structure

o deals with a particular situation.

Look at Figure 3.6. Normally the staff would work in their formal team structure. However, at service time, if there were a large number of starters to be served, members of other teams would join this section to help while they were needed, creating an informal team. Once the first course had been served, the informal team would disband. The staff would return to their formal teams and continue with their work.

Another time when an informal team might be formed is when change is proposed. If a new menu was being developed a Head Chef and the team leaders from each section may meet to suggest dishes and test recipes.

Informal teams may also exist outside the formal workplace. If a member of staff is in hospital, other staff members may become an informal team to organise a schedule of visits and help for that person's family. A group of friends may form an informal team to organise a Christmas or charity event.

Roles and responsibilities of team members

All teams must have a leader. Formal teams have an appointed leader who is recognised by their job title. They may also be paid at a higher rate than the rest of their team.

An informal group will also have a leader. The leader is unlikely to be appointed and could change as and when the tasks to be carried out require different strengths.

The success of a team depends very much on the leader. The leader of a team should:

○ set a good example
○ be respected by all the team members
○ be consistent in decisions made
○ encourage, motivate and support team members.

Try this!
Think of your team leader at work. Do they do a good job? Can you identify what they do to make the team work well together?

How do team members work together effectively?

A good team member will:

○ always be reliable and on time for work
○ be organised, work cleanly and methodically
○ complete all tasks required within a reasonable time
○ help other people to complete their work if necessary
○ share information and learn from other team members
○ communicate clearly with others.

If a team is working effectively it will:

○ complete the required work on time and to a good standard
○ be able to learn new skills and techniques easily
○ communicate well within the team
○ motivate the team members to work harder and be successful
○ work to and achieve a common aim.

The working day is much less tiring and stressful for everyone if teams work together well.

Test yourself!

1 List four benefits of working in a team.

2 Name the two types of team.

3 Give an example of how working in a team can be better than working individually.

Organising your own work

When to ask for help

Sometimes, particularly when starting a new job, you may not be sure what to do. Being uncertain about a task can result from:

○ not being shown how to do it
○ being unsure of the standard expected
○ forgetting how to carry out a task
○ being uncertain if you have sufficient time to carry out a task properly
○ not knowing how to operate equipment necessary to complete the task.

You need to ask for help whenever necessary, particularly at the start of a new job. If you do not, you could:

○ waste materials and time carrying out the task incorrectly
○ injure yourself or someone else
○ produce a sub-standard item
○ irritate other members of your team who then have to rectify your mistake.

Remember!

If you keep asking for help at very frequent intervals your team members and your supervisor may get fed up with you. Pay attention to help that you are given. Make notes so you are sure what to do and have them to hand for next time. Ask questions when the person is helping you, not after they have gone back to their own work. The more you carry out a task, the more confident and skilful you will become.

In the kitchen

Paula had just started to work in the pastry department of a large kitchen. The Pastry Chef asked her to make four dozen bread rolls for lunch service. Paula followed the standard recipe the chef had given her. The recipe made eight dozen rolls so Paula had to reduce the ingredients by half. She thought she had done this correctly and was surprised when the mixture seemed very slow to prove. Instead of asking the chef for advice she carried on. When the rolls came out of the oven they were far too small and extremely hard. They could not be used. The Pastry Chef had to stop what he was doing and make some replacement rolls. He was very cross that Paula had not asked for help as soon as she realised something was wrong.

Figure 3.7 The Pastry Chef was very cross

You need to ask for help when:

○ you are asked to do something you have not done before
○ you are still uncertain about a task you have not carried out very often
○ you cannot find something and have had a thorough look for it
○ you have not understood or remembered instructions you have received.

Helping others

Working in a team, you will be encouraged to help each other. Help is invaluable and your team members will always appreciate support. But remember that help should only be given if:

○ the assistance has been asked for, or your manager or supervisor has asked you to help. People can get upset if others start to take over uninvited, thinking they are helping.

○ by helping, the problem will be solved, not made worse. Too many cooks can spoil the broth! Also you need to be sure that you actually have the necessary skill to help.

○ by helping with one problem, another is not created, e.g. by stopping to help, you cannot finish your own preparations on time.

In the kitchen

Phil had to make 500 savoury tartlets for a cocktail party that afternoon. He was very proud of the tartlets he could make – the Head Chef said they were some of the best he had tasted. He was running short of time to finish them, but working as fast as he could. Mike decided to help him and started to prepare the filling. He did not ask Phil for his recipe. He put together the ingredients quickly without measuring them as he did not think there was time to bother with being precise. As a result there was not enough filling for all the tartlet cases. Phil had to make some more filling with the remaining ingredients, but there were not the correct amounts to make the proper recipe. The Head Chef commented that the tartlets were not as good as usual. Phil was very cross with Mike for interfering and spoiling the high quality of his work. Mike could not understand why Phil was so cross – he thought Phil should have been grateful for the help!

Figure 3.8 Why was Phil cross with Mike?

Using your work time effectively

When working in a kitchen you must have very precise time management. Every chef in a kitchen may have up to three deadlines every day – breakfast, lunch and dinner. Customers will not accept any excuse if their food is not ready – they will go elsewhere to eat, and probably not come back to your outlet again. As a chef you should take a professional pride in keeping to deadlines. In this way you will present a positive image and show that you are competent at the job.

Especially when starting work in a new section of the kitchen, or at a new premises, you need to be very well-organised. To be able to manage your time effectively you must:

o plan out your time to schedule the order of your work
o assemble all the equipment you will need before you start the job
o fill in 'gap' times when items are cooking or resting, with other tasks
o clear and clean as you go – include time for this on your work plan
o include a break in your plan at a suitable time.

Organising your work area

In order to complete tasks on time and to a high standard you need to work in an efficient and organized way. This will give customers a positive image of your company. Part of being organised is planning ahead to make sure you have everything you need for a job before you start – this is called 'mise en place'. Food preparation areas should always be kept clean and tidy in order to comply with legislation, but this will also help you work more efficiently. You also need to position the items you are going to use sensibly on your work area. Remember:

o Leave yourself sufficient space to carry out the task.
o Avoid cluttering your work space with any equipment you are not going to use.
o Use any shelves that may be above or below your work area. Do not overload shelves or position anything on them that might fall off easily.
o Include waste bowls or trays on your list of equipment. They should be big enough to hold trimmings and peelings without overflowing. They should not be so big that they take up too much space on the worktop and cramp the work area.
o If working with high-risk foods, avoid any risk of contaminating any of the items (see page 70, Controlling food safety hazards).
o Make sure you can work in a safe manner so you do not endanger either yourself or others (see Chapter 1, Health and safety).

Figure 3.10 In which area could you work more efficiently?

Try this!   **Worksheet 10**

Write a time plan for a busy day at work. Allow yourself a realistic amount of time to complete the tasks. Schedule a break and time in between tasks for cleaning down. *Did your plan work? Did you find that it helped you become more organised? Did you find that you completed more jobs than usual in the time because you took the trouble to plan it out first?*

Definition

Mise en place: having all equipment and ingredients ready prior to starting a task.

Try this!

At work on a fairly quiet day, test how organised you are!

While you carry out one of your routine preparation jobs, make a note of how many times you have to leave your workplace to fetch items you have forgotten. Time yourself from when you start to get ready until the task is finished.

The next time you have the same job to do, take a few minutes to write out all the supplies and equipment you will need, then get them ready. Time yourself from the start of assembling the equipment to the end of the job and see if you have saved any time – you should have!

Test yourself!

1 You have been following a recipe to make bread rolls for the first time. The instructions state that the mixture must be 'proved'. You do not understand this term. Should you:

   a ask for help?

   b miss that section of the recipe out?

   c throw the mixture away?

   d leave the kitchen in search of a textbook?

2 When preparing several different dishes for lunch service do you:

   a start with the first one on the list and work your way through to the last?

   b start with the most difficult and leave the easiest until last?

   c pick the one you enjoy making most to do first and leave the others until later?

   d decide in advance which is going to take the longest and start with that dish, working out a time plan to include the others?

3 You find that you have had to go back to the stores several times for ingredients and equipment for your current task. You could save time and energy by:

   a assembling all the ingredients and equipment together at the start

   b leaving that task until the end of the day next time

   c asking someone else to collect the items you had forgotten

   d requesting your work area to be moved nearer to the stores.

Supporting the work of your team

To be able to work together as a team it is important that members:

○ each carry out a fair share of the workload

○ all work to the same standard

○ show consideration to each other

○ communicate effectively with one another.

Unfair work practices

One problem that can occur when people work in teams is unfair working. Everyone in a team is expected to contribute fairly to the workload of the team. In a kitchen there is no choice about how much preparation work has to be completed before service – it all has to be done, otherwise the meal service will be affected.

The reason someone may not be pulling their weight in a team at work could be:

○ they are new at the job and cannot work at the necessary speed yet

○ they are not feeling well

○ they have personal problems which are affecting their performance at work

○ they are tired

○ they are lazy

○ they are not keen or interested in their job.

Figure 3.11 Should these chefs be at work?

New staff members are usually given a period of induction and training when they start a new job. They are not often given a full workload to complete. If they are struggling, the team leader should notice this and assign another team member to help them until they can cope.

Staff who are not feeling well should not come to work. They should contact their employer as soon as possible. This is particularly the case with those employees whose jobs involve handling food. Their illness could be transmitted through the food to other staff or customers (see Wounds, illness and infection on page 47).

Sometimes staff come to work because they do not want to let their other team members down. If this is the case, the team leader should either send them home or transfer them to duties not involving food handling until they feel better.

Many people have to deal with personal problems outside work. Sometimes this can affect their performance at work. If this is the case the poorly performing person should be encouraged to see their team leader or someone either at work or outside with whom they can talk about their problem. If nothing is done to help, the person could end up losing their job – which would be an additional problem for them to deal with.

Working in food production is tiring (see Personal cleanliness and hygiene, page 44). If employees do not look after themselves properly they will not be able to continue to do their job well. This can cause them to be persistently late or careless and slow in their tasks. After a while the rest of their team will not tolerate this.

In the kitchen

Tom started a new job in a busy restaurant kitchen. He worked in the vegetable section with two other chefs. Tom found the work quite hard. He was very tired when he got home at the end of his shift, but he still enjoyed going out with his friends later. Most nights he went out and did not come back until after midnight. After a few days he started being late for work. Tom kept oversleeping. At first the two other chefs helped him catch up with his preparation so that he was ready for service. Tom liked the help. It meant it did not really matter if he was late. A couple of weeks went by and then the two other chefs stopped helping Tom. This meant that Tom could not finish his vegetable preparation in time for service. He got into trouble with the Head Chef and received a formal warning for being persistently late for work.

Why did the two other chefs help Tom at first? Why did they stop helping him?

Being reliable and considerate to your other team members is very important.

There are also people who do not pull their weight at work because they are not really interested in the job they do. This situation may result in staff:
○ being noisy
○ being thoughtless
○ being inconsiderate
○ being annoying
○ being careless
○ taking shortcuts
○ producing work of a poor standard.

This affects other members of the team in a bad way.

Consideration to other team members

Occasionally members of a team do not get on together or with the team leader for a variety of reasons. These may include:

○ a personality clash
○ members of the team having different standards and principles
○ individuals not accepting criticism very well.

It may take some time for frictions in a team to settle down. As long as all the team members are considerate and motivated this should eventually happen. A positive attitude is required from everyone concerned.

Figure 3.12 The wrong way to deal with a problem

Figure 3.13 The right way to deal with a problem

Try this!   **Worksheet 11**

Beverley had been working in the kitchen for ten years. She enjoyed her job and knew she was very good at it. She maintained high standards and expected other people to do the same. Beverley did not tolerate fools gladly and she could be very impatient.

Rob started working in the kitchen. It was his first full-time job after completing his college catering course. He did very well at college and won a prize for achievement. He knew he could be very good at his job, and expected to be promoted very soon.

Rob did not agree with some of Beverley's work practices. He told her some of the things she was doing were wrong. This infuriated Beverley. She started to resent Rob and felt that she was being made to look foolish in front of the rest of the staff. One day the Head Chef asked Rob to make a red wine sauce. Rob left the sauce on the stove to cook and went to the stores to fetch some more ingredients. The sauce started to burn. Despite the smell of burning, no one removed the saucepan from the stove. When Rob returned he found the burnt sauce. He was not sure what to do and asked Beverley. Beverley took great delight in telling Rob in a very loud voice that he had ruined the sauce and should have known better than to leave a pan unattended in the kitchen. She reminded him that there was no more red wine left and told him he would just have to make do. Rob swore at Beverley and stormed out of the kitchen.

What approach did Rob have that upset Beverley?
What approach did Beverley have that upset Rob?
If you were the Head Chef, how would you put this situation right?

Remember!
Never:
○ be rude or swear at anyone
○ be malicious or spiteful
○ take people for granted
○ let your standards slip.
Always:
○ show respect for others
○ be enthusiastic
○ be helpful
○ listen carefully to others.

Communication skills

Being able to work well as a team is only possible if you communicate well. This does not just mean talking to each other. Communication can take different forms, including:

- talking face to face
- speaking on the phone
- sending an email
- sending a text message
- writing a message or letter
- body language.

Most communication in the kitchen involves speaking and body language. However, sometimes there is a need to write things down – food orders, stock requisitions, messages for other members of staff.

Talking face to face is the most effective method of communication, as both people can see the expressions on each other's faces as well as hear what they are saying. This helps them understand better.

How to communicate effectively

Most people do not listen carefully to what is being said to them. This is where many problems occur. The best way to find out if someone has understood what you have said is to ask them a question about it. Alternatively, you could ask them to repeat back what you have said to them. If you have been telling them how to do something, you could ask them to do it for you.

The catering and hospitality industry is international. You may have to communicate with someone who does not speak the same language as yourself. To ensure they understand what you are trying to say to them you may need to:

- show them what you mean
- draw a picture to help you explain
- get someone who speaks both languages to help you.

Using the phone at work

Speaking on the phone is something that we are all used to at home. At work communication must be precise and accurate. The phone is used at work because you can receive an instant response to a question from someone who is not in the same area.

Figure 3.14 Listen carefully and be precise

When speaking on the phone you must remember:

○ to speak clearly
○ not to speak too quickly
○ to announce yourself and your position when you answer
○ to smile as you speak (it does make a difference!)
○ to write down any important information you are given
○ to repeat back to the caller any important information to ensure it is accurate. This is particularly important with telephone numbers and prices of commodities, for example.

Always keep a record of:

○ the name of the caller
○ the time of the call
○ the date of the call
○ the contact number to return the call.

Sending an email

Sending a business email should be similar to writing a business letter. These are some of the informal rules to observe:

○ Do not abbreviate or use slang expressions or text language.
○ Always read over the message before you send it to make sure it makes sense.
○ Never use all capitals: IT LOOKS AS THOUGH YOU ARE SHOUTING!
○ Always use a greeting, such as 'Dear Mr Phillips'.

In a kitchen environment emails may be sent internally:

○ to different departments about guest requests
○ to departmental managers about staffing arrangements and new procedures.

or externally:

○ to suppliers with orders
○ to potential suppliers asking for prices and delivery information
○ to service companies to arrange engineers to call.

Figure 3.15 Follow the informal rules when sending an email

Writing a message

It is very important when you prepare a message for someone else to read that:

○ you write as clearly as possible – print if necessary
○ you double-check any names and numbers as you write them down
○ you sign the message with your name and the date and time you wrote it
○ you leave the message in a safe place where you are sure it will be seen by the appropriate person as soon as possible.

Figure 3.16 Write messages carefully

Body language

Body language is the way people communicate with each other without using words, instead they use gestures. It is done subconsciously – without you noticing. You must be aware of the effect body language can have. If you are trying to hide your feelings from someone, be very careful – body language never lies!

Body language differs from culture to culture. If you are working with people from other parts of the world you need to be aware of this. Examples of this include:
- Japanese people greet each other by bowing very low.
- Indian people may move their heads from side to side when they mean 'yes'.

Which method of communication is best to use?

It is important to know which form of communication is best to use on which occasion. As more ways of transmitting information are invented – such as email and text messages – choosing the best method can be difficult.

> **Try this!**   **Worksheet 12**
>
> **Choose the best method of communication for the following examples:**
> - **To get an order to a supplier for delivery the next morning.**
> - **To ask a member of staff to prepare a dish straight away.**
> - **To instruct a member of staff how to garnish a new main course dish.**
> - **To remind a member of staff to start work early the next day.**
>
> *Did your answers cover a range of communication methods? If your answers were exactly the same for each example think carefully. Could any problem or confusion result from your choice of communication method? Would this affect the service to the customer? Could others in the kitchen have to work harder to put the problem right?*

What do all these situations have in common?
- The Head Chef tells you the recipe to use for a new starter about to go on the menu.
- The vegetable supplier tells you the new telephone number to be used to place daily orders.
- The Head Chef asks you to provide a list of the ingredients you need to prepare for the service next week.
- The meat supplier gives you the website address where the up-to-date prices can be found.

- The Head Chef asks you to submit the hours that you worked last week.
- You need to carry out the weekly stock take in your section of the kitchen.

Each of the six tasks above need to be recorded in writing. This may involve:

- typing on a computer
- filling in a form
- writing in a notebook
- jotting down information on a piece of paper.

To be able to carry out all these tasks accurately it is important to write information down for both yourself and others to use in the future.

Test yourself!

Complete the sentences.

1 Sometimes, members of a team may not _____ _____ _____ because they have personal problems at home.

2 Never:
   - be rude or _____ at anyone
   - be malicious or _____
   - take _____ for granted
   - let your standards _____.

3 Always:
   - show _____ for others
   - be _____
   - be _____
   - _____ carefully to others.

4 Complete these guidelines for recording a message:
   - _____ as clearly as possible – _____ if necessary.
   - Double-check any _____ and _____ as you write them down.
   - _____ the message with your _____ and the _____ and _____ you wrote it.
   - _____ the message in a _____ _____ where you are sure it will be _____ by the appropriate person as soon as possible.

Contributing to your own development

How improving yourself helps your team

As you become settled in your job, you may wish to improve your skills and abilities. This may help you to get promoted in your workplace. It may also enable you to move employment and get a better-paid and more challenging job in the future.

The ways that you can develop your skills and abilities include:
○ attending college on a part-time or full-time basis
○ going on short training courses from your workplace
○ working alongside very skilled craftspeople.

If you improve your own skills and abilities this will also help your team. The advantages include:
○ productivity for the whole team may improve
○ you can share your skills with your team mates
○ everyone may become more motivated and creative as a result
○ the reputation of the whole team will be improved.

Feedback from others

Feedback is defined as 'information provided about the quality or success of something'. In the workplace, feedback usually takes the form of:
○ customer opinion about the quality of a meal (often from a customer service questionnaire)
○ the result of an **appraisal** of an employee by a supervisor or manager.

> **Definition**
>
> **Appraisal:** an assessment of performance providing feedback.

Figure 3.17 Feedback may be the result of an appraisal

101

Feedback will often result in a change or reward, for example:

o A negative customer comment about a dish may mean it is removed from the menu.

o A positive appraisal may mean an employee is considered for promotion.

Developing and using a learning plan

A learning plan is a useful way of organising your development. As you progress in your job you may improve your skills and abilities on a formal basis – such as a college course. You may also learn different skills in your everyday work.

A learning plan can help you in two ways:

o It can help you to plan out a career path.

o It can help you organise any formal learning you are undertaking.

Planning out a career path

If you are ambitious and want to own your own catering business or manage a large kitchen, you will need a high level of technical knowledge as well as good business and management skills. To obtain these skills you may need to study several courses. A learning plan will help you map these out so that you take the right courses in the most suitable order – either full-time or part-time. You need to match these courses with appropriate jobs at the right level to help you develop your skills.

It is useful to have the help of a Careers Advisor when using a learning plan in this way.

Formal learning

If you are already studying a course a formal learning plan can be very useful. It will:

o help you order the reading and coursework that you need to complete

o allow you to set realistic targets to achieve these stages in your studying

o help to train you in time management

o help you to keep your learning on track so that you can achieve your ambition.

What you need to set up a formal learning plan

You will need a diary and a notebook. In the notebook you will need to record:

○ your long-term aims – what you want to achieve finally
○ your short-term aims – the achievements you need to fulfil your long-term aims
○ the formal short-term aims that you may have set for you by your workplace or college, e.g. passing your Intermediate Food Hygiene examination, or completing a project on different types of poultry.

In the diary, set yourself some realistic target dates such as:

○ the date you have to take your Food Hygiene examination
○ the date by which you should start revising for the examination
○ the date you should hand in your project
○ a series of dates by which you should have various sections of your project researched, prepared and produced.

By planning your learning in this way, you are giving yourself the best chance of fulfilling all your ambitions. You are also demonstrating to your employer and others that you can be organised, conscientious, focused and reliable. By completing the learning experiences, you acquire knowledge and skill which can be used to help you later in life.

Test yourself!

1 Name three ways in which you could improve your work performance and further your career.

2 What could happen if you had a bad appraisal interview with your manager?

3 What do you need to set up a formal learning plan?

4

Healthy eating

This chapter covers skills and knowledge in the following unit:

○ 7132 Unit 296 (2PR17) Produce healthier dishes

Working through this chapter could also provide the opportunity to practise the following Functional Skills at Level 2:
Functional Maths Interpreting – use and interpret statistical measures, tables and diagrams, for discrete and continuous data, using information communication technology (ICT) where appropriate

In this chapter you will:

Understand how and be able to produce healthier dishes	7132 – 296.1,2

A balanced diet

Everyone is constantly told by the press, doctors and the government that healthy eating is very important. People generally live much longer now that they did fifty or one hundred years ago. On average people also grow taller and weigh more. The amount and variety of food available today is the greatest ever. Many food items are much cheaper than they used to be.

Food provides material that our bodies can convert into heat and energy and can use to grow and repair internal systems.

Food is made up of various amounts of carbohydrate, protein, fat, vitamins, mineral salts and fibre. A balanced diet must contain all of these nutrients in the correct proportions. Lack of any one will affect the body in different ways:

○ Lack of carbohydrate → lower energy levels.
○ Lack of protein → poor growth and healing.
○ Lack of fat → poor health and low energy.
○ Lack of vitamins → poor health.
○ Lack of mineral salts → poor teeth and bones and general health.
○ Lack of fibre → poor digestion.

Figure 4.1 Eating healthily can lead to a longer life

If we eat more food than our bodies require, the excess amounts will:

○ build up fat which is stored on our bodies
○ increase the weight which we have to carry around
○ create an imbalance of chemicals in our bodies (e.g. too much salt or sugar).

This leads to problems such as:

○ obesity (from the build-up of fat)
○ joint problems (from the increase in weight)
○ diabetes, high blood pressure, thyroid problems (from the increase in sugar and from particular types of fat which are much more common now in the food we eat).

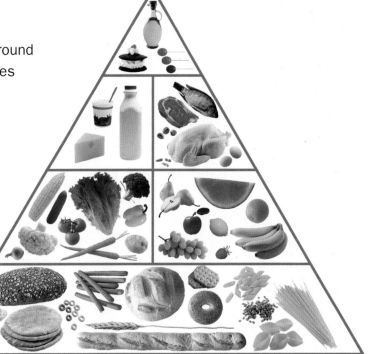

Figure 4.2 A food pyramid

When they are at home, people have the choice of eating healthily. Some people are not in this position and have to eat meals that have been prepared for them. Examples of people in this situation include residents of:

o   hospitals

o   prisons

o   care homes

o   boarding schools

o   residential homes

o   armed forces barracks.

If you work in a food production operation which caters for one of these sectors you have a particular responsibility to ensure that they have a balanced diet.

Nowadays people eat out more than ever before. This places a duty on caterers to ensure that safe, nutritious, healthy choices appear on restaurant menus. Chefs must be aware of the need to offer a choice of dishes with:

o   fewer calories

o   less fat

o   less sugar

o   less salt.

Government guidelines for healthy eating

The government, together with experts from the food industry, regularly carries out investigations into the health of the population. From these investigations it produces a series of reports with recommendations.

A 2005 government report states:

'Good nutrition is vital to good health. Poor nutrition is a recognised cause of ill-health and premature death in England – an estimated one-third of cancers can be attributed to poor diet and nutrition. While there is a high awareness of healthy eating, most people consume less than the recommended amounts of fruit and vegetables but more than the recommended amounts of fat, salt and sugar.'

Marcus says

The diners in our restaurant are now more aware of nutrition than ever before. I would advise chefs to be adaptable and aware that some diners are either unable to eat certain products (such as dairy products, shellfish, or wheat) or simply prefer not to.

Did you know?

In the UK 65 per cent of men and 56 per cent of women – 24 million adults – are either overweight or obese. This is a form of 'malnutrition' – meaning 'bad nutrition' – although this term is more often used to describe people who do not have sufficient food to eat.

The government issued the following guidelines for everyone to follow:
○ Increase the amount of fruit and vegetables eaten to at least five portions per day.
○ Increase the amount of fibre consumed.
○ Reduce the amount of salt consumed.
○ Reduce the amount of saturated fat eaten.
○ Reduce the amount of sugar consumed.

The Food Standards Agency has developed a programme called 'The Balance of Good Health' to show people what proportions and types of foods make up a healthy, balanced diet.

This programme divides foods into five different groups. For each group it gives a recommended daily serving. This will vary slightly according to the age, sex and occupation of the person. The groups are as follows:
○ Bread, other cereals and potatoes – one to two servings per day.
○ Fruit and vegetables – five servings per day.
○ Milk and dairy foods – two to three servings per day.
○ Meat, fish and alternatives – one to two servings per day.
○ Foods containing fat and food containing sugar – one small serving per day.

Remember!
The way you cook food can affect how healthy it is to eat. Chicken breast is a healthy food – but not if it is breadcrumbed and then deep fried!

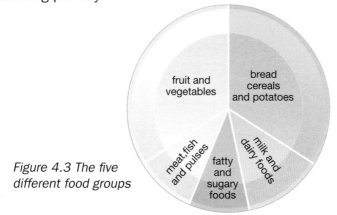

Figure 4.3 The five different food groups

Remember!
Your customers should:
○ enjoy their food
○ eat a variety of different foods
○ eat the right amount to be a healthy weight
○ eat plenty of foods rich in starch and fibre
○ eat plenty of fruit and vegetables
○ not eat too many foods that contain sugar or salt
○ not eat too many foods that contain a lot of fat.

Types and combinations of ingredients that make a healthy dish

Including the following items in a dish will increase its health value:
○ Generous amounts of fruit and vegetables which are an excellent source of vitamins, minerals and fibre.
○ Moderate amounts of meat, fish and dairy foods.
○ Small amounts of fats and oils.
○ Wholegrain items such as oats, wheat and other cereals.

Basic nutrition

Nutrition is the study of the various ways in which food can nourish the body. The human body is very complicated. Nutritional scientists are still discovering ways in which the body uses food. New recommendations about diet are issued when new research has been successfully carried out. These may recommend that we eat more of certain types of food, or identify food items which have been found not to be good for health.

The table below shows which types of food are the best sources of the nutrients that are needed for a balanced diet.

Nutrient	Type of food	Why it is needed
Carbohydrates	Potatoes, bread, pasta, rice – as starch Sweet food and drinks – as sugars	To provide energy
Proteins	Meat, fish, nuts, lentils	For growing and repairing tissues
Fats	Meat, fried food, cakes and pastries	For energy and certain vitamins
Vitamins and minerals	Fruit, vegetables and many other types of food	For general health
Fibre	Fruit, vegetables, unrefined cereals	To aid digestion
Water	Pure water is best but 4 pints per day of water-based liquid (such as low-sugar squash) is recommended	To aid digestion and most other body processes

Figure 4.4 Types of food that provide different nutrients and why they are needed

Try this!
Worksheet 13

Protein is essential for growth and the repair of the body. List five types of food that are high in proteins and five that are low in proteins. You can repeat this exercise for the other basic nutrients too.

Did you know?
A prolonged lack of certain substances may lead to particular illnesses, e.g.:
o a lack of vitamin C leads to a skin condition called scurvy
o a lack of iron leads to a blood condition called anaemia.

The digestive system

The body is able to make use of the food we eat by a process called digestion. Most food contains more than one nutrient. Food needs to be broken down by the body into individual nutrients ready for use.

The digestive system breaks down the food we eat into a substance from which it can remove the nutrients. It does this in a series of stages:

1 Your teeth physically reduce the size of the food. If you do not chew your food well you can put strain on your oesophagus (the tube from your mouth to your stomach).

2 The food is then mixed with saliva, which breaks down starch into simple sugars. This is why if you leave bread or potatoes in your mouth for a while before swallowing they start to taste sweet.

3 In the stomach the food is mixed with gastric juices. These juices are made up of hydrochloric acid and substances called enzymes. These break down the complex structure of protein and curdle any milk present.

4 In the small intestine:
  ○ any remaining starch is converted to glucose
  ○ proteins are converted into a range of amino acids
  ○ fats are broken down into a watery solution ready to move into the intestines.

5 Most nutrients are absorbed into the bloodstream through the lining of the small intestine. The nutrients can then be carried round the body to where they are needed.

6 Bacteria are naturally found in the large intestine and they help the body to process food.

7 Any indigestible matter – such as fibre – continues through the colon and passes out through the rectum and anus. A meal may take 24 hours or more to completely pass through the digestive system.

We need to look at the nutrients in food in more detail to be able to appreciate their importance when creating healthy dishes.

Figure 4.5 The digestive system

Did you know?

If you unravelled your intestines they would be the length of a double-decker bus!

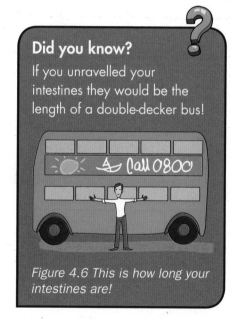

Figure 4.6 This is how long your intestines are!

Did you know?

Some of the acids present in your stomach are as strong as industrial strength cleaner!

Proteins

All proteins are made up from amino acids. There are 22 of them and all are needed by the body to grow and repair itself. When proteins are broken down by the digestive process, the body can manufacture most of these amino acids for itself – but there are a few that it cannot create. These are known as 'essential' amino acids. To ensure the body has all the amino acids it needs it is important to use protein food from both animal and vegetable origins.

These include:

Animal	Vegetable
Meat Game Poultry Fish	Peas Beans Nuts
Eggs Milk Cheese	Wheat products

Figure 4.7 Types of protein

Fats

As well as providing energy, fats also carry certain important vitamins. Both plants and animals contain fats, but they are of different sorts. They include:

Animal fats	Vegetable fats
Butter	Margarine
Cheese	Nuts
Lard	Soya beans
Fish oil	Olive oil

Figure 4.8 Types of fat

Differences between fats are caused by the variety in fatty acids from which they are made. Animal fats are 'saturated' and fish and vegetable fats are 'unsaturated'. Some animal fats also contain vitamins A and D. A manufacturing process called 'hydrogenation' can turn liquid oils into solid fat known as 'trans-fat'. This type of fat can be found in increasing amounts in ready-prepared meals. To be digested successfully all fats have to be broken down into fatty acids and a chemical called 'glycerol'. Animal fats and trans-fats are said to cause a higher amount of cholesterol to be found in the bloodstream.

Carbohydrates

The vast majority of food items in which carbohydrates are found are vegetable. They provide energy for the body. There are two main types of carbohydrates:

o Sugars are very simple for the body to absorb.
  They include:
  – glucose
  – sucrose
  – maltose
  – fructose
  – lactose.

o Starch is difficult to digest unless it has been cooked.
  Sources include:
  – all cereals (such as wheat flour)
  – potatoes
  – pulse vegetables such as lentils.

Vitamins

Vitamins are chemical substances which are very important for health. Without the correct balance of vitamins in your body you may not grow properly and will feel generally unwell. If you take in too large an amount of some vitamins you can poison yourself – but it is extremely unusual for this to happen.

The table below gives more information about the main groups of vitamins.

Vitamin	Type of food	Why it is needed
Vitamin A	Dairy products Fish oils Dark green vegetables	Helps growth and resists infection Helps eyesight
Vitamin B group	Yeast (in bread) Meat Cereals	Helps growth and energy levels Helps the nervous system
Vitamin C	Fresh fruit Green vegetables Potatoes	Helps growth and healing of injuries Prevents gum and mouth infections
Vitamin D	Sunlight Dairy produce Oily fish	Prevents brittle bones and teeth

Figure 4.9 What types of food provide vitamins and why they are needed

Minerals

You may be familiar with minerals such as iron, salt and copper and what they can be used for, e.g. manufacturing. But did you know that the human body needs very tiny amounts of 19 minerals to keep it healthy? However, too much of any mineral can be extremely bad for you. For example, most people in Britain eat far too much salt.

The table below gives more information about the most important minerals.

Mineral	Type of food	Why it is needed
Calcium	Dairy products Fish Bread	Helps bones and teeth grow Helps blood clot
Iron	Meat Green vegetables Fish	Helps keeps the blood healthy
Sodium (salt)	Meat Eggs Fish	Helps keep all the fluids in the body balanced

Figure 4.10 What foods provide minerals and why they are needed

> **Did you know?**
> Thinking uses up less than one calorie per hour!

Calories

All food has a value in numbers of calories. Calories measure the amount of energy food can produce in the body. If the body does not use this energy it tends to be saved as fat. It is useful to know the number of calories in the food you are eating if you are training for a particular sport when you need to use a lot of energy. It is also helpful when you are trying to keep a balanced diet and control your weight.

Figure 4.11 The more active you are, the more calories you will use

Different activities use up different numbers of calories. For example:

o Sitting watching television – 15 calories per hour.
o Walking moderately fast – 215 calories per hour.
o Climbing up stairs – 1000 calories per hour.

Try this!   **Worksheet 14**

When you are next out shopping for food, look at the label of the item you are buying. It will usually tell you how many calories the food will provide. See which food has the highest in value and which has the lowest. The highest value food is likely to be the most fattening!

What makes a balanced diet?

Now that you know the main nutrients that are needed by the body you may be able to understand the problems that people can experience from not eating a balanced diet.

If people eat too much **fat** they are in danger of:
o obesity
o high blood pressure
o heart attacks.

If people eat too much **sugar** they may suffer from:
o tooth decay
o diabetes
o obesity.

If too much **salt** is consumed, people may experience:
o kidney problems
o high blood pressure.

The government's research has discovered that many people have medical problems brought on by eating too much fat, sugar and salt. This is why it is trying to promote a healthier diet and lifestyle for everyone. A healthier diet would include more starchy food, fruit, vegetables and pulses. Why are these important?

Eating **starchy** foods helps:
o the digestive system work better
o provide many of the minerals and vitamins needed for health.

Eating more **fruit and vegetables** helps:
o general health improve
o the digestive system work better
o provide many of the minerals and vitamins needed for health.

Eating more **pulses helps:**
o the digestive system work better
o provide a useful alternative to meat and fish
o reduce the amount of fat consumed.

Did you know?
Most people eat too much salt – probably around one and a half times more than is good for them. Adults should eat no more than one teaspoonful of salt per day.

Remember!
Starchy foods include cereals, bread, pasta and potatoes.

Remember!
Pulses include butter beans, kidney beans, lentils, soya beans and chick peas.

How to interpret food labels

Labels on packaged food now have a great deal of nutrition information. This is to try to help everyone eat a balanced diet. There is also a lot of information about ingredients which is very important for anyone who is allergic to a particular substance (see Allergies, page 42).

The law now states that food labels must contain:
o the name of the food – including any method of processing, e.g. dried peanuts, smoked mackerel
o the weight or volume
o a list of ingredients – in order of weight from largest to smallest
o a use-by date for perishable food or best-before date for preserved food
o storage conditions
o preparation instructions – to ensure the food tastes its best and that it will be thoroughly heated to the safe temperature of 75°C
o the name and address of manufacturer, packer or seller – in case further information is required
o a production lot number – in case there is a problem and the product has to be recalled.

Additional information may also be provided, e.g.:
o nutrition information   o cooking instructions   o serving suggestions.

These are the symbols for the shelf life of frozen foods:

Symbol	Food must be kept at or below	Maximum storage times	Pre-frozen or frozen from fresh
*	–6°C	One week	Pre-frozen food only
**	–12°C	One month	Pre-frozen food only
***	–18°C	Three months	Pre-frozen food only
****	–18°C or colder	Six months	Pre-frozen food; or fresh food frozen from room temperature

Figure 4.12 Shelf life of frozen foods

Allergen information

As well as appearing in the ingredients list, sometimes food types which are known to cause allergy may be listed again in a separate box or highlighted in some other way. Some labels include 'may contain' warnings to indicate the food may contain minute traces of food known to cause an allergic reaction (see Allergies, page 42).

△ **Allergy advice**
Contains milk, wheat, gluten, soya.

! May contain traces of sesame seeds and soya.

WE CANNOT GUARANTEE THAT THIS PRODUCT IS 100% FREE OF SEEDS AS IT HAS BEEN MADE IN A FACTORY THAT USES SEEDS.

☐ Recipe: contains almonds, o cashew nuts and hazlenuts.

Figure 4.13 Food labels must contain warnings about allergens

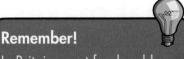

Remember!
In Britain, most foods sold loose do not have to display all the information required by the food labelling laws for packaged foods.

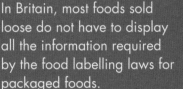

Did you know?
A new European Union law will require certain food ingredients to which many people are allergic to be very clearly labelled. The foods include milk, eggs, peanuts, fish, soya, wheat, sesame and sulphur dioxide.

Creating and presenting healthier dishes

For chefs producing food in residential situations, such as care homes and schools, offering their customers healthy meals is very important. It is also necessary in hospitals, to help patients recover their health quickly.

Figure 4.14 Healthy meals are especially important for hospital patients

Fresh ingredients are better for health

Many commodities now travel a very long distance from where they were produced to where they will be used. The longer the journey, the more the quality of the produce will drop. Salad leaves picked by a farmer and sold in the local market will be much fresher than those grown in Spain, packed up and transported by a lorry, followed by a plane journey and then another lorry trip!

Figure 4.15 Many ingredients travel a long way to get to our tables

Preserved ingredients such as frozen and canned items are useful, but are not usually as healthy as fresh or chilled items which contain more nutrients. The preservation process can destroy some of the nutrients in the food.

Did you know?

A large hospital in the south-west of England produces meals for 720 patients daily and operates a 250-seater restaurant providing lunches for hospital visitors and staff. The chef uses a low-salt convenience stock in the kitchen. Menu items offered to patients include choices suitable for high-energy, diabetic, low-potassium, low-salt and healthy-eating diets.

Did you know?

At the Yew Lodge Hotel in the Midlands, the chefs use seasonal, healthy food and include ingredients such as beans and lentils in dishes. They use sweet potato and carrot mash instead of creamed potato. They allow the customer to choose if they want a sauce with their food.

Preparing ingredients in a healthy way

If fresh ingredients are prepared a long time before they are used, they lose some of their important vitamins and minerals. The quality also suffers as they may become dried-up and stale. Onions prepared too far in advance will lose their flavour and beetroot will 'bleed'. There is also likely to be more waste from food that cannot be used.

Ways of reducing saturated fat in dishes

- Use olive oil or sunflower oil instead of butter.
- Select lean cuts of meat and trim the fat off other cuts.
- Cut chips as thickly as possible as they absorb less fat.
- Avoid glazing vegetables.
- If frying, make sure the oil is hot enough. Otherwise the food will absorb more fat. Food which has been fried needs to be drained on absorbent paper to remove the surplus fat.
- Use fish such as salmon, trout, mackerel and fresh tuna in place of cod, haddock, plaice and tinned tuna.
- Use semi-skimmed or skimmed milk in place of the full-fat type.
- Use a strong cheese so that you can use less of it.
- Use yoghurt, **quark**, crème fraîche or fromage frais in place of cream.

Definition

Quark: A German cheese with the texture and flavour of soured cream.

Ways of reducing sugar in dishes

- Eat plain fresh fruit as a dessert.
- Always use tinned fruit in natural unsweetened fruit juice rather than in syrup.
- Use fresh or unsweetened fruit juices whenever possible.
- In place of fizzy drinks, try fresh or unsweetened fruit juice with sparkling water.
- Cut back on the amount of sugar used to make desserts (except meringues and ice cream – which cannot be made with less sugar).
- Use sugar-free cereals and low-sugar jams where appropriate.
- If appropriate use a sugar substitute or honey.

Ways of reducing salt in dishes

- Add less salt – do not automatically add salt when beginning to cook, only use it to adjust the seasoning at the end.
- Check the labels of any processed foods you use for flavouring dishes. It is surprising how many already contain salt, e.g. mustard, soy sauce.
- Do not combine foods high in salt together in one dish such as bacon, beefburgers, sausages, cheese and ham.
- Combine salty foods with fruit or vegetables which contain potassium. This will help to reduce the effect of the salt.
- Avoid using preserved ingredients that contain high levels of salt such as dried fish, smoked salmon and capers.

Ideas for flavouring dishes using less salt

- Make your own stock. Ready-made stocks or bouillon are often high in salt.
- Use lemon juice, lime juice and balsamic vinegar instead of salt.
- Use lots of fresh herbs and spices.
- Onions, shallots, leeks and garlic all help to flavour food without using salt.
- Freshly ground black pepper can be a popular alternative to salt.

Ways of increasing fibre and starch in dishes

- Use high-fibre, wholemeal or granary bread.
- Use wholemeal flour instead of white flour.
- Use wholemeal pasta and brown rice.
- Include pulses in dishes where appropriate.
- Offer jacket potatoes.

Healthier types of sauces, dressings, toppings and condiments

As fashions change, so do ingredients and methods of cookery and presentation. With so much talk about healthy eating, many establishments are changing how they prepare their sauces. Traditional sauces use flour, butter and cream, but the following styles of sauces are more healthy and are becoming popular:

- Herb, olive and walnut oils and dressings.
- Sauces made from reductions of stocks and flavourings.
- Yoghurt-based dressings.
- Fruit-based sauces and dressings.

> **Did you know?**
> The concentration of salt in soy sauce is twice that of seawater!

> **Did you know?**
> Substituting wholemeal flour for white flour is most successful when making savoury dishes. However, pastry can be very heavy if made with all wholemeal flour. A mix of half wholemeal, half white flour produces a better result.

> **Did you know?**
> Brown rice will take longer to cook than white rice.

Cooking dishes to maximise nutritional value

Vitamins and minerals can be destroyed by long periods of cooking at high temperatures. To preserve its nutritional value, food needs to be cooked quickly. Do not use cooking methods that add fat.

The types of cookery that are the healthiest to use include:

○ grilling
○ steaming
○ baking
○ poaching.

Deep-fried items are popular, and quick and easy to produce, but are very unhealthy. Shallow fry with sunflower oil rather than deep fry with solid fat.

Did you know?

Organic food is produced under strict controls restricting the use of chemicals. Food produced in a more intensive way is not subject to these controls. Crops may have substances used on them such as pesticides (used to kill insects). In high-volume meat production, additives which speed up growth in animals may be used.

Test yourself!

1 Which of the following are nutrients?
   a Fat
   b Carbohydrate
   c Cellulose
   d Additives
   e Vitamins
   f Minerals.

2 Which of these should we eat more of?
   a Bread
   b Vegetables
   c Fruit
   d Sweets
   e Salt
   f Crisps.

3 Which of these should we eat less of?
   a Bread
   b Vegetables
   c Fruit
   d Sweets
   e Salt
   f Crisps.

4 Complete the following sentences:
   a Fromage frais can be used instead of
   _____ .
   b Herbs and spices can be used instead of
   _____ .
   c Honey can be used instead of
   _____ .

5 Which of the following are healthy methods of cookery?
   a Roasting
   b Grilling
   c Deep frying
   d Poaching
   e Steaming.

6 What percentage of the population is overweight – males and females?

5 Cooking methods

This chapter covers skills and knowledge for these cooking methods:

- Boiling
- Steaming
- Blanching
- Poaching
- Stewing and braising
- Frying
- Grilling
- Roasting and baking
- Combination cooking
- Microwaving.

Working through this chapter could also provide the opportunity to practise the following Functional Skills at Level 2:
Functional Maths Analysing – understand and use simple formulae and equations involving one or two operations; use, convert and calculate using metric and, where appropriate, imperial measures

These methods relate to the following units:

Cook and finish basic meat dishes	7132 – 229
Cook and finish basic poultry dishes	7132 – 230
Cook and finish basic fish dishes	7132 – 227
Cook and finish basic shellfish dishes	7132 – 228
Cook and finish basic game dishes	7132 – 231
Make basic stocks	7132 – 238
Prepare, cook and finish basic hot sauces	7132 – 236
Prepare, cook and finish basic soups	7132 – 237
Prepare, cook and finish basic rice dishes	7132 – 239
Cook and finish basic offal dishes	7132 – 232
Cook and finish basic vegetable dishes	7132 – 233
Prepare, cook and finish basic pasta dishes	7132 – 240
Prepare, cook and finish basic pulse dishes	7132 – 241
Prepare, cook and finish basic egg dishes	7132 – 243
Prepare, cook and finish basic bread and dough products	7132 – 244
Prepare, cook and finish basic pastry products	7132 – 245
Prepare, cook and finish basic cakes, sponges, biscuits and scones	7132 – 246
Prepare, cook and finish basic cold and hot desserts	7132 – 249

Cooking methods

Various cooking methods are discussed in this chapter. It gives you important information about the processes and safety issues.

Boiling

Boiling is a wet cooking method which requires food to be **immersed** in a liquid, e.g. water or stock, and cooked by a direct heat source, e.g. gas or electricity, on top of a stove, hob or cooking range. The food is cooked at 100°C as this is the temperature at which water boils. The liquid should be bubbling and moving rapidly. Not all food is suitable for boiling as the cooking action can break delicate food down making it limp and unsuitable for service. For example, courgettes have a high water content and disintegrate if boiled.

Boiling can lower the nutritional value of the food, as some vitamins, e.g. vitamins B and C, dissolve in water and so are absorbed into the hot liquid during boiling.

Boiling has different results depending on whether the food is added to cold liquid which is then heated to boiling point, or whether it is added to liquid that is already boiling.

If food is added to cold liquid before boiling, the natural flavours and goodness are extracted. This process is used to make stocks. It softens hard food, e.g. root vegetables, and prevents damage to items which would lose their shape if placed in rapidly boiling liquid. If food, e.g. small cuts of fish, is plunged into hot liquid, the flavour of the food is sealed in. This method also sets the protein and colour in foods, e.g. green vegetables, and can reduce overall cooking times.

The equipment required to boil food is:
o A pan large enough to hold the food and enough liquid to cover it. The pan can be a saucepan or a large industrial boiler or stock pot.
o Spiders or perforated spoons to remove the food from the liquid. If a large amount is cooked a colander (large strainer) can be used.

Remember!
Safety first! When handling hot equipment:
o wear protective clothing
o have a dry oven cloth to hand to hold hot equipment
o have ready utensils, e.g. tongs, palette knife or a slice to agitate and move the items being cooked.

Definition
Immerse: to cover something completely in liquid.

Simmering

Simmering is similar to boiling, but the liquid is kept at a constant temperature just below boiling point. When a liquid is simmering, the surface of the liquid quivers with a gentle bubbling action. The cooking action is quite slow and is appropriate for dishes or food types that require a longer cooking period. When cooking foods such as meat, cheaper cuts of meat would be suitable for this method.

Video presentation

Watch *Prepare fish stock (2) boil, skim, simmer and strain* to see the difference between boiling and simmering. Also watch *Prepare velouté sauce (2) mix, boil, simmer.*

Steaming

Steaming uses a moist heat to cook. Modern equipment can provide atmospheric pressure (normal steam from boiling water) or forced steam using a high-pressure steamer which cooks the product more quickly.

A steaming vessel can be a specially designed piece of industrial equipment or a simple saucepan with a fitted lid containing a trivet to raise the food above the water. Because the lid of a steaming vessel fits tightly, the steam cannot escape and pressure builds up inside the vessel. The pressure can be regulated by letting out more or less of the steam. The higher the pressure the quicker the item will cook. In Oriental and Asian cookery, a covered wicker basket is used for steaming food.

Figure 5.1 Different types of steamer

Other equipment needed to steam food includes:
○ utensils, e.g. spoons and tongs, to handle the food
○ cloths to protect you from heat
○ containers to place steamed food into.

Steaming is considered to be an extremely healthy method of cooking, as the nutrients within the product are preserved far better than in other cooking methods. Steaming will not colour the food. This method is often used when cooking for people on diets or people who are unwell, because it ensures maximum nutritional content.

Remember!

Steam can be extremely dangerous. It can cause severe scalds if you do not use equipment correctly. You should always turn the steam off and make sure no-one is standing nearby before opening the door of a steamer.

121

Blanching

Blanching is the process in which raw food is immersed in boiling water for a short time, then removed and refreshed in iced water or under cold running water. Blanching is carried out for a variety of reasons:

○ To make it easier to remove the skins of vegetables, fruit and nuts.
○ To make ingredients firmer.
○ To purify ingredients by killing the enzymes that cause the quality of food to deteriorate. Food that has been blanched, e.g. garden peas, can then be stored fresh or frozen for later use.
○ To remove the salt or bitterness from ingredients.
○ To reduce the volume of ingredients.
○ To allow food to be partially cooked, stored and then quickly re-heated. This is a way of speeding up service.

Chips can be blanched in hot oil at 160°C. This means they are thoroughly cooked but not coloured. When they are needed for service they can be quickly plunged in very hot oil to colour them.

Video presentation
Watch the techniques used in *Blanch a tomato to remove the skin* and *Blanch meat bones*.

Poaching

Poaching, a wet cooking method, means to simmer slowly and gently in liquid. The amount of liquid used depends on the dish to be cooked. A whole chicken will require more liquid than a breast, but generally the minimum amount of liquid is used.

The liquid used to poach food is usually boiled first. When the food is added the liquid is not brought back to the boil, but is kept just below boiling point. The cooking liquid may affect the food being poached, e.g. it may add flavour to a food (stock) or its boiling point may be lower (milk). Liquids commonly used in poaching are water, wine, stock and milk. Fish, vegetables, eggs and some offal are examples of food suitable for poaching.

The equipment used to poach poultry is usually a heavy-based pan with a lid. The heat source can be an open flame, a solid or electric hob or oven. If food is poached in the oven (e.g. fish), this is known as 'oven poaching'. It is a speedy and gentle method of poaching. Overcooking food during oven poaching could lead to the food drying out.

When poaching, the food may be only half-covered by liquid. It is a good idea to cover the food, e.g. with a lid or buttered paper. This will keep the moisture in and prevent the food drying out. Once

Video presentation
Poach a salmon fillet teaches you how to do this like an expert.

cooked, poached food must be well drained. Excess liquid could alter the consistency of a sauce added to poached food and spoil it.

Stewing and braising

Stewing and braising are wet methods of cooking in a pot on top of the stove or in the oven. This is a slow cooking method, which allows food to be cooked gently until it is soft and ready for service. In stewed or braised dishes the food and liquid is served together as a dish.

Use a large, heavy-based saucepan or dish, with a minimum amount of liquid covering the food. Bring the liquid to the boil and simmer it slowly. Take care not to burn the base of the pan, as this will spoil the flavour of the dish. Always ensure there is enough liquid in the pan to prevent burning.

> **Remember!**
> Food that is stewed or braised will be hot and dangerous. Use protective clothing and equipment to prevent accidents from spilling hot liquid and burning yourself.

Frying

Frying means cooking in hot fat, e.g. oil or butter. There are four types of frying:

1 shallow frying
2 sauté
3 stir-frying
4 deep-frying.

Shallow, sauté and stir-frying

Shallow, sauté and stir-frying are all versions of a similar frying process. Food is cooked with a small amount of butter or oil. Cooking this way colours the food and makes it more appealing. Stir-frying is usually associated with Asian food dishes. It is a quick cooking method using a wok and hot oil. The food is cut into small, evenly-sized pieces and tossed in hot oil in the wok for a short period of time.

The equipment required for shallow or stir-frying is:

o a sturdy pan with steep sides
o a cloth to protect you from high temperatures
o utensils, e.g. tongs, palette knives, spoons, to move and agitate the food
o a range or hob to provide the heat source. To achieve even cooking you will need to regulate the heat under the pan; gas hobs make it particularly easy to do this.

> **Remember!**
> Hot oil can inflict serious injury. For safety reasons:
> o make sure the food you are frying is free from water and excess liquid, which may cause the oil to spit and possibly burn you when cooking
> o place the food into a hot frying pan away from your body to avoid splashing yourself with hot oil.

>
> **Video presentation**
> Watch the video *Stir-fry beef* to find out more about this cooking method. Watch *Deep-fry goujons* to learn how to do this safely.

Deep-frying

Deep-frying food means immersing it in hot oil in a saucepan or deep fat fryer. The temperature of the oil should be approximately 180°C. Deep-frying will colour the food and give it a crunchy texture on the outside. Inside the food remains moist. This method of cooking is popular for breadcrumbed or battered fish, chicken pieces, chips and onion rings.

The equipment needed for deep-frying is:

- a sturdy pan with a heavy base
- a basket or slotted steel spoon to lift the food out of the oil
- utensils, e.g. tongs to grasp the food
- colanders or absorbent paper to put the food into to allow the excess oil to drain off before serving
- a regulated heat source
- a thermostatically controlled deep fat fryer may also be used.

Looking after the oil is the most important part of deep-frying. Make sure you:

- filter oil daily
- wipe the inside of the fryer thoroughly before replacing the oil
- clean the fryer once a week
- switch off the fryer when not in use
- turn the fryer down during quiet periods: the recommended standby temperature is 93°C
- use the correct utensils for handling food and filtering oil: using iron or copper will cause a chemical reaction and harm the oil.

Remember!

Although chips can be deep-fried straight from the freezer, it is important to shake off all the ice first or the oil will froth dangerously.

Remember!

Always season food after frying, never before.

Chef's tip

Do not use olive oil for deep-frying as it can burn easily at the temperatures required to deep-fry and this will taint the food.

Grilling

Grilling is a dry method of cooking by intense heat from above, below or both. The heat source can be electric, gas or charcoal. Food is placed near the source of heat on bars or on a solid metal plate. If the heat source is above the food, the equipment being used is known as a salamander.

Grilling is an extremely popular, simple method of cooking which is appropriate for tender cuts of meat, offal, poultry, fish and vegetables.

Figure 5.2 Food being grilled on a salamander

Before food is grilled, it is usually seasoned with salt and pepper and sometimes herbs, spices or marinades. Food can be brushed with butter or olive oil to baste it and can be coated in flour to aid the colouring process and give a crispy texture when grilled. Food will colour when grilled, but it is important not to pierce the surface of the food, as moisture or juices will be lost, leaving the food dry. If you overcook food when grilling, it will be dry and tough.

Griddling

Griddling is an American term. It is another form of grilling. The food is placed on a solid iron plate which is heated from underneath. The heat source can be gas, electric or charcoal. Some griddles have bars running across them. This enables the foods to be **charred** or **seared**, providing a distinctive flavour, colour and pattern. Safe procedures must always be followed, as this equipment can cause serious injury.

Too much oil on the griddle can lead to excessive smoke and can hamper the cooking process.

Roasting and baking

These cooking processes make food easy to eat and digest and more appealing to the consumer.

Both use an oven and dry convected heat to cook the food. Ovens can be powered by electricity or gas. Modern combination ovens combine dry and moist heat to ensure the best cooking results. The temperature of the oven will determine the cooking time. The hotter the oven, the quicker the food will colour and cook. A fierce temperature can spoil the food being cooked, so you must regulate it. Food to be baked, e.g. rolls, should be even in size. This ensures they all cook in the same amount of time.

The equipment required to roast or bake dishes includes:

o Sturdy roasting trays of an appropriate size

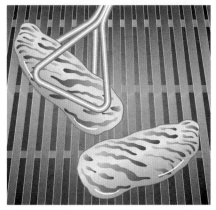

Remember!
Grilling is a quick method of cooking food and the heat must be regulated to prevent the dish burning.

Figure 5.3 Cooking on a griddle

Definition
Charring or **searing:** using the hot bars on a griddle to darken or pattern the item as it is cooking.

Remember!
The temperatures reached when roasting are extreme (120–300°C). Always use oven cloths and personal protective equipment.

○ Cloths to handle hot equipment

○ Suitable utensils, e.g. a perforated spoon or slice, to agitate the food

○ An oven to roast or bake

The difference between baking and roasting is that for roasting, oil is added to aid the cooking process. For example, roasted Mediterranean vegetables have seasoning and oil added to them. The oven heats the oil, which in turn cooks and colours the vegetables. Roasting also requires you to baste. This means taking the oil and juices from the food and pouring them over it at timed intervals to keep it moist.

Baking is a method of cooking in an oven using dry heat. The dry heat within the confined space of the oven creates the best conditions for cooking the dish. When baking, the heat generated within the baked product (e.g. pies, pastries) creates moisture that counteracts the dry convected air. This self-generated moisture keeps the cooked product in optimum condition for serving. No oil or other additional ingredients need to be added, e.g. baked potatoes need only be washed and pricked before placing in the oven.

Combination cooking

Combination cooking means that more than one method of cooking is used in making a dish. For example, a cauliflower cheese gratin uses two cooking methods. Cauliflower is cooked by boiling and then placed in a dish, covered with a cheese sauce and then finished and coloured in the oven or under a grill.

Some cooking equipment is designed to enable combination cooking methods. For example, combination ovens give the benefits of both steaming and convection during cooking. This cooking process ensures the dish remains moist.

Marcus says

There are many different cooking methods that can be used for many different ingredients. Think it through carefully – what do you hope to achieve and what suits your ingredients best? For example, never fry braising steak!

Microwaving

Microwaving is a method of cooking and heating food by using high-frequency power. The energy is used to disturb molecules or particles of food, agitate them and cause friction, which has the effect of heating the food.

Microwave ovens are fast, energy-saving, versatile and easy to operate. Food that is cooked in a microwave oven needs no fat or water. However, microwaves do not brown the surface of the food or make it crispy.

Using a bain-marie

Food can be cooked and kept hot by the bain-marie method. This is done made by placing a pan or bowl of food in a larger pan of boiling water.

This method can be carried out in the oven, on top of the stove or using the kitchen equipment with the same name, a bain-marie. A bain-marie has open wells of water and needs to be heated by steam, gas or electricity to boil the water.

Figure 5.4 A bain-marie

Finishing

Finishing means completing the dish ready for service in line with the dish specification, which will include visual, texture, temperature and taste aspects. Finishing could include, for example, coating the dish with a sauce or foam, or glazing it. It could also include adding a garnish or accompaniment (see below). Finishing is important in order to give the customer the best possible experience.

Try this! **Worksheet 15**
Close your book. How many cooking methods can you name?

Classic dish names

In classic French cooking there were many terms used to indicate a method of cooking, or that a particular ingredient was used in creating a dish to be served alongside the finished dish as an accompaniment. Many of these names are still in common usage and you should be familiar with them.

French term	Meaning
bonne femme	A French term, meaning 'good wife', applied to dishes that are prepared in a simple, family or country way and often served in the container in which they are cooked.
à la meunière	A method of cooking that can be used for all types of fish (whole, filleted or steaks). The fish is lightly floured (hence the name of the dish – meunière means 'miller's wife') and fried in butter. When cooked it is sprinkled with lemon juice, then noisette butter and finally chopped parsley.
à la lyonnaise	Describes various preparations, usually sautéed, characterised by the use of chopped onions which are glazed in butter until golden and often finished off with the pan juices deglazed with vinegar and sprinkled with chopped parsley.
à la florentine	A method of preparation used mainly for fish, white meat or eggs in which spinach and (usually) mornay sauce are included.
a la provençale	Describes numerous preparations inspired by (or arising directly from) the cookery of Provence in which olive oil, tomato and garlic predominate. The provençale garnish for meat or poultry includes either peeled and slowly cooked tomatoes and large mushrooms garnished with duxelles seasoned with garlic, or crushed garlic-flavoured tomatoes with stoned (pitted) olives (black or green), or aubergines (egg-plants) stuffed with a tomato fondue, French (green) beans in butter and chateau potatoes. Provençale sauce (made with tomato, onion, garlic and white wine) is used to dress vegetables, eggs, poultry and fish.
duxelles	A basic preparation of chopped mushrooms, onions and shallots sautéed in butter.
à la grecque	Describes dishes of Greek origin, but is more loosely used for dishes inspired by Mediterranean cuisine. Vegetables à la grecque are cooked in a marinade flavoured with olive oil and lemon and served cold, either as an hors d'oeuvre or an entrée. Pilaf à la grecque consists of rice mixed with sausage, peas and cubes of pepper. Fish à la grecque is coated with a white wine sauce flavoured with celery, fennel and coriander seeds.
à la bordelaise	The name given to a wide range of dishes (eggs, fish, shellfish, kidneys and steak) which use such ingredients as bone marrow, shallots and – significantly – wine (white for fish, red for red meat).
pavé	This word, which literally means 'slab' or 'block', is applied to several dishes but most commonly to a square-shaped cake or dessert made from genoese sponge cake sandwiched with butter cream or squares of rice or semolina pudding. It is also used for a cold entrée, usually a mousse, set in a square or rectangular mould, coated with aspic jelly and garnished with slices of truffle. Pavé also describes a square block gingerbread and a thick piece of prime grilled beef.
à l'italienne	In French classic cuisine this name is given to dishes of meat, fish, vegetables or eggs that are either dressed with Italian sauce (based on a duxelles of mushrooms, ham and chopped herbs) or garnished with artichoke hearts or macaroni. It is also applied to pasta cooked al dente and to many other dishes typical of Italian cookery.

à la piedmontaise	Describes various dishes that include a risotto, sometimes accompanied by truffles. Arranged in a variety of ways – in darioles, in timbale moulds or as croquettes – the risotto is used to garnish poultry, meat and fish. The term à la piedmontaise also refers to dishes of the Piedmont region of northern Italy that do not necessarily feature truffles, such as polenta, ravioli and macaroni. Pastries à la piedmontaise are usually based on hazelnuts, another famous product of Piedmont.
à la milanaise	Food prepared in the style of Milan is generally dipped in egg and breadcrumbs mixed with grated Parmesan cheese, then fried in clarified butter. The name also describes a method of preparing macaroni (served in butter with grated cheese and tomato sauce) and a garnish for meat, made from macaroni with cheese, coarsely shredded ham, pickled tongue, mushrooms and truffles, all blended in tomato sauce. Dishes cooked au gratin with Parmesan cheese are also described as à la milanaise.

Fig 5.5 Commonly used terms for dishes

Test yourself!

1 Are these cooking methods wet or dry? Put a W next to the wet cookery methods and a D next to the dry cookery methods.
   a Simmering _____
   b Braising _____
   c Baking _____
   d Stewing _____
   e Grilling. _____

2 What is the recommended standby temperature for a deep-fat fryer?
   a 90°C
   b 92°C
   c 93°C
   d 95°C.

3 There are four types of frying. What are they?

4 What is the difference between roasting and baking?

6 Vegetables and pulses

This chapter covers skills and knowledge in the following units:

- 7132 Unit 226 (2FP7) Prepare vegetables for basic dishes
- 7132 Unit 233 (2FC7) Cook and finish basic vegetable dishes
- 7132 Unit 241 (2FPC6) Prepare, cook and finish basic pulse dishes
- 7091 Unit 270 Preparation, cooking and finishing of vegetable dishes

Working through this chapter could also provide the opportunity to practise the following Functional Skills at Level 2:
Functional English Writing – use a range of writing styles for different purposes; use a range of sentence structures, including complex sentences, and paragraphs to organise written communication effectively

In this chapter you will:

Understand how and be able to prepare vegetables for basic dishes	7132 – 226.1,2	7091 – 270.1
Understand how and be able to cook basic vegetable dishes	7132 – 233.1,2	7091 – 270.2
Understand how and be able to finish basic vegetable dishes	7132 – 233.3,4	7091 – 270.3
Understand how and be able to prepare basic pulse dishes	7132 – 241.1,2	
Understand how and be able to cook basic pulse dishes	7132 – 241.3,4	
Understand how and be able to finish basic pulse dishes	7132 – 241.5,6	

Identifying vegetables and pulses

Vegetables accompany most meals. In vegetarian dishes they are sometimes the main ingredients. You can probably already identify many different types of vegetables and pulses. What you may not know is where they come from and how to cook them.

Pulses are seeds and pods which are harvested for drying. Commonly used pulses include some types of peas, lentils and beans.

Many items, e.g. chives and potatoes, are available all year round as suppliers obtain them from abroad when they are out of season in this country.

Vegetables and pulses can be split into these categories:
- root vegetables
- bulbs
- flower heads
- fungi
- tubers
- leaves
- stems
- vegetable fruits
- pulses.

Healthy eating

Root vegetables are usually peeled to remove the outer skin before being cooked. They will have been in contact with the soil and may be dirty. However, you can scrub root vegetables with water and cook them with their skins on, as the skin contains valuable nutrients.

Root vegetables

Carrots, parsnips, beetroot, turnips, radishes and swede are all examples of root vegetables. They grow in soil. The root is the edible part of the plant. The stalks grow above the soil and are usually thrown away and not eaten. Root vegetables are a good source of fibre and vitamins A and B. They normally have a firm or hard texture, as this helps them to survive in the soil.

Figure 6.1 Root vegetables: a carrot, b parsnip, c beetroot, d turnip, e radish, f swede

Carrots

Carrots are tapered orange vegetables which vary in size. The younger they are, the smaller and sweeter they are. Carrots are a common addition to many British dishes and are generally boiled or steamed. They are a good source of vitamins A and C.

Swede

Swede is a round vegetable with a thick outer skin. The flesh is yellow and has a distinctive sweet flavour. This vegetable is usually boiled or steamed and can be served diced or mashed.

Turnips

Turnips have a similar shape to swede but are smaller. They may be purple and white or greenish-white depending on the variety. The tough outer skin is peeled away leaving a white flesh, which is usually boiled.

Beetroot

Beetroot is a smaller round vegetable, which is easily recognised by its deep red colour. It is generally used in salads and in soups such **borsch**.

Parsnips

Parsnips look similar to carrots but are a creamy beige colour. They can be roasted in batons to accompany a roast dinner, puréed in a soup, boiled and served as mash or even steamed whole.

Radishes

Radishes are small round vegetables with a red outer skin. They have a bitter flavour and are used in salads or as a garnish rather than for cooking.

Celeriac

Celeriac looks similar to swede but its flesh is white rather than yellow. It has a slightly bitter flavour, a bit like celery. It can be steamed or boiled and served on its own, diced or mashed. It can also be combined with mashed potato.

Find out!

The Scots have a special name for swede or turnip. What is it? These are eaten along with 'tatties' (potatoes) on a special night of the year. Find out what this is.

Definition

Borsch: a traditional Russian soup made with beetroot.

Bulbs

Bulbs grow in soil but their stalks are above the ground surface. They are recognisable by the layers which form at their base. Examples of bulb vegetables include onions, leeks, chives and garlic.

Onions

Onions are probably the most common and popular type of bulb vegetable. They are used in cookery worldwide for a large range of dishes, e.g. casseroles, stir-fries and sauces. Most onions have a dry inedible skin which is peeled and thrown away during preparation. Onions vary in size, shape and colour.

Shallots are small and either red or white. Traditionally they are available between September and October, although now you can get shallots all year round.

Red onions are dark red. They are sweeter in flavour than other onions and are good in salads.

Spring onions are used raw in salads. Some outer layers are removed from the stalk and bulb to remove dirt or damage. They are now available all year round.

Button onions, as the name suggests, are small. They are white. They are used as garnishes in dishes such as coq au vin because they are bite-sized and can be served whole.

Spanish onions are the largest. They are sliced or diced in various dishes, e.g. stews and casseroles, or accompany convenience products, e.g. hot dogs and burgers.

Figure 6.2 Bulbs: a onion, b leek, c chives, d garlic

Figure 6.3 Types of onion: a shallot, b red onion, c spring onion, d button onion, e Spanish onion

Leeks

Leeks have a white base and stem which changes to green at the top. Leeks have a lot of dirt in their layers so it is important to wash and trim leeks properly. Leeks vary in size and can be used in a variety of ways.

Did you know?
The leek is the national symbol of Wales.

Chives

Chives are usually used as a herb or garnish and are not served as a dish. Chives are available all year round.

> **Try this!**
> Leek and potato soup can be served either hot or cold. Make the soup, taste it hot and then cold to see which temperature you prefer.

Most items are now available all year round from suppliers. However, if a supplier gets a product from abroad it will generally cost more.

Garlic

Garlic is a versatile vegetable. It is not usually served on its own but is crushed or sliced and added to dishes such as soups, sauces, meat dishes or marinades to enhance flavour. Garlic is usually grown in France and can vary in size from a standard bulb to jumbo or elephant garlic.

> **Chef's tip**
> Garlic has a very overpowering flavour, which can linger on your hands, breath and clothes. Always ensure you use the correct amount according to the recipe. If you use too much, the dish will be overpowered by the garlic flavour.

Flower heads

Broccoli, asparagus and cauliflower are common examples of flower head vegetables. As the name suggests, the flower head is the part of these plants which is eaten. Flower heads deteriorate quite quickly so it is important to ensure they are fresh.

Figure 6.4 Flower heads: a cauliflower, b broccoli

Cauliflower

A cauliflower has tightly packed florets or flowers making a compact, round, white head. The flower head is usually surrounded by thick green leaves, which are discarded during preparation. Cauliflowers are available all year round, but the price will vary.

> **Did you know?**
> Cauliflower leaves can be used to make soup.

Broccoli

Broccoli is a deep greenish-purple colour. Poor quality is indicated by discoloration – the head starts to seed and goes yellow. The stem from which the florets are cut is edible so by leaving the stem intact with the floret you have a greater yield from the vegetable.

> **Did you know?**
> The consumption of broccoli is associated with reducing the risk of developing some cancers.

Fungi

Not all fungi are edible. In fact some fungi could kill you or your customer if eaten so it is really important to obtain your fungi from a reputable supplier. Most people do not possess the skills to pick their own mushrooms or fungi in a wood; the consequences of picking the wrong fungi, e.g. a death cap, mean it is not worth taking the risk.

Reputable suppliers will have many different types of edible fungi and mushroom available, e.g. grey and yellow oyster, hon-shimeji, field and paris brown. They will vary in price due to their availability and the season.

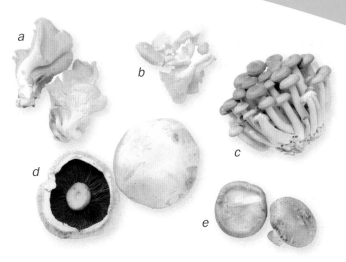

Figure 6.5 There are many types of mushrooms available to caterers, including: a grey oyster, b yellow oyster, c hon-shimeji, d field, e paris brown

Mushrooms

The most commonly used mushrooms are button mushrooms and open flat mushrooms. These are generally white but can be dark brown. Freshness is essential and should be checked before use. Mushrooms must be washed thoroughly as they are found in or around decaying trees and plants or are artificially cultivated in soil heavily treated with manure or animal waste. Mushrooms are usually cooked by frying.

Quorn

This is a high-protein vegetable used by vegetarians as a meat substitute. Quorn is processed from a tiny plant of the mushroom family. It resembles grey mincemeat. It is not suitable for vegans as it contains egg white.

Figure 6.6 A death cap mushroom

> **Try this!**
> **Substitute quorn for minced beef and make a cottage pie in the same way. You will be surprised how similar the taste is.**

> **Remember!**
> Not all fungi are mushrooms. A truffle is also a fungus. It can be black or white, is extremely expensive and is used to add flavour to certain dishes.

Tubers

Tubers are swellings or nodes on the roots of plants. The rest of the plant is discarded for cooking. They grow under the soil. The main vegetable in this group is the potato. Potatoes are round or oval, yellowy-white on the inside with an outer skin, which is peeled or scrubbed before cooking. Sweet potatoes have orange flesh and a sweeter flavour than normal potatoes.

There are at least 40 different types of potato ranging from small Charlotte potatoes to red Desiree potatoes. Maris Pipers make the best chipped potatoes. Potatoes differ in size from bite-sized baby new potatoes to large King Edwards, which can be bigger than your hand.

Potatoes are split into 'new' and 'old'. New potatoes are available between May and August and old potatoes are available between September and April.

Figure 6.7 Potatoes: a baby new potatoes, b maris piper, c desiree

Did you know?
A potato is made up of layers, which can be seen if the potato is cut.

Leaves

Leaf vegetables are the prepared leaves of the plant. They include cabbage, sprouts, spinach and lettuce.

Cabbage

Several varieties of cabbage are commonly used in cooking:

Traditional or **white cabbages** are greenish-white balls of flat leaves tightly packed together. The thick-stemmed leaves are trimmed to aid the cooking process.

Savoy cabbages have a distinct flavour and ruffled appearance. The leaves are green or yellow. They are not as tightly packed as white cabbages.

Figure 6.8 Leaf vegetables: a savoy cabbage, b red cabbage, c spinach, d iceberg lettuce, e green cabbage, f white cabbage

Red cabbages are similar in shape and texture to white cabbages, but the leaves are a deep purplish-red. Red cabbages generally take a little longer than normal cabbages to cook because of their density and the thickness of their leaves.

Sprouts

Sprouts, which we all traditionally turn our noses up at during Christmas, are a type of miniature cabbage with a very distinctive flavour. The small, tightly-packed balls of leaves are attached to the long sturdy stem of the plant. Extremely nutritious, Brussels sprouts are a valuable source of folic acid which is important for pregnant women.

Spinach

When cooked, spinach reduces to a dark-green, soft texture. Because it reduces in volume so much on cooking, a great amount is needed if a large yield is required.

Lettuce

Lettuce is traditionally used in salads. Lettuce must be washed thoroughly, as soil can easily get into the heart. Lettuce leaves should be firm, clean and fresh.

Stems

This group of vegetables includes celery, asparagus and seaweed.

Celery

Celery is the most commonly used stem vegetable. It has a distinctive taste and is often used in salads, although it can be braised or made into soup. The long green stem has a fibrous string-like outer skin, which should be removed to enhance its quality.

Chef's tip
Fruit, e.g. apple, is a good accompaniment for red cabbage.

Chef's tip
Nutmeg is a great addition to spinach.

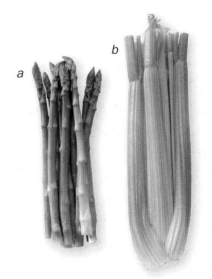

Figure 6.9 Stem vegetables: a asparagus, b celery

Asparagus

The base of asparagus is quite woody, so cut it away. The remaining stem has a small flowering head, which has usually not flowered before cooking.

Seaweed

With the increased interest in Asian cooking, especially Japanese cooking, seaweed is used in many kitchens. Many types of seaweed are used in cooking and it is used in a variety of dishes including salads, ice cream, puddings, bread, soups and stocks. These are some different types of seaweed:

- **Kombu**: also known as kelp, this can be used in rice or bean dishes, or used to make soups or stock.
- **Wakame**: this can be added to soup.
- **Nori**: can be eaten on its own, in soups or sprinkled over food.
- **Arame** and **hijiki**: traditional Japanese seaweeds.
- **Agar agar**: occasionally used in desserts. Processed agar agar can be used as a gelatine substitute for vegetarians.
- **Dulse** and **sea palm**.
- **Samphire**: is a common and popular seaweed which is used to flavour soups and salads.

Seaweeds are very rich in minerals. For example, they contain between seven and 14 times as much calcium as milk, depending on the type of seaweed. Seaweed is eaten cooked, dried or fresh depending on the dish, and can be obtained from Asian restaurant suppliers.

Did you know?

Asparagus is classed as a flower head if just the tips are cooked. However, asparagus is usually cooked whole with its stem.

Chef's tip

Finely shredded deep-fried seaweed is a great accompaniment to an Asian dinner.

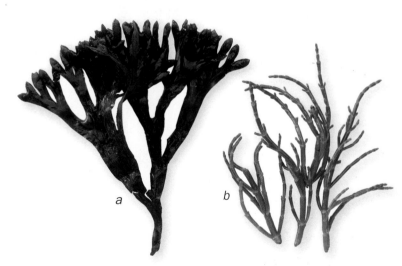

Fig 6.10 Seaweed: a nori, b samphire

Vegetable fruits

These vegetables are the ripened fruit of the plants they grow on. They include aubergines, capsicums (peppers), cucumber, avocados, tomatoes, courgettes, marrow and sweetcorn.

Figure 6.11 Vegetable fruits: a aubergine, b capsicums, c cucumber, d avocado, e beef tomato, f tomato, g cherry tomatoes

Aubergines

Aubergines have a firm to spongy texture. They are bell-shaped and black or purple in colour. They are generally used with other vegetables, e.g. tomatoes, courgettes, garlic and onions for ratatouille. Aubergines can be grilled with olive oil for an hors d'oeuvre (starter) or used as the vegetable layer in moussaka. Aubergines are a Mediterranean vegetable and are a popular element in that style of cookery.

Capsicums

Capsicums are commonly known as sweet peppers. They can be red, orange, green or yellow. The colour depends on the age of the capsicum, i.e. a green capsicum will eventually turn red. These versatile vegetables are used in salads and many Mediterranean dishes. They can also be blanched and stuffed with other food, e.g. rice, to create vegetarian dishes (see page 317).

Cucumbers

Cucumbers are long green baton-shaped vegetables, which are not usually cooked but are used for cold food and salads.

Avocados

Avocados originally came from South America but are now grown in many different countries. They are oval in shape and are a green or brown colour. The skins are tough and inedible. Once peeled, avocados may discolour rapidly. Avocados contain a large seed or stone in the centre. When ripe the flesh feels soft to touch. It can easily be puréed. They have a high fat content for a vegetable.

> **Try this!**
> Take a piece of raw red capsicum and taste it. Now brush it with oil and grill it till the skin is black. Remove the skin and taste the capsicum. The difference is astonishing – the sweet flavour of the capsicum really comes through.

Tomatoes

Tomatoes are very versatile and are used in many dishes and salads. They are instantly recognisable from their round red appearance, although they do come in other shapes as well, e.g. the long plum tomato from Italy. Their colour varies and a good indicator of flavour is a deep red colour. Tomatoes supplied on the vine are considered to be better quality and the flavour should be sweeter. Cherry tomatoes are baby tomatoes and have a sweeter taste than normal tomatoes. Beef tomatoes are the largest variety. They are very fleshy and juicy with a sweet flavour. They are ideal in Greek salad and can be cooked by grilling or shallow frying as an accompaniment to a meal.

Courgettes

Courgettes are similar in appearance to marrows, but they are smaller. They taste quite bland so they are usually sautéed or stir-fried with other vegetables, e.g. onion and garlic, to add flavour. Overcooking courgettes makes them soggy and unattractive.

Marrows

Marrows are much larger versions of courgettes with similar preparation and cooking methods. Marrows are not popular as their high water content makes their flavour quite bland. Overcooked marrows are extremely unappealing and mushy.

Fresh peas and beans

Peas and beans are the seeds (e.g. garden peas) and the seed pods (e.g. mangetout, French beans, runner beans and broad beans) of plants. Vegetables such as garden peas are usually blanched and then frozen.

Some seed pods grow to yield large seeds, e.g. broad beans, from which the pod is discarded and only the seed is used for cooking. Other types, e.g. runner beans and French beans, are picked with the pod and seed still intact and are prepared together. These vegetables contain high levels of vitamin C.

> **Marcus says**
>
> To get the maximum flavour and texture out of fresh vegetables, use items that are in season at the time.

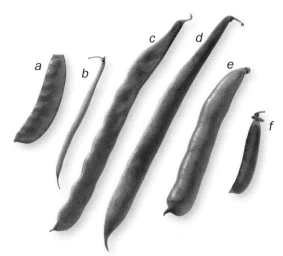

Figure 6.12 a mangetout, b French bean, c flat bean, d runner bean, e broad bean, f garden peas

Mangetout is a pea pod inside which the peas have not yet grown. They are very delicate and do not take long to cook. Quick cooking methods such as stir-frying are suitable for mangetout as they can become wilted and mushy very quickly.

Pulses

Pulses are the edible seeds of plants, harvested for drying.

Pulses, e.g. chickpeas, lentils, split yellow peas, split green peas and beans, can be obtained dried or cooked and canned. The pulses you are likely to use at NVQ Level 2 will be dried, and most of these will need soaking before use. Pulses are a high source of fibre, protein, iron and B vitamins.

Peas

- Split green peas disintegrate easily and are very starchy. They are often used as an ingredient in soups and broths.
- Chickpeas hold their shape well and are used, as with other pulses, in vegetarian dishes. In some parts of the world they are ground into flour to make breads, batters, etc. They have a slightly nutty flavour.
- Marrowfat peas, like split green peas, disintegrate easily and are very starchy. They are often used as an ingredient in soups and broths.

Beans

Many types of beans are available to caterers, e.g. red kidney beans, white haricot beans, mung beans, butter beans, borlotti beans, broad beans and soya beans.

- Red kidney beans contain an enzyme which if not destroyed will cause food poisoning. Rapid boiling for ten minutes destroys the enzyme. This cooking time enables the heat to penetrate the bean and kill the enzyme.
- Haricot beans are used in baked beans.
- Butter beans are also known as lima beans. They are large, flat and yellowy-brown. They have a buttery taste when cooked.
- Borlotti beans are similar to kidney beans and are a good substitute for kidney or haricot beans in dishes. They are very moist and tender and have a nice texture in dishes.

Try this!   **Worksheet 16**
Close your book and list as many vegetables as you can for each category.

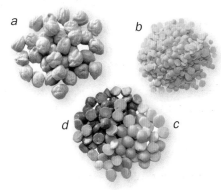

Figure 6.13 Dried pulses: a chickpeas, b lentils, c split yellow peas, d split green peas

Healthy eating
Pulses contain no saturated fats and are a healthy alternative to meat.

Remember!
Red kidney beans must always be boiled for at least ten minutes before use.

o Soya beans are high in fat and protein. Soya bean products are increasingly popular. They are processed into flour, milk, meat substitutes (e.g. tofu or tempeh), margarine and even soy sauce.

Lentils

Lentils are the seeds of a small branching plant. They resemble small peas. They can be used whole or split and do not necessarily need to be soaked before cooking. Lentils are rich in protein. They are named and identified according to their colour: red, yellow, green and brown. Red and yellow lentils disintegrate when cooked, while green and brown remain whole.

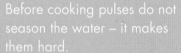

Find out!   **Worksheet 17**

Find more information about pulses. For each type of pulse write a description, a note of its uses, nutritional information and any other key facts you discover.

How to judge quality of vegetables and pulses

It is essential that you can select good quality vegetables for use. Always consider size, shape, colour, smell, damage and texture. If you are unsure about the quality of any vegetable you should consult your supervisor. The table below lists vegetables and the quality points to look for.

Marcus says

Before cooking pulses do not season the water – it makes them hard.

Vegetable or pulse	Quality points
Potato	No excessive soil, no eyes or roots growing from the tuber, no weeping, bruising or damage to the skin. Good even size for type required.
Carrot	Good tapered straight shape, vibrant orange colour, no woody appearance, no insect or spade damage or wrinkling of skin.
Turnip	Firm with no damage to the exterior. Outer skin is not wrinkled, no insect or spade damage. Pliable to touch.
Swede	Firm with no insect or spade damage to the exterior. Outer skin is not wrinkled and pliable to touch.
Parsnip	Firm with no insect or spade damage to the exterior. Outer skin is not wrinkled. Pliable to touch.
Radish	Even size, good red colour. No insect or spade damage to outer surface. Healthy fresh-looking green leaves.
Celeriac	White, firm with strong smell and rough, mottled outer skin.
Onion	Firm and dry exterior, no moisture at top. No sign of stem growth.
Garlic	Firm and dry exterior, no moisture at top. No sign of stem growth.

Chives	Good green colour, no discoloration, no signs of wilting.
Spring onion	Bulb and stem clean in appearance, no damage to stem, leaves or bulb. No slime, no moist leaves.
Leek	No excessive soil, no damage or slimy feel to exterior layers or leaves.
Cabbage	No discoloration, damage or wilting. Clean and fresh appearance.
Courgette	Dark green skin, no bruising or damage to the exterior surface. Firm flesh.
Marrow	No bruising or damage to the exterior surface. Firm flesh.
Sprouts	Compact leaves, no yellow discoloration, clean fresh appearance.
Lettuce	No wilting leaves, no excessive soil, no contamination from insects such as snails and slugs. Colour should be bright and vibrant.
Spinach	Crisp leaves, fresh appearance, no slimy leaves, deep green colour.
Cauliflower	Tightly packed heads, no discoloration or damage to the head. Leaves surrounding the flower head intact and not wilting. Not too many leaves.
Broccoli	Fresh green colour, no discoloration (yellow). Tight florets. Stems firm and crisp, not spongy or flexible.
Asparagus	Green pointed shoot on a white stem. Firm flower heads, good size, base not too woody, no discoloration or damage.
Celery	Firm stems with no damage or discoloration to the vegetable. Stems tightly packed together. Breaks crisply when separated.
Mushrooms	No slime or bad odour. Clean and dry, no discoloration to the cap.
Tomato	No damage to skin, firm to touch, good colour.
Avocado	Good green or brown colour, skin firm but with some give to show ripeness. No damage to exterior.
Aubergine	Firm, no damage or soft spots.
Cucumber	Long firm and straight. Skin clean and a good green colour. No sign of wilting or wrinkling. No soft spots.
Capsicum	No wrinkling, good vibrant colour, no soft spots or damage.
Broad bean	Pods undamaged and not too large. Evenly sized.
Mangetout	Crisp, flat, evenly sized pods, good green colour, no discoloration.
Peas	Plump and crisp, no discoloration.
Runner beans	Even size, not too big, good green colour, no discoloration, snaps crisply when broken.
French beans	Even size, not too big, good green colour, no discoloration, snaps crisply when broken.
Dried pulses	Free from contaminants such as insects; feels clean, dry and smooth.

Figure 6.14 Quality points to look for in vegetables and pulses

Worksheet 18

Try this!
Close your book. List the quality points you should look for in a delivery of fresh vegetables.

Food value and healthy eating

Pulses and vegetables are an essential part of a healthy, well-balanced diet. The wrong cooking method or cooking time will affect the nutritional value of the food so it is important to understand and apply the correct preparation and cooking methods.

Most vegetables contain large amounts of vitamins B and C. These vitamins dissolve in water; therefore over-boiling vegetables to a mush means they will not be as nutritious.

The table below identifies the nutritional value of vegetables.

Type	Fats (grams per 100g)	Protein (grams per 100g)	Carbohydrates (grams per 100g)	Vitamin content
Potato	0.2	3.9	31	B, C
Carrot	0.3	0.6	7.9	A, B, C, K
Turnip	0.3	0.9	4.7	B, C
Swede	0.3	5.0	1.9	B, C
Parsnip	1.1	1.8	12.5	B, C, K
Beetroot	0.3	0	9.0	A, B, C
Radish	0.1	0.8	2.9	C
Onion	0.2	1.2	7.9	B, C
Garlic	1.0	7.0	15.0	C
Spring onion	1.0	2.0	3.0	B, C
Leek	0.5	1.6	2.9	B, C
Cabbage	0.5	2.1	3.9	B, C
Courgette	0.4	1.8	1.8	C, K
Sprouts	1.0	2.8	2.0	A, C, K
Lettuce	0.3	0.7	1.9	C
Spinach	0.8	2.8	1.6	A, B, C, K
Cauliflower	0.9	3.6	3.0	B, C, K
Broccoli	0.9	4.4	1.8	A, B, C, K
Asparagus	0.6	2.7	1.1	C

Celery	0.3	0.3	0.9	C
Mushroom	0.5	1.8	0.4	B, C, K
Tomato	0.4	0.7	2.8	A, B, C
Avocado (145g)	28	2.0	2.0	B, C, E
Aubergine	0.4	0.9	2.2	B
Cucumber	0.1	0.7	1.5	C
Capsicum	0.4	1.0	6.4	A, B, C
Broad beans	0.8	5.1	5.6	B, C
Peas	0.7	4.8	7.8	B, C
Runner beans	0.4	1.6	2.0	A, C
Haricot beans	1.6	21.4	49.7	B
Lentils	1.5	24.0	48.8	B
Soya beans	7.3	14	5.1	B
Chickpeas	5.4	21.3	49.6	C

Figure 6.15 Nutritional value of vegetables

Preparation tools and techniques

Washing

Vegetables grow in, on or above the ground. They can become contaminated by the soil, which contains many types of harmful bacteria, e.g. *Clostridium perfringens* and *Bacillus cereus*, so it is important to wash them carefully. Also, insects and other animals, e.g. slugs, can be trapped within the leaves. Another reason for washing vegetables is to remove any residue from chemicals and pesticides, which may have been sprayed onto the vegetables to deter birds and insects.

It is important to inspect the product first to make sure it is the right quality. Then strip away any unnecessary leaves or remains from when the vegetable was joined to the plant, e.g. removing the tomatoes from the vine.

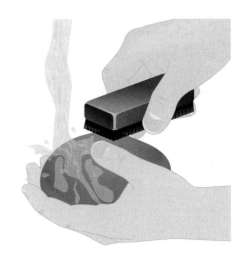

Figure 6.16 A brush can be used to clean potatoes

Next wash the vegetables in cold running water. The type of vegetable will determine how robustly you clean it. You may use a brush to scrub the mud from potatoes but you would be more careful washing a tomato. Some delicate leaves, e.g. spinach, may need repeated soaking to get them clean. Once the items have been washed thoroughly, they should be drained of any excess water.

Peeling

Peeling is the removal of the outer layer of a food item (which is generally inedible or unappealing) to reveal the edible flesh beneath, e.g. peeling a swede will reveal the yellow flesh. Peeling also improves the presentation of the vegetable.

Not all vegetables need to be peeled. Vegetables such as tomatoes, cucumbers, mushrooms, beans, mangetout, capsicums, cabbage and spinach grow above the ground, and their outer skins are edible. They do not need to be peeled unless it is a dish requirement.

Vegetables which grow in or on the soil often develop tough outer skins. These need to be washed and then peeled. As a general rule, root vegetables and tubers require peeling. Some fruit vegetables, e.g. avocados, also need peeling due to the toughness of their skin.

The tools used to peel vegetables vary from a hand vegetable peeler, a 3-inch vegetable knife to a 7-inch vegetable knife. Carrots require a hand peeler, whereas a turnip will need to be peeled using a 7–10-inch vegetable knife. Always use a brown board when peeling vegetables.

Large industrial equipment may be used to peel vegetables such as potatoes. Potatoes are usually required in large quantities, so rather than peeling hundreds of potatoes by hand, a potato rumbler can be used. This is a large mechanically operated drum which has a rough interior and spins at a fast rate. Water is flushed through the rumbler constantly. The rapid spinning of the drum removes the skins of the potatoes. The water washes them and also washes away the peelings. This process saves a lot of time. Potatoes can also be purchased pre-prepared. Any discoloured potatoes should be reported to your supervisor.

Video presentation

Watch *Washing and peeling vegetables.*

Remember!

In all cases, if you are unsure of how to peel an item, seek assistance from your supervisor.

Figure 6.17 Tools used to peel vegetables

Figure 6.18 Potato rumblers are a quicker way of peeling large quantities of potatoes.

For vegetables such as broad beans or peas, peeling means to shell the whole vegetable from its pod. Break open the pod, and remove the peas or beans and wash them.

Figure 6.19 Shelling fresh peas

Rewashing

Constantly handling vegetables when peeling may mean they become re-contaminated with soil or other impurities. Re-washing the vegetable after peeling or other preparation methods will remove any unwanted impurities and leave it ready for the next stage. This process is good practice when food handling.

Cutting

Cutting vegetables into the required size or shape is a necessary part of preparing vegetables. Many vegetables need to be cut into bite-sized pieces, which may also speed the cooking process.

There are many different cuts which can be applied to vegetables (but not usually pulses). To cut you need a knife and a chopping board. The knife should be appropriate to the task. The board should be brown, stable and flat. If you are doing a classic cut, you should start by trimming the vegetable so that it is stable on the chopping board. You should then make initial cuts to bring the vegetable into pieces of roughly the right size and shape for the cut you are doing.

Traditional French cuts

There are six traditional French cuts for cutting vegetables:
○ **Jardinière:** trim, slice, cut into baton shapes 15mm × 4mm.
○ **Macedoine:** trim, slice, cut into dice 5mm × 5mm × 5mm.
○ **Julienne:** trim, slice, cut into thin strips like matchsticks, 3–4cm in length by 2–4mm thick.
○ **Mirepoix:** trim, chop roughly into pieces of no specific shape or size, although they are normally quite large pieces.
○ **Paysanne:** trim into desired shape, thinly slice into squares, circles and triangles of about 1cm in diameter.
○ **Brunoise:** trim, slice into thin strips like matchsticks, cut strips into small dice, 2mm × 2mm × 2mm.

> **Try this!** **Worksheet 19**
>
> Draw a simple sketch of the vegetable cuts to scale then find out five uses for each.

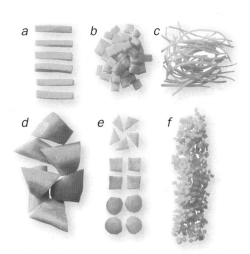

Figure 6.20 Traditional French cuts: a jardinière, b macedoine, c julienne, d mirepoix e paysanne, f brunoise,

Mastering these cuts takes time because they are very precise and a lot of skill is involved. Good knife skills are essential for a chef, and practising these cuts is good preparation for developing other knife skills.

Clumsy knife skills and poorly cut vegetables will detract from the presentation of a dish. They could even affect the cooking, as larger pieces will cook more slowly than smaller ones.

Slicing

Slicing is a general term for cutting food with a knife. Vegetables such as onions are usually sliced. If the bulb is whole, slicing across the diameter of the onion will create onion rings. Halving the bulb will produce slices of onion, which are suitable as general garnish, e.g. with steaks.

Slice to the specific size or shape stated in the recipe. Slicing can be done by hand or by a mechanical food processor, depending on the size of the catering outlet.

Trimming

Trimming is the removal of food parts not required for a particular dish. For vegetables this includes peeling, removing the thick stems in the centre of cabbage leaves and removing the outer leaves of a cauliflower.

Grating

Root vegetables and other vegetables of a firm texture may be grated to yield fine strands of vegetable. Carrots are grated for salads and coleslaw.

A grater is a metal utensil which has a sharp rough surface and is perforated. As a vegetable is passed over this surface, strands of it are shaved through the perforations. Graters come in all shapes and sizes, from hand graters to industrial machinery which will grate large quantities in a short space of time. Food processors normally have grating utensils.

Video presentation

Choosing the right knife and *Sharpening a knife* will give you important background information. *Classic cuts* shows you how these essential cuts are made.
Watch *Preparing and chopping an onion* to see a skilled chef doing this.
Watch *Preparing leeks* for a demonstration of trimming.

Remember!

At all times ensure your own and others' safety. Never use any equipment you have not been trained on how to use.

Figure 6.21 An industrial food processor

Soaking

Pulses are generally dried. They need soaking or reconstituting before cooking. This means soaking them in water to put the water content back into the vegetable to make it soft.

The type of pulse will determine how long it should be soaked for. Usually pulses should be soaked in twice the volume of water to pulses and between 4 and 8 hours.

It is advisable to soak pulses in the fridge as warm temperatures during the soaking process can have an adverse effect on them.

Once pulses have been soaked they should be re-washed, as there will be some sugars in them which are hard to digest.

Cooking methods, tools and equipment

Blanching

Blanching is used to kill the enzymes in vegetables that cause their quality to deteriorate. Blanching can also be used to remove skins from vegetables and nuts.

To blanch vegetables immerse them in boiling water for between ten seconds and two minutes depending on the type. Remove them from the boiling water and refresh them (make them cool again) by immersing them in iced water or running cold water over them.

Once drained, vegetables which have been blanched may be stored fresh or frozen for later use or the next stage of preparation.

Over-blanching a vegetable will cook it for too long and the quality will be affected. If a tomato is blanched for too long the flesh after peeling will be very mushy and unsuitable for use.

Have to hand:
- a cloth to stop you burning yourself
- a pan with boiling water
- a spider or perforated spoon
- a perforated basket if the quantity is large enough
- an industrial boiler if the quantity is large enough
- a container with iced water or cold running water.

Remember!
Vegetables should not be prepared too far in advance because they will deteriorate quickly and lose vitamins. Some vegetables, e.g. potatoes, carrots, parsnips etc., should be kept in cold water because they will discolour. Others, e.g. Brussels sprouts, cauliflower, broccoli etc., should be put in a covered container in the refrigerator.

Video presentation
Blanch a tomato to remove the skin shows you how to do this.

How to blanch tomatoes to remove their skins

Use a paring knife to remove the eye of the tomatoes. Make a cross-incision on the underside of the tomatoes.

Use a slotted spoon to plunge the tomatoes into boiling water for ten seconds.

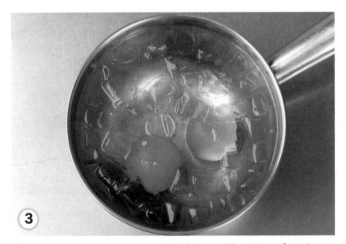

Remove the tomatoes and immediately refresh them in a bowl of iced water.

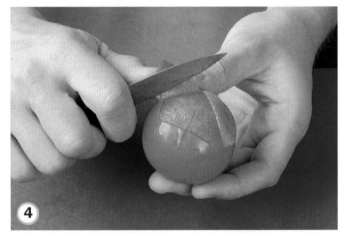

When cool, the skin should easily peel away with the help of a paring knife.

Capsicums can also be blanched to remove their skins. Oil rather than water is used because the skins are very tough and difficult to remove. There are three ways to remove the skins:

1 Brush the capsicum with oil and grill it until the skin is black, then peel it off.
2 Deep-fry the capsicum until the skin comes off.
3 Roast the capsicum, then deep-fry it and put it in a plastic bag. The skin will come off.

The equipment needed for blanching capsicums is either a grill or a deep fryer, a spider or perforated spoons, cloths and suitable trays to lay out the vegetables. For more information see page 122.

Ratatouille

tomatoes	200g
onion, diced	100g
garlic, chopped	hint
green capsicums	100g
red capsicums	100g
olive oil	50ml
herbes de Provence	good pinch
courgettes	200g
aubergines	200g
salt and pepper	to taste
chopped parsley	good pinch
Cooking time	1 hour
Serves	10–12

Preparation	4
Cooking skills	2
Finishing	2

Method

1 Blanch the tomatoes (see method above). The skin should split for easy removal. Peel off the skin and chop including the seeds.
2 Chop the onion and garlic.
3 Clean the capsicums, cut into small strips.
4 In a large cooking pot with thick bottom, put in olive oil, onions and chopped garlic. Add the capsicum. Cover to keep in the moisture. Cook for 20 minutes, stirring frequently, and add olive oil as necessary to prevent burning.
5 Add the peeled tomatoes and herbes de Provence. Stir well and cook for another 15 minutes.
6 Cut the aubergines and courgettes into chunky bite-size pieces.
7 Add the aubergine and courgettes to the pot. Cook for another 25 minutes.
8 Season to taste and garnish with parsley.

Boiling

Not all vegetables are suitable for boiling, e.g. courgettes have a high water content and will disintegrate if boiled. Vegetables which are suitable for boiling include:

○ potatoes
○ carrots
○ runner beans
○ broad beans
○ dried pulses, e.g. lentils, beans and peas
○ fresh peas

- broccoli
- cauliflower
- beetroot
- Brussels sprouts
- cabbage
- parsnips
- turnip
- swede.

Boiling lowers the nutritional value of the vegetable. Vitamins B and C are commonly found in vegetables. These vitamins dissolve in water and are absorbed into the hot liquid during boiling.

Over-boiling can leave a vegetable limp and lifeless, so correct cooking times are important to ensure a good-quality product. Different types of vegetables have different cooking requirements. For more information see page 120.

Boiling root vegetables and tubers

The flesh of root vegetables and tubers, e.g. potatoes, is firm and dense. The boiling process breaks down the structure of the vegetable, making it pleasant and easy to eat. These types of vegetables should be put into cold water and brought to the boil. They will need boiling for 15–20 minutes. Test them by inserting a sharp implement, e.g. a skewer, into the flesh. It should enter easily. Some root vegetables, e.g. carrots, should not be too soft. They should still be quite firm with a slight crunch.

Remember!

Root vegetables must be cooked in cold water brought to the boil. Green vegetables must be cooked in water that is already boiling.

Glazed baton carrots

carrots	600g
butter or margarine	50g
sugar	15g
salt	to taste
chopped parsley	good pinch
Serves	6–8

Preparation	2
Cooking skills	2
Finishing	2

Method

1 Wash and peel the carrots and cut them into **batons**.
2 Place them in a pan and add the butter, sugar and salt.
3 Add enough water to half cover the carrots.
4 Cover them with a lid until the liquid boils.
5 Remove the lid. **Skim**.
6 Serve in a hot dish, season to taste and sprinkle with chopped parsley.

Definitions

Baton: a cut of a vegetable, evenly sized 2.5cm long × 0.5cm × 0.5cm.
Skim: to remove any surface impurities from a liquid using a spoon or similar implement.

Boiling stem vegetables

Asparagus is expensive and care must be taken to cook it correctly. The shoots should be cut to an even size, removing the tough ends. The tips cook quicker than the stem so use a special asparagus kettle which boils the stem and steams the tips. If an asparagus kettle is not available, bundle the stems, tie them with string and cook them standing up in a wide pan.

Figure 6.22 An asparagus kettle

Asparagus and prosciutto

			Preparation	2
			Cooking skills	2
			Finishing	2

fresh asparagus	1kg
salt	5ml
prosciutto, cut into thin slices	250g
parmesan cheese, grated	60ml
butter	200g
Oven temperature	180°C
Cooking time	8–10 minutes
Serves	10

Method

1. Preheat the oven to 180°C.
2. Clean the asparagus, cutting off the tough ends. Add salt to the boiling water. Place the asparagus in the water, cover and cook for five minutes.
3. Lift out with tongs and drain the asparagus on paper towels.
4. Divide the asparagus into bundles, wrap each bundle with two strips of prosciutto, securing with a toothpick or similar implement.
5. Place the asparagus and ham bundles in a greased ovenproof dish and sprinkle with the parmesan cheese.
6. Heat in the oven for three minutes.
7. Melt the butter in a saucepan. Put the bundles on a warm serving plate and pour melted butter over them.

Boiling leaves

Leaf vegetables are less dense and require a much shorter boiling time. They should be added to water that is already boiling and cooked for only a few minutes. This also helps to reduce the amount of vitamins and minerals lost during the cooking process.

Boiling pulses

Pulses are usually cooked by boiling. Red kidney beans must always be boiled for ten minutes to kill off poisonous enzymes contained in them before they are used. Pulses are usually boiled before being made into other dishes, e.g. hummus, fritters and rissoles.

Cooking times for pulses vary:
- Borlotti beans: 1 hour
- Haricot beans: 1–1½ hours
- Broad beans: 1½ hours
- Lentils: 15–30 minutes
- Chickpeas: 1–1½ hours
- Dried peas: 45 minutes
- Kidney beans: 1 hour
- Soya beans: 30–45 minutes.

Steaming

Many vegetables are suitable for steaming. The vegetables that are most often cooked this way are:
- potatoes
- carrots
- cauliflower
- broccoli
- asparagus
- swede
- turnip
- Brussels sprouts
- beans and peas.

Steaming will not colour the vegetables but will enhance their colour as long as they are not overcooked, e.g. broccoli will be greener, carrots will be more orange. For more information see page 121.

Healthy eating
Steaming is healthier than any other method of cooking vegetables and pulses.

Stewing

Most vegetables are suitable for stewing, either on their own or as an accompaniment to meat in meat stews. Root vegetables need longer cooking times than softer vegetables such as aubergines. Care must be taken to ensure the dish is not overcooked. A vegetable curry is a good example of a stewed vegetable dish, as are ratatouille and petit pois français (which is made from peas, lettuce and small onions).

All pulses are suitable for stewing, and chickpea curry is a suitable meat substitute in an Indian restaurant. For more information see page 123.

Remember!
Steam can be extremely dangerous. It can cause severe burns if you do not use equipment correctly.

Mixed bean curry

Preparation	3
Cooking skills	2
Finishing	2

dried red kidney beans	50g
dried black-eyed beans	50g
dried haricot beans	50g
dried flageolet beans	50g
vegetable oil	30ml
cumin seeds	5ml
mustard seeds	5ml
cloves of garlic, crushed	2
onion, finely chopped	1
ginger	2.5cm piece
fresh green chillies, chopped	2
curry paste	30ml
chopped tomatoes, canned	400g
tomato purée	30ml
water	250ml
fresh coriander, chopped	30ml
Cooking time	2¼ hours
Serves	10

Method

1 Soak all the beans in water overnight.
2 Drain the beans and put them in a heavy-based saucepan with at least double the volume of cold water.
3 Bring to the boil and boil vigorously for ten minutes, then simmer for 60–90 minutes or until the beans are soft.
4 Heat the oil in a pan and fry the cumin, mustard seed, garlic, onion, ginger and chillies until the onion is soft.
5 Stir in the curry paste.
6 Add the tomatoes, tomato purée and water. Adjust the seasoning and simmer for five minutes.
7 Add the drained beans and coriander. Cover with a lid and simmer for 30 minutes until the sauce has thickened.
8 Serve and garnish with extra coriander.

Frying

Nearly all vegetables are suitable for shallow- or stir-frying. Different vegetables have different textures and cooking times will vary. For more information see pages 123–124.

Mixed vegetable stir-fry

vegetable oil	15ml
clove of garlic, chopped	1
ginger	2.5cm piece
baby carrots	225g
broccoli florets	350g
asparagus tips	175g
spring onions	125g
green cabbage	175g
light soy sauce	30ml
apple juice	15ml
sesame seeds, toasted	15ml
Cooking time	10 minutes
Serves	4–6

Preparation	4
Cooking skills	2
Finishing	2

Method

1 Heat the oil in a wok and sauté the garlic over a low heat.
2 Raise the heat. Add the ginger, carrots, broccoli and asparagus tips and stir-fry for four minutes.
3 Add the spring onions and green cabbage and stir-fry for another two minutes.
4 Drizzle over the soy sauce and apple juice and toss over the heat for one to two minutes.
5 Sprinkle the sesame seeds on top and serve.

Courgettes provençale

courgettes	600g
garlic clove	1
olive oil	25ml
chopped tomatoes	300g
salt and pepper	to taste
chopped parsley	
Cooking time	6 minutes
Serves	6–8

Preparation	2
Cooking skills	2
Finishing	2

Method

1 Wash the courgettes and slice them to 5mm thickness.
2 Crush and chop the garlic.
3 Use olive oil to mask bottom of a heated pan then fry the garlic off with the courgettes. Only a little colour should be achieved.
4 Add the tomatoes and season to taste.
5 Serve sprinkled with chopped parsley.

Sautéing

This method of frying means cooking quickly in a small amount of hot fat. The food is tossed in the pan so that it browns all over.

Did you know?
The name comes from the French word 'sauter' which means 'to jump'.

Mushroom sauce

onion, chopped	20ml
butter	60g
flour	4 tbsp
salt	½ tsp
beef stock or consommé	500ml
fresh mushrooms, sliced	250g
pepper	⅛ tsp
Cooking time	15–20 minutes
Serves	4–6

Preparation	2
Cooking skills	3
Finishing	2

Method

1 Over a medium to low heat, sauté the onion in three-quarters of the butter.
2 Add the flour and salt, cook the roux until the flour and butter are smooth and blonde.
3 Add the beef stock or consommé, reboiling each time liquid is added to the mixture.
4 Sauté the mushrooms in the remaining butter.
5 Add the mushrooms to the sauce.
6 Bring to a boil once again, adjust seasoning with salt and pepper.
7 Serve immediately.

Deep-frying

The most commonly used deep-fried vegetable is chipped potatoes.
Pulses are also deep-fried, e.g. fritters.

Falafels

dried chickpeas	150g
onion, chopped	1 large
cloves of garlic, chopped	2
parsley, roughly chopped	60ml
cumin seeds	5ml
coriander seeds	5ml
baking powder	2.5ml
vegetable oil	500ml for deep-frying
salt and pepper	to taste
pitta bread	
salad	
natural yoghurt	
Oil temperature	180°C
Cooking time	3 minutes
Serves	approx. 6

Preparation	4
Cooking skills	2
Finishing	3

1 Soak the chickpeas in a bowl of water overnight.
2 Put the chickpeas in a large pan and cover them with water. Make sure they are covered by 5cm of water.
3 Bring to the boil and boil for ten minutes. Then simmer for 60–90 minutes until soft.
4 Put the chickpeas in a food processor. Add the onion, garlic, parsley, cumin seeds, coriander seeds and baking powder. Process until a fine paste is formed.
5 Shape the paste into walnut-sized balls.
6 Deep-fry in batches.
7 Serve with pitta bread, yoghurt and salad.

Lyonnaise potatoes

potatoes	2kg
olive oil	20ml
onions, thinly sliced	4
garlic, chopped	2tbsp
butter	50g
salt	to taste
ground white pepper	to taste
fresh parsley, finely chopped	1 tbsp
Oven temperature	200°C
Cooking time	10 minutes
Serves	8

Preparation	2
Cooking skills	2
Finishing	2

Method

1. Peel potatoes and cut into ½-inch slices. Place in a pot and cover with water.
2. Bring to the boil. Allow to boil for 2 minutes, then drain and set aside.
3. Heat a large ovenproof frying pan over a medium heat. Pour in olive oil, then add onions.
4. Sauté until lightly caramelised, 8 to 10 minutes. Stir in garlic and sauté until onions are deep brown and garlic is soft.
5. Place pan back on stove over a low heat. Melt the butter and sauté the potatoes until they are cooked and have a good golden colour.
6. Add the onions for the last 5 minutes.
7. Bake in a preheated oven for 10 minutes.
8. Season with salt and pepper and sprinkle with chopped parsley just before serving.

Vegetable tempura

For the tempura batter

cornflour	100g
egg yolks	2
egg whites	2
ice cold water	60ml
seasoning	to taste
Serves	4

Method

1 Sift the cornflour and seasoning into a bowl and make a well.
2 Put the egg yolks and water into the well and mix gently to form a batter – do not beat.
3 Allow to stand for 15 minutes.
4 Whisk the egg whites until stiff and fold into the mixture.
5 Use immediately.

Vegetables for tempura

Vegetables suitable for tempura include broccoli florets, cauliflower florets, asparagus spears, strips of capsicum (peppers, red, green, yellow), french beans and mangetout.

The vegetables may be used raw, after washing and drying, or slightly blanched, but they need to retain their 'bite'.

1 Prepare the tempura batter to stage 3 and leave to rest.
2 Portion, wash and dry the vegetables to be used.
3 Heat the deep fat fryer oil to 170°C.
4 While the oil is heating, finish the batter.
5 Dip the vegetables into the batter and deep fry until light golden brown.
6 Drain and serve.

Grilling and griddling

Grilling and griddling are quick cooking processes. For more information see pages 124–125. Vegetables are usually brushed with butter or oil to aid the colouring process and to prevent the vegetable from drying out. Your skill and experience are required to identify when vegetables are cooked. Cooking times vary depending on the type and thickness of the vegetable. Suitable vegetables for grilling and griddling are:

Definition
Duchesse potatoes: mashed potato piped onto trays, and then grilled before service.

- mushrooms
- onions
- tomatoes
- aubergines
- capsicums
- asparagus
- pre-prepared potato dishes such as **duchesse potatoes**.

Baking and roasting

Both processes make vegetables and pulses easy to eat and digest and more appealing to the consumer. For more information see page 125. Some vegetables and pulses suitable for roasting and baking are:

- potatoes
- carrots
- lentils (when making a loaf or vegetarian dish).
- capsicums
- parsnips

Remember!
Overcooking vegetable or pulse dishes by grilling will make the food dry out.

Boulangère potatoes

potatoes (Marie Piper are best)	400g
onions, finely sliced	150g
vegetable or chicken stock	250ml
butter	50g
fresh parsley, chopped	2 tbsp
salt and ground pepper	to taste
Oven temperature	200°C
Cooking time	1 hour 30 minutes
Serves	4

Preparation	2
Cooking skills	1
Finishing	1

Method

1 Preheat an oven to 200°C.
2 Wash, peel and rewash the potatoes.
3 Cut the potatoes into 2cm thick slices. Save the best slices for finishing the top of the dish.
4 Lightly cook the onions without colour in a little butter.
5 Grease a deep ovenproof dish and arrange the potatoes and onions layer by layer. Season with salt and ground pepper between each tier of potatoes.
6 Neatly arrange the saved potato slices on the top.
7 Pour in the stock just covering the potatoes.
8 Add a few knobs of butter on the top of the potatoes.
9 Place in the oven for approximately 25–30 minutes until lightly browned.
10 Lower the heat to 170°C and press the potatoes down flat occasionally.
11 Continue to cook for approximately 1 hour until the liquid has almost been absorbed.
12 Brush with melted butter and serve with chopped parsley if desired.

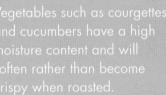

Did you know?
Vegetables such as courgettes and cucumbers have a high moisture content and will soften rather than become crispy when roasted.

Potatoes dauphinoise

mixture of milk and whipping cream	250ml
salt	¾ tsp
pepper	½ tsp
garlic, minced	1 clove
potatoes	1kg
gruyère cheese, grated	200g
Oven temperature	190°C
Cooking time	45 minutes
Serves	8

Preparation	3
Cooking skills	3
Finishing	2

Method

1. In a heavy saucepan, combine the milk and cream, salt, pepper and garlic.
2. Bring the liquid to the boil over a medium heat.
3. Immediately remove from the heat. Set aside and keep warm.
4. Peel the potatoes and then using a sharp knife or mandolin, cut into very thin slices.
5. Pour 75ml of the milk mixture into a greased 10-inch (25cm) dish. Layer with half of the potato slices, overlapping slightly. Repeat this layering.
6. Pour remaining milk mixture over the top of the potatoes.
7. Cover the potatoes with gruyère cheese.
8. Bake in the oven for about 20 minutes or until milk mixture starts to bubble up the sides. Using a spatula, press down the potatoes to submerge.
9. Bake for about 25 minutes longer or until potatoes are tender and the top is golden brown.
10. Let the dish stand for 15 minutes before serving.

Find out!
What country is the dish potatoes dauphinoise associated with?

Remember!
Always use a dry cloth when handling trays from the oven to reduce the risk of burning yourself.

Roast potatoes are a popular dish for Sunday roast lunch. To make roast potatoes, peeled potatoes are covered in oil and put into a hot oven. The oil fries the potatoes while in the oven, producing brown and crispy potatoes ready for the table.

Roast potatoes

potatoes	5kg
oil	75ml
salt	to taste
parsley	for garnish
Oven temperature	190–200°C
Cooking time	60–90 minutes
Serves	10–15

Preparation	2
Cooking skills	2
Finishing	2

Method

1 Pre-heat the oven.
2 Wash, peel and re-wash the potatoes.
3 Cut the potatoes into even sizes.
4 Fry and colour the potatoes in shallow hot oil.
5 Season the potatoes with salt. Place them on a tray and put them in an oven.
6 Baste the potatoes at regular intervals.
7 When they are soft inside and crisp on the outside, place them in a dish. Sprinkle them with parsley and serve.

Braising

A vegetable dish such as braised celery is started on the top of a stove. The vegetable can be fried to give colour (brown braising) or left as it is (white braising), before being added to a liquid, e.g. white stock or jus-lié (see Chapter 11). The ingredients are brought to the boil, covered with a lid and then placed in an oven.

Vegetables suitable for braising are:

- celery
- onions
- artichokes
- pulses, e.g. chickpeas
- stuffed cabbage
- leeks.

For more information see page 123.

Combination cooking

A cauliflower cheese gratin dish is a good example of combination cooking as it uses two methods of cooking. The cauliflower is boiled, then put in a dish and covered with cheese sauce. It is finished and coloured in the oven or under a grill. For more information see page 126.

Cauliflower cheese

cauliflower	1 whole
butter	25g
plain flour	25g
mustard powder	½ tsp
warm milk	300ml
cheddar cheese	150g
salt and pepper	to taste
Oven temperature	180–200°C
Cooking time	20–30 minutes
Serves	4–6 depending on size

Method

1. Cut the cauliflower into florets. Cook the cauliflower by boiling or steaming and place it in an ovenproof dish.
2. Melt the butter in a pan.
3. Add the mustard powder and flour.
4. Cook into a white roux.
5. Add the warm milk and make sure there are no lumps.
6. Add the grated cheese and stir until smooth. Season to taste.
7. Pour the sauce over the cauliflower and bake it in the oven until a good glaze appears.
8. Sprinkle with chopped parsley and serve.

Duchesse potatoes

potatoes	500g
butter	25g
egg	1
salt	pinch
Oven temperature	230°C
Cooking time	2-3 minutes
Serves	4

Preparation	2
Cooking skills	1
Finishing	2

Method

1 Wash, peel and rewash the potatoes.
2 Cut into even sized pieces.
3 Place into a suitable sized pot, cover with cold water, add a little salt, cover with a lid.
4 Bring to the boil and then simmer until cooked.
5 Drain off the water, cover and return to a low heat to dry out the potatoes.
6 Pass through a medium sieve into a clean stainless steel bowl.
7 Add the egg and stir in well with a wooden spoon.
8 Mix in butter and correct the seasoning.
9 Place the mixture into a piping bag with a large star nozzle and pipe out onto greased baking sheets into neat spirals about 2cm diameter and 5cm high.
10 Place into a hot oven at 230°C (Gas 8) for 2–3 minutes in order to firm the edges slightly.
11 Remove from the oven and brush with egg wash.
12 Brown under salamander or in a hot oven, and serve.

Marquise potatoes

Preparation 2
Cooking skills 2
Finishing 2

duchess potato mixture (see above)	400g
tomato concassee	100g
egg wash	to coat
parsley, chopped	garnish
Oven temperature	230°C
Cooking time	2-3 minutes
Serves	4 (two nests per person)

Method

1. Pipe the duchess mixture through a large star nozzle into the shape of round nests approximately 6cm in diameter and 2cm in height on to a lightly buttered baking sheet.
2. Put the nests into a hot oven for 2–3 minutes to slightly dry and harden the surfaces.
3. Remove from the oven, brush with egg wash and fill the centre of each nest with the tomato concassee.
4. Return to the oven to brown the potato to a golden colour and heat the tomato (approx 15–20 minutes).
5. Sprinkle with chopped parsley and serve.

See page 168 for tomato concassée.

Croquette potatoes

Preparation 2
Cooking skills 2
Finishing 2

duchess potato mixture (see above)	400g
flour	
egg wash	for coating
white breadcrumbs	
parsley sprigs	garnish
Serves	4 (three croquettes per person)

Method

1. Place the duchess mixture onto a floured board and roll into a cylinder 2cm wide.
2. Cut into equal sized pieces (approx 5cm) allowing 3 per portion.
3. Coat each piece completely in flour, then egg wash and finally breadcrumbs.
4. Reshape as necessary with a palette knife.
5. Place in frying basket and deep fry at 185°C until golden brown.
6. Drain well, garnish with a sprig of parsley and serve.

Meat and potato croquettes (Durham cutlets)

duchess potato mixture (see above)	100g
cooked minced beef (other cooked meats could be used instead)	200g
onion, chopped and sweated	50g
parsley, chopped	10g
egg yolk	1
seasoning	to taste
flour egg wash white breadcrumbs	} for coating
Serves	4 (one cutlet per person)

Method

1 Mix the potato mixture, cooked minced meat, chopped sweated onion, egg yolk and parsley together.
2 Season to taste and divide into four equal portions.
3 Shape into a suitable shape (round, oval or cutlet form).
4 Coat thoroughly with flour, egg and breadcrumb, and reshape as necessary.
5 Deep or shallow fry until heated through and golden brown (approximately 4–6 mins at 175–190°C).
6 Drain and serve.

Sauté potatoes

potatoes, boiled or steamed with their skins on, even sized	400g
oil	40g
seasoning	to taste
parsley, chopped	garnish
Serves	4

Preparation	1
Cooking skills	2
Finishing	1

Method

1 Peel the potatoes and cut into slices approximately 3mm thick.
2 Heat the fat in a heavy frying pan, add the potatoes and fry to a golden brown colour, tossing occasionally.
3 Drain off fat, lightly season and serve sprinkled with chopped parsley.

Variations: Sauté potatoes can have a range of ingredients added to make a variety of dishes (e.g. fried onions (Lyonnaise), artichokes (Mireille), garlic (provencal), rosemary (romarin) or mustard seeds (moutarde)).

Tomato concassé

tomatoes	
water, for boiling	
iced water, for cooling	

Preparation	1
Cooking skills	1
Finishing	1

Method

1 With a paring knife, score the tomatoes with an X at the opposite end to where the stem was once attached.
2 Immerse tomatoes in boiling water for 30 seconds or until they start to blister.
3 Plunge them into iced water immediately until cold.
4 Peel off the skin and cut in half crossways.
5 Hold the tomato halves cut side down and squeeze to rid them of their seeds and water.
6 Dice to the required size ready for further use.

Holding and serving

Holding vegetables and pulses at the right temperature is very important. The Food Safety Act 1990 states that hot food must be served and held at a temperature of at least 63°C. Cold salads must be served at or below 5°C. These temperatures make sure that potentially harmful bacteria will not multiply and harm the consumer.

If vegetables must be kept warm (e.g. if they are bulk cooked), they can be stored in a thermostatically controlled hot cupboard for no longer than 90 minutes. Ideally, however, food should be served freshly cooked so it is at the optimum temperature of 63°C and above. If the dish is covered in tin foil it will hold heat for a short period.

Test yourself!

1 What are the six traditional French cuts of vegetables?

2 What general quality points should you check for in vegetables and pulses? Write a description.

3 What particular quality points should you check for in the following vegetables and pulses?
  a Potatoes
  b Radish
  c Courgette
  d Mangetout
  e Dried pulses.

4 What should you do if you have any problems during the preparation of vegetables or pulses?

5 What are bulbs?

6 What are root vegetables? Write a description.

7 Which vitamins are water-soluble?

8 What should you do if you have any problems during the cooking of vegetables or pulses?

9 What is blanching?

10 What equipment do you need to blanch tomatoes?

11 At what temperature should vegetables be deep-fried?

12 Why must kidney beans be boiled rapidly for ten minutes before use?

7

Meat and offal

This chapter covers skills and knowledge in the following units:

- 7132 Unit 222 (2FP3) Prepare meat for basic dishes
- 7132 Unit 229 (2FC3) Cook and finish basic meat dishes
- 7132 Unit 225 (2FP6) Prepare offal for basic dishes
- 7132 Unit 232 (2FC6) Cook and finish basic offal dishes
- 7091 Unit 268 Preparation, cooking and finishing of meat dishes

Working through this chapter could also provide the opportunity to practise the following Functional Skills at Level 2:
Functional ICT Finding and selecting information – evaluate fitness for purpose

In this chapter you will:

Understand how and be able to prepare meat for basic dishes	7132 – 223.1,2	7091 – 268.1
Understand how and be able to cook basic meat dishes	7132 – 229.1,2	7091 – 268.2
Understand how and be able to finish basic meat dishes	7132 – 229.3,4	7091 – 268.3
Understand how and be able to prepare basic offal dishes	7132 – 225.1,2	
Understand how and be able to cook basic offal dishes	7132 – 232.1,2	
Understand how and be able to finish basic offal dishes	7132 – 232.3,4	

You will learn to cook basic meat and offal dishes, including:

- classic roast beef
- steak and kidney pudding
- liver and onions.

Types of meat

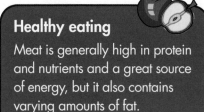

Figure 7.1 Domestically farmed animals

Meat is the flesh of domestic farmed animals. It is taken from the carcass in various cuts and joints. The following types of meat are relevant to your NVQ Level 2 award:

○ beef

○ veal

○ lamb and mutton

○ pork

○ ham

○ bacon.

Beef

Beef is a red meat from cattle. Cattle are usually slaughtered between the ages of 18 months and two years. Different breeds of cattle (Aberdeen Angus, Welsh Blacks, Hereford, Sussex and shorthorn) may be used and the quality of the beef can vary according to the age and type of cattle.

Once the animal is slaughtered, the carcass is hung for between 7 and 21 days. A carcass which has been hung for longer will produce a more tender meat as the natural enzymes within the carcass will start to break down the meat tissue. This hanging process is strictly controlled in both temperature and process and regular checks are carried out so there is no risk to consumers. The outcome is tender meat for cooking.

Figure 7.2 Aberdeen Angus cattle produce high-quality beef

Cuts and joints of beef

The quality of meat varies depending on which part of the **carcass** the meat is taken from. You must know where on an animal a cut of meat is from, as this will have a bearing on how the meat is cooked, as well as its preparation method.

After **slaughter** the head is removed and the carcass is split in half lengthways giving two sides. Figure 7.3 is of a side of beef, showing where the different cuts and joints are to be found.

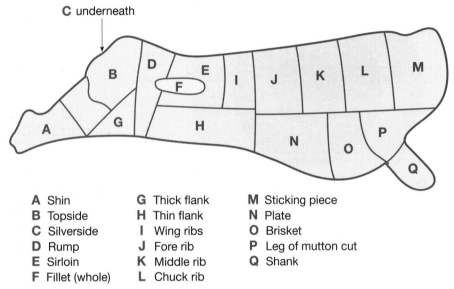

A Shin	**G** Thick flank	**M** Sticking piece
B Topside	**H** Thin flank	**N** Plate
C Silverside	**I** Wing ribs	**O** Brisket
D Rump	**J** Fore rib	**P** Leg of mutton cut
E Sirloin	**K** Middle rib	**Q** Shank
F Fillet (whole)	**L** Chuck rib	

Figure 7.3 The different cuts and joints that can be found on a side of beef

The table below gives more information on the cuts and joints from Figure 7.3 that you will use most often. It provides information on cooking methods and suitable portion sizes. Each cut or joint has a distinctive shape. Remember these shapes to help you recognise the different cuts.

Position	Name of cut/ joint	Appearance	Suggested cooking methods	Weight per portion
A	Shin		Boiling, stewing	180g
B	Topside		Roasting, braising, stewing	180–200g
C	Silverside		Roasting, braising, stewing, boiling	180–200g

Healthy eating

Lean cuts of beef (less than 5 to 9 per cent fat), are almost as healthy as a chicken breast. In some cuts such as fillet, beef has only 1g more saturated fat than a skinless chicken breast.

Healthy eating

Beef is extremely high in nutrients, especially vitamins B12 and B6, riboflavin and iron.

D	Rump	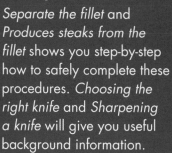	Roasting, braising, grilling, frying	180–360g
E	Sirloin		Roasting, grilling, frying	180–300g
F	Whole fillet, chateaubriand, tournedos, filet mignon		Roasting, grilling, frying	120–360g
G	Thick flank		Braising, stewing	180g
H	Thin flank		Boiling, stewing	180g
J	Fore rib from which rib-eye steak can be cut		Roasting (whole fore rib), grilling, shallow frying (rib-eye steak)	120–210g
O	Brisket		Braising, boiling, stewing	120–210g
Q	Shank		Stewing	120–160g

Figure 7.4 Identifying and preparing the different cuts and joints of beef

Checking beef quality

When checking beef before preparation you must make sure it is of the right quality. A poor-quality piece of meat will inevitably end up as a poor-quality dish. If you are unsure about the quality, always check with your supervisor.

The following points should be considered when checking the quality of beef:

○ It should have a fresh aroma and not smell stale or unpleasant.
○ There should be a sufficient amount of fat in proportion to the meat present.

Did you know?

If stored correctly, a well-aged sirloin steak (7–21 days) will be brown rather than the normal red colour, but it will be perfectly safe and extremely tender.

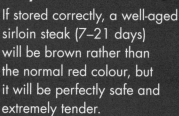

Video presentation

Separate the fillet and *Produces steaks from the fillet* shows you step-by-step how to safely complete these procedures. *Choosing the right knife* and *Sharpening a knife* will give you useful background information.

○ The fat should be smooth and creamy in colour.

○ The meat should be clean and bright in appearance. It should not look slimy.

○ Flecks of fat run through some cuts of meat, this is called 'marbling'.

○ It should be an appropriate temperature (1 to 5°C if fresh and −18 to −25°C if frozen) and stored correctly.

○ It should be firm and a deep red colour with a sheen.

○ It should be the correct cut or joint for the dish you are preparing.

Problems with beef are usually associated with the condition and quality of the meat. Cattle are now subject to rigorous checks by vets prior to slaughter.

Remember!
Meat may well have a lot of fat or glands on it as well as bones still within the cut or joint, and as the chef you will need to know how to prepare it. Some cuts of meat are expensive, so mistakes can be costly.

Definition
Cull: to kill an animal.

Veal

Veal is the flesh of a calf (usually **culled** at three months of age). The meat is classed as white meat and is usually pale pink as the calf's diet is cow's milk. The texture of the meat is fine and lean because of the age of the animal.

Cuts and joints of veal

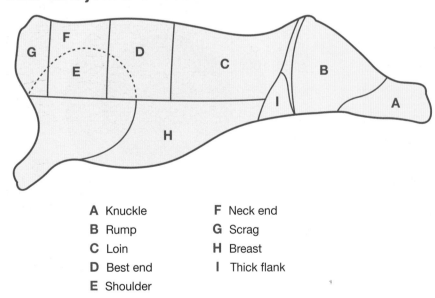

A Knuckle	**F** Neck end
B Rump	**G** Scrag
C Loin	**H** Breast
D Best end	**I** Thick flank
E Shoulder	

Figure 7.5 The different cuts and joints on a side of veal

The table on page 175 lists the cuts and joints from Figure 7.5 that you will use most often. It provides information on cooking methods and average weights of each cut.

Position	Name of cut/joint	Suggested cooking methods	Average weight
A	Knuckle	Boiling, stewing	1–2kg
B	Rump from which escalopes can be cut	Roasting, frying, braising	4–6kg
C	Loin	Roasting, frying, braising, grilling, griddling	4–6kg
D	Best end	Roasting, frying, braising, grilling, griddling	5–7kg
E	Shoulder	Roasting, braising, stewing	3–5kg
F	Neck end	Boiling, stewing	3–4kg
H	Breast	Stewing	2–3kg
I	Thick flank	Roasting, frying, braising	6–8kg

Figure 7.6 Preparing the different cuts and joints of veal

Checking veal quality

Issues regarding selection, quality and potential problems concerning the use of veal are similar to those of beef as the origins are the same (see pages 173–174).

Lamb and mutton

Lamb is meat from domestically farmed sheep which are less than 12 months old. Meat from sheep over the age of 12 months is classed as mutton.

The breed of sheep used for lamb and mutton is varied and can depend on the region. The meat from sheep usually has a delicate, sweet flavour and the flesh can vary in colour from pink to a deep red. The fat is usually quite hard and white in colour.

Lamb can be slaughtered at three different ages. This will have a bearing on the colour and flavour of the meat. The ages are:
o 30–40 days, weighing 8–10kg
o 70–150 days, weighing 20–25kg
o 180–270 days, weighing 30–40 kg.

Mutton can be from rams (male sheep) or ewes (female sheep). Rams produce better quality mutton than the ewes, whose meat is of an inferior, fattier quality. The best quality mutton is taken from a **castrated** ram over 12 months old.

Did you know?
The loin and best end of veal are joints, which are used in the same manner as lamb (see page 174).

Did you know?
Lamb or mutton generally has a higher fat content than beef. Its calorific value can be as much as 250 calories per 100g of meat.

Healthy eating
Lamb and mutton are a rich source of protein and vitamin B12.

Definition
Castrated: testes removed before sexual maturity.

175

Cuts and joints of lamb

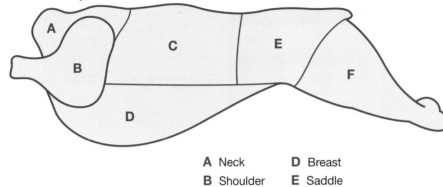

A Neck	**D** Breast
B Shoulder	**E** Saddle
C Best end	**F** Leg

Figure 7.7 The different cuts and joints on a side of lamb

The table below identifies the cuts and joints from Figure 7.7. It provides information on cooking methods (which are explained later) and average weights of each cut.

Position	Name of cut/joint	Appearance	Suggested cooking methods	Average weight
A	Neck		Boiling, stewing	0.5–1kg
B	Shoulder		Roasting, braising, stewing	3–5kg
C	Best end		Roasting, braising, stewing	2–3kg
D	Breast		Roasting, stewing	1–2kg
E	Saddle		Roasting, grilling, frying	3–5kg
F	Leg		Roasting, grilling, frying	3–5kg

Figure 7.8 Identifying and preparing the different cuts and joints of lamb

Did you know?

Vitamins B and C are water-soluble, so cooking lamb in a wet dish such as a navarin (lamb-based stew) will reduce the vitamin B and C content.

Chef's tip

Rosemary is a good ingredient to add flavour and to garnish lamb dishes. It is also used with game and for sweet dishes such as poached pears.

Checking lamb quality

Prior to preparing lamb, its suitability and quality should be checked. Consider the following:

○ It should have a fresh aroma and not smell stale or unpleasant.

○ There should be a sufficient amount of fat evenly spread in proportion to the meat present.

○ The fat should be smooth, creamy in colour and brittle (flaky).

○ The meat should be a dull red colour, with a clean appearance and no slimy exterior.

○ It should be at an appropriate temperature (1 to 5°C if fresh and −18 to −25°C if frozen) and stored correctly.

○ It should be the correct cut or joint for the dish you are preparing.

> **Chef's tip**
>
> Lamb and mutton do have a high fat content and consequently you may need to regularly skim the fat from the top of a dish such as an Irish stew.

Pork

Pork is a very popular meat taken from pigs. It is consumed in vast quantities throughout Europe. Other products such as ham and bacon are also produced from pork meat.

Male pigs are known as boars, females as sows and piglets as suckling pigs. A pig is usually slaughtered at the age of 10–12 months. Pigs are usually intensively fattened. The yield of meat from the carcass is generally quite high. Domesticated pigs for farming have shorter legs and a stockier appearance than wild pigs. There are many different breeds of pig farmed for their meat. The most common are the white Yorkshire, western white, Danish Landrace and Belgian Pietrain.

> **Healthy eating**
>
> Pork is high in protein. Nutrients such as the B vitamins and other minerals such as zinc are evident in pork.

Cuts and joints of pork

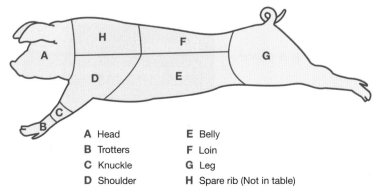

A Head	**E** Belly
B Trotters	**F** Loin
C Knuckle	**G** Leg
D Shoulder	**H** Spare rib (Not in table)

Figure 7.9 The different cuts and joints on a side of pork

The table below identifies the cuts and joints from Figure 7.9 that you will use most often. It provides information on cooking methods and weights of cuts and joints.

Position	Name of cut/joint	Appearance	Suggested cooking methods	Average weight
A	Head		Boiling	2–3kg
B	Trotters		Boiling	0.5kg
C	Knuckle		Boiling	1–2kg
D	Shoulder		Roasting, boiling	7–9kg
E	Belly		Roasting, boiling	2–3kg
F	Loin		Roasting, grilling, frying	4–6kg
G	Leg		Roasting, boiling	6–8kg

Figure 7.10 Identifying and preparing the different cuts and joints of pork

Checking pork quality

The following quality points should be checked before using a piece of pork:

o It should be lean and pale pink.
o There should not be any slimy residue on the exterior of the meat.
o The smell should be pleasant and not overpowering.
o The fat should be evenly spread over the meat joints, but not in excess.
o The skin is very tough and this should be smooth and free from coarse hairs.

Remember!
Care must be taken when handling pork as it may contain harmful parasitic worms, and other harmful bacteria. The threat of **cross-contamination** is ever present if you do not use the correct skills when preparing and cooking pork. Washing your hands is essential after handling pork as the bacteria can infect any cuts or abrasions you may have on your hands.

Definition
Cross-contamination: the transfer of harmful bacteria from one food source to another by the food handler using the same equipment for different tasks, not cleaning their tools properly or not washing their hands before handling another food type.

- It must have been stored correctly prior to use, either in a fridge (at the bottom to prevent any blood dripping onto other food) or in a freezer.
- It should be at an appropriate temperature (1 to 5°C if fresh and −18 to −25°C if frozen) and stored correctly.
- It should be the correct cut or joint for the dish you are preparing.

Ham

Ham is usually a cured and cooked prime leg of pork (e.g. York ham). Some hams can be eaten raw after they have been cured, e.g. Parma and Serrano ham. A curing or preserving process is applied to ham before cooking.

Gammon is a type of ham, but here the leg is not removed from the carcass until brining cures the carcass.

These are the different curing or preserving processes:
- Brining: injecting a salty liquid solution into the joint.
- Dry cure: rubbing a dry salt mixture onto the joint.
- Smoking: hanging in a room over a slow-burning regulated wood fire.

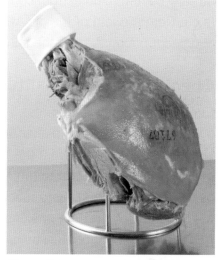

Figure 7.11 A York ham on a ham stand

Figure 7.12 What sort of curing process is being used here?

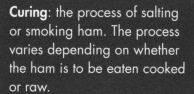

Definition

Curing: the process of salting or smoking ham. The process varies depending on whether the ham is to be eaten cooked or raw.

The time taken to cure the meat is usually three days, but this can vary depending on the type of ham required and whether the ham is to be eaten raw.

Checking ham quality

The quality points to be considered for ham are the same as for pork (see page 178) except that ham is ready to eat.

Chef's tip

Make sure you soak ham in water to extract the excess salt from the meat before cooking.

Bacon

Bacon usually comes from a large pig bred specially to produce bacon called a 'baconer'. The meat is cured (salted in brine) or smoked. There are two types of bacon: green, which is usually unsmoked bacon, and smoked. Bacon is usually cooked by frying and grilling but if kept in larger joints, as opposed to rashers, it can be boiled.

Cuts of bacon

There are usually four cuts from a baconer pig: back bacon, streaky bacon, middlecut bacon and gammon steaks. Back bacon is cut from the loin of the pig, while streaky is cut from the belly. Middlecut bacon is from the loin and the belly.

Checking bacon quality

Consider the following points:

○ Streaky bacon has a higher fat content than back bacon because it is taken from the belly.
○ Bacon should be firm to touch and dark pink.
○ It should not be slimy to touch.
○ It should not have an unpleasant smell.
○ The fat should normally be creamy, but smoking can give the fat a brown tint.

Chef's tip

Pineapple rings are often served with gammon steaks. The sweetness of the fruit counteracts the saltiness of the meat.

Types of offal

Offal is the edible organs and parts taken from domestic farm animal carcasses. It is usually cooked in the same way as meat. The following types of offal are relevant to your NVQ:

○ oxtail
○ kidney
○ heart
○ tongue
○ liver
○ sweetbread.

You will need to know what parts of the animal offal comes from, as this will have a bearing on how the offal is prepared and cooked.

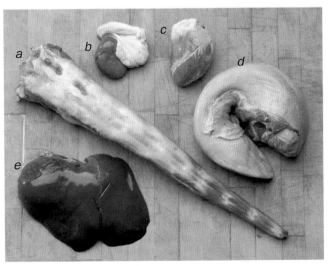

Figure 7.13 a oxtail, b kidney, c heart, d tongue, e liver

Find out! 　　　　　　　　　**Worksheet 20**

Find out about other types of offal, e.g. ox tongue and lamb hearts. How big are they? How much do they weigh? How are they cooked? Find a recipe for each type.

Liver

Liver is taken from many different types of animal and can be cooked in a variety of ways, but it is usually fried, grilled or braised. The size of the liver varies depending on the size of the animal which it comes from. Calf's liver is the most popular type, followed by lamb's liver. Ox liver is also used, but it is lower in quality and has a much stronger flavour. Pig's liver is also used, but generally in braised dishes and pâtés.

Checking liver quality

The following quality points should be checked before using a piece of liver:

○ It can deteriorate quite quickly if not stored correctly, so it is important that it is stored at the correct temperature (see Pork quality on page 178 for temperatures).

○ It should be deep red, have a clean appearance and smell pleasant.

○ Signs of discoloration, bad smells and a slimy appearance are indicators of poor quality.

Kidney

Kidneys are organs which vary in size depending on the animal from which they are taken. Calf's kidneys are the best quality. Lamb and pig kidneys are also good. Ox kidneys are used, but these take longer to cook and need to be blanched before cooking. See page 122. The usual cooking methods for kidneys are frying, grilling and braising.

Checking kidney quality

Consider the following points when selecting a kidney:

○ It should be clean, reddish brown and have a pleasant aroma.

○ The kidney should not feel slimy.

○ The kidney should be below 5°C prior to preparation.

○ If encased in fat the fat should be a creamy colour.

Remember!
Offal may have a lot of fat or glands on it as well as bones left inside it, and as the chef you will need to know how to prepare it.

Healthy eating
Liver has a high level of vitamins and minerals especially vitamins A, B and C, and iron.

Did you know?
Liver is at its best if cooked and served pink.

Healthy eating
Kidney is high in vitamins A and K and has a strong flavour.

Sweetbreads

Sweetbreads are the throat and pancreas glands of calves and lambs. Lamb sweetbreads are usually an average weight of 100g. Calf sweetbreads can weigh as much as 500g.

Checking quality of sweetbreads

These are the points to consider when checking the quality of sweetbreads:

o They are usually creamy white.
o They should be soft to touch, dry and clean.
o A good aroma is a sign of quality.

> ### Find out!
> **Worksheet 21**
>
> Find out and record why vitamins B6, B12, C and the minerals iron, riboflavin, zinc and protein are important for health and which types of meat and offal contain them.

Preparing meat and offal dishes

Preparation methods

The table below lists the most popular cuts for each type of meat or offal.

Meat or offal	Cut or joint
Beef	Dice, steaks, strips
Veal	**Escalopes**, cutlets
Lamb	Leg, cutlets, chump chops, shoulder
Mutton	Dice
Pork	Chops, cutlets, dice, leg, loin
Bacon	Rashers, gammon
Ham	Slices
Kidney	Sliced, diced
Liver	Sliced
Sweetbreads	Sliced, pressed

Figure 7.14 Popular cuts of meat and offal

> ### Healthy eating
> Sweetbreads are a very good source of protein.

> ### Remember!
> If you have a piece of offal which you think may be of poor quality, you should inform your supervisor.

> ### Marcus says
> Freshness is vital for offal, although some cuts of meat can be aged.

> ### Definition
> **Escalopes:** large thin slices of meat cut from the leg of pork or veal, or the breast of poultry such as turkey. An escalope is batted to flatten it before cooking. Because they are very thin, escalopes cook quickly.

Cutting

It is essential that the correct knife and equipment is used and that you observe safe working procedures.

Ask yourself:

○ Have I been trained to cut this food item?
○ Do I know what to do next? (If not, ask!)
○ Have I got the right knife?
○ Is my knife sharp enough?
○ Am I using the correct board?
○ Am I dressed correctly?
○ Have I selected the right equipment?
○ Is my workstation tidy and suitable to prepare the food?

If your answer is 'Yes' to all of the above questions, it is safe to proceed.

In most cases a red chopping board is used for raw meat and the knife could be a red 7-inch boning knife, 10-inch chef's knife or 12-inch steak knife. Generally, you will need a knife with a sturdy blade so that it does not move when you are cutting the meat, as this could cause an accident. For slicing and dicing you will need a knife with a large heel.

Boning

Boning enables meat to be presented better and carved more easily. It creates a cavity which can be stuffed to add flavour. There are two types of boning: **external boning** and **tunnel boning**. Following external boning, the cavity is filled and the joint tied to form a good shape. Tunnel boning is a more delicate and complex method.

How to tunnel bone the thigh bone from a leg of lamb

1 Find the H bone. This is part of the pelvic bone at the top of the leg of lamb.
2 Cut around the H joint at the top of the leg.
3 Separate the H joint from the ball joint and remove it.
4 Cut around the exposed ball joint.
5 Holding the knife almost flat against the bone, scrape and cut to ease the flesh away from the bone. As you do this, turn the leg inside out to make it easier.
6 Turn the meat back on itself so the skin is facing outwards again. There should not be any damage to the exterior of the joint as this will spoil the appearance.

Remember!
Make sure you use the correct knife and chopping board for the procedure, that your work space is clean and tidy and your hands are washed prior to cooking.

Remember!
Always cut away from yourself for safety reasons.

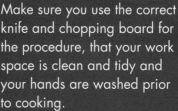

Definition
Boning: to remove the bones from a joint of meat.
External boning: to remove bones by cutting through the skin to expose the flesh and bone and then to cut away the bone from the meat.
Tunnel boning: to remove the bones from a bird or joint by cutting the flesh away from the bone without cutting through the skin.

7 Stuff and tie the joint. See pages 190 and 192.

Dicing

Meat which is off the bone can be diced. The meat or offal is cut into square cubes or evenly sized pieces to allow it to cook evenly.

How to dice beef

  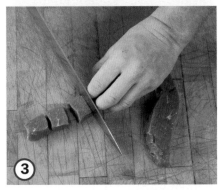

① Use a 10-inch chef's knife. Cut across the beef (here a thick flank) to leave thick slices. You can trim off the end of each slice to neaten it.

② Cut each slice into strips. Trim the end of each strip to make a neat square end.

③ Cut each strip into dice. Ensure they are evenly sized. Store on a tray and refrigerate until required.

Dicing is appropriate for dishes such as beef casseroles, navarins and blanquettes, where the meat is usually of a poorer quality and therefore requires longer cooking, e.g. braising, stewing and boiling.

Offal does not often need to be diced, but if it does, the process is the same.

Video presentation
Slice and dice chuck steak shows this being done.

Slicing

Slicing means to cut across a piece of meat or offal. Carving is a method of slicing cooked meat for presentation. If you cannot slice the meat correctly, then your final dish will not have the best presentation possible. Slicing is usually carried out by hand, but an electric slicer can be used for cooked, slightly frozen or raw meats.

Slicing meat requires patience and skill. The meat or offal may be raw or cooked. In either case you must hold your knife and the food firmly. You must use the correct knife and it must be sharp.

The carving knife should not be serrated as that could tear the meat. You should carve away from yourself for safety. Holding the

Figure 7.15 Sliced kidney and sliced liver

joint firmly on a secure carving board will aid you when serving the customer and helps in maintaining a professional image.

How to slice ham off the bone

1 Cut straight across the neck of the joint near the bone.

2 Slice off the outer skin and excess fat.

3 Turn the board 180°. Cut the meat across the joint towards the bone.

4 Arrange the slices on a plate as you cut them.

5 Continue slicing until you reach the bone.

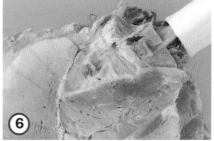

6 When you reach the bone turn the ham over and slice the other side.

Portioning

Portioning means cutting meat into the correct size, weight or shape during preparation or for it to be served. The correct size and amount depends on the dish. Slicing up a sirloin into individual steaks is portioning the meat.

The term is also used if carving cooked roasted meat, pies and other meat dishes before service. By cutting the cooked dish into servings (portions) a guaranteed **yield** of that dish is achieved. Portion sizes depend on the commodity. For example:

- A portion of carved roast lamb leg should weigh approximately 120–150g.
- A grilled rump steak would be one per portion as the steaks were pre-cut.
- Sliced liver fried with bacon and onions may be portioned so that each customer has three slices per portion.

Chef's tip

The advantage of portioning your meat or offal before cooking is that you have a guaranteed number of servings for cooking and have enough food to feed everyone.

Definition

Yield: to produce a certain number of portions.

Trimming

Trimming means cutting away bone, excess fat, sinew or glands. Trimming improves the presentation of the meat or offal.

Beef has the skin removed, but sometimes there is a lot of fat lying around or in the meat which needs to be removed. Sirloin has a large area of sinew under the fat layer and above the meat layer. This fat and sinew must be removed. This process can be a little time-consuming as it is important to complete this task correctly, safely and without losing excess amounts of quality meat.

Healthy eating

If fat is trimmed from meat it can make it a healthier option.

Video presentation

Trim a best end of lamb shows shows you more skills.

How to remove the fat and sinew from a sirloin

① This is the underside of the sirloin. The thick outer layer of fat is removed from the sirloin to reveal the sinew tight to the flesh.

② Using the point of a boning knife, lift and cut away the sinew. With the blade pointing upwards at a 45° angle, you will ensure only the sinew is removed. Push away the chain from the meat using your thumb. Cut the chain off.

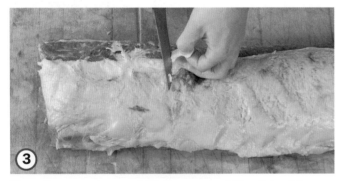

③ Turn the meat over. Lift the end of the fat with your fingers. Slice the fat away with a sawing motion.

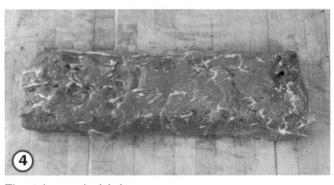

④ The trimmed sirloin.

You must observe the following safe working procedures:

○ Ensure your workplace is clean and tidy.

○ Use a red chopping board for raw meat.

○ Use a 10-inch chef's knife.

○ Always cut away from yourself to avoid accidents if the knife slips.

○ Have a container ready to put the trimmings into and a dish to put the finished product into.

How to trim liver

Liver varies in size. It is surrounded by a fine, transparent membrane which should be removed, because if it is left on during the cooking process it will shrink. The liver may also have some small glands (green or brown jelly-like spheres) and tubes or gristle. These should also be removed before cooking. After trimming, liver should be cut into even thin slices – cut at a slant or angle. This is to ensure consistent cooking.

> **Remember!**
>
> Some trimmings may be suitable for stock, so do not just throw your trimmings in the bin.

> **Video presentation**
>
> *Prepare a whole lamb's liver* shows you how to trim and slice a liver. Also watch *Prepare a chicken liver.*

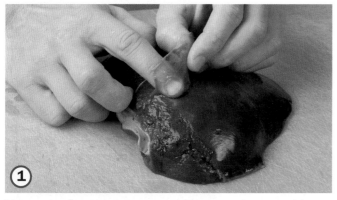

① Use your fingers to remove the membrane without damaging the liver.

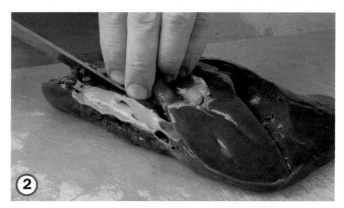

② Remove excess fat, glands or valves. You will be left with a deep red liver with a soft gelatinous texture.

How to trim kidneys

Kidneys are usually cut through the centre to expose the white core, which must be removed. If large enough, they can be sliced thinly before cooking. Like liver, kidneys are surrounded by a membrane, which if left on during the cooking process will shrink, so this should be removed. They may also have some small glands (green or brown jelly-like spheres) and tubes or gristle, all of which should also be removed before cooking.

Pressing

Sweetbreads are usually blanched before cooking by bringing them to the boil. They are then washed, dried and pressed before being cooked. Calves' sweetbreads are sometimes passed through flour, egg and breadcrumbs then shallow-fried.

Mincing

Mincing means passing meat or other ingredients through a piece of equipment which cuts and grinds the product into a fine texture. Mincing meat enables cheaper cuts of meat to be used and cooked using quick cookery methods, such as grilling or frying.

Minced meat can vary in quality depending on fat content of the meat and the cut of meat minced. Cheaper cuts of minced beef are mixed with onions and seasoning to make burgers. Minced fillet steak is high-quality and low in fat compared to other cuts. It is used to make steak tartare, which is eaten raw.

Mincing or grinding is used to make sausages. The meat is finely minced and then blended with other ingredients to make sausagemeat. Sausage skins are then filled with sausagemeat.

Another word for minced meat is forcemeat, as the meat is forced through a mincing machine, changing its appearance and texture.

Skinning

Pork and bacon have a very tough skin, which is usually scored (for crackling) or removed or to expose the fat layer beneath, which is in turn removed to an acceptable level. To remove the skin from a pork loin you need a sturdy firm-bladed knife. The process is the same as removing the fat from a sirloin of beef, but the pork fat is tougher.

Video presentation
Watch *Prepare kidneys* to see the skills you need.

Video presentation
Watch *Prepare sweetbreads* to find out more.

Figure 7.16 Minced beef

Video presentation
Now watch *Prepare pâté from minced liver.*

Try this!
Rather than throwing away the skin from the pork loin, replace it over the skinned loin when roasting as it keeps the pork moist and the skin crisps into a tasty accompaniment.

How to remove the skin from a pork loin

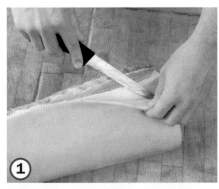

① Keep the knife blade away from you and make a cut to separate the skin from the fat.

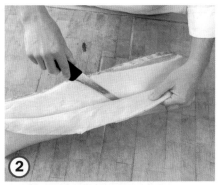

② Remove the skin by cutting across the horizontal loin. Use gentle sweeping motions.

③ At the edge make sure you cut away only skin and not meat. The bone edges give you a clear cutting guide. Do not remove too much fat as this aids the cooking process and keeps the meat moist.

Coating

Coating can be as simple as covering a piece of liver in seasoned flour during preparation. It can also refer to covering meat e.g. a veal escalope in flour, egg and breadcrumbs to meet the requirements of a dish.

Coating with seasoned flour

This is commonly done when preparing pieces of offal for cooking, e.g. liver and kidneys. Each piece of meat or offal is dipped in a dish of seasoned flour, then the excess is shaken off. The flour helps to give colour to the meat or offal when it is fried.

Coating with flour, egg and breadcrumbs

Nearly all types of meat and offal can be coated in flour or breadcrumbs. The dish requirements will dictate whether or not this is necessary. Before you begin have ready three separate bowls: one bowl of well-seasoned flour, one bowl of beaten egg and one bowl of fine breadcrumbs. You should always follow the process below to make sure that the meat or offal is evenly coated.

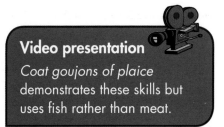

Video presentation
Coat goujons of plaice demonstrates these skills but uses fish rather than meat.

189

How to coat a pork escalope with seasoned flour, beaten egg and breadcrumbs

1 Coat the pork with seasoned flour.

2 Gently pat the pork to remove the excess.

3 Put the pork in the beaten egg. Make sure it is completely covered.

4 Allow the excess to run off. Clean your hands.

5 Put the pork in the breadcrumbs. Ensure it is well coated. Gently pat off the excess.

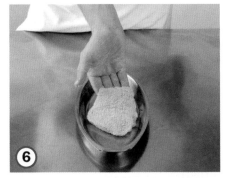

6 Put the breadcrumbed portion on a suitable tray until it is required for cooking.

Once the meat or offal has been coated, it must be cooked fairly soon or the coating will become soggy. Do not stack portions of breadcrumbed products on top of each other as they may stick together and affect the appearance of the coating. Use greaseproof paper to layer many portions of coated meat or offal.

Coating meat in flour, egg and breadcrumbs helps it to remain moist during cooking, as it is sealed within a crispy coating, e.g. pork schnitzels.

Stuffing

Stuffing meat adds to its flavour, appearance and texture. Stuffing is added to the meat during the preparation stage. Ingredients such as meat, vegetables, rice and even fruit can be used for stuffing.

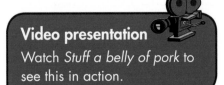

Video presentation
Watch *Stuff a belly of pork* to see this in action.

How to stuff a pork belly draft

Before you begin, make light cuts in two-thirds of the skin to improve the flavour of the finished product. Trim the belly to form a square.

① Trim to remove any excess fat.

② Make the stuffing into a sausage shape. Put it in along the centre of the meat and spread it out.

③ Start to roll the meat around the stuffing.

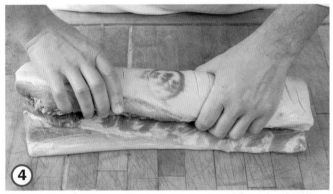

④ Continue to roll. The skin with the light cuts in it should be uppermost. Tuck the uncut skin inside the cut skin.

The equipment and tools used to stuff meat are:

o Boning knife

o Chopping board

o Piping bag to fill cavities in the meat (optional)

o Spoons to prevent unnecessary handling of stuffing

o String to tie the joint

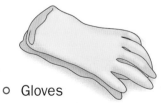

o Gloves

Before stuffing meat, it is important to check the quality of the product. If necessary, wash and dry the meat before stuffing. The stuffing or filling should always be at the correct temperature, which is 1–5°C. The meat should also be at this temperature. If possible, do not handle the filling – use a piping bag or spoon.

Tying

Tying holds meat joints together before cooking, e.g. roast topside of beef, boned leg of lamb or stuffed pork loin. Tying the meat joint with butcher's string means it retains its shape during cooking, especially if the meat joint is stuffed. Untied, the stuffed joint would fall apart and the quality of the dish would be affected. Strands should be tied about a thumb's width apart. Tying a joint also provides you with a guide to portion sizes and portions will not fall apart. Do not tie the meat too tight. If you do, the juices from the meat will be forced out during cooking and leave the meat dry.

> **Remember!**
> Temperature is important when preparing meat or offal. The meat may contain harmful bacteria, which multiply rapidly at room temperature. Adding hot filling to a cool pork loin could lead to food poisoning.

How to tie a stuffed pork belly draft

① Pass butcher's string under the meat in the middle and tie a simple slip knot. The string should be quite loose. Cut the string.

② Tie a string at each end. These should be a little tighter.

③ Fill in with more strings approximately a thumb's width apart. Keep the knots aligned as it is easier to remove the string afterwards.

Seasoning and marinating

Seasoning

Seasoning is the addition of ingredients such as salt, pepper and spices that help to bring out the flavour. Adjusting the quantities of seasoning will affect the flavour but you must be careful; too much of some seasonings, like salt, can make the dish or ingredients inedible.

If the meat you are preparing is for a wet cooking method, e.g. a casserole, navarin (a rich slow-cooked lamb or mutton stew) or blanquette (a French stew made from white meat, e.g. veal, lamb or poultry), the meat should be seasoned before cooking but the overall seasoning of the dish should be adjusted after cooking when all the flavours have combined.

Marinating

Marinating is a method used to preserve or flavour foods. It involves combining a cooked or uncooked liquid with the meat. The liquid is called a marinade. It contains ingredients which change and improve the flavour of the meat. The meat can be left in the marinade for 30 minutes to 48 hours. The meat should be covered completely by the marinade.

Some marinades are cooked and then cooled before being combined with the meat. Most marinades are cold and can be created very quickly to flavour meat or offal.

Did you know?

The term **marinade** comes from the Latin word *marinus*, which means marine (sea) and refers to the salt water used to preserve food for Roman sailors.

Storage

Meat and offal, especially pork, can contain harmful bacteria and parasitic worms. This means that prepared meat or offal must be stored correctly before, during and after preparation:

○ Ensure that raw meat or offal is covered and stored at the bottom of a refrigerator. This will prevent any blood or liquid dripping onto other food.

○ Clearly label the meat which has been prepared. The label should include the date so that it is possible to determine its shelf life.

○ Store prepared meat and offal at 1 to 5°C.

○ Do not stack prepared pieces of meat on top of each other as it can affect the appearance and quality of the end product. Food poisoning by cross-contamination can be caused if one meat is mixed with another type.

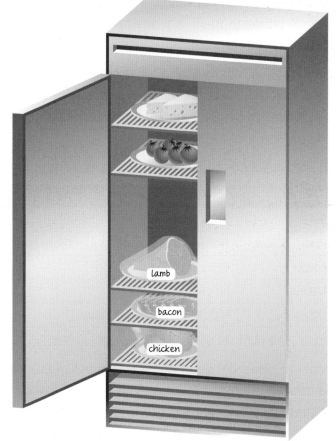

Figure 7.17 Always store your meat safely at the bottom of the fridge to avoid contaminating other food

193

Cooking and finishing meat and offal

Cooking methods

After meat or offal has been prepared it is important that the correct cooking method is used to ensure a quality dish. The cooking method chosen will depend on the dish required. A chef must work in a safe manner and use the correct tools, techniques and methods. The temperature of cooked meat and offal is also very important, as it will have a bearing on the quality of the served dish. Food safety may be at risk if meat or offal are not cooked to the correct temperature.

Boiling

Tougher cuts of meat are normally boiled or cooked by other wet methods. Boiling is a simple process and does not require a lot of skill, although there is a need to **skim** the liquid to remove impurities and fat.

Boiling foods means that a lot of nutrients will be lost as they are water soluble. However, as the liquid may be used or consumed with the meat not all these nutrients will be wasted. For more information see page 120.

The table lists cuts of meat and offal that are most often boiled.

Meat or offal	Cut or joint
Beef	Shin, thin flank
Pork	Trotters, cheeks, belly, gammon, ham
Lamb	Shin, shanks
Mutton	All cuts
Offal	Kidneys and sweetbreads

Figure 7.19 Cuts of meat and offal suitable for boiling

Cooking times are determined by the cut of meat and the dish to be cooked. Always refer closely to the menu or recipe; if you are unsure ask your line manager, head chef or supervisor.

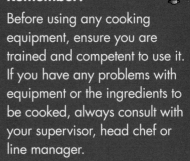

Remember!

Wet cooking methods are used for tough fibrous meats or offal.
Dry cooking methods are used for tender cuts of meat and offal.

Remember!

Before using any cooking equipment, ensure you are trained and competent to use it. If you have any problems with equipment or the ingredients to be cooked, always consult with your supervisor, head chef or line manager.

Figure 7.18 Boiling is a wet method of cooking meat using liquids like water or stock

Definition

Skim: to remove any surface impurities from a liquid using a spoon or similar equipment.

Video presentation

To see how to skim watch *Prepare fish stock (2) boil, skim, simmer and strain.*

Creamed sweetbreads

sweetbreads	450g
onion	1 small
carrot	1 medium
parsley stalks	bunch
bay leaf	1
salt and pepper	to taste
butter or margarine	40g
flour	60ml
milk	300ml
lemon juice	squeeze
chopped fresh parsley	to garnish
Cooking time	45 minutes
Serves	4

Preparation	2
Cooking skills	3
Finishing	2

Method

1 Put the sweetbreads, onion, carrot, parsley stalks, bay leaf and seasoning in a saucepan with water to cover and simmer gently for 15 minutes until tender.
2 Drain the sweetbreads, keeping 300ml of the liquid for later use.
3 Melt the butter in a saucepan, stir in the flour and cook gently for a minute. Remove from the heat and gradually add the milk and cooking liquid.
4 Bring to the boil, stirring until thickened and add lemon juice.
5 Add sweetbreads to the sauce and simmer gently for five to ten minutes.
6 Garnish with parsley.

Boiled gammon

piece of gammon or collar	
carrots	2 medium
onions	2 medium
bay leaf	1
black peppercorns	4
parsley or onion sauce to garnish	
Cooking time	depends on size; 2kg would take 60–80 minutes
Serves	12–14

Preparation	1
Cooking skills	1
Finishing	1

Method

1 Weigh the joint to calculate cooking time. Put in a pan of water and bring to boil. Drain off the liquid (this removes excess salt).
2 Place the joint in a large saucepan with the other ingredients, cover with cold water and bring to the boil. Keep removing any scum that forms at the surface of the liquid.
3 When cooked, cool slightly before removing the rind.
4 Serve hot and sliced with parsley or with onion sauce as an accompaniment.

Honey roast ham (after boiling)

Preparation	1
Cooking skills	1
Finishing	2

boiled gammon (see above)

honey or brown sugar

cloves (optional)

Oven temperature	200°C
Cooking time	20 minutes

Method

1 When the ham is cooked, remove the pan from the heat.
2 Leave the ham in the cooking liquid until it is cool enough to handle.
3 Remove the ham from the cooking liquid. Take off the skin and any excess fat.
4 Score the remaining surface fat in a criss cross design and baste with honey.
5 Bake in a hot oven for approximately 20 minutes until glazed to a rich golden brown colour.

Variations – instead of using honey, the ham can be scored, studded with cloves and then sprinkled with soft brown sugar and baked as above.

Steaming

Steaming will not colour the meat and it will look quite natural. Meat is not usually steamed unless it is combined with other ingredients to make a dish such as steak and kidney pudding. For more information see page 121.

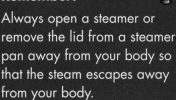

Remember!

Always open a steamer or remove the lid from a steamer pan away from your body so that the steam escapes away from your body.

Steak and kidney pudding

		Preparation	3
Cooking skills	2
Finishing	1

stewing steak	550g
ox's kidney	225g
onion	1 medium
chopped fresh parsley	30ml
plain flour	45ml
lemon rind, grated	1
salt and pepper	to taste
self-raising flour	275g
shredded suet	150g
butter or margarine for greasing	27g
Cooking time	5 hours
Serves	6

Method

1 Place the beef and kidney in a bowl with the onion and chopped parsley. Sprinkle in the flour and lemon rind and season with salt and pepper.
2 Mix the self-raising flour and suet and a pinch of salt. Stir in about 200ml of water and mix into a dough.
3 Roll out the dough and line a greased 1.7 litre pudding basin with the dough, leaving a piece big enough to top the basin.
4 Spoon the meat mixture into the lined pudding basin, add 120ml of water and seal the top of the basin using the remaining dough rolled out. Ensure the mix is well sealed by the dough by dampening the edges and rubbing them and turning in the edges to form a collar.
5 Cut a piece of greaseproof paper and foil and butter one side of the paper and lay it over the top of the basin and then tie the edge of the paper around the bowl. Then cover with the foil.
6 Place the pudding in a steamer and steam for about five hours. If using a saucepan steamer, ensure you check that the water does not boil away.
7 To serve, uncover, place on a serving dish and garnish with parsley.

Stewing

Stewing meat allows you to produce a good-flavoured dish from cheaper cuts of meat, e.g. mutton or beef shin. For more information see page 123.

Blanquette de veau

veal	700g
onions	2 medium
carrots	2 medium
lemon juice	a squeeze
bouquet garni	1
salt and pepper	to taste
butter or margarine	25g
plain flour	45ml
egg yolk	1
single cream	30–45ml
bacon rolls, cooked	4–6
chopped fresh parsley	to garnish
Cooking time	90 minutes
Serves	6

Preparation	4
Cooking skills	2
Finishing	3

Method

1 Put the meat, onions, carrots, lemon juice, bouquet garni and seasoning into a large saucepan with enough water to cover. Cover and simmer for one hour or until the meat is tender.
2 Strain off the liquid, reserving 600ml. Keep the meat and vegetables warm.
3 Melt the butter. Mix in the flour.
4 Gradually add the liquid, ensuring the liquid is boiled after every addition. Cook until the sauce thickens.
5 Adjust seasoning, remove from heat and add egg yolks and cream.
6 Add the meat, vegetables and bacon rolls and reheat without boiling.
7 Serve garnished with parsley.

Frying

It is essential to control the temperature and regularly turn and check meat during frying. Pork must always be cooked right through. Red meat and offal can be cooked to the customer's requirements. For more information see pages 123–124.

Liver and onions

Preparation	2
Cooking skills	2
Finishing	2

butter or margarine	25g
lamb's or calf's liver	450g
onions	450g
salt and pepper	to taste
mixed herbs (optional)	2.5ml
flour	for coating
Cooking time	5–10 minutes
Serves	4

Method

1 Melt the butter in a frying pan, add the onions and fry till brown. Add the herbs and seasoning. Cover and simmer for ten minutes.
2 Add the sliced liver to the onions and increase the heat slightly. Continue cooking for five to ten minutes.
3 Transfer to a warmed serving dish and serve.

Shallow-frying and stir-frying

Only good-quality meat should generally be fried, usually in a sauté pan or frying pan.

To stir-fry meat, cut it into thin strips and place them into very hot oil in a wok. Cook the meat very quickly – normally for no longer than two to six minutes.

> **Find out!** Worksheet 22
>
> List as many meat dishes as you can that require stir-frying, deep-fying or shallow-frying.

> **Remember!**
> Thicker pieces of meat will take longer to cook. For example, a sirloin steak will take longer than thin strips of pork for a stir-fry.

> **Remember!**
> Hot oil can inflict serious injury if you are not careful during cooking.

> **Video presentation**
> Watch the clip *Stir fry beef* to see this dish being made.

Cooking steaks

The fact that customers have different requirements in terms of how they want their steak to be cooked means that it is important that you clearly understand how to cook steaks correctly. The table below shows the core temperatures required to achieve different degrees of cooking:

Customer requirement	Core temperature	Description
Rare	Maximum 50°C	Sealed on the outside, bloody inside. Texture soft. Blood runs from steak.
Medium	55-60°C	Brown on the outside but still quite pink in the centre with blood running out. Soft to touch.
Medium to well done	63-68°C	Well browned with a slight touch of pink at the centre. Firm to touch. Less blood.
Well cooked	Over 75°C	Dark brown, no pink flesh and firm to touch.

Some customers will request a 'blue' steak. This is where the steak is put on the grill or into a pan and immediately turned over and then removed. The core temperature never gets above 28°C. The term 'blue' comes from the blue tinge which the meat has after this has been done. This dish is less popular these days and some restaurants will not serve it.

Garnishes and sauces

Steaks are often served with a choice of sauces and accompaniments. The following sauces are often served with steak.

○ Blue cheese sauce
○ Chasseur sauce (mushrooms, shallots, white wine and tomatoes and herbs)
○ Mushroom sauce
○ Pepper sauce
○ Red wine sauce

Commonly served acccompaniments include onion rings, watercress and straw potatoes.

Pork medallions with cider, cream and mustard sauce

olive oil	1 tbsp
pork fillet, cut into 3 medallions	150g
salt and freshly ground black pepper	to taste
sultanas	1 tbsp
cider	50ml
wholegrain mustard	1 tbsp
double cream	75ml
fresh chives, chopped	1 tsp
Serves	1

Preparation	2
Cooking skills	2
Finishing	1

Method

1 Heat the oil in a frying pan over a medium-high heat. Season the pork medallions on both sides with salt and freshly ground black pepper and fry for 3–4 minutes on each side, or until beginning to turn golden-brown.
2 Add the sultanas, cider, mustard and cream and simmer until reduced and thickened. Season, to taste, with salt and freshly ground black pepper.
3 To serve, place the pork into a serving dish and sprinkle over the chives.

Pork escalope with calvados sauce

pork escalope	4 × 100g
onions	50g
butter	50g
calvados	30ml
double cream	125ml
chopped basil, sage, rosemary, chives	pinch of each
salt	pinch
cayenne pepper	pinch
eating apples	2
cinnamon	pinch
lemon	1
brown sugar	25g
butter (melted)	25g
Serves	4

Method

1. Core and peel the apples.
2. Cut into ½ cm (¼ inch) thick rings and sprinkle with a little cinnamon and a few drops of lemon juice.
3. Place onto a baking sheet, sprinkle with brown sugar and a little melted butter and caramelise under the salamander grill (or in the top if a hot oven).
4. Lightly sauté the escalopes on both sides in the butter.
5. Remove from the pan and keep warm.
6. Add the chopped onions to the pan, cover with a lid and cook gently without colouring (use a little more butter if necessary).
7. Strain off the fat, leaving the onions in the pan and deglaze with the calvados.
8. Reduce by half; add the cream, seasoning and herbs.
9. Reboil, correct the seasoning and consistency and pass through a fine strainer on to the meat.
10. Garnish with the slices of caramelized apples.

As an alternative, calvados can be replaced with twice the amount of cider and reduced by three quarters. Add a crushed clove of garlic and 1 tablespoon of french mustard.

Kidney stroganoff

lamb kidneys	600g
oil	20ml
butter	30g
shallots, finely chopped	30g
brandy	15ml
cream	400ml
juice of half a lemon	
seasoning	to taste
parsley, chopped	garnish
Serves	4

Preparation	3
Cooking skills	2
Finishing	2

Method

1 Remove the outer 'skin' from the kidneys and split into two lengthwise.
2 Remove the white core and slice the kidney into four.
3 Season the kidneys and fry for 2–3 mins in butter. Remove the kidneys from the pan with any excess fat.
4 Add the finely chopped shallots to the pan and cook without colour. Drain off the fat.
5 Add the brandy to the pan and flame.
6 Add the cream to the pan, season lightly and allow to reduce by half.
7 Correct the seasoning and finish with the lemon juice.
8 Replace the kidneys in the pan and reheat gently – do not boil.
9 Serve garnished with a little chopped parsley.

Grilling

Beefsteaks, lamb cutlets, pork chops, veal, liver and kidneys can all be grilled, but you must ensure that the cut of meat is appropriate. See the table on page 205.

The meat can be placed on a tray or directly onto a clean grill. The meat may even be on skewers, e.g. kebabs. The meat is usually brushed with butter or oil (olive) to baste the meat during grilling. Meat such as pork, which has been marinated, is suitable for grilling. The heat colours the meat and helps to develop flavour.

The cooking time will vary depending on the type and thickness of the meat and it must be cooked to at least 63°C at the centre. Cooked grilled meat or offal should be firm to touch and resistant to pressure. Beef and lamb are an exception to this rule, as they can be served pink. For more information see page 124.

Healthy eating

Grilling is a healthy way of cooking meat as some of the fat drips from it.

Barbecued pork spare ribs

Preparation	3
Cooking skills	2
Finishing	2

vegetable oil	30ml
onions	2 medium
garlic clove	1
tomato purée	30ml
malt vinegar	60ml
dried thyme	1.25ml
chilli seasoning	1.25ml
honey	45ml
beef stock	150ml
pork spare ribs	1kg
Oven temperature	190°C
Cooking time	1¾ hours
Serves	4

Method

1. Heat the oil in a saucepan, add the onions and cook for five minutes until softened.
2. Add all the remaining ingredients, except the spare ribs, and simmer gently for ten minutes.
3. Place the spare ribs in a roasting tray in a single layer and brush with a little of the sauce.
4. Roast in the oven at 190°C for 30 minutes.
5. Pour off the excess fat and spoon the remaining sauce over the ribs.
6. Cook for a further 1¼ hours, basting occasionally.

Griddling

Some griddles have bars running across them. This enables the meat to be **charred** or **seared**, providing a distinctive flavour and colour. Too much oil on the griddle can lead to excessive smoke and can hamper the cooking process. For more information see page 125.

Any type of meat or offal that can be grilled can also be griddled. The table below identifies what cuts from the meat types are suitable for grilling and griddling.

Meat or offal	Prime or tender cuts or joints
Beef	Rump, sirloin, fillet
Veal	Loin, best end
Lamb	Best end, saddle
Pork	Loin
Bacon	Gammon, loin
Offal	Liver, kidneys

Figure 7.19 Cuts of meat and offal suitable for grilling and griddling

Definition

Charring or **searing**: using the hot bars on a griddle to mark a pattern on the meat as it is cooking.

Roasting

Roasting meat gives a joint a good natural flavour and colours it nicely through the cooking process which adds to the appearance of the final dish. Meat such as lamb or beef can be rare, well-done or medium. This refers to how much the meat is cooked. Pork must always be well cooked. Undercooked pork runs the risk of giving someone food poisoning.

Place meat for roasting in a sturdy tray with handles. Roasting is normally started at a temperature of 200–210°C. The heat is then turned down to 160–180°C once the meat has coloured. Oven cloths and personal protective equipment must be used. A probe should be used to check that the centre of the joint of meat has reached an acceptable temperature and is safe to eat. The temperature is usually 63°C.

A probe is not always available. If this is the case, the juice from the meat can be used to test its condition. If the juice is pink and the meat is pork then continue to cook. A well-done joint of meat cooked throughout will have juices that run clear. Touch is another test. A resistant surface indicates that the meat is cooked.

Marcus says

Ensure the correct cooking method is used for the particular cut of meat. For example, lamb shoulder cannot be pan fried as it would be almost inedible – it needs to be slow cooked.

Let the meat relax for 30 minutes before carving to allow the meat to cool slightly and make it tenderer to eat. This is particularly important with red meat, e.g. lamb and beef.

The roasting times for the main types of meat are as follows:
o Beef: 20 minutes per 450g plus 20 minutes.
o Lamb: 15–20 minutes per 450g plus 20 minutes.
o Pork: 25 minutes per 450g plus 25 minutes.
o Veal: 20 minutes per 450g plus 20 minutes.

The table below lists the types of meat and cuts suitable for roasting.

Meat	Cut or joint
Beef	Rump, topside, sirloin, fillet, ribs
Veal	Cushion, best end
Lamb	Best end, leg, shoulder, chops, saddle
Pork	Loin, leg, ribs, belly, shoulder
Bacon	Gammon

Figure 7.20 Cuts of meat suitable for roasting

Classic roast beef

piece of beef (sirloin, rib, rump or topside)	2kg
beef dripping (optional)	50g
salt and pepper	to taste
mustard powder (optional)	5ml
horseradish sauce	
Oven temperature	200–210°C until meat has coloured, then 160–180°C
Cooking time	See guidelines above
Serves	8–10

Preparation	1
Cooking skills	2
Finishing	2

Method

1 Weigh the meat and calculate the cooking times.
2 Place the meat in a shallow roasting tin, preferably on a grid with the thickest layer of fat uppermost.
3 Add beef dripping if the meat is lean, season with salt, pepper, and mustard if preferred.
4 Roast the joint at 180°C for the calculated time, basting occasionally.
5 Remove from the oven and allow to rest for 20 minutes before carving. Serve with horseradish sauce.

For more information see page 125.

Baking

Steak and ale pie

For the short crust pastry:

flour	200g
salt	pinch
lard	50g
butter	50g
ice cold water	2–3 tbsp

For the pie mix:

chuck steak, diced	200g
mushrooms, quartered	100g
oil	50ml
onion	100g
stock	125ml
beer	125ml
seasoning	to taste
worcester sauce	few drops
tomato puree	2 tbsp
parsley	1 tsp
cornflour	10g
Oven temperature	200°C
Cooking time	35–40 minutes
Serves	4

Method

1 Sieve the flour and salt.
2 Rub in the fat (butter and lard) to a sandy texture.
3 Add sufficient water to make a fairly firm paste.
4 Handle as little as possible and allow to rest.
5 Cut the meat into 2cm squares.
6 Heat the oil in a frying pan, add the meat and quickly brown on all sides.
7 Drain the meat in a colander.
8 Lightly fry the onions in the same oil.
9 **Deglaze** the pan with the red wine.
10 Place the meat, onion, mushrooms, worcester sauce, tomato puree, parsley and the liquid in the pan, season lightly with salt and pepper.
11 Bring to the boil, skim, then allow to simmer gently until the meat is tender (1 hour 30 minutes to 1 hour 45 minutes).
12 Dilute the cornflour with a little water, stir into the simmering mixture, reboil and correct seasoning.
13 Place the cooled mixture into the prepared pie dish, cover with pastry, egg wash and bake at 200°C for approximately 35–40 minutes.

> **Definition**
>
> **Deglaze**: to add wine or stock to a pan used for frying in order to lift the remaining sediment to make a sauce or gravy.

Steak and kidney pie

For the short crust pastry:

flour	200g
salt	pinch
lard	50g
butter	50g
ice cold water	2–3 tbsp

For the pie mix:

chuck steak, diced	200g
kidney, diced	50g
oil	50ml
onion	100g
stock	125ml
red wine	25ml
seasoning	to taste
worcester sauce	few drops
tomato puree	2 tbsp
parsley	1 tsp
cornflour	10g
Oven temperature	200°C
Cooking time	35–40 minutes
Serves	4

Preparation	3
Cooking skills	2
Finishing	1

Method

1 Sieve the flour and salt.
2 Rub in the fat (butter and lard) to a sandy texture.
3 Add sufficient water to make a fairly firm paste.
4 Handle as little as possible and allow to rest.
5 Cut the meat into 2cm squares.
6 Heat the oil in a frying pan, add the meat and quickly brown on all sides.
7 Drain the meat in a colander.
8 Lightly fry the onions.
9 Deglaze the pan with the red wine.
10 Place the meat, onion, worcester sauce, tomato puree, parsley and the stock in the pan, season lightly with salt and pepper.
11 Bring to the boil, skim, then allow to simmer gently until the meat is tender (1 hour 30 minutes to 1 hour 45 minutes).
12 Dilute the cornflour with a little water, stir into the simmering mixture, reboil to thicken and correct seasoning.
13 Place the cooled mixture into the prepared pie dish, cover with pastry, egg wash and bake at 200°C for approximately 35–40 minutes.

Lancashire hotpot

Preparation	3
Cooking skills	2
Finishing	2

dripping (oil may be substituted)	30g
seasoning	to taste
middle neck of lamb cut for stewing	600g
potatoes, peeled and sliced (3mm thick)	600g
onions, peeled and sliced	600g
white stock (brown stock may be used instead)	1 litre
parsley, chopped	garnish
Oven temperature	230°C
Cooking time	1½–2 hours
Serves	4

Method

1. Heat the dripping in a frying pan. Lightly season the meat and fry in the dripping to lightly colour and seal on both sides.
2. On the bottom of a deep earthenware dish or casserole place a layer of potatoes, then one of onions, season and then add a layer of fried meat.
3. Repeat the layers, finishing with a neat layer of overlapping potatoes.
4. Pour in sufficient stock to come just beneath the surface of the top layer of potatoes.
5. Brush over the surface with melted dripping (or butter). Thoroughly clean the edges of the dish before cooking.
6. Put in a hot oven (230°C) until lightly coloured.
7. Reduce the heat (180°C) and cook slowly until tender(1½–2 hours). Press the surface down occasionally with a fish slice to maintain the appearance of the dish and prevent the top layer drying out.
8. Brush the top layer with a little more melted fat just before service and sprinkle with chopped parsley.

Moussaka

onions	50 g
garlic	1 clove
butter/ margarine or oil	25g
tomato puree	25g
minced lamb	400g
demi-glace	125ml
aubergines	200g
tomatoes	200g
flour	25g
oil	60ml
breadcrumbs	25g
parmesan cheese, grated	25g
melted butter	25g
béchamel sauce	500ml
cinnamon	¼ tsp
oregano	¼ tsp
egg yolks	2
allspice	pinch
nutmeg	pinch
Oven temperature	230°C
Cooking time	20–30 minutes
Serves	4

Method

1 Finely chop the onions and garlic.
2 Sweat off in butter without colouring.
3 Lightly colour the minced lamb, add tomato puree, then add the **demi-glace** and bring to the boil. Simmer until cooked. Add cinnamon and oregano.
4 Season the mixture. It should be fairly dry.
5 Peel the aubergines and cut into ¼ inch slices.
6 Pass the slices through seasoned flour.
7 Fry the slices in shallow hot oil on both sides and drain.
8 Peel the tomatoes and cut into ¼ inch slices.
9 Place the mixture of lamb into an earthenware dish. Layer with tomatoes and then aubergines.
10 Season with salt and pepper.
11 Pour over the béchamel sauce. Add two egg yolks to the sauce.
12 Sprinkle with breadcrumbs, cheese and melted butter.
13 Gratinate in a hot oven at 230°C–250°C until golden brown.
14 Sprinkle with chopped parsley and serve.

See page 308 for béchamel sauce.

Definition

Demi-glace: a sauce which is made up of equal quantities of brown stock and brown sauce (espagnole sauce), reduced by a third until the consistency coats the back of a spoon.

Braising

The benefits of this cooking method are that the meat is very tender, flavours are able to merge and it allows cheaper, tougher cuts of meat to be used. The thickening agent for the liquid used when braising dishes is flour. A white or brown roux will be made and cooked into a sauce relevant to the dish. For more information see page 123.

Combination cooking

Lasagne is an example of a meat dish cooked using combination cooking. First the meat is **sealed** then it is stewed and finally it is finished by baking in the oven. For more information see page 126.

Combination ovens

A combination oven uses dry heat and an injection of steam to keep the food moist during cooking e.g. lamb chops can easily become dry if overcooked in an ordinary oven. In a combination oven, the steam coupled with the convection heat will help to keep the meat moist and good to eat. For more information see page 126.

Hot holding, finishing and serving

Once you have worked hard to prepare and cook a dish it is important to serve it with the correct garnish and at the right temperature.

Hot holding

Holding the meat at the right temperature is also about being compliant with the law. The Food Safety Act 1990 states that hot food must be served and held at a temperature of at least 63°C. This temperature makes sure that potentially harmful bacteria will not multiply and harm the consumer.

Food is usually held at the correct temperature by either storing in a hot cupboard or hotplate which is above 63°C. Be aware that you may only hot hold food for a maximum of 90 minutes. Keep checking the condition of the food whilst hot holding as it can tend to become dry if it is not monitored correctly.

> **Did you know?**
> The thickening agent for the liquid used when braising dishes is flour. A white or brown roux will be made and cooked into a sauce relevant to the dish.

> **Definition**
> **Sealing:** lightly cooking meat on all sides in order to seal in the flavour and juices and add colour. It is usually done prior to putting the meat in a stew or braised dish.

Finishing

Finishing a meat or offal dish correctly is very important. You should always check a dish before it is served and ask yourself the following questions:

○ Is the meat or offal at the correct temperature for service?

○ Does the dish have the correct flavour?

○ Does it need more seasoning?

○ Do I have the correct **garnish** or accompaniment for the dish?

○ Do I have the right equipment to finish and serve the dish?

The following are all appropriate garnishes for meat dishes:

○ Other cooked ingredients such as Yorkshire pudding for roast beef.

○ Accompaniments and sauces appropriate to the dish, e.g. apple sauce for pork or mint sauce for lamb.

Definition

Garnish: adding the final touches required to enhance a dish.

Yorkshire pudding

Preparation	1
Cooking skills	1
Finishing	–

plain flour	125g
salt	pinch
egg	1
milk	200ml
vegetable oil	30ml
Oven temperature	220°C
Cooking time	40–45 minutes
Serves	4–6

Method

1 Add the flour, salt and egg in a bowl and mix.
2 Add half the milk and beat until smooth.
3 Add the remaining milk and beat until smooth.
4 Put a small amount of oil in a small roasting tray and pre-heat it in the oven.
5 Pour the batter into the hot tray and cook until risen and golden brown.

Serving

The equipment required to finish and serve meat can include:

○ serving platters (earthenware, plate or metal)

○ serving utensils, e.g. spoons, tongs, slices or forks.

The surface of a dish should be clean and presentable and maintained in an appropriate condition during service so that it is appealing to customers.

The final dish needs to be appealing to you and your customer. This is an aspect of catering where your flair will play an important part in shaping your career.

Figure 7.20 Serving is as essential as the preparation and cooking in creating an appealing dish

Test yourself!

1 Where should a pork joint be stored and at what temperature?

2 What is offal? Name two different types.

3 What is the most preferred type of liver used in offal dishes?

4 Which meats are classed as high risk?

5 What are the quality points to check for when selecting a pork loin for roasting?

6 What is the minimum temperature for pork to be cooked to?

7 Why is it important to cook pork thoroughly?

8 What type of pig does bacon come from?

9 What are sweetbreads?

10 What are the accompaniments for roast beef, lamb and pork?

8 Poultry

This chapter covers skills and knowledge in the following units:

- 7132 Unit 223 (2FP4) Prepare poultry for basic dishes
- 7132 Unit 230 (2FC4) Cook and finish basic poultry dishes
- 7091 Unit 269 Preparation, cooking and finishing of poultry dishes

Working through this chapter could also provide the opportunity to practise the following Functional Skills at Level 2:
Functional English Reading – Read and summarise, succinctly, information/ideas from different sources; identify the purpose of texts and comment on how meaning is conveyed

In this chapter you will:

Understand how and be able to prepare poultry for basic dishes	7132 – 223.1,2	7091 – 269.1
Understand how and be able to cook basic poultry dishes	7132 – 230.1,2	7091 – 269.2
Understand how and be able to finish basic poultry dishes	7132 – 230.3,4	7091 – 269.3

You will learn to prepare and cook basic poultry dishes, including:

- sauté chicken bonne femme
- poached breasts of chicken with mushroom sauce
- chicken in white wine sauce.

Types of poultry

What is poultry?

Poultry is the generic term used for domestic farmyard birds, e.g. chickens, ducks and turkeys. Geese and guinea fowl are also included in this group. Poultry is an increasingly popular source of protein, because it is versatile and adaptable in modern cooking.

Figure 8.1 Poultry includes many different species of bird (duck, turkey, chicken, guinea fowl, goose)

Chicken is the most popular type of poultry. It can be found in most domestic fridges as well in restaurants and industrial kitchens worldwide.

Quality points

The following quality points apply to all poultry:

○ There should be no bruises or cuts on the skin of the bird.

○ The skin should be dry and not slimy.

○ Good-quality poultry should be odourless or at least have a fresh smell to it.

○ The bird should be the right size for the dish you are to prepare. For example, a chicken for roasting should be about 1.3kg. Other birds, e.g. duck or turkey, can vary in weight but you should check the size against the requirements of the dish.

○ The **cavity** should not contain any excess blood or yellow fat, nor show any signs of damage to the inside of the carcass.

Remember!

If you are unsure or have a problem with the poultry you are preparing or cooking then always seek advice from your supervisor, line manager or head chef.

Did you know?

Corn-fed chickens are yellow. The cooked fat has a yellow tinge to it because of the food the bird is fed.

Definition

Cavity: the hollow space left inside the bird once all the innards have been removed.

Potential problems

Poultry is a high-risk food, as it can contain harmful bacteria, e.g. salmonella. Bacteria can multiply if poultry is not stored or cooked correctly and this could lead to food poisoning. It is important to follow these food safety guidelines strictly:

○ Poultry should be stored correctly at an appropriate temperature (1 to 5°C if fresh and –18 to –25°C if frozen).
○ Always store raw meat on the bottom shelf of the refrigerator to stop the juices dripping onto the shelves below.
○ Thoroughly defrost frozen poultry before cooking. Otherwise the meat in the thickest parts may not be cooked through and the harmful bacteria could remain.
○ Always cook poultry to a temperature of above 63°C.
○ Check there is no sign of uncooked flesh before serving.

Chicken

Chickens are farmed or reared in three different ways:

1 **Free-range**: the birds are usually left to roam freely.
2 **Battery**: an intense method of farming where the birds are kept packed in pens with little if any freedom of movement.
3 **Organic**: birds are fed on natural and traditional foods. Information is always readily available regarding organic poultry from either the label or organisations relevant to the product.

There are many types of chicken for cooking; the most common are shown in the table below.

> **Did you know?**
> Chicken is high in protein and full of vitamins, especially vitamin B.

> **Healthy eating**
> The breast meat of chicken is low in fat and the leg meat has lower fat content than other more traditional red meats. The young age of the chicken (12 weeks) means that the meat is tender and very adaptable.

Type	Description	Average portion yield	Appearance
Poussin	4–6-week-old bird	1	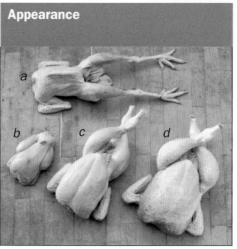
Double poussin	6-week-old bird	2	
Roasting chicken	12–14-week-old bird	4–8	
Boiling fowl	Older bird, over 14 weeks	6–8	
Large roasting chicken	Young fattened cockerel	8–12	

Figure 8.2 Types of chicken for cooking

a boiling fowl, b poussin, c roasting chicken, d capon

The bird you will most commonly prepare is the traditional roasting chicken, which may come pre-packed. It can range in size from 1.3kg to 3kg. The chicken will have already been plucked and cleaned of its innards. It will therefore be ready for dish preparation and cooking.

A chicken can be cooked:
○ whole
○ **jointed** from the carcass into two breasts and two legs (see page 221)
○ cut into eight pieces for sautéing (see page 222–224).

Checking quality of chicken

When selecting chicken for use in the kitchen, it is important to check for the following quality points:
○ It should be plump and of appropriate size (1.3kg–3kg).
○ There should not be any damage, breaks, blemishes or bruising.
○ It should be clean, with a fresh smell and it should not be slimy to the touch. An unpleasant odour indicates that the chicken may be unsuitable for use.
○ Make sure there is minimal fat and that the cavity does not contain a high proportion of yellow fat inside it, as this indicates poor quality or an old bird.

Using the wrong type of chicken will result in a poor quality dish and affect your kitchen's reputation. For example, you should not use a boiling fowl if you are supposed to be producing roast chicken.

Healthy eating
A skinless chicken breast is an appropriate low-fat meat option as part of a healthy well-balanced diet. A chicken breast has only 120 calories per 100g.

Definition
Jointed: cuts of poultry removed from the carcass during preparation, e.g. legs and breasts.

Remember!
Chicken breasts can be expensive so there must not be too much wastage during preparation.

Duck

It is believed that duck was first domesticated in China hundreds, maybe thousands, of years ago. Today many types of duck are reared for cooking. Some commonly used types of duck are:
○ Pekin or Long Island
○ Barbary or Muscovy
○ Aylesbury.

Barbary and Aylesbury are the most commonly used ducks in cooking. The Aylesbury duck has a higher fat content than the Barbary duck. Ducks are generally quite large birds. They should have long plump breasts and smaller legs in proportion to the breasts. The flesh is usually a deep red.

Figure 8.3 Duck breasts. Note the deep red flesh

Cuts of duck

Duck is versatile and can be prepared and cooked in many ways:

o It can be cooked whole.

o It has two breasts and two legs which can be jointed from the carcass.

Duck has a rich flavour, well-suited to sweet accompaniments.

Checking quality of duck

When selecting a duck for use check for the following points:

o The skin is light in colour.

o The duck is plump, especially in the breast region.

o The skin must be clean and free from damage, blemishes or bruising.

o It should smell fresh.

Turkey

Turkeys were originally discovered in the Americas. They used to be eaten only at festive occasions, e.g. Christmas or Thanksgiving. However, turkey is now widely available all year round. It is a versatile meat. It must be cooked correctly – overcooked turkey can be very dry.

Turkeys are either farmed intensively or as free-range birds. A free-range bird will have a plumper breast and smaller legs in comparison with intensively-farmed or battery-farmed turkeys.

Cuts of turkey

Turkeys can be purchased frozen or fresh, whole or in cuts, e.g. breasts or legs. A turkey is generally a large bird. Individual birds can vary dramatically in size from 3 to 11 kilos. Even a single breast joint will provide a large amount of meat. A turkey can be cooked in different cuts:

o It can be cooked whole.

o The legs can be removed and the rest of the turkey cooked – turkey crown.

o It has two legs and two breasts which can be jointed from the carcass.

Did you know?

Peking duck is roasted duck, which has been shredded. It is served in a light pancake with strips of spring onion and cucumber and plum sauce. Bombay duck is not duck at all. It is a dried fish!

Healthy eating

Duck contains a lot of fat, so should not feature too regularly in a healthy diet. It is a good meat choice for special occasions.

Healthy eating

Duck is high in protein, B vitamins and some minerals.

Figure 8.4 A turkey

Checking quality of turkey

When selecting a whole turkey check for the following points:

- It has a plump breast of firm flesh.
- There are no breaks, blemishes, bruising or other damage.
- It is clean. There should not be any slime and it should smell fresh.

Preparing poultry dishes

Preparation methods

Checking the poultry

A good-quality bird will give you a better chance of a good dish.

It is essential to check the quality of the poultry before use for food safety reasons (see Quality points, page 217). Remember that you should always:

- Check the appearance.
- Check the smell.
- Check the size – is it appropriate for the dish you are cooking?
- Check the cavity. Sometimes the edible innards (offal) of the bird are left inside but usually they are cleaned and re-packed in a separate bag.
- Wash the cavity if necessary to remove any unwanted residues.

Trimming

Trimming means removing the bones, fat and connective tissue from the poultry. Trimming improves the presentation of the meat.

Trimming is carried out using a knife so you must observe safe working procedures as follows:

- Ensure your workplace is clean and tidy.
- Use a red chopping board for raw meat.
- Use a 10-inch chef's knife to trim the poultry.
- Always cut away from yourself to avoid any accidents if the knife slips.
- Have a container ready to put the trimmings into and a dish to put the finished product into.

Healthy eating
As with chicken, turkey is a lean meat source, high in protein, vitamin B and other minerals, e.g. zinc, magnesium and iron.

Did you know?
The innards found within the poultry cavity are known as giblets. They can be used to make a stock for gravy.

Healthy eating
If fat is trimmed from the poultry, it can make a healthier eating option.

Remember!
Some trimmings may be suitable for stock so do not just throw trimmings in the bin.

Cutting and chopping

It is essential that the correct knife and equipment is used and that you observe safe working procedures.

Ask yourself:

○ Have I been trained to cut this poultry?
○ Do I know what to do next? (If not, ask!)
○ Have I got the right knife?
○ Is my knife sharp enough?
○ Am I using the correct board?
○ Am I dressed correctly?
○ Have I selected the right equipment?
○ Is my workstation tidy and suitable to prepare the poultry?

If your answer is 'Yes' to all of the above questions it is safe to proceed.

In most cases a red chopping board would be used for raw poultry and the knife would be a red 10-inch chef's knife. This knife has a sturdy blade and a large heel. Used correctly it is the most suitable for this task. Other suitable knives could include a boning knife, but this would be used for more specialist preparation methods, e.g. **tunnel boning**.

Portioning

The advantage of **portioning** the poultry before cooking is that you have a guaranteed number of servings. If you are preparing chicken for 200 people then portioning will assure you at an early stage that you have enough food to feed everyone.

Marcus says

All birds, from quail to turkey, have the same bone structure, which makes preparation fairly straightforward once mastered for one type. You just need to vary the utensils and level of force depending on the bird, not your technique.

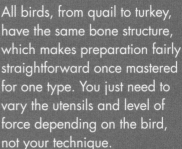

Definition

Tunnel boning: removing the bones without breaking the skin of the bird.

Definition

Portioning: cutting meat into the correct size for it to be served. The correct size depends on the dish being made. Poultry is usually cut into four pieces (two breasts and two legs). If the poultry is a poussin (see table on page 216) it may also be prepared for grilling.

How to portion a chicken into four

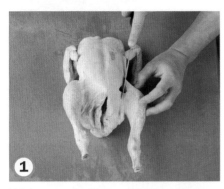

1 With your knife make small cuts at the top of the leg where it is attached to the main carcass.

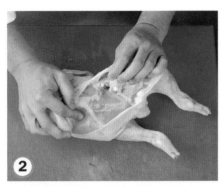

2 Dislocate the leg by popping the leg joint out of the socket and pulling back the leg.

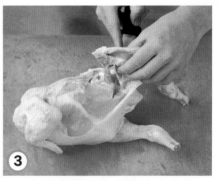

3 Cut the leg away from the carcass by following the natural line of flesh. Make sure you remove the oyster. Repeat on the other side.

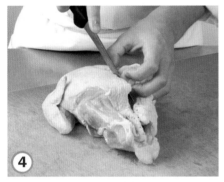

4 To separate the two breasts follow the natural line of the breast bone and cut down through the carcass and wing joint. The wings remain attached.

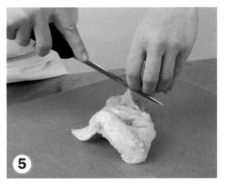

5 Trim each breast to remove any sinew, bone or excess fat.

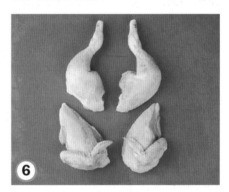

6 You will be left with two breasts and two legs.

Dicing and slicing

These methods of cutting are used for meat which is off the bone. Dicing makes you think of square cubes but with poultry, evenly sized pieces of any shape are needed. Cutting poultry into evenly sized pieces allows the meat to cook evenly. Dicing and slicing into strips is appropriate for stir-fries. A thin slice of meat, such as chicken, is sometimes called an émincé. A dish consisting of thin slices of left-over meat covered with a sauce is called an émincé.

The principles listed on page 222 should be followed to ensure personal and food safety when dicing poultry meat.

Remember!
Throughout this process ensure you work safely with the knife. Always work away from you, so if you slip you do not inadvertently stab yourself. If you are unsure of any process seek advice from your line manager.

Cutting poultry for sauté dishes

Sautéing is a relatively quick method of cooking and therefore the meat must be cut into small manageable pieces of approximately the same size in order to ensure even cooking. This preparation method is carried out on whole chickens.

How to cut a chicken into eight pieces for sauté

1

Make sure all the giblets have been removed. Clean the cavity – if necessary wash it out under cold running water and wipe it with a kitchen towel.

2

To remove the wishbone, pull the skin back around the neck area. Use an 8–10-inch chef's knife to rub the flesh on each side to expose the wishbone. You can see where the wishbone is joined to the shoulder blade.

3

Using the point of the knife cut through the bone on each side.

4

Run your finger along each side of the bone to the top. At the top there is an oval-shaped piece of bone attaching the wishbone to the breast. Pinch this and pull to remove the wishbone.

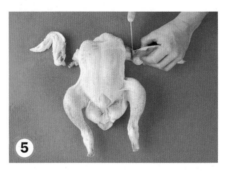

5

Cut above the wing joint. Scrape flesh back to expose a clean bone.

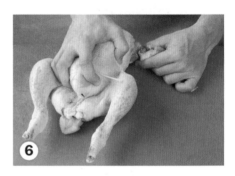

6

Snap off the wing at the joint. Repeat on the other side.

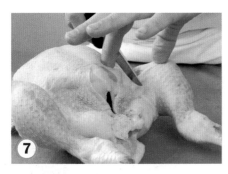

7 Pull out the leg and make a small cut through the skin to expose the flesh.

8 Push the thigh backwards to expose the bone. Hold the leg and pop the bone from the socket.

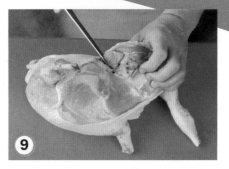

9 Work around the small piece of flesh on the back. This is the 'oyster'.

10 Remove the leg. Repeat to remove the second leg (2 pieces).

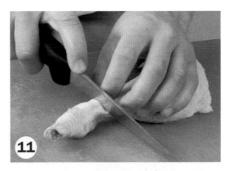

11 Cut the flesh at the bottom of the drumstick and scrape it back to the joint.

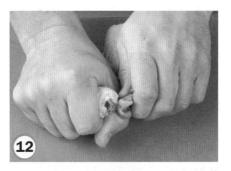

12 Snap the joint, leaving a small piece of clean bone exposed.

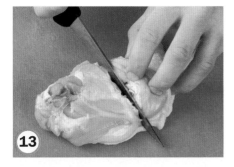

13 Smooth the skin. Put the meat skin side down. There should be a visible line of fat. Using this as your guide, cut through between the drumstick and thigh. Repeat on the other leg (4 pieces).

14 Remove the ball joint from each drumstick. Press down with the heel of the knife to cut off the bone. Repeat with the other leg.

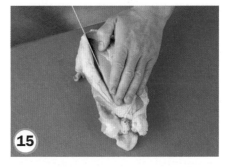

15 Have the cavity end towards you. Follow the feather lines along the breast, cutting through the shoulder.

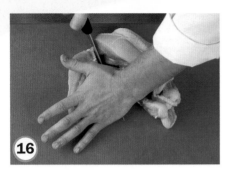

16 Put your hand over the front of the knife to steady it. Push the knife down to cut right through the bones. Remove the wing with part of the breast. Repeat on the other side (6 pieces).

17 Turn the chicken onto its side. Cut the remaining carcass from the breast.

Video presentation

Prepare a whole chicken for sauté shows a professional chef working through this process.

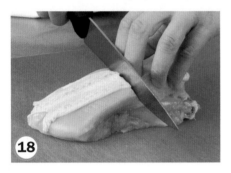

18 Cut across the breast bone. You will need to press on the heel of the knife to cut through the bone.

19 Reassemble the 8 portions on a tray, tidying the skin as you do this.

Boning

Boning is usually carried out so the legs of a bird can be stuffed, e.g. the thigh bone of a turkey, although a whole bird can also be boned out. It is much easier to carve a joint that has been boned and it also looks more attractive. There are two types of boning: tunnel boning and external boning.

External boning means cutting through the flesh to the bone and then removing the bone using a boning knife (a knife with a sturdy, tapered blade about 7-inches long). The cavity can then be filled and the joint tied to form a pleasing shape. Tunnel boning is a more delicate and complex method.

Definition

Boning: to remove the bones from a joint of meat or poultry.

Remember!

Be very careful when boning poultry so that you do not cut yourself.

Figure 8.5 A boning knife

How to tunnel bone a thigh bone from a turkey leg

1 Cut around the ball joint at the top of the leg.
2 Holding the knife almost flat against the bone, scrape and cut
  along the thigh bone to manipulate the flesh away from the bone.
  Turn the leg inside out as you do this to make it easier.
3 Once the joint above the drumstick is exposed, cut through the
  joint to remove the thigh bone.
4 Turn the leg back in so the skin is facing outwards again. There
  should not be any damage to the exterior as this would spoil the
  appearance of the finished dish.
5 Stuff the leg.

Stuffing or filling

Stuffing or filling poultry adds to the flavour, appearance and texture
of the dish. Stuffing, e.g. sage and onion, is often put into the neck
cavity. Legs can also be filled or stuffed. Before stuffing a cavity it is
important to check it to ensure the quality of the bird. If necessary,
wash and dry the inside of the cavity. The stuffing or filling should
always be at the correct temperature, which is 1–5°C. If possible do
not handle the filling; use a piping bag or spoon.

Remember!

Temperature is important
when preparing poultry. The
meat may contain harmful
bacteria, which multiply
rapidly at room temperature.
Adding hot filling to a cool
chicken cavity could lead to
food poisoning. Always allow
hot fillings or stuffing to cool
below 8°C before adding
them to the poultry.

How to stuff a turkey breast

1

2

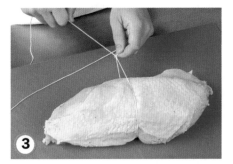

3

Remove the breast from the turkey. Cut into the fattest part of the breast along its length. This cut almost slices all the way through the breast, creating a pouch or envelope effect.

Put the cooled stuffing in this 'envelope' or 'pouch', using a spoon or your hands, as long as they are clean.

Tie the breast back to its original shape before cooking, using butcher's twine or another similar string. Do not use plastic-based string as this can melt and contaminate the meat.

How to stuff a leg

1 Remove the thighbone from the bird. This gives a natural cavity.
2 Put the stuffing in this cavity.
3 Sew, tie or wrap the leg in foil so that it keeps its shape during cooking.

Equipment and tools used to stuff a bird:

○ suitable knife
○ chopping board
○ piping bag to fill cavities in the meat
○ spoons to prevent unnecessary handling of stuffing
○ string to tie the bird or joint
○ gloves, which the food handler can use when stuffing poultry.

Seasoning and marinating

Seasoning

Seasoning is the addition of various ingredients, e.g. salt, pepper, and certain spices and herbs, to give a particular flavour to a dish or type of food. Adjusting the quantities of seasoning will affect the flavour, but you must be careful. Too much of some seasonings, e.g. salt, can make the dish or ingredients inedible.

A chicken or turkey for roasting is usually seasoned before cooking, during the preparation stage. If the poultry you are preparing is for a **wet method** of cookery, e.g. stewing or braising, the poultry should

Video presentation
Watch *How to stuff a chicken leg for ballotine* to see how its done.

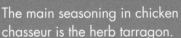

Did you know?
The main seasoning in chicken chasseur is the herb tarragon.

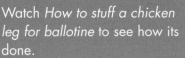

Definition
Wet method: a dish which is cooked and served in a liquid.
Dry method: a dish which is cooked using a dry method of cookery (e.g. roasting, grilling).

be well-seasoned before cooking. The overall seasoning of the dish should be adjusted after cooking when all the flavours of the ingredients in the casserole have combined.

Marinating

Marinating is used to preserve or flavour foods. Marinating poultry is done by combining a cooked or uncooked liquid with the bird or joints in a dish. The liquid is called the marinade. It contains ingredients which will alter and enhance the flavour of the poultry. The poultry can be left in the marinade for between 30 minutes and 48 hours, depending on the dish. The poultry should be covered completely by the liquid.

Some marinades are cooked and then cooled before being combined with the meat. Most marinades, however, are cold and can be created very quickly using ingredients necessary to flavour the meat.

Some marinades are used after the meat has been removed from them to create a sauce to accompany the dish. Tandoori is a well-known chicken dish in which the sauce is created from the marinade.

As a chef you can experiment with creating your own marinades by combining flavours and adding those to different base ingredients, e.g. poultry.

Did you know?
Marinating can prolong the shelf life of poultry, as it may cure the meat.

Basic marinade for chicken

Preparation	1
Cooking skills	1
Finishing	–

chicken	1 portioned into 4 or 8
salt and pepper	to season
chopped shallots	2
thyme	1 sprig
bay leaf	1
chopped parsley	1 tablespoon
garlic clove, crushed	1 small
clove	1 small
black peppercorns	12
lemon juice	from 2 lemons
olive oil	375ml
Serves	4

Method

1 Season the chicken with salt and pepper.
2 Mix the other ingredients together in a bowl. Add the chicken and make sure it is covered in marinade.
3 Cover the dish and put it in a refrigerator for 2–12 hours.

Coating

Coating poultry can be as simple as covering it in seasoned flour during preparation. It can also refer to covering a piece of poultry in flour, egg and breadcrumbs to meet the requirements of a certain dish, e.g. Chicken Kiev.

Coating with seasoned flour

This is commonly done when preparing pieces of poultry for sauté. Dip each piece of poultry in a dish of seasoned flour and shake off the excess. The seasoned powder combines with the poultry to create a well-coloured and crisp texture when sealing the meat.

Coating with flour, egg and breadcrumbs

Coating poultry in flour, egg and breadcrumbs for Chicken Kiev allows the garlic butter to be held in the poultry leg or breast during cooking. A breadcrumb coating adds a different texture to the dish.

Always follow this process to make sure the poultry is evenly coated:

1 Take three bowls: one bowl of well-seasoned flour, one bowl of beaten egg and one bowl of fine breadcrumbs.
2 Coat the poultry with the flour and shake off any excess.
3 Place it in the beaten egg mix. Make sure the poultry is completely coated in egg mix. Shake off the excess.
4 Place it in the breadcrumb bowl. Make sure the meat is well coated.
5 Put the breadcrumbed poultry on a suitable tray until required for cooking.

Once the poultry has been coated it must not be left very long before cooking or the coating will become soggy. Do not stack portions of breadcrumbed products on top of each other or the quality of the coating and its appearance will be affected. Use greaseproof paper to layer many portions of coated poultry.

> ### Find out!
> **Worksheet 23**
> List as many poultry dishes as you can that are coated in flour, egg and breadcrumbs.

> **Remember!**
>
> It is important to use the correct tools, equipment and techniques when preparing poultry in order to ensure safety, to meet the dish requirements and to be economic, efficient and reduce wastage.

Chicken Kiev

chicken breasts	2
butter	50g
lemon juice and zest	½ lemon
garlic clove	1
chopped parsley	20g
salt and pepper	to taste
flour	50g
white breadcrumbs	100g
eggs, beaten	2
watercress as garnish	
Cooking time	8–10 minutes
Serves	2

Preparation	2
Cooking skills	2
Finishing	1

Method

1. Flatten the chicken breasts slightly.
2. Mix the butter, salt and pepper, lemon juice, crushed garlic and chopped parsley in a bowl.
3. Shape the butter mixture into fingers to fit inside the breasts.
4. Cut a pouch in each chicken breast big enough to put the butter in.
5. Put the butter into the chicken breasts and cover it with the surrounding flesh.
6. Coat each chicken breast in flour, egg and breadcrumbs. Make sure none of the chicken meat is left exposed. Refrigerate for one hour.
8. Deep-fry the chicken breasts for about six minutes until golden brown. Finish in a hot oven if required.
9. Serve with watercress.

Trussing

To **truss** a bird, use a trussing needle and butcher's string. A trussing needle is a long steel needle with a curved sharp end that is adapted for passing through poultry carcasses. Butcher's string is sturdy and will not alter when heat is applied. There are several ways to truss a bird and one method is shown below.

Definition

Trussing: a method of securing the bird in an appropriate shape during the cooking process.

How to truss a chicken

Use a string that is approximately four to five times the length of the bird.

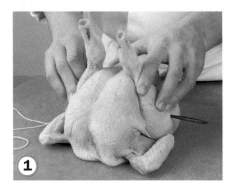

1 Insert the needle between the drumstick and the thigh on one side, through the cavity and out between the thigh and drumstick on the other side.

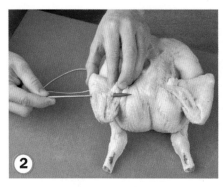

2 Turn the bird over and pass the needle between the two wing bones.

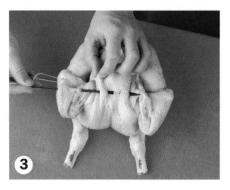

3 Sew down the neck flap.

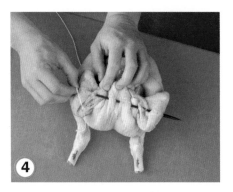

4 Come back through the opposite winglets.

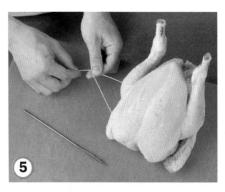

5 Tie securely producing a neat shape.

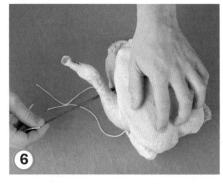

6 Insert the needle through the leg below the bone. Go through the cavity and exit through the other leg below the bone.

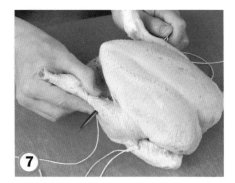

7 Go back through, just above the bone.

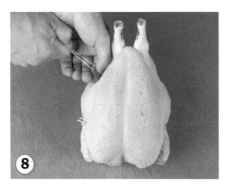

8 Pull the string tight to produce a nice neat shape and tie off.

9 A trussed bird.

Storing prepared poultry

Poultry can contain harmful bacteria, e.g. salmonella. This means it is necessary to store poultry correctly before, during and after preparation:

○ Ensure that raw poultry is stored at the bottom of a refrigerator. This will prevent any blood or liquid dripping onto other foods.
○ Clearly label poultry which has been prepared. The label should include the date so that it is possible to determine its shelf life.
○ Store prepared poultry at 1–5°C.
○ Do not stack prepared poultry on top of each other as it can affect the appearance and quality of the end product.

Cooking and finishing poultry dishes

Cooking methods

After poultry has been prepared correctly, it is important that the correct cooking method is used to ensure a quality dish. The cooking method adopted depends on the dish required. As the chef, you must make sure that you work in a safe manner and that the correct tools, techniques and methods are used.

It is useful to remember that a tough and fibrous bird is best cooked using wet methods of cookery, e.g. stewing, braising or boiling. For tender poultry, dry methods of cooking are appropriate, e.g. roasting, grilling, etc. Overcooking poultry makes it dry and unappealing to eat.

Steaming

For information on steaming, see page 121. See also recipe for chicken liver paté on page 238.

Poaching

White stock is usually used to poach poultry. See pages 122 and 256 for more information. To test whether the poultry is cooked, prick the meat gently. The juices should run clear or white.

Video presentation
Prepare a whole chicken for roasting takes you step-by-step through this procedure. You could also watch *Prepare a chicken for spatchcock.*

Chef's tip
Adding carrots and onions to the poaching liquor can give a delicate flavour to a poultry dish. Leeks and fennel are other good flavours for poultry.

Poached breasts of chicken with mushroom sauce

Preparation	2
Cooking skills	2
Finishing	2

skinless chicken breasts	4
white stock	350ml
butter	25g
mushroom sauce	500ml
mushroom caps	8
salt and pepper	to taste
chopped parsley	to garnish
Cooking time	30 minutes
Serves	4

Method

1. Poach the chicken breasts in white stock for 20 minutes.
2. Slice the mushroom caps.
3. Shallow fry the mushroom caps in butter.
4. Heat the mushroom sauce.
5. Garnish the poached chicken breasts with the cooked mushroom caps, **napper** with the sauce and decorate by sprinkling the chopped parsley over it.

Definition

Napper: a French term meaning to coat or mask a tray of food.

Stewing

Stewing allows you to produce a good-flavoured dish from cheaper cuts of poultry, e.g. the legs or thighs. Vegetables and stock can be added and cooking slowly enables the flavours to infuse or merge.

Towards the end of the cooking time, you may need to thicken a stewed poultry dish. This can be done by **reducing** the liquid so it thickens itself or by using a roux or starch-based sauce method (see Chapter 11). For more information on stewing see page 123.

Definition

Reducing: to boil the liquid rapidly until it reduces in volume.

Coq au vin (chicken in red wine)

chicken	1	**For the garnish:**	
oil	50ml	button mushrooms	100g
bouquet garni	1	lardons of bacon	100g
red wine	100ml	button onions	100g
chicken stock	50ml		
meat glaze	12g		
butter	25g		
flour	25g		
heart-shaped croutons, fried	4		
chopped parsley	to garnish		
Oven temperature	140–160°C		
Cooking time	1–1½ hours		
Serves	4		

Method

1. Cut the chicken for sauté (see page 222).
2. Put the oil in a pan and heat it until there is a blue haze. Put the chicken in the pan.
3. Season chicken and **seal** and colour it quickly.
4. Remove the chicken and place it in a stewing vessel with the bouquet garni.
5. Sauté the onions, mushrooms and lardons in the same pan the chicken was coloured in.
6. Deglaze the pan with the wine and stock. Bring it to the boil.
7. Pour the liquid over the chicken and put a tightly fitting lid over the dish. Cook it in the oven until the chicken is tender.
8. Remove the chicken and garnish it with the mushrooms, lardons and onions.
9. Reduce the sauce by a third and add the meat glaze.
10. Put the butter and flour into a clean bowl. Combine the butter and flour into a paste (beurre manie).
11. Add small amounts of the paste to the liquid.
12. As the liquid boils whisk to obtain the required consistency: thick enough to coat the back of a spoon.
13. Adjust the seasoning.
14. Pour an appropriate amount of the sauce over the chicken and garnishes.
15. Serve with the fried croutons on top, sprinkled with chopped parsley.

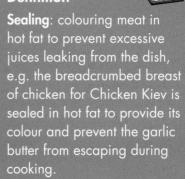

Definition

Sealing: colouring meat in hot fat to prevent excessive juices leaking from the dish, e.g. the breadcrumbed breast of chicken for Chicken Kiev is sealed in hot fat to provide its colour and prevent the garlic butter from escaping during cooking.

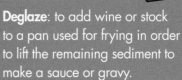

Definition

Deglaze: to add wine or stock to a pan used for frying in order to lift the remaining sediment to make a sauce or gravy.

Frying

Regular turning and checking of the poultry during frying is essential to ensure that the food is cooked right through. Remember that thicker pieces of meat will take longer to cook. For example, chicken drumsticks will require longer cooking than thin strips of breast.

Deep-frying

Pieces of poultry which are deep-fried must be closely monitored to make sure they are thoroughly cooked. Temperature probing or piercing the flesh at the thickest part to see if blood runs from the joint is a good indicator.

Shallow-frying, sautéing and stir-frying

Only good-quality poultry should be used for sauté as the pan is deglazed and a sauce is made from **residues**.

> **Definition**
> **Residue**: the content left in the pan once the poultry has been cooked or sealed, including liquid and solid materials which all contain intense flavours which enhance a dish.

> **Definition**
> **Bonne femme**: dishes that are prepared in a simple rustic style and often served in the container they were cooked in.

> **Definition**
> **Turned potatoes:** potatoes that are cut into a barrel shape before cooking.

Sauté chicken bonne femme

Preparation	4
Cooking skills	3
Finishing	3

chicken cut for sauté (see page 205)	1
lardons of bacon, blanched and sautéed	100g
white wine	100ml
demi-glace	400ml
button onions for garnish	100g
cocotte potatoes	100g
salt and pepper	to season
Cooking time	45 minutes
Serves	4

Method

1 Sauté the chicken. Ensure that the poultry is cooked and coloured evenly. Keep an eye on the poultry as you do not want it to burn; regulate the heat if necessary. Fry off the lardons in the same pan, until they have a slight golden brown colour.
2 Deglaze the sauté pan with the wine.
3 Reduce the liquid by half.
4 Add the demi-glace, adjust the seasoning if required, add the garnishes (lardons, **turned potatoes** and onions), and serve.

For stir-frying, the poultry is cut into thin strips and cooked very quickly – normally for no longer than three to six minutes. This maintains its tenderness and succulence.

Find out!   **Worksheet 24**

List as many poultry dishes as you can that require stir-frying, deep-frying, sautéing or shallow-frying.

For more information in frying see pages 123–124.

Grilling

Chicken or duck breasts are often grilled. When grilling poultry the meat can be placed on a tray or directly onto a clean grill plate. The poultry may be on skewers if you are preparing kebabs. Poultry is usually brushed with butter or (olive) oil to **baste** the meat during grilling. Poultry which has been marinated (see page 227) is suitable for grilling.

Chicken and other poultry must be cooked to at least 63°C. Cooked grilled poultry should be firm to touch and resistant to pressure. Duck breast is an exception to this rule, as it is usually served pink. An average duck breast takes 12 minutes to cook correctly. Overcooking poultry by grilling will make the meat dry and tough. For more information see page 124.

Griddling

A little oil may be used to assist in griddling, or the poultry itself may have been marinated with a little oil before cooking. For more information see page 125.

Roasting

Roasting usually changes the colour of the meat and adds to the meat's appeal. When roasting poultry, place the bird or jointed bird into a hot oven to colour and then turn the temperature down to allow the bird to roast slowly. This keeps the meat moist.

Roasting times for poultry are:
○ Chicken: 200–230°C for 20 minutes per 450g plus 20 minutes.
○ Turkey: 180°C for 15–20 minutes per 450g plus 20 minutes.
○ Duck: 180°C for 30 minutes per 450g.

For more information on roasting see page 125.

Remember!
Grilling poultry is a healthy way of cooking food, as the meat does not absorb much fat. A grilled skinless chicken breast contains only 120 calories per 100g.

Definition
Baste: to moisten with liquid, fat, gravy, etc.

Roast chicken, turkey or duck

Preparation	2
Cooking skills	2
Finishing	3

turkey, chicken or duck	one whole bird
oil	25–35ml
salt and pepper	to season
bed of root	1
Oven temperature	200–230°C for 20 minutes, reducing to 190°C for the remaining time
Cooking time	See page 217 for roasting times
Serves	4 if chicken or duck 6–12 if a turkey

Method

1 Wash the poultry and remove any excess fat.
2 Coat the bird in oil, season and put it on a **bed of root** on its side.
3 Roast for 20 minutes. Reduce the heat. Turn the bird onto its other side. Continue to turn at intervals of 20 minutes to obtain good even colour all over the bird.
4 Finish cooking breast side up.
5 Check internal temperature to ensure bird is cooked correctly.
6 Serve roast chicken with gravy, bread sauce, game chips and watercress. Serve roast turkey with cranberry sauce. For a duck, a fruit-based sauce such as orange or plum is a lovely accompaniment.

Combination cooking

Combination cooking means that more than one method of cooking is used in making a dish. For example, chicken croquettes are a dish where the poultry is boiled or poached, then diced and bound with other ingredients, e.g. mashed potatoes, flour, egg and breadcrumbs, and then deep-fried. See page 126 for more information.

A combination oven uses two different methods of cooking within the same oven. An example of its use is for turkey, which if roasted whole can easily become dry when cooked in an ordinary oven. In a combination oven, the steam coupled with the convection heat will ensure the meat remains moist and of good eating quality.

Video presentation

Watch *Prepare a whole chicken for roasting* before following this recipe.

Definition

Bed of root: chopped root vegetables which act as a base to put the bird on to prevent sticking and burning on the tray.

Video presentation

Prepare a paté from minced liver shows you step by step how to make a liver paté. You could also watch *Prepare a chicken liver*.

Traditional Chicken Maryland

Preparation 1
Cooking skills 2
Finishing 2

For the chicken:

flour for coating	
fresh breadcrumbs	225g
salt and freshly ground black pepper	
chicken breasts	4
eggs, beaten	2
oil, for frying	
butter	30g
streaky bacon	4 rashers

For the sweetcorn fritters:		**For the banana fritters:**	
flour	100g	vegetable oil, for deep frying	
egg	1	plain flour	175g
sweetcorn	200g	ice-cold water (for batter)	about 100ml
water	150ml	bananas, cut into thick chunks	3
salt	1 pinch		
Oven temperature	180°C		
Cooking time	15 minutes		
Serves	4		

Method

1 Preheat the oven to 180°C.
2 For the chicken, place breadcrumbs in a bowl and season well with salt and freshly ground black pepper.
3 Season the chicken, coat in flour and dip into the beaten egg, then the breadcrumb mixture, to coat all over.
4 Heat the oil in a frying pan and fry the chicken for about 12 minutes over a medium heat, turning frequently, until crisp and golden-brown.
5 Dot the chicken breasts with butter, place onto a baking sheet and transfer to the oven. Bake for ten minutes, or until the chicken is completely cooked through.
6 For the banana fritters, place the vegetable oil into a deep, heavy-bottomed saucepan and heat until a small cube of bread sizzles and turns golden when dropped into it.

7 Place the flour into a bowl and add enough water to make a smooth batter. Dip the banana pieces into the batter to coat.
8 Carefully place the bananas into the hot oil and deep fry for 4–5 minutes, or until crisp and golden-brown.
9 Sieve flour in a bowl and add salt.
10 Make a well in the centre, add egg and milk and gradually incorporate.
11 Beat to a smooth batter.
12 Add sweetcorn (which should be fully drained if using canned).
13 Using a tablespoon, place a tablespoon of the mixture into hot fat, cooking for 3 minutes. Turn over half way through.
14 Grill the streaky bacon until coloured and slightly crisp.
15 To serve, garnish the cooked chicken maryland with the sweetcorn, banana fritters and the streaky bacon.

Chicken liver pâté

butter	20g
onion, chopped	30g
garlic, chopped	1 clove
lean pork, diced	100g
fat pork, diced	100g
chicken livers	300g
bay leaf	1
thyme	1 sprig
chervil	1 sprig
nutmeg, mace, allspice	pinch of each
parsley stalks	small bunch
seasoning	to taste
brandy	50ml
double cream	30ml
unsmoked bacon, thinly sliced	300g
Oven temperature	175°C
Cooking time	1 hour
Serves (approx.)	6–8

Method

1 Melt the butter in a heavy frying pan and add onions and garlic. Allow to sweat without colour until soft.
2 Add the fat pork and lean pork and cook until sealed with minimum browning.
3 Add the herbs and spices and the chicken livers, which need to be sealed without cooking through.
4 Remove the pan from the heat, take out the bay leaf and herb stalks.
5 Pass the mixture through the fine plate of a mincer and then a fine sieve.
6 Add the brandy and cream, mixing in well, and correct the seasoning.
7 Line the terrine with the thinly sliced bacon allowing extra length over the sides to fold over the top so that the mixture is fully enclosed.
8 Fill the terrine with the mixture and fold the bacon slice ends over the top neatly. Cover with the lid of the terrine.
9 Place the terrine in a deep tray half full of hot water and cook in a moderate oven (175°C) for approximately 1 hour. To test if thoroughly cooked, pierce with a needle, which should emerge clean and hot if the pâté is adequately cooked in the centre.
10 While the pâté is cooling, remove the lid and place a suitably sized block of plastic or wood (thoroughly wrapped in foil or cling film) on the surface of the terrine with a 1 kg weight on the top to compress the mixture.
11 If the pâté is required to be displayed whole, dip the container in hot water and turn out.
12 Otherwise, keep chilled and serve slices as required, usually accompanied with freshly made toast.

Hot holding, finishing and serving

Once you have worked hard to prepare and cook a dish, it is really important to be able to serve it with the correct garnish and at the right temperature.

Hot holding the poultry at the right temperature is also about complying with the law. The Food Safety Act 1990 states that hot food must be served and held at a temperature of at least 63°C. This makes sure that potentially harmful bacteria will not multiply and harm the consumer.

Finishing the poultry dish correctly is very important. You should always check a dish before it is served and ask yourself the following questions:

○ Is the poultry at the correct temperature for service?
○ Does the dish have the correct flavour?
○ Does it need more seasoning?
○ Do I have the correct garnish for the dish?
○ Do I have the right equipment to finish and serve the dish?

You can finish poultry by:

○ coating it with a sauce, e.g. duck is often coated with orange sauce
○ glazing it by brushing it with butter, oils or dish residue to add an attractive gloss, e.g. a barbecue marinade.

Find out!

Worksheet 25

List as many garnishes as you can that would be suitable for the following dishes:

○ Roast chicken
○ Chicken bonne femme
○ Chicken Maryland
○ Turkey fricassee
○ Roast turkey
○ Peking duck
○ Duck in orange sauce
○ Roast duck.

Garnishing means adding the final touches to enhance a dish. Appropriate garnishes for poultry dishes are other cooked ingredients, e.g. bacon rolls, stuffing and bread sauce for roast chicken, or a sprinkling of parsley over a casserole to add colour.

Serving

The equipment required to finish and serve poultry includes:
○ serving platters (earthenware or metal)
○ serving utensils, e.g. spoons, tongs, slices or forks.

The service area for a dish should be clean, presentable and appealing to customers at all times.

Test yourself!

1 State two actions to be taken when a problem is encountered with quality of poultry.

2 List two ingredients which can be used to garnish a roasted chicken.

3 What is the correct holding temperature for cooked poultry?
   a 62°C
   b 63°C
   c 64°C
   d 65°C

4 What internal temperature should poultry be cooked to?
   a 62°C
   b 63°C
   c 64°C
   d 65°C

5 State two ways to reduce fat in poultry dishes.

6 List five different types of poultry.

7 Complete the following sentences.
   When selecting a duck for use, check the following points:
   a The skin is _____ in colour.
   b The duck is _____, especially in the _____ region.
   c The skin is _____ and free from _____, _____ or _____.
   d It smells _____.

8 What do the following words mean? Write a definition for each.
   a Trimming.
   b Portioning.

9 What is the correct temperature for stuffing or filling?
   a 1–5°C
   b 2–6°C
   c 3–5°C
   d 5–8°C.

10 For how long would you roast the following birds?
   a A chicken weighing 3kg.
   b A chicken weighing 1.5kg.
   c A turkey weighing 5.5kg.

9

Fish and shellfish

This chapter covers skills and knowledge in the following units:

- 7132 Unit 220 (2FP1) Prepare fish for basic dishes
- 7132 Unit 227 (2FC1) Cook and finish basic fish dishes
- 7132 Unit 221 (2FP2) Prepare shellfish for basic dishes
- 7132 Unit 228 (2FC2) Cook and finish basic shellfish dishes
- 7091 Unit 267 Preparation, cooking and finishing of fish dishes

Working through this chapter could also provide the opportunity to practise the following Functional Skills at Level 2:
Functional ICT Developing, presenting and communicating information – use appropriate field names and data types to organise information

In this chapter you will learn how to:

Understand how and be able to prepare fish for basic dishes	7132 – 220.1,2	7091 – 267.1
Understand how and be able to cook basic fish dishes	7132 – 227.1,2	7091 – 267.2
Understand how and be able to finish basic fish dishes	7132 – 227.3,4	7091 – 267.3
Understand how and be able to prepare shellfish for basic dishes	7132 – 221.1,2	
Understand how and be able to cook basic shellfish dishes	7132 – 228.1,2	
Understand how and be able to finish basic shellfish dishes	7132 – 228.3,4	

You will learn how to prepare and cook basic fish and shellfish dishes, including:

- sea bass with capers
- deep-fried cod in batter
- moules marinière.

Types of fish and shellfish

Types of fish

White flat fish

This category includes the following types of fish:

o dover sole

o brill

o halibut

o turbot

o lemon sole

o plaice.

White flat fish have white flesh and are flat. Turbot, brill and halibut are very large flat fish, but are readily available from suppliers and popular in many fine restaurants. The cuts of flat fish are different to those of round fish.

Figure 9.1 a Dover sole, b brill, c halibut, d turbot, e lemon sole, f plaice

White round fish

The following types of white round fish are included at NVQ Level 2:

o cod

o hake

o haddock

o monkfish

o whiting

o huss.

These round fish are relatively common in UK coastal waters. Like flat fish, their flesh is white but the cuts are different.

Figure 9.2 a cod, b hake, c haddock, d monkfish, e whiting

Oily fish

This category includes the following fish:

○ mackerel

○ salmon

○ trout

○ tuna

○ herring

○ sardines

○ anchovies.

All oily fish are round and the flesh is darker than that of white fish. White fish contain oil, but only in their livers, whereas oily fish have oil throughout their bodies.

Oily fish are usually cooked by dry methods such as grilling or baking.

Figure 9.3 a mackerel, b salmon, c trout

Types of shellfish

Crustaceans

Crustaceans included in NVQ Level 2:

○ prawns

○ shrimp.

Other types of crustacean often used in cooking :

○ crab

○ lobster

○ crayfish

○ langoustine (Dublin bay prawn).

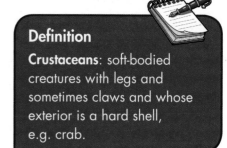

Definition

Crustaceans: soft-bodied creatures with legs and sometimes claws and whose exterior is a hard shell, e.g. crab.

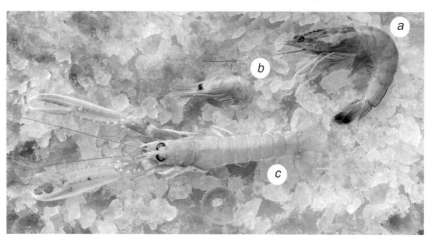

Figure 9.4 a tiger prawn, b shrimp, c langoustine

Molluscs

Molluscs included in NVQ Level 2:

o mussels

o cockles

o clams

o squids (a cephalopod).

Other types of mollusc used in cooking:

o oysters (a bivalve mollusc)

o scallops (a bivalve mollusc).

Quality of fish and shellfish

Figure 9.5 a parlourdes clams, b amande clams, c mussels

Fish and shellfish can be obtained fresh, canned, salted, pickled, vacuum-packed or frozen. It is best to purchase only fresh fish and shellfish. Once killed, fish and shellfish will deteriorate very quickly if not stored correctly. If you are unsure of the quality of the fish or shellfish, do not use it. Ask your supervisor for advice.

The quality points below can indicate freshness in all types of fish (whole, fresh or frozen):

o The eyes should be clear and raised, not sunken.

o It should not smell of ammonia or have an unpleasant smell.

o There should be slime on it and its skin should be moist.

o Its gills should be bright and pink.

o It should be firm in texture.

o It should have no external damage, e.g. cuts, damaged fins.

o The scales should be firmly attached and shiny.

o It should be kept at the correct temperature (–18 to –25°C for frozen, under 5°C for fresh).

o If frozen, there should be no evidence of freezer burn.

o Once thawed it should have firm flesh.

Listed below are quality points for shellfish, alive and frozen:

o It should be kept at the correct temperature (–18°C or below for frozen, under 5°C for fresh).

o There must be no freezer burn on the flesh or skin.

o Fresh shellfish should be alive.

o The open shells of mussels or clams will close if tapped. If they do not, discard them.

o It should have a fresh salty smell.

Definition

Molluscs: soft-bodied creatures contained in a hard shell, e.g. mussels.

Healthy eating

Fish is a healthy food source in its natural state. The addition of rich ingredients may make it unhealthier (e.g. cream sauces) but generally the flesh of fish is a healthy source of protein.

Did you know?

All fish and shellfish contain high levels of vitamins A, B and D.

Did you know?

Fish contains high levels of monosaturated fat, which has no impact on cholesterol levels.

○ All claws and legs should be intact and not damaged.

○ Live shellfish, e.g. lobster, should be lively not limp.

○ There should not be too many barnacles on the shells.

○ Shellfish should be a good weight in proportion to their size.

Find out!

Worksheet 26

Visit a fish market or supermarket and make a list of all the types of fish and shellfish. Categorise the fish into flat, round and oily. Categorise the shellfish into cephalopods, bivalves or univalves.

Video presentation

Watch *Quality points of fish* to see this.

Remember!

Any shellfish that has its shell open before preparation is probably dead.

Preparing fish and shellfish

Preparation methods

Washing

Washing fish and shellfish is important during the preparation phase. Washing should be carried out regularly during preparation as fresh fish can be quite messy and the washing process should be thorough. Fish and shellfish should be run under cold water. The reasons fish and shellfish should be washed:

○ To remove impurities such as sand and other physical contamination.

○ To wash any slime away from the skin before preparing.

○ To wash away any liquid which may have built up while being stored.

○ There may be blood or traces of scales or stomach contents after gutting and these must be removed.

○ The shells may have had barnacles removed, so washing will remove any loose debris.

○ To keep them clean.

Marcus says

When preparing fish and shellfish be careful with any cuts or abrasions on your skin. Infections can result, so remember to scrub your hands afterwards!

Shelling

Shelling means removing the shell to leave the soft edible flesh of the mollusc or crustacean. While shellfish can be cooked with their shells intact, some dishes require the shell to be removed. Oysters must have their shells opened before being served raw. Scallops may have the shell removed.

How to shell a prawn

Prawns may be shelled before or after cooking. The process in both cases is the same.

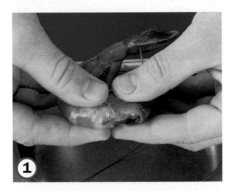

1

Pull the head from the prawn. Put it in a separate bowl.

2

Starting from the underside, peel away the shell in a rolling motion. The body will separate from the shell.

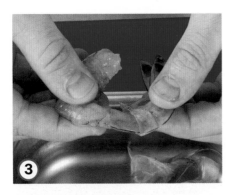

3

The tail section will require a gentle pull to extract it from the shell.

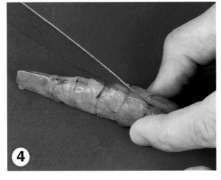

4

Make a shallow cut along the back of the prawn to expose the intestinal tract.

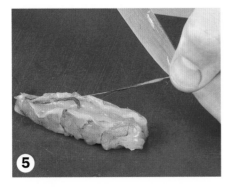

5

Grasp the intestinal tract between your thumb and the blade of a paring knife. Gently extract ensuring the entire tract is removed.

6

Rinse the prawns and put them in a clean bowl until required.

Video presentation

You could now watch *Prepare prawns* to see this being done.

How to prepare mussels

1 Purge mussels in a container of cold water for several hours.

2 Mussels must only be used if they are perfectly fresh. Check each one by tapping it against the side of the sink.

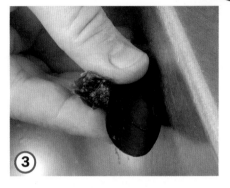

3 The shell of a fresh mussel should be closed or should close when tapped to indicate it is still alive. Discard any that do not close.

4 Wash under cold running water while scraping with a small paring knife to remove barnacles.

5 Remove the byssus threads by pulling with your fingers or use your thumb and the paring knife.

Video presentation
You may wish to watch *Prepare mussels* to see this being done.

How to remove a mollusc from its shell

Shellfish open their shells when cooked. Removing a mollusc is simple. Use either your hands or a small knife to pull the mollusc from its attachment.

Cuts

Numerous cuts can be taken from flat and round fish. The table below identifies these.

Cut	Description of cut	Appearance
Fillet	This is flesh which is free from skin and bone. It is usually the whole fillet and will therefore vary in size. A plaice fillet will be much smaller than that of a salmon.	
Supreme	A piece of fillet that has been cut across a large fillet at an angle. This cut is usually reserved for larger types of fish such as cod or salmon.	
Goujon	A strip cut from a large fillet. A goujon is usually coated in breadcrumbs before cooking.	
Paupiette	A flattened piece of filleted fish, which is then stuffed and rolled.	
Delice	A neatly folded and trimmed flat fish fillet.	
Medallion	Similar to a supreme but trimmed further to form a round or oval shape. (Monkfish is often cut into medallions.)	
Darne	A slice cut across the bone from a round fish.	
Tronçon	A finger-shaped cut from a flat fish across its body width. The thickness will vary depending on the type of flat fish.	

Figure 9.6 Different cuts of fish

Try this!   Worksheet 27

Look at the table above. Cover up the writing. Can you identify the photographs of the different cuts?

Video presentation

For guidance on how to make these cuts watch: *Prepare a whole halibut and cut tronçons; Prepare a whole cod and cut darnes; Cut supremes of salmon; Prepare paupiettes of plaice; Prepare delices of plaice; Cut goujons of plaice.*

Trimming

Trimming fish means to remove the fins, gills, eyes, head and scales. Gills, eyes and fins are usually removed by cutting them out or off using kitchen scissors. Kitchen scissors are used as they are robust and sturdy.

Shellfish (e.g. mussels) have byssus threads (threadlike attachments) hanging from their shells. They use these to attach themselves to rocks or other static structures. Use a knife to pull away these strings, and wash the shellfish again.

Video presentation

Watch *Trim a whole salmon* for more information.

How to remove the scales from a fish

Here we use a medium-sized serrated knife which is suitable for the removal of scales from a large fish such as salmon. A filleting knife would be more suitable for a smaller fish, e.g. herring or trout. Fishmongers sometimes use a special type of wire brush.

Lay the fish on a blue chopping board. Cut off the fins using fish scissors.

Scrape the knife blade against the scales of the fish in the opposite direction to that in which they lie. Ensure you hold the fish firmly by the tail to prevent accidents. This scraping motion will lift the scales and any surplus slime from the fish's body. Wash the fillet.

Filleting

Filleting is a complex knife skill, which is an essential part of preparing fish. Filleting is the removal of the flesh from the bones and skin. For large fish this helps with portion control.

The equipment and tools used for filleting fish are:

o a blue chopping board, secured to a flat work surface
o suitable filleting knife with a sharp, flexible blade
o container for waste products
o tray for the fillets
o tweezers to remove pin bones (small bones) left in the fillet
o kitchen scissors which can be used to trim away fins.

Figure 9.7 The tools required for filleting fish

The process for filleting a flat fish is different from that of filleting a round one. Usually the preferred knife to use is a 7-inch blade which is flexible to aid the filleting process. If the flat fish is large (e.g. a turbot), a knife with a sturdy blade is needed for safety.

How to fillet a flat fish (plaice)

Lay the fish flat on the chopping board. Cut around the head with the point of the knife until you reach the lateral line.

Cut down the central lateral line until the knife reaches the rib bones. Then cut along the lateral line as far as the tail.

Bending the flexible blade, sweep the knife smoothly against the bones to remove the flesh. Cutting motions will leave flesh on the bone and affect the presentation of the fillet.

Cut the fillet away from the fins and place it on a tray. Turn the fish round and remove the other fillet in the same manner.

Trim up the fillet to remove the fins.

How to fillet a round fish (salmon)

The fish must already be gutted and trimmed.

1

Lay the fish flat on the chopping board. Use a knife which has at least a 7-inch flexible blade and is sharp. Cut behind the fins and gills to give access to the backbone.

2

Cut along the backbone of the fish around the rib cage. Lift the fillet off the bones as you are cutting.

3

Continue to cut, lifting the fillet off the bones.

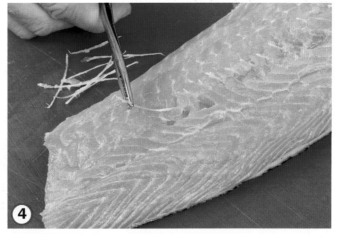

4

Place the fillet on the chopping board. Run your fingers along the flesh to locate any pin bones and remove them using tweezers.

Repeat the process on the other side of the fish.

Try this!   Worksheet 28

Close your book and write down the five steps you should follow to fillet a flat fish.

Video presentation
Watch *Fillet a salmon* to see this in action.

Skinning

While skin is usually edible on fish, some dish requirements mean that it needs to be removed. This is quite difficult. When skinning, you must not damage the flesh of the fish, so specific knife techniques are needed.

Skinning usually occurs once the fillets of the fish have been removed. The exception is a whole flat fish. In this case the whole skin is removed by making an incision at the tail and then pulling the skin from the flesh to the head.

The equipment needed for skinning is:
○ a blue chopping board
○ a flexible filleting knife
○ salt or a clean cloth
○ a container for waste products
○ a tray to place the skinned fillets on.

Video presentation
Watch a skilled chef at work in *Skin a salmon fillet*.

How to skin a fillet

To provide grip when you grasp the tail end of the fillet either dip your fingers in some salt before you begin or use a cloth to hold the tail.

① Place the fillet on the chopping board. Cut into the end of the tail section until the knife is touching or lying on the skin at an angle of 45°.

② Take a firm hold of the tail skin and keep a firm grip on the knife. Use a sawing action, moving both the skin and knife at the same time. You will see the fillet come away from the skin and the angle of the knife will mean that no flesh will remain on the skin.

③ Trim any untidy pieces of fillet away to leave a neat, clean skinned fillet.

Preparing a whole fish

Fish such as trout, salmon, sole and plaice can be prepared whole ready for cooking.

How to prepare a whole round fish

1 Remove the eyes and gills.
2 Gut the fish (removing innards).
3 Remove the scales and trim the fins.
4 Wash thoroughly.

How to prepare a whole flat fish

1 Remove the eyes and gills.
2 Gut the fish.
3 Remove the skin (see skinning on page 252).
4 Wash thoroughly.

Coating

This is when the fish – either whole or in portions – is covered in an outer coating of batter, flour, egg and breadcrumbs or seasoned flour.

The purpose of this coating is:
○ to protect the delicate flesh inside (this the main reason)
○ to enhance the appearance of the fish dish
○ to meet recipe requirements.

Some fish dishes that are coated are:
○ cod in batter – the fish is coated in batter
○ plaice meunière – the fish is coated in flour
○ goujons of plaice – the fish is coated in flour, egg and breadcrumbs.

Batter is a mix of eggs, flour and liquid which can be water or milk, or even beer. When deep-fried batter forms a crispy coating around the fish. When cooked it is usually golden brown.

Flour is usually seasoned and when fried it provides a golden coating. The flesh can still be seen.

Flour, eggs and breadcrumbs provide a golden crispy coating when shallow- or deep-fried.

Video presentation
Coat goujons of plaice (pané l'ànglaise) shows you how to coat goujons in seasoned flour, beaten egg and breadcrumbs.

Marinating

Marinating is a technique used to flavour fish. It can be done by combining a cooked or uncooked liquid or paste with the fish in a dish. The liquid or paste is called a marinade. It contains ingredients which will alter and enhance the flavour of the fish which is being marinated.

The fish can be left in the marinade for short or long periods. The fish should be covered completely by the liquid or paste.

If a whole fish is used (e.g. trout), incisions can be cut into the body of the fish to allow the flavour of the marinade to merge into the fish.

Did you know?

Marinade ingredients can include yoghurt, olive oil, garlic, curry pastes, lemon juice, and fresh herbs.
The combination of these ingredients makes excellent barbecue dishes.

Tools and equipment

The tools and equipment relevant to the preparation of fish and shellfish at NVQ Level 2:

o Blue chopping board

o Filleting knife

o Oyster knife to open oysters

o Kitchen scissors for trimming fins and gills

o Tweezers for removing small pin bones from fillets

o Plastic trays to lay fish on

o Salt to use when grasping fish for skinning

Storage

The storage of fish and shellfish before preparation is very important, as these food types are high-risk and can cause serious food poisoning if not handled correctly.

Storage before use

Fresh fish must be stored in a refrigerator at below 5°C. It will remain fresher longer if stored on ice.

Fresh shellfish must be stored in a cold room or refrigerator, covered with a damp cloth. Tanks will prolong the life of the shellfish, but generally it should be used on the day it is purchased or received for best quality.

Frozen fish and shellfish must be wrapped correctly and frozen at -18°C or below. Defrosting fish and shellfish should be done in a controlled way, by putting the items into a fridge or cold room inside a container. This is because leaving these items out at room temperature may cause harmful bacteria to multiply rapidly.

Storage once prepared

Shellfish should really be prepared and cooked immediately; however, this is not always possible. Once any fish or shellfish has been prepared, if it is not required for immediate use it must be put back onto the bottom shelf of a refrigerator below 5°C, covered and labelled with the date on it.

Cooking and finishing basic fish and shellfish dishes

It is important to note that most shellfish dishes are washed, cooked and then prepared.

Cooking methods

Boiling

Boiling is the most common method of cooking shellfish. Fish are not usually boiled – poaching is the more appropriate technique.

Marcus says

Remember when cooking salmon, which can be eaten raw, that it doesn't need to be cooked all the way through. It will continue to cook even when it's off the heat!

Moules marinière

mussels, washed and scraped	1kg
fish stock	200ml
dry white wine	100ml
onion, finely diced	50g
lemon juice	a squeeze
salt and cayenne pepper	to taste
beurre manie	30g
chopped parsley	to garnish
Cooking time	25–35 minutes
Serves	2

Method

1 Put mussels, stock, wine, onion, lemon juice, and seasoning in a pan. Cover with a lid and bring to the boil.
2 Cook for a few minutes, then remove the shellfish. All the shells should be open. Discard any which are closed.
3 Bring the liquor to the boil.
4 Add the **beurre manie** in small pieces to thicken the liquid.
5 Serve the sauce over the mussels. Sprinkle with parsley.

Definition

Beurre manie: Equal quantities of plain flour and butter mixed together to form a paste and added to a boiling liquid in small quantities as a thickening agent.

Steaming

All types of fish and shellfish are suitable for steaming. Steamed fish is often eaten by people on diets or people who are unwell because it ensures maximum nutritional content.

Poaching

Poaching is a common cooking method for fish. The amount of liquid used is dependant on the size of the fish cut or the shellfish to be cooked. A whole salmon will clearly need more liquid than a salmon darne.

The equipment used to poach fish should be a heavy-based pan with a lid, or a lipped tray, which will hold liquid. If using a tray, place buttered greaseproof paper over the food to keep the fish moist and prevent it from drying out.

All poaching is started on the top of a stove, but some poached fish can be finished in an oven.

Did you know?

Fish and shellfish can be cooked in their natural state. However, many dishes combine other ingredients, e.g. soups, chowders, curries, stews and casseroles. The nutritional value may alter if different ingredients are added, e.g. calorific content may increase if fish and shellfish are mixed with dairy items.

Fish stock or a court bouillon (see Chapter 11) is usually the appropriate liquor used to poach fish and this fish stock takes 30 minutes to prepare and cook.

When poaching fish or shellfish, bring the liquid to the boil and then simmer gently. The liquid may form part of a sauce to accompany the dish.

There are two types of poaching: deep poaching and shallow poaching.

Deep poaching is when a whole fish or cut is totally immersed in a special pan called a fish kettle (see Figure 9.9). The skin is left on to protect the flesh of the fish but it is removed later on. The liquid in which the fish or shellfish is poached is more acidic than when poaching in the conventional manner.

Shallow poaching is when the fish or cut is placed in a tray or pan. Liquid, either stock or milk, is added but does not cover the whole fish or cut. The liquid is brought to the boil the dish may be finished in the oven.

Before putting the dish in the oven, a cartouche (buttered piece of greaseproof paper) is placed over the fish to keep the steam in and to keep the fish moist during cooking.

Frying

Deep-frying

Fish or shellfish are usually coated in a batter (fish and chips) or breadcrumbs (scampi or goujons) before being deep-fried. These coatings provide a crisp texture to fish and shellfish and protect them from being damaged by the hot oil. Coatings include batters and breadcrumbs.

Batters consist of flour, eggs and baking powder or yeast mixed with water, milk or beer. The yeast or baking powder **aerates** the batter and makes it lighter.

Breadcrumbs – the fish is coated in flour and dipped in egg wash (beaten egg) before being passed through fresh breadcrumbs. The coating is sealed by the hot oil, keeping the fish or shellfish (scampi) moist. Breadcrumbs colour very quickly, so the temperature has to be checked carefully. Breadcrumbed fish can be deep-fried and then finished in the oven.

Video presentation

See how to poach salmon in court bouillon in *Poach a salmon fillet.*

Figure 9.8 A fish kettle is the perfect tool for deep poaching a whole fish

Chef's tip

Whole fish should be placed in cold court bouillon to cook. Fish cuts should be placed in hot court bouillon, as the heat seals the outer part of the cut, trapping the juices inside immediately.

Definition

Aerate: to introduce air into a mixture or liquid, making the texture lighter.

All fish can be deep-fried, as can many types of shellfish, e.g. cod, plaice, scampi (langoustines) and prawns (coated). Hot oil cooks the fish quickly. However, if the oil is too cool it will take longer to cook the fish and more fat will be absorbed. A thermostatically controlled deep fat fryer is required to deep-fry fish.

Deep-fried cod in batter

		Preparation	2
		Cooking skills	2
		Finishing	2

cod fillets	250g
seasoned flour	50g
vegetable/corn oil	to fill friture two-thirds
frying batter	75ml
salt and pepper	to taste
lemon wedges	2
parsley sprigs	
Cooking temperature	180°C
Serves	2

Method

1   Pass the fillets through the seasoned flour and shake off any excess.
2   Heat the oil.
3   Place the floured fillets in the frying batter. Allow a few seconds for any excess to run off and then place into hot oil.
4   Cook until golden brown in colour.
5   Remove with a spider, drain off excess oil from the battered fillet, add salt and pepper to taste and serve with lemon wedges and a deep-fried parsley sprig.

Shallow-frying

Shallow-frying in a frying or sauté pan can make a fish or shellfish dish more appealing and also add colour to the product. Plaice coated in seasoned flour with the addition of a nut butter sauce (beurre noisette) is a traditional recipe for shallow-frying, called 'à la meunière'.

Fish and shellfish can be shallow-fried in pieces (medallions) as steaks, darnes, troncons, and even whole (trout). The length of cooking time will vary. A whole trout will take significantly longer to cook than monkfish medallions. Sometimes fish is quickly **seared** in hot fat to give it a crisp outside and give a subtle additional flavour.

Video presentation

Watch *Deep fry goujons* to see a chef cook this dish and use a deep fat fryer safely.

Remember!

Safety when deep-frying is crucial as fat fires can cause major damage. Always have a fire blanket in the area in case of fire and never use a friture or industrial fat fryer if you have not been trained.

Chef's tip

When shallow-frying always lay the fillets in the pan presentation-side down first as the oil is cleaner and free of any impurities, apply colour, then turn over to avoid over-handling.

Definition

Seared: cooked quickly in hot fat to add colour.

Some fish dishes require no coating on the fish. Shellfish such as prawns may be shallow-fried with just the addition of some chilli or garlic.

Fish such as sea bass should be placed skin-side down first and cooked until crisp and golden.

To shallow-fry fish you will need:
o a fish slice or palette knife and other utensils such as tongs to turn the fillets or shellfish
o trays and wires to place the cooked fish or shellfish on.

Grilling

Overcooking fish or shellfish by grilling will make them dry. Your skill and experience is required to identify when the fish is cooked. (Firm flesh, correct core temperature, correct colour, crispy skin are all signs.)

Cooking times will vary depending on the type and thickness of the fish cut.

Preparation	3
Cooking skills	2
Finishing	2

Grilled sea bass with capers

sea bass	4 fillets, each about 175g
salt and pepper	to taste
melted butter	25g
chopped parsley	15g
tiny capers	55g
shallot, finely chopped	1
garlic clove, sliced	1
grain mustard	2 teaspoons
lemon juice	¼ lemon
Cooking time	12–15 minutes
Serves	4

Method

1 Lightly oil a suitable tray for grilling.
2 Season the flesh side of the fish then lay the fillets skin-side up on the tray.
3 Brush the fish with melted butter.
4 Place the fish under a heated grill for about four minutes until just done (depending on the thickness of the fish flesh).
5 Place all the remaining ingredients into a pan and gently warm through.
6 Check the seasoning then pour the capers mixture over the cooked fillet and serve.

Most fish are suitable for grilling, as are crustaceans like prawns. Other shellfish like cockles, whelks and mussels are not usually grilled.

Some fish cuts that have been coated in breadcrumbs may also be grilled. Dip the fish in melted butter and breadcrumbs rather than flour, egg and breadcrumbs.

To grill whole fish and large fillets, score or make incisions on the skin side of the fish to enable the heat to penetrate the whole fish. Trout is a good example of a whole fish suitable for grilling.

Baking

Baking tends to dry out the fish, so various methods are used to keep the fish moist:

o Wrap the fish in foil.
o Place the fish or cut into a greaseproof bag (en papillote).
o Stuff the inside of the fish so moisture steams through the fish.
o Wrap pastry around the fish (en croute).
o Bake the fish in a sauce.
o Combine steam and dry heat in a combination oven.

<table>
<tr><td>

Remember!

When handling hot equipment:
o wear protective clothing
o have a dry oven cloth to hold hot equipment
o have ready utensils such as tongs, palette knife or a slice to agitate and move the item.

</td></tr>
</table>

Figure 9.9 Preparing a fish en papillote is just one way of protecting it during baking

<table>
<tr><td>

Try this!

As Asian foods are becoming more and more popular, try cooking fish with spices. Marinate some white cod fillets or other white fish with tandoori paste and natural yoghurt for 60 minutes and then bake in an oven. Served with rice and a salad it makes for a great alternative fish dish at a barbecue or a dinner.

</td></tr>
</table>

Remember!

Always use a dry cloth when handling trays from the oven to reduce the risk of burning yourself.

Fish pie

warm milk	500ml
butter/margarine	50g
flour	25g
fish (cod, salmon, smoked haddock)	400g
prawns (preferably raw)	100g
egg, hard boiled	2
parsley, chopped	1 tbsp
seasoning	to taste
potatoes	450g
Oven temperature	180°C
Cooking time	20 minutes
Serves	4

Preparation	2
Cooking skills	2
Finishing	2

Method

1. Melt 25g of butter/margarine in a thick bottomed pan, add the flour and stir to form a blond roux.
2. Gradually add the milk, stirring all the time, to prevent any lumps forming in the sauce.
3. Cook the sauce out.
4. When cooked out, strain into a clean pan, correct the seasoning and keep hot.
5. Wash, peel and cut the potatoes into cubes. Place into salted water and bring to the boil. Simmer until cooked.
6. Cut the fish into 1 inch cubes. Add to the sauce.
7. Chop the hard boiled egg. Add to the sauce.
8. Add the prawns and correct the seasoning. Add chopped parsley.
9. Place mixture in a casserole dish.
10. Drain the potatoes; mash them with a little butter and seasoning until smooth. Place into a piping bag.
11. Carefully pipe over the fish mixture.
12. Brush with egg wash.
13. Bake in a hot oven until golden brown, for approximately 20 minutes.

An alternative topping: wholemeal breadcrumbs, grated cheese, chopped mixed herbs and seasoning, mixed together and placed over the fish mixture.

Thai fish cakes in coconut sauce

white fish fillets (cod or haddock)	450g
spring onions	5
garlic	3 cloves
red chillies	2
fresh ginger, grated	1 tsp
lemon grass	1 stalk
fish sauce	2 tablespoons
white pepper	to taste
onion, thinly sliced	1
coconut milk	1 tin
fresh basil, chopped	small bunch
sugar	2 tbsp
oil, for frying	
Serves	4

Method

1 Skin the fish and remove bones. Place the fish, spring onions, garlic, 1 red chilli, lemon grass and half the ginger in a food processor and blend to a smooth paste.
2 Add half the fish sauce and white pepper and a little water to make a smooth paste.
3 Heat some oil in a pan or wok and fry tablespoon sized flattened patties of the fish mixture.
4 Cook till golden brown on both sides and set aside.
5 Fry the onion until golden brown.
6 Add the coconut milk and the rest of the chillies and ginger, simmer for ten minutes.
7 Add the rest of the fish sauce, basil and sugar.
8 Return the fish cakes to the sauce and heat through.
9 Serve with plain boiled rice.

Thai poached salmon

long grain rice	125g
Thai red or green curry paste	1 tbsp
coconut cream	200ml
skinless salmon fillets	2
fine green beans, trimmed	handful
fresh coriander leaves	handful
Serves	2

Preparation	1
Cooking skills	1
Finishing	1

Method

1 Heat a medium sized frying pan. Add curry paste and cook, stirring, for a few seconds. Gradually stir in the coconut cream and bring to a simmer.
2 Add salmon fillets, cover and simmer for 7–8 minutes, turning the fish over halfway.
3 Cook rice according to the packet instructions.
4 Blanch green beans in a pan of simmering water until just tender. Drain and divide between 2 hot serving plates.
5 Stir some fresh coriander leaves into the sauce. Top the beans with the salmon, spooning over the sauce. Garnish with coriander and serve with the cooked rice.

Grilled mackerel and mustard sauce

mackerel	4
seasoned flour	50g
salt and pepper	to taste
melted butter or oil	2 tbsp
mustard sauce	500mls
serves	4

Preparation	2
Cooking skills	1
Finishing	1

Method

1 This dish can be made with fillets of mackerel or whole mackerel. In both cases these are grilled.
2 Remove the head and clean the fish.
3 Fillet the fish carefully. (See page 250.) Wash and dry.
4 Trim off all fins and excess rib bones, trim the tail.
5 Wash well and dry.
6 Pass the fillets through seasoned flour. Shake off all excess flour.
7 Place the fillets on a greased baking tray, flesh side down.
8 Brush with melted butter or oil.
9 Grill on both sides under the salamander.

Mustard sauce

margarine, butter or oil	50g
plain flour	50g
milk	500ml
diluted English mustard	to taste
seasoning	

Method

1 Melt the margarine, butter or oil in a thick bottomed pan.
2 Add the flour and mix in to make a roux.
3 Cook out for a few minutes over a gentle heat without colouring.
4 Gradually add the warmed milk and stir until smooth.
5 Allow to simmer for 20–30 minutes. Correct the seasoning.
6 Add the mustard.

Serving

Fish and shellfish are high-risk foods. They must be cooked to a temperature of 63°C or above (except for oysters which are eaten raw).

Once cooked and held at service temperature of 63°C, fish will dry out quickly. Therefore it is important to cook and serve fish and shellfish as required or to order.

Garnishes for fish and shellfish are specific to the dish requirement. Garnishes are used to make the finished dish look more appealing. Accompaniments are other sauces or foods used to enhance the finished dish, or are simply good to eat with the cooked fish. Some traditional garnishes and accompaniments for fish and shellfish:

o Tomato sauce (accompaniment)
o Lemon slices or wedges (garnish)
o Parsley chopped or deep-fried (garnish)
o Tartare sauce (accompaniment)
o Brown bread and butter (accompaniment)
o Hollandaise sauce (accompaniment)
o Beurre noisette (accompaniment).

Try this!   **Worksheet 29**

Using your book, the Internet and any other resources complete the crossword.

Test yourself!

1 Name three different types of shellfish.

2 What are the categories of fish?

3 What equipment is used to trim the fins of fish?

4 What equipment is required to fillet a round fish?

5 List three quality points to look out for when selecting fresh fish for preparation.

6 What equipment is used to poach a whole salmon?

7 What cooking methods are applicable to shellfish?

8 List some traditional accompaniments and garnishes for fish and shellfish.

9 What should you do if any problems occur while cooking fish or shellfish?

10 Game

This chapter covers skills and knowledge in the following units:

- 7132 Unit 224 (2FP5) Prepare game for basic dishes
- 7132 Unit 231 (2FC5) Cook and finish basic game dishes

Working through this chapter could also provide the opportunity to practise the following Functional Skills at Level 2:
Functional ICT Finding and selecting information – evaluate fitness for purpose

In this chapter you will:

Understand how and be able to prepare game for basic dishes	7132 – 224.1,2
Understand how and be able to cook basic game dishes	7132 – 231.1,2
Understand how and be able to finish basic game dishes	7132 – 231.3,4

You will learn to cook basic game dishes, including:

- venison medallions with cherries
- rabbit fricassee.

Types of game

Game animals have been hunted to provide food for man as far back as history goes. Nowadays most of our meat comes from domesticated animals. Game animals are still hunted for sport, but usually only during the open hunting season (June–September for venison, August–December for grouse), although most game meats are now available all year round through specialist suppliers.

Problems can sometimes occur with freshness of game meat. If the carcass appears badly damaged it should be reported to your supervisor and replaced with a more suitable piece of meat.

Game is generally divided into two categories: furred and feathered.

> **Definition**
> **Game:** wild animals or birds which are hunted for food.

Furred game

Game animals with fur include:

Roebuck (small deer or fawn)

Wild boar

Rabbit

Hare

> **Marcus says**
> Only buy and use game in season and beware of the pellets!

> **Healthy eating**
> Game meats are generally lower in calories and have less fat content than farmed meats (e.g. beef, lamb and pork). They are easily digested, as the meat fibres are short and fine. The meat is high in protein.

Figure 10.1 Game animals with fur

Venison

Meat from deer is called venison. There are four types of deer used for food in the UK – roe deer, fallow deer, red deer and sika deer.

Venison is one of the more common game meats. It is likely to come pre-prepared, jointed and packed. Specialist butchers may butcher cuts for you if requested.

Cuts and joints

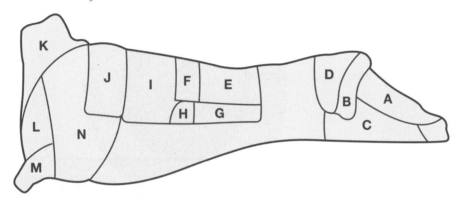

A	Silverside	H	Mignon
B	Rump	I	Cutlets
C	Thick flank	J	Chuck rib
D	Topside	K	Neck
E	Loin	L	Plate
F	Best end	M	Shin
G	Fillet	N	Shoulder

Figure 10.2 The different cuts and joints you can get from deer

The table below identifies the cuts and joints from Figure 10.2 that you will use most often. It provides information on cooking methods (which are explained later).

Position	Cut	Gives	Cooking methods
A–D	Haunch	Joints (silverside, topside, thick flank, rump) Dice/mince Escalopes	Roasting, braising Stewing Frying, grilling
E, F	Saddle	Joint (best end of loin, loin) Chops Noisettes	Roasting Sautéing, grilling, braising Sautéing
E	Best end of loin (quarter)	Chops/cutlets	Frying, sautéing, braising
F, H	Fillet, mignon (from under the saddle)	Steaks/medallions	Sautéing, frying
M	Shin	Dice/mince	Stewing
K	Neck	Dice/mince Neck chops	Stewing Grilling, frying
N	Shoulder	Joints Dice/mince	Roasting Braising, stewing

Figure 10.3 Identifying and preparing the different cuts and joints of venison

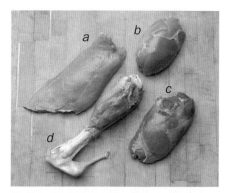

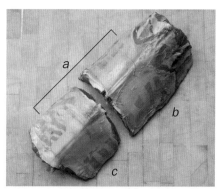

Figure 10.4: a silverside, b thick flank, c top side, d shin

Figure 10.5: a saddle, b best end, c loin

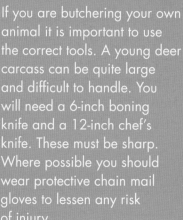

Figure 10.6: loin fillet

Figure 10.7: fillet, mignon

Figure 10.8: neck chops

Quality points

Consider the following points when checking the quality of venison:

○ It should be dry and firm.

○ It should be very dark red in colour.

○ It should have a good amount of flesh (if on the bone) and have a close-grained texture.

○ It should be lean with very little fat.

○ It should smell gamey and aromatic. It should not smell musty.

Rabbit and hare

Cuts

Rabbit and hare can now be found in many supermarkets and butcher shops all year round. These are usually sold whole, skinned and ready for use. Rabbits are generally used for stews and fricassee, so the cuts are quite simple.

Figure 10.9 Compare this rabbit and hare. Notice that the hare is much larger than the rabbit.

Quality points

Consider the following points when checking the quality of rabbit:

○ It should have pink meat with no bruising.
○ It should be well covered in meat.
○ It should have a nice rounded back.
○ Its ribcage should be easily pressed and broken.
○ On a young animal, the ears should be easy to tear.

Younger rabbits (around six to eight months old) are best. The flavour of the meat is the same for all rabbits, but cooking times increase with age, as the meat becomes tougher.

You should check for very similar things when choosing a hare but note the following differences:

○ The meat is a lot darker than a rabbit.
○ It is larger than a rabbit.
○ The best meat is from a young hare (one year old).
○ Hare legs are larger, tougher and more fibrous, best used for stewing and braising dishes.

Healthy eating
Rabbit and hare can be a very healthy meat to use as they contain very little fat.

Did you know?
The dish jugged hare is thickened with the blood from the hare.

Preparation

Skinning

Before being prepared for basic dishes, furred game must be skinned.

Skinning an animal is traditionally done by hand using a very sharp skinning knife. The animal is hung and bled to ensure there is no blood left in the carcass, then cut open along the stomach line to remove the internal organs. The skin is pulled away from the flesh with the aid of the knife, usually from the rear to the head.

Rabbits and hares can have their fur removed easily by sliding the hand between the fur and the flesh. A knife is only used to open the stomach line and cut the fur away from the feet and neck.

There are machines available to skin larger animals like deer and cows. The carcasses are cut into joints. The joints are placed on a conveyor belt system and fed into the machine. This turns the joints against a blade which removes the skin.

How to skin a rabbit

A rabbit will usually have had its entrails removed before purchase because it keeps better if they have been removed.

> **Definition**
> **Skinning**: removing fur or skin from a furred animal in preparation for use in cooking.

> **Video presentation**
> You can watch *Prepare a whole rabbit* if you would like to see this process.

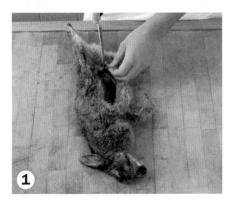

① Lie rabbit down. Extend the opening in the belly with the point of a sharp knife. Be careful not to cut the flesh underneath.

② Ease the skin from the flesh along and around the cut.

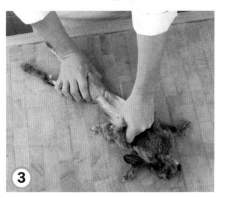

③ Pull the skin over each hind leg so that the flesh of the lower part of the animal is completely freed. Holding the lower body firmly, pull the skin up and over the front quarter.

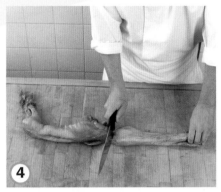

Use a sharp knife to remove the head. Then cut off the front and back feet.

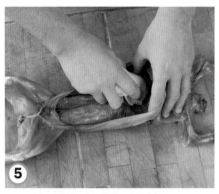

Clean out the cavity very carefully to remove all traces of blood.

Hanging

Game meat needs to hang to allow it to mature. Hanging gives the meat a stronger flavour, also called a gamy flavour. The longer you hang the meat the more gamy the flavour becomes. Hanging also makes the meat tender. This is because various enzymes and microbes in the flesh break down the tissue. Venison and hare are hung from their feet with the fur still on.

The table below shows the length of time furred game can be hung for.

Game type	Hanging time
Venison	6–8 days
Hare or rabbit	2–3 days

Figure 10.10 Recommended hanging times

Portioning

The method below can be used to portion a rabbit or hare. Always remember to wash out the cavity in cold running water. If you want to portion the meat into more than four pieces you can cut the back (saddle) into three or four equal-sized pieces.

Did you know?
Rabbit can be cooked straight after skinning and paunchiing. Hanging is not essential.

Did you know?
You can cook a rabbit whole over a camp fire following skinning and cleaning.

Chef's tip
A 2.5–3.5 kg hare will yield six to eight portions.

How to portion a rabbit into 4 pieces

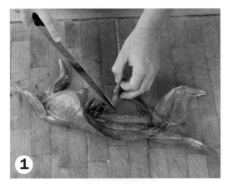

1 Using a chef's knife cut away the flap of flesh just below the rib cage.

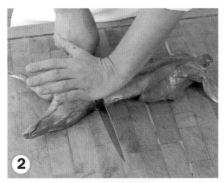

2 To remove the hind legs cut through the vertebrae just above where the hind legs join the backbone.

3 Cut through the rib cage and vertebrae just below the shoulder to remove the front legs.

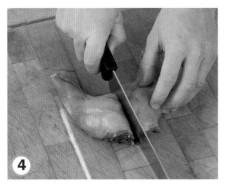

4 Position the knife between the hind legs.

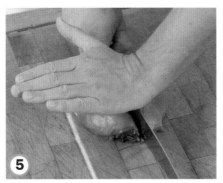

5 Split the backbone in two.

6 Position the knife between the front legs and split the neck and shoulders in two.

7 Take the saddle and reshape it by tucking the flaps underneath then cut it in half across the vertebrae.

8 The rabbit is now ready for the next process.

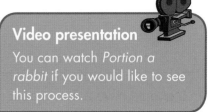

Video presentation
You can watch *Portion a rabbit* if you would like to see this process.

Feathered game

Game birds with feathers include:

Figure 10.11 Feathered game

Game birds

Game birds are very similar to domestic poultry. The styles of cooking are almost the same. The main difference is that the game bird can be hung, giving it a richer, stronger flavour.

Quality points for game birds

Consider the following points when checking the quality of game birds:

○ It should have a firm breast cage with a flexible breast bone.
○ There should be no tears in the skin.
○ The meat should have no patches of blue, which show bruising.

Some game birds are hunted for sport. This means some birds may have small holes in the skin. There may also be shot from the shotgun cartridge in the meat. This must be removed carefully before cooking. Use a small pair of tweezers or a small sharp pointed knife for this task.

Figure 10.12 You should always check for shot when preparing a game bird

Preparation

Hanging

Prior to plucking, the meat needs to hang to allow it to mature. Feathered game hang from their beaks or necks with feathers still on. Pheasant, grouse and quail should be hung for 3–4 days.

Plucking

All birds must be **plucked** in preparation for cooking. This can either be done by hand or by machine.

When plucking by hand, the bird is held tightly and the feathers are pulled away from the skin until none are left.

There are two machine methods: dry and wet.

The wet machine holds and dips the bird into hot water (50°C) for two to three minutes only. If you leave it any longer the skin begins to cook. The bird is then put onto the machine which has a series of rubber fingers on a barrel. The barrel spins and the fingers move over the bird to remove the feathers.

Definition

Pluck: to remove the feathers from a game bird, either by hand or by machine.

Did you know?

Pigeon can be cooked straight after skinning or plucking and cleaning. Hanging is not required.

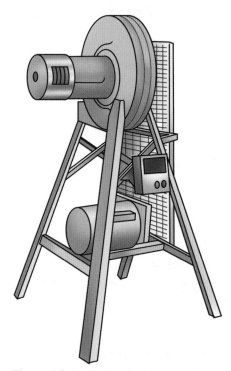

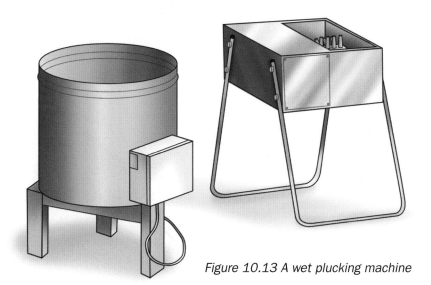

Figure 10.13 A wet plucking machine

Figure 10.14 A dry plucking machine

The dry machine is made of a cylinder with a set of gripping blades that rotate at high speed. The bird's skin is held close to the spinning blades, which grip the feathers and pull them off into a bucket. This machine can pluck a pheasant in around 60 seconds and a large chicken in about 3 minutes.

Figure 10.15 A plucked partridge

Trussing

Most game birds can be bought whole, **dressed**, **trussed** and ready to use.

Smaller birds (e.g. quail or snipe) are served whole, one bird per portion. The cavities must be washed out before preparation.

A trussed game bird sits better on the roasting tray and is easier to baste and turn in the oven. You must remove the trussing twine before service.

Dressing

If you are dressing the birds yourself, you must ensure that the cavities have been cleaned thoroughly to remove any blood or tissue. All **innards** must be removed by hand carefully by placing your forefinger, index finger and thumb into the cavity and pulling out the innards.

You must clean the cavity under cold running water, until the water runs clear with no innards or blood deposits remaining. Do not use hot water!

The flavour can be improved by marinating the bird. This is often done before stewing or braising the meat. You can stuff the cavities and breasts with a variety of fillings and forcemeat stuffings.

Stuffed game bird breast is often sautéed and served over a bed of vegetables, usually two whole breasts to a portion as the breasts are small.

The methods of cutting, portioning and slicing game birds are the same as for farmed poultry (see Chapter 8).

Definition

Dressed: birds that have been cleaned, plucked and trussed.

Innards: the internal organs of a bird.

Truss: to thread one or two pieces of string or twine through the body of a game bird or poultry using a trussing needle, then tying them. This holds the legs and wings in place during cooking or following stuffing.

Figure 10.16 Grouse

Figure 10.17 Pheasant

Video presentation

Watch the techniques used in *Prepare a whole chicken for roasting* and apply them to game birds.

Cooking

Venison

Young deer (12–18 months old) can be cooked without marinating. However, most recipes for braising or stewing venison require marinating before cooking. This helps to improve the flavour of the meat and stops it getting tough and dry. The length of time the meat should be marinated varies with the age of the meat, but a good rule of thumb is 8–12 hours.

Roast venison should be cooked for 6–8 minutes per kg. This is enough to just cook the meat through, leaving a little moisture when cut.

Cooking times will vary if you are grilling, griddling or shallow pan-frying venison steaks. A 100–150g steak will take 2–3 minutes on each side.

Venison is often served with a strong sauce (e.g. pepper- or mustard-based). These sauces help to bring out the full flavour of the meat.

Chef's tip

When roasting venison it is a good idea to use lardons or to bard the joint in bacon fat. This keeps the meat moist while cooking, as venison has very little fat of its own.

Venison medallions with cherries

Preparation	2
Cooking skills	3
Finishing	3

venison medallions (from the fillet)	8 × 90g
salt and pepper	to season
butter	60g
stoned red cherries	200g
red wine	120ml
cinnamon	½ tsp
cornflour or arrowroot	as required
Cooking time	5–8 minutes
Serves	4

Healthy eating

Game meat is often fried or sautéed. A healthier way to cook these dishes is to use fats or oils that are low in saturates. Using less salt and grilling rather than frying the meat also makes these dishes healthier.

Method

1 Lightly season the venison medallions and fry quickly in butter in a frying pan for around two minutes on each side. Remove from the pan and keep warm.
2 Put the cherries, red wine and cinnamon in a pan. Cook until soft. Drain when soft. Reduce the juice and thicken with cornflour or arrowroot until the sauce is thick enough to coat the back of a spoon.
3 Add the cherries to the thickened sauce.
4 Arrange the medallions on a small flat plate. Spoon a little sauce over each one. Serve the remaining sauce in a sauceboat.

Rabbit and hare

You should roast a whole (1.5–2kg) rabbit for 1–1½ hours, turning and basting regularly. You can also roast hare.

Rabbit fricassee

rabbit, jointed	1
butter	60g
flour	30g
water	approx. 1 litre
salt and pepper	to season
onions, diced	80g
mushrooms, cooked	60g
egg yolk	1
cream	150ml
Cooking time	1½ hours
Serves	4

Preparation	4
Cooking skills	3
Finishing	4

Method

1 Fry the meat joints in a saucepan in the butter without colouring.
2 Sprinkle with flour and cook for a few minutes.
3 Moisten with the water (half cover the meat). Add some salt and pepper and simmer for 30 minutes.
4 Add the onions and cook for a further 15 minutes.
5 Drain the meat and onions in a sieve (but keep the sauce). Put the meat back into the saucepan with the cooked mushrooms and onions and keep warm.
6 Strain the sauce and reduce to coat the back of a spoon.
7 Whisk in the **liaison** of egg yolk and cream.
8 Add the rabbit and other ingredients and gently reheat.
9 Serve decorated with heart-shaped croutons.

Chef's tip
A 1–1.5 kg rabbit will yield four portions.

Definition
Fricassee: a light reduced meat stew, bound with a liaison of cream and egg yolks.
Liaison: this is used to bind or thicken a sauce, and is often based on egg yolks and cream.

Game birds

Game birds are usually **barded** or cooked with fruits like apple, as they contain very little fat. They can be cooked using similar methods to farmed poultry. These methods include:

- roasting (pheasant, quail, pigeon, grouse, partridge)
- pot roasting (pheasant, quail, pigeon, grouse)
- braising/casserole (pheasant, partridge, pigeon).

The breasts of the larger birds may be removed, stuffed and pan-fried or braised. These are often served with a sauce.

Game birds should be presented for the table with the breast uppermost, whether served whole or as a sautéed or grilled breast.

Cooking times for game birds are as follows:
- **Pheasant**: 10–12 minutes per kg if roasted, 25–30 minutes per kg if casseroled.
- **Partridge**: 20–30 minutes roasted, 2–2½ hours if casseroled.
- **Small birds (pigeon, quail, woodcock)**: 10–15 minutes if roasted (whole), 45–60 minutes if casseroled.

> **Definition**
>
> **Barding**: to place strips of fat onto or around a piece of meat while it cooks to slowly release juices over the meat. Mainly used for meats that have little of their own fat.

Figure 10.18 Quail

> **Find out!**   **Worksheet 30**
>
> Find at least one recipe for: rabbit, venison, pheasant, quail, woodcock, partridge and grouse.

Storage

Prior to skinning, venison, hare and rabbit should be stored in a cool, well-ventilated room; the ideal temperature is between 5°C and 10°C. If possible they should hang until required. Game birds should also be stored in the same way after being plucked, dressed and prepared.

Problems can occur if game meat is hung too long and begins to deteriorate. If it is not kept cool, dry and covered, the skin can dry out further and become leathery to the touch. However, some customers prefer the taste of well-hung meat, so it is always good to check with your supervisor if you are unsure of the quality of any piece of game meat.

You generally do not need to hang game meat which is to be used for mincing or making sausages. Game meat is also used mixed together in dishes such as game pie or royal game soup. The mixture of textures and flavours makes for a unique dish.

Once prepared, if the meat is not cooked immediately it should be covered, labelled and placed in a refrigerator until required. Marinated meats can be stored in a cool, ventilated room or placed into a refrigerator. These must also be labelled and covered.

Try this! **Worksheet 31**

See how many of the game-related words you can find in the wordsearch.

Test yourself!

1 Name two types of furred game.

2 Complete the following sentences for quality points for venison:
   a It should be _____ and firm.
   b It should be very _____ _____ in colour.
   c It should have a good amount of _____ and have a _____-_____ texture.
   d It should be _____ with very _____ fat.
   e It should smell _____ and _____. It should not smell _____.

3 For how long should you roast a whole rabbit?

4 List two quality points for game birds.

5 What should you do if you suspect game meat is not fresh?

6 Explain how a dry plucking machine works.

7 Explain why you hang game.

8 What age of hare gives the best meat?
   a Four to six months
   b Six to eight months
   c Ten months
   d 12 months.

9 Name two game animals that do not need to be hung before eating.

10 Explain the reasons for barding a game bird.

11

Stocks, soups and sauces

This chapter covers skills and knowledge in the following units:

- 7132 Unit 236 (2FPC1) Prepare, cook and finish basic hot sauces
- 7132 Unit 237 (2FPC2) Prepare, cook and finish basic soups
- 7132 Unit 238 (2FPC3) Make basic stocks

Working through this chapter could also provide the opportunity to practise the following Functional Skills at Level 2:
Functional Maths Representing – understand, use and calculate ratio and proportion, including problems involving scale

In this chapter you will:

Understand how and be able to prepare basic hot sauces	7132 – 236.1,2
Understand how and be able to cook basic hot sauces	7132 – 236.3,4
Understand how and be able to finish basic hot sauces	7132 – 236.5,6
Understand how and be able to prepare basic soups	7132 – 237.1,2
Understand how and be able to cook basic soups	7132 – 237.3,4
Understand how and be able to finish basic soups	7132 – 237.5,6
Know how and be able to make basic stocks	7132 – 238.1,2

You will learn to cook basic stocks, soups and hot sauces, including:

- white beef stock
- white fish stock
- clear soup (consommé)
- purée of lentil soup
- cream of cauliflower soup
- béchamel sauce
- velouté sauce
- tomato sauce.

Basic stocks

A stock is a broth that is used as a braising liquid, a sauce base or as liquid for soup. A good stock should have a delicate flavour and a high proportion of natural gelatine. A gelatinous stock gives richness and body to a preparation without masking the flavours of the basic ingredients.

Stock is made by slowly simmering bones and/or vegetables with **aromatic** herbs in a juice, e.g. water or wine. During cooking the flavours of the meat, vegetables and herbs are released into the liquid. After cooking, the solid ingredients and any grease are removed and the liquid is strained until it is clear.

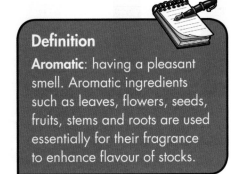

Definition

Aromatic: having a pleasant smell. Aromatic ingredients such as leaves, flowers, seeds, fruits, stems and roots are used essentially for their fragrance to enhance flavour of stocks.

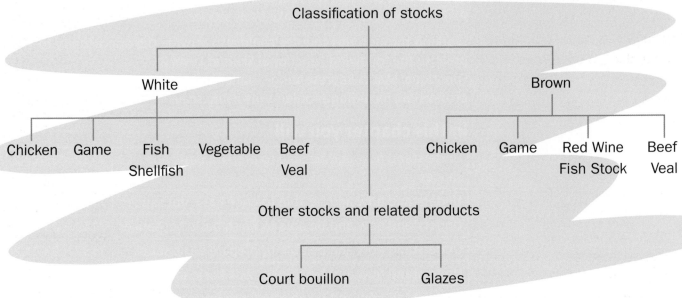

Classification of stocks

- White
  - Chicken
  - Game
  - Fish / Shellfish
  - Vegetable
  - Beef / Veal
- Brown
  - Chicken
  - Game
  - Red Wine / Fish Stock
  - Beef / Veal
- Other stocks and related products
  - Court bouillon
  - Glazes

Figure 11.1 Classification of stocks

Types of stock

Stocks can be made from many different ingredients. The stocks covered in the NVQ Level 2 are: vegetable, chicken, fish, game and beef.

Stocks can be either white or brown. For a white stock, the ingredients are simply added to the stock pot. White stock is used as a liquid to make soups, white stews and **velouté** sauce for poached poultry and fish dishes. For a brown stock, any bones are roasted and the vegetables are sautéed before being added to the stock pot. Brown stock is used as a liquid in soups, brown sauces, brown stews and for braising large cuts of meat.

Definition

Velouté: a stock-based white sauce that is thickened with a white roux.

Vegetable stock or nage

This is a light neutral base, which can be used in many soups and sauces. It can be used with other stocks and is suitable for use in vegetarian cookery. For maximum flavour do not strain the vegetables out immediately after cooking, but allow them to steep in the stock for up to 24 hours. Vegetable stock is used as a liquid for soups, sauces and for all preparations in vegetable cooking such as braised rice.

Chicken stock

This is a very versatile stock. It should have a good amber colour, without being too strong in taste. If a stronger-tasting stock is required, boil the stock until the quantity of stock is reduced to half to produce double chicken stock. Use fresh carcasses and winglets and if possible add boiling fowl, which may be removed later. Some recipes may need a darker or brown chicken stock. To make this, roast chicken carcasses in a hot oven for 15–20 minutes until golden brown (remembering to turn them frequently) and drain off the fat before using. Sauté any vegetables used to a golden brown and drain this also before using.

Fish stock

The best bones to use for fish stock are turbot and sole. Other fish bones can be oily, strong and even taste of ammonia, although hake, haddock and cod can be used. Always remove the eyes and gills, as these can have an effect on the flavour and colour of your stock. Also remember to rinse the fish bones and trimmings under cold water to remove traces of blood. Fish stock is used in the preparation of soups, fish sauces, velouté or white wine sauce. Fish stock is also used for shallow poaching and braising fish.

Fish stock can also be prepared with red wine for poached fish dishes.

Veal stock

This forms the base of many sauces. It is possibly the king of stocks, offering excellent body, richness and colour with a subtle flavour. As the bones are large they should be chopped smaller to enable them to release their flavour. It is possible to produce a white or a brown stock from these bones, but careful roasting of the bones will give a stock greater colour and flavour.

Did you know?
The ideal temperature for the following is:
cooking of stock 100°C
(except fish stock) 98°C
holding of stock 75°C
storage of stock 4°C.

Healthy eating
o Do not use salt or any other seasoning in the preparation of stocks as the natural salt from the ingredients is sufficient.
o Make sure that all fat is removed from the meat and poultry bones before preparing stock.
o Always blanch the bones and refresh them in cold water to remove any excess fat (except fish bones).

Marcus says
Soups need to be seasoned at the beginning of the cooking process for the full flavours to develop.

Stocks should not be seasoned as they are a base ingredient and will be seasoned later.

Don't over season sauces at the start – once reduced down the seasoning will taste stronger than when there was more liquid.

Game stock

A rich brown game stock can be produced from any furred or feathered game. Chop the bones into smaller pieces so that they can release more of their flavour. Roast the bones in a hot oven or sauté them until golden brown. Sauté the vegetables and drain them before use. Game stock is used to produce sauces to accompany a game dish.

Beef stock

Beef stock can be produced in the same way as veal stock. Beef stock is not very versatile and is best suited for use in beef dishes.

Other stocks and related products

Court bouillon

This is a light aromatic stock of vegetables, herbs, spices and white wine vinegar. It is used for poaching fish, crabs and other shellfish. This stock can be used two or three times before being discarded. Like other stocks it may be cooled and frozen for use at a later date.

Glazes

A glaze ('glace' in French) is a concentrated stock which is made through a process of reduction. It is used to enrich the flavour of sauces and dishes such as Parisienne potatoes. Before the stock is reduced, it should be passed through a very fine sieve or better still a piece of wet muslin cloth. Care should be taken through the reduction period to remove any scum that rises to the surface. This will help the glaze achieve its characteristic shine. The consistency of the glaze should be just flowing when warm and solid when refrigerated.

> **Healthy eating**
> o Avoid rapid boiling of stocks as fats are emulsified and dissolved in the liquid making it milky and unhealthy.
> o Avoid adding butter or oil while frying vegetables and bones for brown stocks. Always use the natural fat on the bones to give colour by roasting them in the oven.

Try this!   **Worksheet 32**

Close your book. List as many types of stock as you can remember.

Ingredients and equipment

White stock

White stock is a broth which has no colour. It has white meat bones and aromatic vegetables as a basis. The ingredients used are:

○ chicken, beef, veal or game
○ carrots, onions, leeks or celery
○ thyme, bay leaf or parsley stalks
○ liquid: water or white wine.

Remember!

If a small quantity of stock is required from a large pot in the refrigerator, never dip a utensil into it that is warmer than the stock itself.

Brown stock

This is a broth which has a light brown colour. The other term used to describe this stock is 'estouffade', which is a reduced brown stock. It has browned meat bones and sautéed aromatic vegetables as a basis. The ingredients used are:

○ chicken, beef, veal or game
○ carrots, onions, leeks, celery or garlic
○ thyme, bayleaf or parsley stalks
○ liquid: water.

Equipment

The equipment needed to make a stock:

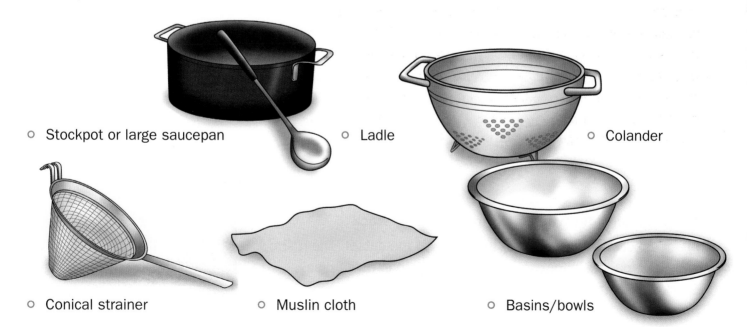

○ Stockpot or large saucepan
○ Ladle
○ Colander
○ Conical strainer
○ Muslin cloth
○ Basins/bowls

In addition, for a brown stock, a roasting tray or frying pan is needed.

Recipes for basic stocks

The minimum cooking times for different types of stock are:

○ Vegetable stock – 30 minutes.
○ Chicken stock – 2 hours.
○ Fish stock – 20 minutes.
○ Game stock – 2 hours.
○ Beef stock – 4 hours.

Preparation	2
Cooking skills	2
Finishing	2

White beef stock

For the stock:		For the bouquet garni:	
beef shin bones	2kg	leeks	120g
water, cold	6 litres	celery	120g
carrots	240g	parsley stalk and root	30g
onions, stuck with two cloves	120g	bay leaf	1
		sprig of thyme	1
Cooking time	4 hours		
Makes	5 litres		

Method

1 Cut or break the bones into 10cm pieces. Remove any marrow.
2 Wash and place into stock pot and add 6 litres of cold water. Bring to the boil and **skim** off the scum.
3 Add 100ml of cold water and wipe the sides of the stock pot clean with a damp cloth.
4 Add the vegetables whole, and the bouquet garni.
5 Allow the stock to simmer gently for six hours, during which time the fat which rises to the surface must be constantly skimmed off. The vegetables should be removed from stock after three hours.
6 Pass the stock through a muslin.
7 Reboil and place aside to cool.

Points to consider when making white beef stock

All fat should be removed from the bones at the outset. The marrow should be put aside for use as a separate dish or as garnish. Stock should only simmer; if it is allowed to boil, it will become milky or cloudy.

Chef's tip

Six to eight hours is the maximum time required to extract the full flavour – if cooked too long the flavour will suffer. Bones from which the flavour has been extracted may be re-boiled for a further six hours to produce jelly.

The vegetables and bouquet garni should be easily accessible – tie bouquet garni to the handle of the pot with a long string and if there is a large quantity of stock, tie vegetables in a muslin or net. If allowed to remain in the pot too long the vegetables will begin to disintegrate and/or lose their colour into the liquid, causing the stock to discolour. Discard scum. Save the fat which can be later clarified and used as dripping, for braising.

Do not allow any fat to remain on the surface as this will stop the heat escaping and may cause the stock to 'turn', that is, become sour.

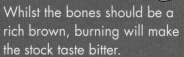

Chef's tip
Whilst the bones should be a rich brown, burning will make the stock taste bitter.

Brown beef stock

Preparation	2
Cooking skills	2
Finishing	2

good meaty bones, beef or veal, and trimmings of meat	2kg
beef fat	60g
carrots, diced (mirepoix) and fried	240g
onions, diced (mirepoix) and fried	240g
bouquet garni	1
ham bone	240g
water	6 litres
Oven temperature	250°C
Cooking time	6–8 hours
Makes	5 litres

Method

1 Cut or break the bones into 10cm pieces and place in a roasting tray. Add the trimmings and fat.
2 Roast the bones and trimmings in a hot oven until a rich brown colour.
3 Remove bones from fat and place in a stockpot. Cover with 6 litres of water, bring to the boil and skim.
4 Add the fried carrot and onion, the bouquet garni and the ham bone.
5 Allow the stock to simmer for six hours, skimming from time to time to remove the fat.
6 Strain through a muslin, reboil and use as required.

Brown game stock

Preparation	2
Cooking skills	2
Finishing	2

neck and breast of venison	2kg
trimmings of hare	1kg
old pheasant or partridge	1kg
carrots	180g
onions	180g
white beef stock or water	6 litres
dry white wine	0.5 litre
mushroom trimmings	120g

For the bouquet garni:

leeks	120g
celery	120g
parsley stalk and root	30g
bay leaf	1
sprig of thyme	1
Oven temperature	250°C or 425°F
Cooking time	2–3 hours
Makes	5 litres

Method

1. Tie the meat and truss the game birds.
2. Make a **bed of roots** with the carrot and onion in the bottom of the roasting tray.
3. Place the meat and game on top of the vegetables in the roasting tray with a little **dégraisse** and brown quickly in the oven.
4. Transfer meat and game to a stockpot.
5. Pour off the fat from the roasting tray and deglaze the tray by pouring on the wine and a little stock and allowing it to simmer until all sediment has been dissolved.
6. Add the deglaze to the stockpot, together with the rest of the stock or water.
7. Bring to the boil, skim and add the remainder of the ingredients.
8. Simmer for three hours, skimming from time to time, strain, reboil and use as required.

Definitions

Dégraisse: the liquid fat which is removed from the surface of simmering stock using a ladle by the process of skimming.

Bed of root: chopped root vegetables which act as a base to put the bird on to prevent it sticking and burning on the tray.

Video presentation

Prepare a whole chicken for roasting will show you how to truss a bird.

Try this!

Worksheet 35

Close your book and list as many types of white and brown stock as you can.

Preparation	2
Cooking skills	2
Finishing	2

White fish stock

onions to slice	250g
butter	50g
fishbones:	
bones and trimmings of sole, whiting, turbot, brill and halibut, thoroughly washed before using	5kg
parsley stalks and root	30g
thyme sprig	1
bay leaves, small	2
white mushroom trimmings, well-washed	200g
lemons for juice	1–2
white peppercorns	approx. 20
white wine (optional)	300–400ml
water	5 litres
salt	20g
Cooking time	20–30 minutes
Makes	approx. 5 litres

Method

1 Peel and slice the onions, blanch, refresh and strain.
2 Melt the butter in a thick-bottomed saucepan. Add the onions and gently cook without colour five to ten minutes.
3 Add parsley, mushroom trimmings, lemon juice, thyme, bay leaf and chopped fish bones. Cover with buttered greaseproof paper and a lid.
4 Cook gently on the side of the stove for 15–20 minutes. This will reduce the volume of the bones so less water will be required and the stock will be stronger and better quality.
5 Add the white wine, water and salt. Bring to the boil, cover with a lid and simmer for 15–20 minutes.
6 Add peppercorns in the last five minutes; skim.
7 Pass stock through a muslin and reserve until required.

Note:
After gently cooking the fish bones for 20 minutes (end of step 3 above) you will notice that there is an extraction of juices at the bottom of the pan. These juices are reduced fish stock. They can be strained off and used for enhancing the flavour of fish sauces. Wine or water is then added to the bones to make a stock as in steps 5–7 above.

Chef's tip
Twenty minutes will extract all the flavour from the bones; excess cooking will make the stock bitter and cause it to deteriorate.

Chef's tip
Only use white mushroom trimmings, as any black pieces will discolour the finished product.

Video presentation

Watch *Prepare fish stock (1) sweat* and *Prepare fish stock (2) boil, skim, simmer and strain* to see this being made.

Holding, serving and storing stocks

Stocks for immediate use are held in a bain-marie at 75°C. Stocks not required for immediate use should be chilled as quickly as possible. When cooling stock, the pan should be raised on a trivet so that cold air can circulate round the pan. When cold, the pan should be covered with greaseproof paper and labelled with the type of stock and date. Stocks should be stored at 4°C in the refrigerator. The most efficient method of storing stock is to reduce it to a glaze. This prolongs the storage life of stocks.

Test yourself!

1 Name four different types of stock.

2 Give four important points to remember about preparation and cooking of white and brown stock.

3 What are the reasons for:
   a white fish stock being cloudy
   b brown chicken stock tasting bitter
   c white beef stock lacking flavour
   d brown vegetable stock being greasy.

4 What are the cooking times for the following stocks:
   a Fish stock
   b White chicken stock
   c Brown beef stock
   d Vegetable stock.

5 State four quality points to look for in the finished stocks.

6 Match the correct temperature to the activity in the preparation of stock:
   a Cooking   4°C
   b Holding   100°C
   c Storage   75°C.

Basic soups

Types of soup

There are many different types of soup:

○ **Unpassed soups** such as Scotch broth, Chicken broth or Rabbit broth.

○ **Clear soup (Consommé)** is a **clarified** stock that uses egg whites, finely minced shin of beef and vegetables. In fact, clarification is not essential if the stock is prepared perfectly by simmering the liquid over a period of time and continuously skimming any impurities that rise to the top.

○ **Purées**, where the main ingredient of the soup gives a name and body to the end product e.g. purée of lentil.

○ **Cream soups**, where vegetables are pureed and added to the béchamel sauce which gives body to the soup. Velouté is another name for a soup when velouté sauce replaces béchamel sauce.

○ **Bisque** is a unique term given to the preparation of soup made from shellfish such as lobster or crab.

○ **Cold soups** can be from clear soup such as jellied consommé or from vegetables and fruits such as potage vichyssoise, gazpacho soup and chilled cherry soup.

Did you know?

The word 'soup' derives from 'sop' – originally the bread over which a broth or other liquid was poured.

Definition

Clarification: the process used to purify stocks, making the cloudy liquid clear using egg whites and albumen from the minced lean shin of beef.

Find out!   **Worksheet 33**

Find three recipes for each soup category: unpassed, purée, clear, bisque, cream, velouté and cold soup.

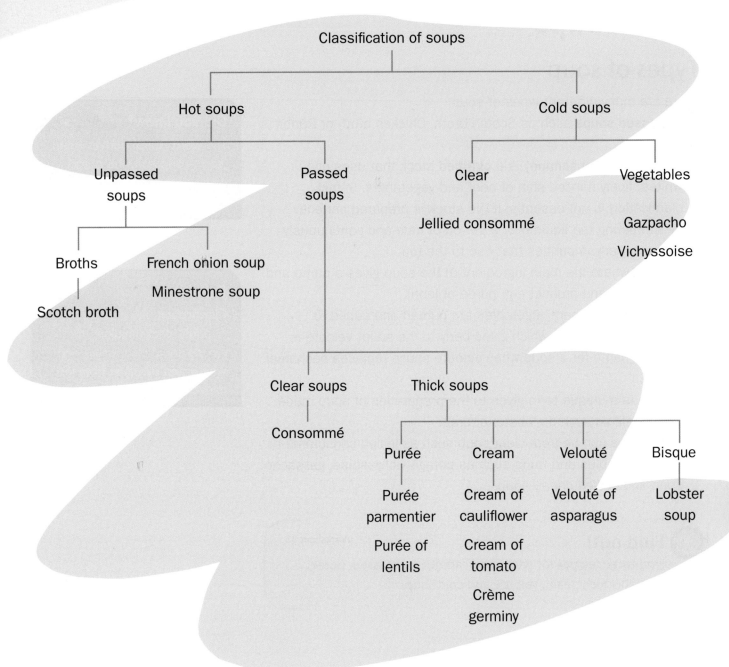

Figure 11.2 Classification of soups

Thickening agents for soups

The table below shows the thickening agents used in different types of soups.

Thickening agent	Types of soup
Barley Beans, pasta Rice Lentils	Scotch broth Minestrone Bisque Game soup
Main ingredient of the soup, e.g.: Potatoes Lentils Beans	 Purée parmentier Purée of lentils Bean soup
White roux	Cream soup
Blond roux	Cream of tomato soup
Brown roux	Brown windsor soup
Béchamel sauce	Cream of cauliflower or celery
Velouté sauce: Chicken Fish	 Velouté of asparagus Velouté of lobster
Espagnole (basic brown) sauce	Kidney soup
Fresh cream and egg yolk liaison	Crème germiny
Breadcrumbs	Gazpacho

Figure 11.3 Thickening agents used in different soups

Healthy eating

o Use an alternative to a roux in the preparation of cream and velouté soup. The soup could be thickened with cornflour.

o Replace butter in the preparation of the roux with vegetable fat or margarine.

Liquids used in the preparation of soups

Type of liquid	Types of soup
Water	Lentils Beans
White stock	Chicken Beef or veal Fish Vegetable
Brown stock	Game Beef or veal
Vegetable and fruit juices	Tomato Beetroot Orange
Beer and wines	Swedish bean soup Consommé (Clear soup) Oxtail soup

Figure 11.4 Liquids used in different soups

Garnishes and accompaniments

Garnishes are defined as food items which are served in the soup.

Garnishes	Soups
Julienne	Velouté of celery
Brunoise	Scotch broth
Paysanne	Minestrone
Small florets of cauliflower	Cream of cauliflower soup
Savoury pancake julienne	Consommé
Rice	Cream of tomato soup
Tapioca	Cream of green pea soup

Figure 11.5 Garnishes

Accompaniments are food items which are served separately alongside soups.

Accompaniments	Soups
Croûtons	Purée soups, e.g. Purée of lentil soup
Croûtes	Clear soups, e.g. minestrone soup
Cheese straws	Turtle soup, Lobster bisque
Grated parmesan cheese	Minestrone soup, French onion soup
Duck patties	Borsch soup

Figure 11.6 Accompaniments

> **Definitions**
>
> **Croûtons**: 1cm cubes of white bread, shallow-fried to a golden brown colour in clarified butter.
>
> **Croûtes**: sliced bread flutes toasted or evenly baked in the oven to a golden brown colour.

Finishing of soups

Finish	Soups
Knobs of butter	Purée soups
Fresh cream	Cream soups
Fresh cream and egg yolk liaison and knobs of butter	Velouté soups
Wines White wine Red wine	Fish soup Red haricot bean soup
Fortified wines Sherry Madeira Port Marsala	Consommé Turtle soup Oxtail soup Consommé **Bisques**

Figure 11.7 Finishing of soups

> **Definition**
>
> **Bisque**: a shellfish soup where the shellfish is puréed to add flavour.

Equipment used in the preparation of soups

The equipment you will need when preparing soups includes:

- large saucepan
- sauteuse
- wooden spatula
- wooden spoon
- ladles
- conical strainer
- colander
- sieves and **wooden mushroom**
- pestle and mortar
- whisks
- balloon whisk
- chopping board
- set of knives
- muslin cloth
- tammy cloth
- bain-marie.

> **Definition**
>
> **Wooden mushroom**: a piece of equipment used to press the solid cooked food ingredients through a sieve to make a purée.

Figure 11.8 Equipment used in the preparation of soups

Soup recipes

Unpassed soup

Preparation	4
Cooking skills	4
Finishing	2

Minestrone soup

haricot beans	80g
butter	60g
small lardons, blanched	100g
onions, chopped	250g
white of leek, paysanne	200g
celery, paysanne	100g
carrots, paysanne	250g
cabbage, paysanne	250g
turnips, paysanne	250g
salt and pepper	to season
white chicken stock	3 litres
bouquet garni	1
peeled potatoes, **paysanne**	400g
french beans, in lozenges	100g
peas	100g
patna rice	50g
spaghetti	50g
tomato purée	10ml
tomatoes for **concassées**	400g
garlic cloves, crushed	2
fresh pork fat, finely chopped, lard gras	60–80g
parsley, finely chopped	20ml
fines herbes	
grated parmesan served separately	
bread rolls or toasted sliced flûte bread served separately	
Cooking time	1 hour
Serves	6–8

Method

1 Wash and soak haricot beans overnight in a cool place. Cook separately for about one hour.
2 Put the butter and small lardons into a thick-bottomed saucepan. Gently cook and very lightly colour. Add the onions, leek, celery, carrots, cabbage and turnips.
3 Season lightly. Cover with greaseproof paper and cook slowly without colouring for 30–40 minutes, stirring occasionally.
4 Add the stock, bouquet garni, potatoes, French beans, peas, patna rice and spaghetti.

Definition

Concassées: finely diced skinned tomato flesh. The tomato is blanched, refreshed, peeled, deseeded and roughly chopped. Concassée is widely used as an ingredient in other dishes.

Fines herbes: a mixture of aromatic herbs such as chervil, tarragon, chives and parsley.

Paysanne: a small cut of vegetables in a variety of shapes, such as triangles, squares, circles and oblongs.

Chef's tip

Other herbs which may be added with the parsley and fines herbes are sage leaves, basil, marjoram and chives.

Did you know?

Minestrone soup is from Italy. It is sometimes called 'minestra'. There are several variations of recipes according to the regions.

5 Cook until all the ingredients are tender. Add tomato purée. Mix in well, remove the bouquet garni.
6 Add the cooked haricot beans; and the add tomates concassées. Reboil, taste for seasoning. Rectify the thickness. The consistency of this soup should be fairly thick.
7 Crush the skinned garlic with finely chopped pork fat, adding chopped parsley and fines herbes. Toss in little hot butter then added to the soup, mixing in well with a ladle.
9 Serve with toasted shredded bread or rolls, or toasted sliced flûte bread and grated parmesan cheese as an accompaniment.

Chef's tip
Consommé can be prepared by using a variety of stocks such as chicken, game and veal. There are numerous classic garnishes which can be added to finish the soup.

Clear soup

Clear soup (*Consommé*)

Preparation	3
Cooking skills	4
Finishing	3

minced shin of beef	1kg
egg white	1
mirepoix of onions	125g
mirepoix of carrots	125g
mirepoix of celery	125g
mirepoix of leeks	125g
cold, white beef stock	5 litres
bouquet garni	1
peppercorns	15–18
salt	to season
Cooking time	3 to 4 hours
Serves	6–8

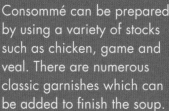

Did you know?
Clear soup should never be boiled as this makes it cloudy. If it gets cloudy, the process of clarification must be repeated.

Healthy eating
Make sure clear soups are free from traces of fat.

Method

1 Soak the minced shin of beef in cold water for about 20–30 minutes, adding salt to withdraw blood. Add egg white and mix well.
2 Prepare the mirepoix of onions, carrots, celery and leeks. Add these vegetables to the beef and cover with good beef stock.
3 Add bouquet garni and peppercorns.
4 Bring it just to the boil slowly over a gentle heat, stirring occasionally.
5 Give a last stir and let the consommé simmer gently over a low heat. Cook it for approximately two hours without stirring.
6 Strain the consommé through a muslin cloth.
7 Use kitchen paper squares to remove all fat from the top.
8 Check the seasoning and colour, which should be a delicate amber.
9 Bring the consommé just to the boil again and serve in a warm soup tureen.

Purée soup

Purée of lentil soup

lentils, red	250g
butter for vegetables	40g
pork or bacon rind	30–40g
onion, diced	30–40g
carrot, diced	30–40g
water	1.25 litres
bouquet garni	1
salt	to season
butter, clarified	40g
milk, boiling	150–200ml
bread for croûtons	100g
Cooking time	1 hour
Serves	6

Preparation	2
Cooking skills	2
Finishing	2

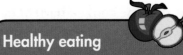

Healthy eating

o Purée soups are healthier than cream of velouté soups.
o Avoid the use of fresh cream, butter or cream and egg yolk liaison to finish the soups.
o Avoid over-seasoning the soups.
o Serve toasted croûtons instead of croûtons shallow-fried in butter.

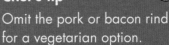

Chef's tip

Omit the pork or bacon rind for a vegetarian option.

Method

1 Wash the lentils well and soak for half an hour.
2 Lightly sauté the diced bacon or pork rind in 25g butter, using a thick-bottomed pan.
3 Add the diced carrot and onion, lightly colour.
4 Add the strained lentils and stir. Cook gently for 10–15 minutes.
5 Add water and bouquet garni. Cover with a lid, simmer until the lentils are tender and fully cooked, add salt in the last ten minutes.
6 Remove bouquet garni. Pass the soup through a sieve.
7 Reboil, pass through a fine chinois.
8 Reboil, taste for seasoning. Check the thickness, adding a little boiling milk if necessary. The consistency of the soup should be like thick double cream.
9 Add the clarified butter (15g) to complete the soup. Check the seasoning and add salt, if necessary.
10 Serve croûtons separately.

Cream soup

Cream of cauliflower soup

Preparation 1
Cooking skills 2
Finishing 2

white of leek	500g
butter	300g
cauliflower, without leaves	2kg
water or cauliflower stock or white stock	2 litres
bouquet garni	1
béchamel, boiling	3 litres
cream, boiling	600ml
salt and pepper	to season
sprigs or leaves of chervil	
Cooking time	1 hour
Serves	6–8 portions

Method

1 Wash and shred the white of leek. Cook in half the butter without colouring.
2 Wash the cauliflower. Reserve 300g of cauliflower in small florets to be boiled and used for garnish.
3 Shred the bulk of cauliflower. Add to the leeks, mix well and season. Cover and continue to cook without colouring, until tender.
4 Add the liquid and the bouquet garni. Simmer for 15–20 minutes.
5 Remove the bouquet garni. Pass the soup through a sieve. Reboil and add boiling béchamel. Mix well, taste for seasoning. Pass through a fine chinois. Reboil then add the boiling cream and work in the rest of the butter.
6 Finally, add small cooked florets of cauliflower. The vegetable stock can be used to adjust the consistency of the soup. Taste again for seasoning. Cover and keep hot in a bain-marie.
7 Add the chervil on serving.

Chef's tip

Cooked leftover plain boiled cauliflower may be used for economy.
Blanched shredded onions can be used instead of leeks.

Cream of tomato soup

bacon trimmings	50g
onions, mirepoix	50g
carrots, mirepoix	50g
margarine	100g
flour	125g
tomato purée	220g
white stock	2 litres
bouquet garni	1
salt	to taste
pepper	to taste
double cream	100ml
For the gastric:	
vinegar	30ml
sugar	20g
Serves	10
Cooking time approx.	1 hour

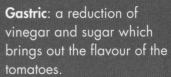

Definition

Gastric: a reduction of vinegar and sugar which brings out the flavour of the tomatoes.

Sippets: 5mm cubes of bread, baked or fried to a golden brown colour.

Method

1 Cut bacon trimmings into 5mm dice.
2 Put margarine, bacon trimmings and mirepoix of onions and carrots in a pan. Sweat the meat and vegetables.
3 Add the flour. Make a blonde roux.
4 Remove the pan from the heat and add the tomato purée.
5 Place the pan back onto the heat and slowly add the hot stock.
6 Mix well in between each addition of stock to prevent the soup going lumpy.
7 When all the stock has been added and mixed in, add the bouquet garni. Season.
8 Bring to the boil and simmer for 1 hour.
9 Strain through a conical strainer.
10 Boil again and skim. Correct the consistency. Adjust the seasoning to taste.
11 For the gastric place the sugar and vinegar in a clean pan. Bring to the boil and reduce slightly. Add small amounts to the soup.
12 Add double cream just before service. Do not re-boil or the cream will curdle.
13 Serve with sippets.

Velouté soup

Velouté of asparagus

white of leek	500g
celery	50g
butter	100g
salt and pepper	to season
asparagus stock	2.5–3 litres
asparagus stalks (optional)	
bouquet garni	1
velouté chicken	3 litres
lemon juice and cayenne	to flavour

For liaison:

yolks of eggs	4
cream	400ml
butter	100g

For garnish:

green asparagus tips	250–300g
sprig of chervil	
Cooking time	1 hour
Serves	6–8 portions

Method

1 Wash and shred the leeks and celery; if they are old, blanch them. Cook slowly in 100g of butter, no colour, for 15–20 minutes. Season and stir occasionally.

2 Add asparagus stock and any available cooked asparagus stalks, both reserved from the cooking of same. Add bouquet garni and velouté. Simmer for 20–30 minutes covered.

3 Put the egg yolks, cream and butter in a china or plastic bowl. Prepare a liason.

4 Pass soup through a sieve, reboil. Taste for seasoning, then gradually pour onto prepared liaison. Mix thoroughly.

5 Reheat to thicken, without boiling. Add lemon juice and cayenne.

6 Pass through a fine chinois or tammy cloth with pressure, reserve in a soup bain-marie, covered; do not allow to boil.

7 Garnish with cooked green tips of asparagus, carefully mixed into the soup. Add sprigs of chervil at the moment of service.

Quality points to look for in finished soups

1 The colour and appearance is correct for the type of soup.
2 Correct consistency, in other words a proportionate amount of liquid added to the main ingredient.
3 Garnishes and accompaniments are consistent size and shape and are cooked correctly.
4 Well seasoned and appropriately finished.
5 Served at the correct temperature, hot or cold, depending on the type of soup.

Did you know?

The ideal temperature for the following is:

cooking of soup	100°C
holding of soup	75°C
service of soup	65°C
storage of soup	4°C.

Test yourself!

1 Name four different types of soup as they will appear on the menu.

2 Identify the main differences between the following:
   a Purée and cream soups
   b Broth and consommé
   c Velouté and cream soups.

3 Indicate the correct temperatures for the following:
   a Cooking of soup
   b Holding of soup
   c Service of soup
   d Storage of soup.

4 State four quality points to look for in the finished soup.

5 Suggest four ways of preparing, cooking and finishing basic soups to make them healthier.

6 Indicate the main difference between a garnish and an accompaniment. Give an example of each.

7 Indicate the finishing of the following soups:
   a Cream
   b Purée
   c Velouté.

8 Name four different thickening agents used in the preparation of basic soups.

Basic sauces

Types of sauces

Marinades were originally used to preserve and tenderise meat. Later they were also used to improve the flavour of dishes. Creative chefs transformed these marinades into sauces, to moisten a stew or accompany roast meats. Some sauces were originally devised to disguise the strong flavours of meat and game. Others, for example a creamy purée of beans or peas, helped to balance the saltiness of preserved meats.

The seventeenth-century in France was the 'golden age' of sauce creation. During that period famous chefs developed a small group of basic sauces, also known as 'mother sauces', from which hundreds of variations came. The original mother sauces were stock-based brown sauce, velouté, milk-based béchamel and hollandaise made from egg yolks. Another basic sauce was added a century later when tomatoes arrived from the New World. At first chefs believed that the scarlet flesh of the tomato was deadly poison. Soon they realised that the flesh can easily be broken down and made into a **piquant** purée sauce.

Did you know?
The word 'sauce' comes from the Latin 'salsus', meaning 'flavoured with salt'.

Definition
Piquant: a pleasant, sharp taste.

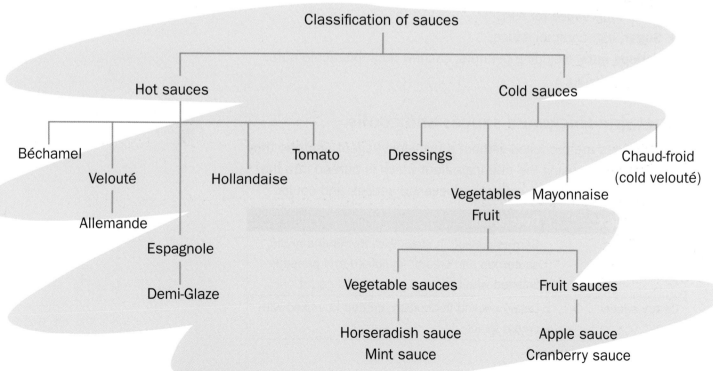

Figure 11.19 Classification of sauces

Thickening sauces

Thickening agents

Thickening agents used in the preparation of sauces include the following types:

1 **Roux**. This is an equal mixture of fat and flour, cooked slowly to break down the starch cells in the flour and allow thickening to take place. There are three types of roux:
    o white (used for e.g. Béchamel sauce).
    o blond (used for e.g. Velouté sauce).
    o brown (used for e.g. Espagnole sauce).
2 **Egg yolks**. These are used for hot and cold sauces, e.g. hollandaise sauce (hot), mayonnaise sauce (cold).
3 **Beurre manie**. This is a mixture of butter and flour kneaded together to form a paste. Small pieces of this mixture are dropped in boiling liquid and whisked together to form a sauce.
4 **Bread**, e.g. bread sauce.
5 **Vegetables and potatoes**.
6 **Fresh fruit**, e.g. apple sauce, cranberry sauce.
7 **Cornflour and fécule** (starch from potatoes). These are used to thicken roast gravy (jus-lié).
8 **Butter**. This is used in an emulsified form, e.g. butter sauce, white wine sauce for fish.
9 **Sugar**, e.g. caramel sauce.
10 **Various nuts**, including peanuts, cashew nuts, pistachio nuts, e.g. Satay sauce.

Vegetable-thickened sauces and coulis

Some sauces are produced without a thickening agent. Instead they are thickened by using the title ingredient which is puréed into the sauce, as in the case of vegetable-thickened sauces and coulis.

Type of sauce	Description
Carrot sauce	Carrots cooked in stock with thyme and garlic, sauternes and cream; liquidised and passed; finished with brunoise of blanched carrot.
Celery sauce	Celery cooked in bouillon, puréed in, mixed with cream sauce.

Fennel sauce	Fennel cooked in white stock with pernod, enriched with cream and butter.
Red capsicum coulis	Red capsicums cooked with garlic and shallots; moistened with white wine and cooked in vegetable stock before **liquidising** and passing through a fine sieve.
Tomato coulis	Tomatoes cooked with vinegar, tomato purée and olive oil. Processed and passed through a fine sieve.

Figure 11.10 Vegetable-thickened sauces

Fruit-thickened sauces

Type of sauce	Description
Apple sauce	Peeled apples cooked with sugar, water, lemon juice and a little cinnamon. Can be enriched with butter.
Cranberry sauce	Cranberries cooked in water, orange juice and port with sugar.
Gooseberry sauce	Gooseberries cooked with sugar and puréed.
Cherry sauce	Reduction of port wine, mixed spice and orange juice; with redcurrant jelly and stoned cherries.

Figure 11.11 Fruit-thickened sauces

Pulse-thickened sauces

These purée-type sauces can be made with any pulse vegetable. They require some hard physical work as they need to be passed firmly through a fine sieve to remove the fibrous outer shells.

Puy lentil sauce: puy lentils cooked in stock with shallots, garlic and thyme, liquidised and passed through a fine sieve.

Miscellaneous sauces

Some sauces fail to fit into any of the groups mentioned and are put into the miscellaneous group. Sauces that may appear here include:
- Bread sauce: thickened by the starch from bread.
- Curry sauces: the word 'curry' comes from the Tamil word for sauce.
- Sweet and sour sauce: thickened using arrowroot.

Did you know?
Although the term 'coulis' is usually referred to as a fruit sauce it is sometimes used to describe some vegetable sauces.

Definition
Liquidising or **blending**: to mix two or more ingredients together in the food processor or liquidiser.

Preparing sauces

Liquids used

1 White stock (see page 286)
2 Brown stock (see page 287)
3 Milk, cream and yoghurt
4 Vegetable and fruit juices
5 Water, beer, wines (white and red), vinegar, various oils, lemon juice
6 Meat juices
7 Court-bouillon.

Flavourings used

- Herbs: parsley, thyme, chives, chervil, tarragon, marjoram, basil, bay leaves, oregano, mint and rosemary.
- Spices: black peppercorns, white peppercorns, nutmeg, cloves, saffron, mace, allspice, cayenne pepper, juniper berries.
- Bouquet garni: the following, tied in a bundle: thyme, bay leaf, parsley stalk, celery stick, piece of leek, green.
- Mirepoix of vegetables: roughly diced onions, carrots and celery.

Equipment required

The equipment you will need when preparing sauces:

- saucepans
- sauteuse
- wooden spatula
- wooden spoon
- ladles
- conical strainer
- colander
- sieves and wooden mushroom
- pestle and mortar
- whisks
- balloon whisk
- chopping board
- set of knives
- muslin cloth
- tammy cloth
- bain-marie.

Common faults when making sauces

Type of sauce	Common faults
Fruit/pulse/vegetable thickened sauce	Not using enough fruit/pulse/vegetable or using too much. Cooking time too short. Cooking temperature too high. Insufficient liquid.
Cream thickened sauce	Heat too high, causing it to burn. Over-**reducing**. Under-reducing. Using the wrong type of cream: double cream is usually the correct cream to use. Using aluminium pans, which discolour the sauce.
Jus	Over-reducing. Under-reducing. Too much thickening agent in the case of jus-lié. Fat not drained from tray, resulting in a greasy jus. Not skimmed. Not strained.
Reduction	Under-reduced. Over-reduced. Not skimming. Seasoning too soon, causing the salts to concentrate. Placing over too low a heat. Reducing at the wrong stage, e.g. while bones are in the liquid.
Brown stock	Bones not browned enough. Bones browned too much. Boiling too rapidly, causing it to go cloudy. Not skimming enough. Using unfit bones. Not cooling quickly.
White stock	Boiling too rapidly. Not skimming enough. Seasoning with salt. Using unfit bones. Too much liquid in relation to bones.
Meat glaze	Over-reducing, producing a bitter glaze. Not straining. Seasoning and becoming too salty, if there are enough natural salts. Under-reducing. Not skimming.

Figure 11.12 Faults in preparing sauces

Healthy eating

- Use an alternative to roux as a thickening agent in the preparation of hot sauces.
- Replace butter in roux with vegetable fats or margarine.
- Ensure that the stocks used for sauces are free from traces of fat.
- Do not use butter, fresh cream or egg yolks to finish the sauces.
- Reduce the level of salt and seasoning in the sauces.
- Avoid the use of alcohol in finishing the sauces.

Definition

Reduce: to concentrate or thicken a sauce. This is done by boiling it to make the water evaporate and reduce the volume of the sauce.

Hot sauces

Béchamel

When preparing béchamel sauce, the 'boiling out' process gives body and stability to the sauce. This is especially important if the sauce is used as a base for soufflés. If the sauce has thickness, but no body or stability, a soufflé will tend to 'spew', or sink.

Béchamel sauce

butter	480g
flour	480g
boiling milk	4 litres
salt	30g
white pepper	pinch
grated nutmeg	pinch
onion, studded with cloves	1
sprig of thyme	1
Cooking time	30 minutes
Makes	4 litres

Preparation	1
Cooking skills	2
Finishing	2

Method

1. Use the butter and flour to make a white roux and cool it.
2. Gradually add the boiling milk, stirring vigorously. Make sure the sauce is quite smooth before adding each small quantity of milk. If this instruction is not followed – or the milk is added too quickly – the sauce will become lumpy.
3. When all the milk has been added, bring to the boil – still stirring – then remove to the side of the stove. Add the seasoning, onion and thyme. Allow to cook gently for one hour.
4. Remove from the heat. Pass through a tammy cloth.
5. Cover with a circle of buttered paper from which the centre has been cut out.
6. Place to one side to cool. If required hot, place in a bain-marie with a few small knobs of butter on top to prevent a skin forming.

Video presentation

For guidance on how to make a roux watch *Prepare velouté sauce (1) make roux.*

Espagnole sauce

Espagnole is the basic sauce for many others. As good sauces cannot be produced from faulty bases, the espagnole must be right from the word 'go'. Therefore, the brown stock used must be of a good flavour, good colour and clear. Do not burn the roux or it will give a bitter flavour to the sauce.

The finished sauce should be 'bright', smooth and clean. The vegetables must be removed before they break up and cloud the sauce. The scum must not boil back into the sauce.

Make sure your strainer and pots are quite clean – many good sauces have been ruined by **passing** them into a dirty saucepan or through an unclean strainer.

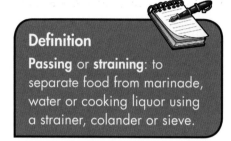

Definition

Passing or **straining**: to separate food from marinade, water or cooking liquor using a strainer, colander or sieve.

Espagnole sauce

dripping or white fat	480g
flour	480g
brown beef stock	10 litres
carrots	480g
onions	480g
sticks celery	60g
tomato purée *or*	120g
fresh tomatoes, crushed	1kg
bouquet garni	1
Cooking time	16 hours
Makes	5 litres

Preparation	2
Cooking skills	2
Finishing	2

Method
1 Use the dripping or white fat and flour to make a brown roux and cool it.
2 Add boiling brown stock gradually, making sure that the stock and roux are smoothly combined before adding more. Stir vigorously with a wooden spatula. This prevents the cooking flour from becoming lumpy.
3 When all the stock has been added, stir until the sauce boils and then put the pan on the side of the stove to simmer gently. Allow to simmer for eight hours, skimming any thick scum and fat.
4 Make a mirepoix of the carrots, onions and celery by dicing. Fry them to a golden colour in a little clean fat. Add this, the bouquet garni and the tomato purée or the fresh tomatoes and continue simmering for a further two hours.
5 Remove from the heat. Pass through a fine strainer (chinois).
6 Simmer the sauce for a further six hours, skimming constantly.
7 Strain and put aside for further use.

Velouté

Velouté sauce

butter	480g
flour	480g
white veal stock	6 litres
salt	to season
white mushroom liquor	400ml
Cooking time	45–60 minutes
Makes	5 litres

Preparation	2
Cooking skills	3
Finishing	3

Method

1 Use the butter and flour to make a blond roux and cool it.
2 Gradually add the boiling stock to the roux as described in espagnole.
3 Reboil, stirring well.
4 Add the mushroom liquor and allow to simmer for one hour, removing any scum during the process.
5 Remove from the heat. Pass through a tammy cloth or fine strainer. Coat with a little butter to prevent skin formation and put aside for future use.

Allemande sauce

white veal stock	400ml
velouté of veal	1 litre
egg yolks	5
mushroom liquor	400ml
lemon juice	from ½ lemon
cream	400ml
butter	60g
Cooking time	30–45 minutes
Makes	1 litre

Preparation	2
Cooking skills	4
Finishing	4

Method

1 Place the veal stock, velouté, mushroom liquor and egg yolks together in a thick-bottomed sauté pan. Mix well.
2 Reduce to one litre over an open flame while stirring and keeping the bottom clear from burning with a spatula.
3 Add the cream and reboil.
4 Remove from stove and work in the butter. Add the lemon juice.
5 Pass through a fine strainer or a muslin.
6 Cover with a buttered circle of greaseproof paper with a small hole in the centre through which the steam escapes.

Video presentation

Watch *Prepare velouté sauce (1) make roux* and *Prepare velouté sauce (2) mix, boil and simmer* to see this being made.

Chef's tip

Velouté should not be milky in appearance but should be bright and have body.

Chef's tip

To make mushroom liquor, first wash mushroom stalks and trimmings. Put them in a buttered pan with a few drops of lemon juice. Cover them with buttered paper and sweat them out. Finally, strain off the moisture.

Tomato

Tomato sauce

Preparation	4
Cooking skills	2
Finishing	3

diced bacon trimmings, blanched	80g
butter	125g
diced carrots for mirepoix	80g
diced onions for mirepoix	80g
plain flour	125g
tomato purée	300g
garlic, crushed cloves	2
white stock	3 litres
bouquet garni	1
salt	to season
pepper	to season
sugar	15g
Cooking time	2 hours
Makes	2 litres

Method

1. Place the butter and bacon into a thick-bottomed straight-sided pan. Allow to colour slightly.
2. Add the diced onion and carrot. Cook gently and lightly colour.
3. Add the flour and mix well.
4. Cook to a blond roux, then cool a little.
5. Add tomato purée and garlic.
6. Gradually add the boiling stock, mixing well.
7. Add the bouquet garni and salt.
8. When boiling remove the spoon, clean inside the saucepan with a palette knife.
9. Cover with a lid. Simmer for one hour.
10. Pass sauce through a sieve with pressure. Reboil, check the thickness and seasoning.
11. Add sugar to counteract the acidity of the tomato purée.
12. Pass the sauce through a fine chinois into a sauce bain-marie.
13. Butter the surface, cover with a lid, keep hot in the bain-marie.

Chef's tip

For large amounts this sauce can be cooked in a moderately hot oven.

 Find out!　　　　　　　　　　**Worksheet 34**

Find as many derivative sauces as you can for each of the following basic sauces: béchamel, velouté, espagnole, hollandaise and tomato.

Gravy

This is made from the meat juices after roasting, e.g. chicken, beef, lamb or pork. Gravy should not really be thickened. A good-quality gravy should be free from fat and have a strong meaty taste.

The flavour of gravy can be improved by the addition of alcohol such as white wine or red wine. It is normally served as an accompaniment with roast meat and poultry and the dish is described as 'au jus'.

Definition

Jus: juice.

Jus-lié

This is a rich, smooth and lightly thickened sauce made from meat juices. The thickening agent used in the preparation of Jus-lié is cornflour or arrowroot.

Did you know?

Jus-lié can also be prepared by just reducing rich brown stock to a shiny glaze. The gelatinous nature of brown stock will help to thicken the sauce.

1 Mix the cornflour or arrowroot with a little cold water and then add slowly to the rich brown stock or reduced meat juices from the pot-roasting tray.
2 Bring to the boil and simmer for 20–25 minutes.
3 Strain through a conical strainer and use.

Temperatures for the cooking, holding and serving of sauces are:
- Cooking of sauces   100°C
- Holding of sauces   75°C
- Service of sauces   65°C
- Storage of sauces   4°C.

Finishing sauces

Methods of finishing sauces include:
- Monter: this method involves finishing the sauce with a few pieces of butter at the last minute prior to serving, e.g. white wine sauce for fish dishes or Madeira sauce for tournedos.
- Adding whipped double cream: this is folded into warm sauce as a glazing for a fish dish.
- Adding fresh cream and egg yolk liaison: to finish sauces for dishes such as Chicken fricassee.
- Adjusting consistency: e.g. adding potato flour diluted in cold water to meat juices from the roasting tray, e.g. Jus-lié.
- Garnishing: e.g. adding short julienne of gherkins to Sauce charcutière.
- Seasoning: e.g. adding mustard to Mustard sauce.

Try this!   **Worksheet 35**

How many of the words can you find in the wordsearch?

Storage

All sauces should be strained through a conical strainer or fine chinois. In some cases, the sauce might have to be passed through a muslin or tammy cloth.

Sauces which are to be used immediately should be stored in a bain-marie with a few knobs of butter placed on top to stop a skin forming. Cover the bain-marie with a lid and label it. Sauces which are prepared for later use should be stored in a bowl and covered with a circle of buttered greaseproof paper from which the centre has been removed. This is to allow heat to escape. The bowl should be raised on a trivet to allow air to pass round and under it to speed cooling. When cold – and only when cold – the sauces may be placed in a refrigerator. The sauce bowl should be labelled and dated. Sauces should be used in rotation – first in, first out.

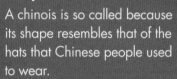

Did you know?
A chinois is so called because its shape resembles that of the hats that Chinese people used to wear.

Test yourself!

1 Name four basic sauces.

2 What is the difference between:
   a Béchamel sauce and velouté sauce?
   b Gravy and jus-lié?
   c Espagnole sauce and tomato sauce?

3 What is the correct the temperature for:
   a cooking of sauces?
   b holding of sauces?
   c service of sauces?
   d storage of sauces?

4 State four quality points to look for in the finished sauces.

5 Name four different thickening agents used in the preparation of sauces.

6 State four different methods of finishing sauces.

7 Write down four different ways of making healthier sauces.

8 Give two uses of each of the following basic sauces:
   a Béchamel sauce
   b Espagnole sauce
   c Velouté sauce
   d Tomato sauce.

12

Rice, pasta, grain and egg dishes

This chapter covers skills and knowledge in the following units:

- 7132 Unit 239 (2FPC4) Prepare, cook and finish basic rice dishes
- 7132 Unit 240 (2FPC5) Prepare, cook and finish basic pasta dishes
- 7132 Unit 247 (2FPC12) Prepare, cook and finish basic grain dishes
- 7132 Unit 243 (2FPC8) Prepare, cook and finish basic egg dishes

Working through this chapter could also provide the opportunity to practise the following Functional Skills at Level 2:
Functional ICT Finding and selecting information – recognise and take account of copyright and other constraints on the use of information; evaluate fitness for purpose of information

In this chapter you will:

Understand how and be able to prepare basic rice dishes	7132 – 239.1,2
Understand how and be able to cook basic rice dishes	7132 – 239.3,4
Understand how and be able to finish basic rice dishes	7132 – 239.5,6
Understand how and be able to prepare basic pasta dishes	7132 – 240.1,2
Understand how and be able to cook basic pasta dishes	7132 – 240.3,4
Understand how and be able to finish basic pasta dishes	7132 – 240.5,6
Understand how and be able to prepare basic grain dishes	7132 – 247.1,2
Understand how and be able to cook basic grain dishes	7132 – 247.3,4
Understand how and be able to finish basic grain dishes	7132 – 247.5,6
Understand how and be able to prepare basic egg dishes	7132 – 243.1,2
Understand how and be able to cook basic egg dishes	7132 – 243.3,4
Understand how and be able to finish basic egg dishes	7132 – 243.5,6

You will learn to cook basic rice, pasta, grain and egg dishes, including:

- risotto
- baked rice pudding
- ravioli
- Scotch oatcakes
- millet croquettes
- Spanish omelette.

Rice

Rice is a type of grain which grows on dry and wet land. It has been a food source for well over 3,000 years and is the second largest cultivated food source in the world.

Rice is grown in many countries, but mainly in China, India, Bangladesh, Africa and America. Rice can be eaten hot or cold, and used in savoury or sweet dishes.

Rice seeds are covered in a husk or tough outer skin. The seeds are milled to remove the husk and produce brown rice. With further milling the **germ** and the **bran** of the plant are removed, producing white rice.

Types of rice

The three main types of rice available are long grain, short grain and round grain.

Long grain rice is shaped like a narrow missile with a point. It is ideal for use with plain boiled rice dishes or savoury dishes. The grains remain separate during cooking because it has a tough hard texture and holds its shape. It is usually white and slightly see-through. Long grain is the rice most usually found in kitchens. When cooked, long grain rice has a light fluffy texture.

Short grain rice is round and looks a little like wheat. When cooked, it has a softer texture than the long grain type and the grains stick together easily. It has a light colour, sometimes golden but normally creamy white. Because this rice sticks so well, it is ideal for risotto and paella dishes.

Round grain rice is very much like short grain rice. When cooked, it has a soft texture, is almost see-through and goes sticky. It is used mainly for sweet rice dishes like puddings and is also known as pearl or pudding rice.

Although rice is broken down into long, short and round grain categories, these categories also contain different types of rice and have many differernt names and uses.

Figure 12.1 A rice plant growing in a paddy field

> **Definition**
> **Germ**: the heart of the seed.
> **Bran**: the hard outer layer of the rice seed.

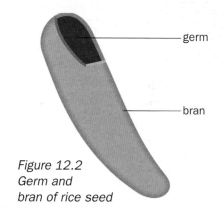

Figure 12.2 Germ and bran of rice seed

germ

bran

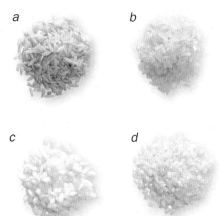

Figure 12.3 Types of rice: a brown long grain, b long grain, c round grain, d arborio

a

b

c

d

You will come across the main types when shopping for rice, and these include brown basmati, jasmine, japonica and arborio; all of these types of rice are available in most supermarkets.

Other rice types that are not so well know are carnaroli, vialone nano, baldo and carolina rice.

Brown rice: This is a very nutritious long grain rice. It has a sandy colour. When cooked, brown rice has a chewy texture with a mild nutty flavour.

Basmati: This is an Indian long grain rice. It is sometimes called the king of rices because of its great flavour; when cooked it has a nice aromatic quality and is best used as plain boiled rice to accompany spicy dishes.

Japonica: This is a Chinese long grain rice often used in sushi dishes; it is almost black and when cooked has a nutty mushroom-type flavour. It can be used in stir-fries and casseroles, but also as a stuffing.

Arborio: This is an Italian round pearl grain rice; it is most often used in risotto dishes but can also be used in puddings.

Vialone nano: This is an Italian short grain rice ideal in risotto, paella and puddings. This rice should ideally not be washed before use.

Jasmine: This is Thai long grain rice; when cooked it is less sticky that most other long grain rices and is best suited to plain boiled or fried rice dishes.

Carnaroli and baldo: These are Italian short grain rices mainly used in risotto and paella dishes; they are also good for puddings.

Carolina: This is an American white long grain rice; it is perfect for plain boiled rice, fried rice and use cold in salads.

Quality points for rice

Most rice, dried pasta and grains come packed and treated and are usually quite clean, but you must still check their quality.

When selecting rice it is very important to check for imperfections. Before using rice, dried pasta or grains always check the following:
- It has been correctly stored, off the ground in a waterproof container or a storage bin that has a lid.

Healthy eating
Brown rice is high in fibre and is a much healthier alternative to white rice.

Marcus says
Cooked rice is a high risk food, so be sure to employ the correct cook, chill, reheat methods to avoid any food safety issues.

Remember!
If you find problems with any ingredient you should:
- inform your supervisor or line manager immediately
- ask your supervisor for a substitute or replacement ingredient
- never use the problem ingredient
- separate the problem ingredient from the others before use.

- It has been stored in a cool well-ventilated store free from damp.
- It does not have any other physical contaminants, e.g. stones or anything that may have fallen into the storage container.
- If it is still in the original packaging, that it is free from tears, rips or general damage.

Preparation methods

It is important to check the dish requirements before you begin preparing your dish. You should check what type of rice you need (long, short, round, brown) and the quantity you require, as this reduces unnecessary wastage.

Before cooking rice, wash it under cold running water to remove unwanted starch left over from milling and packaging. Also, as rice is tightly packed the grains rub against each other and leave a fine floury substance in the packet which needs to be removed. Washing the rice before cooking means it is less likely to stick.

It is important to weigh rice carefully to reduce wastage as rice gets larger and fluffs up as it cooks.

Cooking methods

Boiling

Boiling is the easiest and most usual way to cook rice. It is an ideal way to cook rice for serving with curries or meat dishes.

The rice (usually long grain) is plunged into boiling salted water for 15–20 minutes. When the rice is light and fluffy, but still with a little bite, it is cooked. Drain the rice in a colander and wash it off well to remove starch before service.

To safely store boiled rice for use in cold dishes, e.g. salads, drain the boiled rice under cold running water in a colander until cooled, allow to drain then put it in a covered container and refrigerate until required.

Steaming

Steamed rice is popular in Chinese-style cookery. It is simple and quick, and most types of rice can be steamed. Steamed rice is eaten plain or used as a garnish for meats and fish.

Did you know?
For a main dish the ideal portion of uncooked rice is 65g (2½ ounces) per person.

There are two ways to steam rice. The first way is to put washed rice over boiling water in a steamer; this takes 20–40 minutes.

The second, and more common, way is to combine boiling and steaming. Put the rice into a pan and cover it with 1½ times as much water. Cover with a tight-fitting lid, bring to the boil, then turn down the heat and cook until all the water has been absorbed by the rice or evaporated.

Stewing

Rice can be stewed in stock, water or milk. Set up as for boiling but keep the rice on the heat until most of the liquid has gone. It is important to keep stirring to prevent the rice sticking to the side or bottom of the pan.

Frying

Countries like China, Nepal and India use fried rice as part of many of their dishes. After you have boiled rice you can fry it, which is a good way to give the rice flavour. You can add other ingredients, e.g. vegetables or meat.

Fried rice

rice	5kg
oil	1 tsp
Cooking time	25 minutes
serves	40

Preparation	1
Cooking skills	1
Finishing	1

Method

1 Boil and cool the rice.
2 Put the cooked rice in a deep frying pan with some oil or butter or margarine.
3 Heat it over a low heat and stir often to stop it sticking.

Find out! Worksheet 36

Visit the website for 'The Cook's Thesaurus' and go to the rice section. A link has been made available at www.heinemann.co.uk/hotlinks. Just follow the links and enter the express code 9257P. Choose ten types of rice and find out:
o country of origin
o uses
o cooking method and time
o a recipe for each.

Egg fried rice

		Preparation	1
rice	5kg	Cooking skills	2
eggs	25	Finishing	1
Cooking time	25 minutes		
Serves	40		

Method

1. Boil and cool the rice.
2. Lightly scramble the eggs in a frying pan.
3. Add the cooked rice, season and mix with the egg.

Baking

This method is best suited to puddings. The best rice to use is round or short grain.

Milk is the most common liquid used with baked rice and forms the basis of rice pudding. Put the rice into the boiling liquid. Other ingredients may be added to help flavour the rice. Put this mixture into an oven and bake until the liquid has been soaked up by the rice.

Baked rice pudding

		Preparation	1
milk	500ml	Cooking skills	1
round grain or pearl rice	160g	Finishing	1
sugar	120g		
nutmeg, grated	pinch		
Oven temperature	190°C		
Cooking time	30–35 minutes		
Serves	4		

Method

1. Put the milk into a medium-sized milk pan. Bring the milk to the boil and slowly add the rice. Remember to stir while you add the rice. Allow to boil for one minute.
2. Take off the boil. Slowly add the sugar and nutmeg.
3. Pour the mixture into an ovenproof baking dish, then put the dish into a medium/deep baking pan.
4. Pour boiling water into the baking pan so that it comes 1cm up the side of the baking dish, creating a bain-marie.
5. Cook in a preheated oven.
6. Remove the pudding from the oven, allow it to cool slightly.
7. Clean the outside of the dish and serve.

Braising

The common term for this method of preparing rice is pilaf or pilau. Long grain rice is the best type to use.

To prepare dishes such as pilaf, paella or risotto, sweat the rice in butter or oil to begin the cooking process. This coats the rice in fat. Add liquid, e.g. water or stock, and braise in an oven or over heat.

Pilaf or pilau of rice

Preparation	2
Cooking skills	1
Finishing	2

onions, finely chopped	80g
butter	40g
white long grain rice, washed	260g
stock or water	750ml
Oven temperature	200°C
Cooking time	16–18 minutes
Serves	4

Method

1. Using a deep frying pan, sweat the onions in half the butter, being careful not to brown them.
2. Add the washed rice and stir until it becomes almost transparent.
3. Add the boiling stock or water and season.
4. Place a cartouche (buttered greaseproof paper) on to the liquid and rice, cover with a lid and put the pan into a preheated oven. Alternatively, transfer the rice and liquid to an ovenproof dish and proceed as before.
5. Remove the pan or ovenproof dish from the oven and allow the rice to stand for five minutes.
6. Stir in the remaining butter with a fork to separate the grains and transfer the rice to a serving dish.

Microwaving

Rice can be reheated in a microwave but you must be very careful as it is a high-risk food. (See below.)

Video presentation

If you would like to find out more about sweating food watch *Prepare fish stock (1) sweat.*

Did you know?

Au gras is cooked in the same way as pilaf rice but the rice is cooked with fat bouillon stock of chicken or beef.

Did you know?

Medium or long grain rice absorbs up to three times its weight in liquid.

Risotto

onion, finely chopped	30g
cooking oil	30g
short or round grain rice	350g
white stock	1.5 litres
salt	to season
bay leaf	1
butter	15g
finely grated Cheddar or Parmesan cheese	60g
Cooking time	15 minutes
Serves	5

Method

1 Using a medium-sized pan, sweat the finely chopped onions in the oil. Do not let them colour.
2 Add the rice and heat through.
3 Add the stock, season well and bring to the boil.
4 Add the bay leaf and simmer gently over a low heat. Stir frequently as the stock is absorbed by the rice.
5 When the rice is cooked, stir in the butter and grated cheese.
6 Serve sprinkled with grated cheese.

Chef's tip

Here are some interesting variations on this basic dish:
Mushroom risotto
Add 300g porcini mushrooms or ceps (fresh) and 25g diced ceps.
Vegetable risotto
Add 2 courgettes, ½ celery stalk, ½ leek, 100g fresh peas, 100g broad beans. Reduce liquid to 1.2 litres but add 100ml white wine.
Asparagus risotto
Add 500g asparagus (diced).

Safe use and storage of rice

Safe service and storage of rice dishes, whether hot or cold, is very important. The following points must be remembered:

○ Hot rice dishes should be served at a minimum of 63°C. If you are hot-holding the dish for any length of time, e.g. on a hotplate, it should be kept at or above this temperature.

○ Reheated rice should have a core temperature of 75°C before service. Only reheat rice once.

○ Rice for service as a cold dish should be served at a temperature of 5°C and eaten as soon as possible afterwards.

Remember!

Rice is a high-risk food. Make sure the rice is properly cooked, cooled and stored.

○ When using pre-cooked rice for dishes, e.g. salads, it is important that the rice has been properly stored in a refrigerator at a temperature of 3°C–5°C.

○ Any rice stored after cooking should be covered and labelled showing the date.

○ Do not use rice that has been refrigerated for more than three days (check label for the date).

Test yourself!

1 Write down three cooking methods for long grain rice.

2 At what temperature should rice be served when used as an ingredient in a hot dish?
   a 60°C
   b 65°C
   c 73°C
   d 75°C.

3 What temperature must reheated rice reach before service?
   a 60°C
   b 65°C
   c 73°C
   d 75°C.

4 Why is brown rice a healthier option than white rice?

5 What is the best rice to use for puddings?
   a Long grain rice
   b Round grain rice
   c Brown rice
   d Arborio.

6 What weight is an ideal portion of uncooked rice?
   a 55g
   b 60g
   c 65g
   d 70g.

7 Draw and label a diagram showing the parts of a rice seed.

8 Which four ingredients do you need to make a Baked rice pudding?

9 Rice is grown in many countries. Write down the names of three of them.

10 Before cooking rice what should you do?

Pasta

Traditionally, Italian pasta is made from wheat flour, eggs and oil. Sometimes water is used instead of eggs. The ingredients are mixed together and kneaded like dough. Pasta may be flavoured during the mixing stage by adding purées of vegetables, which can also colour it.

Types of pasta

Pasta has many varieties and comes in many shapes. Some well-known pasta varieties are spaghetti, cannelloni, macaroni, tortellini and ravioli. Pasta can be eaten plain, filled with vegetables, meat or cheese, fish and shellfish or simply eaten with a sauce.

Fresh pasta

Common colours for fresh pasta:
- Light yellow: the colour for fresh pasta. It has a plain taste.
- Green: this pasta may have had spinach added. It is called pasta verde.
- Red: this comes from adding tomato purée and is called pasta rossa.

More colours can be created by adding unusual ingredients:
- Black: add diluted cuttlefish ink.
- Purple: add beetroot juice.
- Brown: add bitter chocolate powder.

Once mixed, the fresh pasta is kneaded, shaped, filled, rolled or cut as needed. Fresh pasta can easily be formed into different shapes.

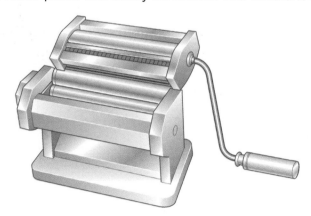

Figure 12.4 A pasta machine rolls the dough very thin

Did you know?
It is quite common for people, especially when young, to have an allergy to eggs.

Did you know?
'Pasta' is an Italian word meaning 'paste' or 'dough'.

Chef's tip
Fresh pasta dough should be smooth to touch with an elastic feel.

Did you know?
You can buy machines to roll out pasta very thin. It can then be cut into shapes, sheets or strips.

Basic pasta dough

Preparation	1
Cooking skills	2
Finishing	–

flour (durum wheat flour, plain flour, brown flour or semolina)	500g
salt	pinch
eggs *or*	5
cold water	200ml
oil	15ml
Serves	10

Method

1 Sift the flour with the salt.
2 Make a bay, add the eggs *or* water. Add the oil and mix to a stiff paste.
3 Knead together well and allow to relax for 20 minutes.
4 Dust with a little flour or semolina to reduce sticking and use as required.

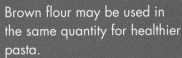

Healthy eating

Brown flour may be used in the same quantity for healthier pasta.

Marcus says

If making fresh pasta, use free range eggs to improve colour and texture. Be sure to use the best quality pasta flour to gain the best results.

Dried pasta

Dried pasta is simply fresh pasta that has been dried. Dried pasta has a long shelf life. Generally, the plain unfilled dried pasta, e.g. conchiglie or spaghetti, can be kept for as long as two years provided it is kept dry and covered. Other dried and filled pasta such as tortellini lasts less time. Always check the 'use by' dates on the package before use (see page 114).

Shaped pasta

Fresh, kneaded pasta dough can be shaped by hand or using a machine. The dough comes out in the selected shape and is cut to size ready for drying or cooking.

Figure 12.5 Tortellini being shaped around a finger

In the table are examples of some popular pasta shapes:

Pasta shapes	Description of use
Rigatoni	Very good for heavier sauce dishes, e.g. bolognese or thick cheese sauce.
Cannelloni	Stuffed, covered with a sauce and baked.
Spaghetti	Good with almost any sauce, and can also be stir-fried after it has been boiled.
Linguine	A thin, long flat shape, good with sauce or in a salad.
Twists or rotini	The twist can hold meat, vegetables or cheese. This shape is ideal baked, as a pasta salad or stir-fried.
Farfalle	A 'butterfly' shape – ideal with a light sauce.
Vermicelli	Like thin spaghetti, this is ideal with light sauces.
Penne	This shape is a good choice to mix with a sauce, or use in a soup or salad.

Figure 12.7 Popular pasta shapes

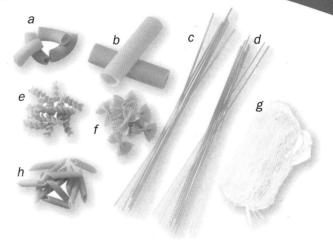

Figure 12.6 Pasta shapes: a rigatoni; b cannelloni; c spaghetti; d linguine; e twists; f farfalle; g vermicelli; h penne

Flat pasta

To make flat pasta, e.g. tagliatelle or lasagne, the dough is rolled very thin and then cut to a required shape: long strips, short strips or square sheets. The pasta dough can be passed through a machine which will flatten and cut it, or rolled out using a rolling pin and cut with a sharp 9-inch chef's knife.

Stuffed pasta

Stuffed pasta dishes are very popular as the pasta shapes are filled with meat, vegetables or cheese. This type of pasta makes an excellent meal on its own.

Stuffed pasta includes cannelloni, tortellini and ravioli, all of which can be served with a sauce and can be baked.

Cannelloni can be bought dried and filled with the stuffing of your choice. To make fresh cannelloni, follow the steps below.

1 Roll out some pasta dough to 10cm squares, 1.6mm thick.
2 Take a piping bag with a 12.5mm nozzle and pipe your filling in a line down the centre of the square.
3 Lightly egg wash one side of the square and roll it up like a sausage roll.
4 Put the cannelloni in a dish and cover it in a sauce ready for baking. Alternatively, you can cook flat sheets of cannelloni in boiling water for 15 minutes, drain them and serve with a separate sauce.

Figure 12.8 Rolled stuffed cannelloni ready for cooking

Quality points for dried pasta

The quality points for dried pasta are the same as those for rice. See page 316.

Cooking methods

To cook fresh pasta, plunge it into boiling salted water for 3–8 minutes depending on the variety. Filled pasta takes around two minutes longer to cook. Stir pasta regularly during cooking.

Cook dried pasta in the same way but for 8–15 minutes.

Certain varieties of pasta may be combined with other ingredients and baked, e.g. lasagne.

It is important to test pasta while cooking. To test whether pasta is cooked, remove a piece of pasta from the pan and taste it. It should be firm with no floury taste but still stiff enough to need chewing. This is called 'al dente'. It is easy to overcook pasta. When overcooked, pasta becomes stodgy, swells up, and then breaks apart.

Pasta can be cooked and cooled for use in salads or pre-cooked and used at a later date for stir-fries. This is called blanching. See page 122 for more information about blanching.

Boil the pasta, strain it in a colander and refresh it under cold running water until cold. Store it covered in a refrigerator until it is needed.

Chef's tip
Dried pasta cooking times can vary. Always follow the instructions on the packet carefully.

Many pasta dishes are finished or accompanied by sauces, which can be light or heavy. These are some common sauces:

○ **Carbonara**: a light binding sauce with a cream base, cooked bacon pieces or Parma ham. This sauce is traditionally seasoned with crushed black peppercorns. It has many varieties. Many chefs like to include mushrooms and onions to change the flavour of the sauce.

○ **Napoletana** or **Neapolitan**: a tomato-based sauce, which is quite thick and often has other ingredients, e.g. ham, onions, mushroom, garlic, and herbs such as oregano or thyme. This sauce is often poured over the pasta allowing the customer to mix the sauce into the dish themselves.

○ **Bolognese** or **Bolognaise**: traditionally this is a minced meat-based sauce; it contains a little tomato or tomato purée, onions, garlic and herbs, and is usually served with spaghetti.

○ **Pesto**: a green sauce made with a mixture of olive oil, crushed pine nuts, basil and parmesan cheese. It can be served with pasta or Italian bread.

Try this!

Worksheet 37

Write out how to cook perfect pasta.

Spaghetti bolognaise

Preparation	1
Cooking skills	2
Finishing	2

onions, chopped	60g
olive oil	30ml
lean minced beef	280g
garlic clove, crushed	1
tomatoes, peeled and diced	220g
mixed herbs	pinch
beef jus	280ml
salt and pepper	to season
spaghetti	600g
Parmesan cheese (grated)	60g
Cooking time (sauce)	45 minutes
Cooking time (spaghetti)	15–18 minutes
Serves	5

Method

1 Sweat the onions in the oil until tender. Do not colour them.
2 Add the garlic and the minced beef.
3 Cook until the beef separates into individual small pieces, then add the tomato and mixed herbs.
4 Add the beef jus and bring to the boil. Season and simmer for 30 minutes.
5 Boil the spaghetti in salted water for 10–15 minutes for dried pasta, 5 minutes for fresh pasta. When cooked, drain in a colander and lightly refresh under cold water.
6 Heat the butter in a shallow saucepan. Add the spaghetti, season well and stir until thoroughly reheated.
7 Place the spaghetti in a serving dish with the hot bolognaise sauce in the centre. Serve with more Parmesan cheese.

Chef's tip

For speed of service, pasta can be blanched and then cooled in iced water and held until needed. When required it can be reheated quickly. See page 122 for more information on blanching.

Ravioli

pasta dough	250g
egg	1
filling of your choice (savoury mince, ricotta cheese, **duxelle**, shrimp and lemon, tofu)	100g
tomato sauce	200ml
Cheddar or Parmesan cheese, grated	30g
Cooking time	15–20 minutes
Serves	5

Preparation	2
Cooking skills	1
Finishing	1

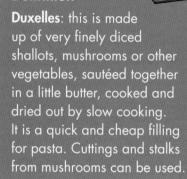

Definition

Duxelles: this is made up of very finely diced shallots, mushrooms or other vegetables, sautéed together in a little butter, cooked and dried out by slow cooking. It is a quick and cheap filling for pasta. Cuttings and stalks from mushrooms can be used.

Method

1 Divide the dough into two equal pieces and roll out each piece to 1.5mm thick. Keep the pieces an even size.
2 Cover one piece in egg wash.
3 Put the filling into a piping bag.
4 Pipe portions of filling the size of a hazelnut 2.5cm apart onto the egg-washed piece of dough.
5 Cover with the second piece of dough and press down between each row of filling in both directions.
6 With the blunt end of a 2.5cm round cutter, press down around each portion of filling.
7 Cut the dough into equal-sized squares with the filling in the centre of each square.
8 Cook in boiling salted water for 10–15 minutes. Remove and drain in a colander.
9 Arrange the ravioli neatly in a baking dish and cover with the tomato sauce.
10 Sprinkle with cheese and lightly grill until the cheese melts.
11 Serve immediately.

Safe use and storage of pasta

The safe use and storage of pasta is the same as that of rice.
See page 321 for detailed information.

Pasta has a short shelf-life after cooking because of its high water
content. Use refrigerated pasta within two days. (Check information
on the label for the date.)

Test yourself!

1 List the three main ingredients used to make pasta dough.

2 Give two cooking methods for pasta.

3 What happens to pasta when it is overcooked?

4 How many days can you keep pasta in a refrigerator?
   a One day
   b Two days
   c Three days
   d Four days.

5 What is Neapolitan sauce?

6 For how long should you cook fresh pasta?
   a 1–5 minutes
   b 2–8 minutes
   c 3–8 minutes
   d 5–10 minutes.

7 For how long should you cook dried pasta?
   a 5–10 minutes
   b 8–15 minutes
   c 10–15 minutes
   d 15–20 minutes.

8 Which of these pasta types can be stir-fried after it has been boiled?
   a Penne
   b Farfalle
   c Linguine
   d Spaghetti.

9 Which of these pasta types has a 'butterfly' shape?
   a Penne
   b Farfalle
   c Linguine
   d Spaghetti.

Grains

Grains are also known as cereals. They are grown in greater quantities worldwide than any other crop. They are cheap to produce.

Grains are the main source of carbohydrates for many developing countries but also contain some protein, fats and vitamins.

Types of grain

Barley

Barley is a cheap, very nutritious food. Barley is a good ingredient for soups and stews, where it is used to thicken the dish.

Two types of barley are available:

○ **Pearl barley**: the most common form of barley. Pearl barley is stripped of a nutritious bran layer during processing, leaving just the 'pearl' inside. Even with this bran layer taken off, pearl barley is still a nutritious food.

○ **Pot barley or whole grain barley**: processed exactly like pearl barley, but the bran layer is left on. This type of barley is the most nutritious.

Pearl and pot barley are very common in health food stores as they are normally sold in their natural form.

Figure 12.9 Processed pearl barley grains

Buckwheat

Buckwheat has a nutty, earthy flavour and gives dishes a rough texture. Buckwheat seeds are triangular after processing and are a light golden colour. It is commonly ground down into flour and used to make everything from pancakes and tortillas to bread and noodles. The seed when ground into flour is gritty and dark and makes an excellent healthy substitute to normal flours. Buckwheat is also popular in some countries, e.g. America and Scotland, as a breakfast cereal.

Corn or maize

This is the only grain that is normally eaten as a fresh vegetable. Corn is high in vitamin A, fibre and other nutrients. Corn is also known as maize in some countries.

Healthy eating
Buckwheat is high in fibre and protein but very low in fat.

Did you know?
Buckwheat is free from gluten, so it is perfect for people with a gluten allergy. For more information on gluten see page 347.

Corn bought fresh and raw in its husk (leafy outer covering) is called 'corn on the cob'. When buying corn on the cob fresh, break off one kernel (piece of corn) and bite it; the kernel should have a slightly sweet taste and be crisp. If the corn has no taste and is very dry, it is overripe.

Polenta

Polenta is made from ground corn called cornmeal. It looks like flour and can be rough or finely ground. It can be yellow or white. Polenta is very popular in Italy and is used in all sorts of recipes.

Polenta is most often served with simple meat dishes like pork chops, sausages or steaks. See page 334 for cooking instructions.

Figure 12.10 Polenta

Oats

Oats are highly nutritious. They contain protein, fat, iron, potassium, B vitamins and carbohydrates. They are high in fibre. Oats have a pleasant, nutty flavor and are fawn in colour.

Oats can be ground down into a meal and used to coat meat or fish. They can be rolled or crushed during processing and used to make breakfast cereals, e.g. porridge or muesli. They can also be used as an ingredient in biscuits or in crumble topping for pudding.

Millet

Millet is very similar to wheat. It can be bought with its outer husk (hull) on or off. Millet seeds can be used to make flour, or used as part of breakfast cereals like muesli. The seeds are very tasty when toasted. Millet can be found in health food shops and is quite cheap.

Figure 12.11 Rolled oats

Healthy eating
Millet is very high in protein but is gluten-free.

Did you know?
Millet flour is very popular in India where it is used to make a flattened bread called bhakri.

Wheat

Wheat is used mainly in making flour; most flour available in the supermarkets is made from wheat. It can be used as grain in salads and also as an ingredient in pilaf dishes, muesli and cereal bars.

Wheat grain that has not been ground into flour has a nutty flavour. It is high in nutrients and gluten.

Wheat is also processed into other ingredients like bulgar, semolina and couscous:

- **Bulgar**: made from whole wheat that has been soaked and baked to speed up cooking time. It can be used as an ingredient in soup, bread and stuffing. It is a popular dish in the Middle East where it is used to make pilaf dishes. Bulgar comes whole, or cracked into fine, medium, or coarse grains. It is very high in nutrients and can be used as an alternative to couscous or rice.

- **Semolina**: wheat that has been roughly ground or milled. It is often boiled and made into a pudding with sugar or another sweetener, e.g. jam. It can be flavoured with vanilla and eaten hot or cold.

- **Couscous**: similar to semolina, but the wheat is ground a little finer. It is used as a side dish to meat or served under a stew or casserole. It is a very popular dish in Africa, Morocco and the Middle East where it is served with vegetables or as a separate side dish. To prepare couscous, soak it in cold water, then drain and wash it before steaming in a steamer or **couscousier**. Couscous can be served with meat or vegetable dishes.

Figure 12.12 Bulgar wheat

Quinoa

Quinoa is pronounced 'keen wah'. It is mostly used as an ingredient for breakfast cereals, but can also be cooked in the same way as rice. Quinoa contains more protein that any other grain. It is described as a perfect food because of the balance of nutrients.

Figure 12.13 A couscousier

Find out!   **Worksheet 38**

Look at the list of grains: barley, buckwheat, corn/maize, polenta, oats, milet, bulgar, wheat, couscous, semolina, quinoa.

Can they be used for:

- classic main course dishes
- garnishes
- desserts?

Definition

Couscousier: a tall pot where stews or vegetables are cooked in the bottom and a smaller pot sits above with the couscous in it. The couscous cooks by steaming and absorbs the flavour from the meat or vegetables below it.

Quality points for grains

The quality points for grains are the same as those for rice. See page 316 for more information. In addition, look for signs of pest infestation. Grains are a favourite food for vermin and other pests. Check the grains for signs of mould, especially if the grains is stored somewhere near moisture.

Problems

See page 316 for more information about what to do if you have problems with ingredients. Report any signs of pest infestation immediately.

Safe use and storage of grains

The safe use and storage of grains is the same as that of rice. See page 321 for more information. Grain dishes that are cooked and finished may be frozen for later use. Put them in a suitable dish and cover them. Label with the date of cooking and freezing, and place in a freezer. Thaw the dish properly before re-use.

Cooking methods

Boiling and simmering

Most grains can be boiled. Both types of barley take around one to two hours to cook, usually by boiling or simmering, although pot barley can take up to three hours to become soft.

Polenta is normally boiled and quick-cook polenta can take as little as five minutes. Traditional polenta can take as long as an hour to cook. Polenta may be served hot and creamy with a little butter added. Extra ingredients, e.g. cheese, can be added just before service.

Oats can be made into porridge, a hot breakfast cereal, if you boil them in milk or water.

Quinoa can be boiled, stewed or baked. It is an ideal replacement for rice and can be treated in much the same way. It takes about 15 minutes to cook.

Pilaf of pot barley

chicken or beef stock	440ml	
pot barley (or pearl barley)	240g	
spring onions, roughly chopped	3	
celery stick, roughly chopped	1	
mushrooms, sliced	220g	
salt and pepper	to season	
Cooking time	15 minutes	
Serves	4	

Preparation 2
Cooking skills 1
Finishing 1

Method

1 Cook the barley in the simmering stock for approx. 45–50 minutes.
2 Drain the barley well and keep it warm. Keep around 100ml stock back.
3 Put the stock in a pan.
4 Add the spring onion and celery. Cook until the celery is soft.
5 Add the mushrooms. Cook until most of the liquid has gone.
6 Add the cooked barley. Mix gently.
7 Season with salt and pepper and serve.

This recipe can also be served cold as a salad.

Frying

Boiled polenta can be allowed to harden and then sliced and sautéed or fried before serving.

Grilling

Hardened polenta can also be sliced and grilled or fried before serving.

Baking

Millet croquettes

cooked millet	480g
celery, finely diced	120g
carrot, finely grated	60g
onion, finely diced	120g
chopped parsley	60g
dill	10g
oregano	5g
flour	120g
water	220ml
Makes	8–10 × 90g croquettes
Oven temperature	170°C
Cooking time	25 minutes

Preparation	2
Cooking skills	1
Finishing	1

Chef's tip
This recipe can be used for vegans.

Method

1 Put the millet, celery, carrots, onion, parsley, dill and oregano into a bowl. Mix.
2 Add the flour. Gradually add the water and mix.
3 Form the mixture into even cigar-shapes, each 4cm long and approx. 90g.
4 Place on a lightly greased tray and bake.

Basic simple cornbread

cornmeal	240g
wheat flour	240g
baking powder	20g
corn oil	50ml
water	330ml
sugar	30g
salt	pinch
Serves	8
Oven temperature	170°C/350°F
Cooking time	20 minutes

Preparation	1
Cooking skills	1
Finishing	1

Method

1 Put all the ingredients into a bowl and mix well.
2 Put in a greased casserole dish.
3 Bake in the oven.

Scotch oatcakes

flour	60g
salt	pinch
baking powder	20g
oatmeal or rolled oats	300g
margarine	90g
milk	150ml
egg wash	1 beaten egg
Oven temperature	190°C
Cooking time	25 minutes
Makes	up to 10 cakes

Preparation	2
Cooking skills	1
Finishing	–

Method

1 Sift the flour into a bowl.
2 Add the salt, baking powder and oatmeal or rolled oats. Mix together.
3 Rub in the margarine until the mixture has sandy texture.
4 Make a well. Add the milk and mix to a stiff paste.
5 Allow to rest for one hour.
6 Roll out to 5mm thick and cut into 75mm circles with a crimped cutter.
7 Place on greased trays and egg wash lightly.
8 Bake.

Test yourself!

1 Explain the importance of using the correct tools, equipment and techniques when preparing dishes containing grains.

2 Briefly explain how grain dishes should be stored.

3 Describe the action to take if you find any ingredient for your dish not suitable.

Eggs

Bird eggs are a common food source. Many varieties of eggs can be cooked and eaten, e.g. eggs from ostriches, quails, ducks and chickens. The eggs most commonly used in cookery are chicken's or hen's eggs. They can be either white or brown, but they look exactly the same inside and taste the same when cooked. Eggs are very nice on their own poached, fried or scrambled, and they are also found in all sorts of recipes, e.g. bread dough, batter, pasta and cakes.

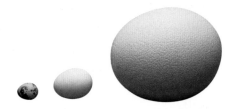

Figure 12.14 Quail, chicken and ostrich eggs

The egg has a yellow centre called a yolk, which is surrounded by albumen, which usually called 'the white of the egg'. The yolk and albumen are covered by a shell which can be easily broken.

The contents of the egg can be used together in dishes, such as sponge cakes that need both yolk and white, or separated, e.g. meringue only uses the white while béarnaise sauce needs just the yolk.

Egg whites make a good raising agent. Egg white proteins break and expand when whipped, forming elastic-walled cells that trap air. The air expands when subjected to heat.

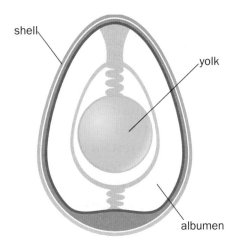

Figure 12.15 The parts of an egg

The main protein in egg white is called albumen. This protein can be strengthened with the addition of an acid, e.g. lemon juice. Strengthened albumen is used when making meringues and royal icing as it provides more body.

Egg yolk proteins bind and thicken. The proteins are less stable than those of the egg white. When exposed to excessive heat, they harden and separate from the yolk's fat and water molecules, causing the yolk to separate and **curdle**.

The setting temperatures of eggs are as follows:

○ Egg white starts setting at a temperature of 62°C and sets completely at a temperature of 70°C.

○ Egg yolk starts setting at a temperature of 65°C and sets completely at a temperature of 70°C.

○ The whole egg, white and yolk mixed, starts setting at a temperature of 63–65°C and sets completely at 70°C.

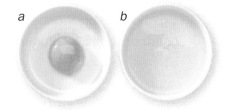

Figure 12.16 Separated eggs: a egg yolk, b egg white

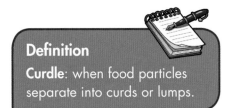

Definition
Curdle: when food particles separate into curds or lumps.

Eggs are available in their shells, as pasteurised whole eggs, pasteurised egg yolks, pasteurised egg whites, and even dried.

Raw eggs are the most common and have the most uses. However, they are a high-risk food, being associated with salmonella food poisoning. The following rules should be followed when using them:

○ Wash your hands after handling eggs.
○ Store fresh eggs in cool dry conditions.
○ Purchase fresh eggs from reputable suppliers.
○ Do not store fresh eggs with strong-smelling foods, because the shell is porous and can absorb smells from other foods.

An average hen's egg weighs about 50g and can be white or brown. Weight is used to measure the size of eggs. See the table below

Size	Very large	Large	Medium	Small
Weight	Larger than 73g	63g–73g	53g–63g	Under 53g

Figure 12.17 Egg sizes

Quality points for eggs

Make these checks when selecting eggs for your dish:

○ The eggs are clean and free from dirt. If the shell has dirt on it, gently wash it with cold water.
○ There are no cracks in the shell.
○ Eggs in their shells have been stored in a dry cool room.
○ Eggs that have been shelled or separated have been covered and kept in a refrigerator.

Make these checks when cracking eggs:

○ The yolk of the egg is a nice bright yellow. Occasionally it may have a blood spot. This is not dangerous and the yolk can be used.
○ The white of the egg is a see-through off-white colour.
○ They have very little smell. If the egg does have a strong smell, throw it away.

Did you know?

Eggs are often used as a symbol of life and fertility. Many ancient philosophers saw eggs as a symbol of the world and its four elements: the shell represented the earth, the white represented water, the yolk represented fire; and the air sac represented air.

o No shell gets into the egg yolk or white as this can be unpleasant for the customer later. If you notice shell in the raw egg after cracking or separating, gently remove it with a fork or spoon.

o Before and after handling and preparing eggs for dishes, you must wash your hands.

Problems

See page 339 for more information.

Cooking methods

Boiling

It takes eight to ten minutes to hard-boil an egg; this means that the yolk and white of the egg are cooked solid. Hard-boiled eggs can be served hot in their shell or cooled and used as garnish, in a salad or as a sandwich filling. They can be combined with other ingredients to form dishes such as Scotch eggs (cooked boiled egg, wrapped in sausagemeat and breadcrumbs, then deep-fried and finished in an oven). For more information on boiling see page 120.

> **Marcus says**
> When poaching, frying or boiling, use fresh eggs to make sure the white and yolk do not separate. Older eggs can be used for other cooking methods such as baking.

How to boil an egg

1 Bring the water to boil and gently put the eggs into the water, using a perforated spoon or a basket.
2 Set a timer, or use a watch or clock, and simmer for 8–10 minutes, depending on how well cooked the eggs need to be for the finished dish.
3 Remove the eggs from the water.
4 If serving hot, place into an egg cup.
5 If using the eggs as part of a cold dish or garnish, cool them immediately under cold running water for a few minutes then store refrigerated in their shells until required.

Soft-boiling

Soft-boiled eggs have a runny yolk and a fully cooked or set white. Follow the same cooking method as boiled eggs, but reduce the time to three to four minutes.

Soft-boiled eggs cannot be used cold. They are usually eaten hot for breakfast.

Frying

See page 123 for more information on frying. Shallow-frying can be difficult as eggs cook very quickly when fried.

How to shallow-fry an egg

1 Put a little oil or butter in a shallow frying pan and gently heat it.
2 Crack an egg into the pan. The egg will begin to cook straight away. The white will go very white, and the yolk will harden.
3 Gently remove the egg from the pan and serve.

Fried eggs can be served as part of a meal, e.g. breakfast, or served as an accompaniment with meat, e.g. gammon steak. They can also be eaten on their own as a snack with some bread.

Poaching

See page 122 for more information on poaching. Poached eggs are cooked in water with a little vinegar added. The acid in the vinegar helps to set the protein in the egg.

How to poach an egg

1 Put some water, a splash of vinegar and a pinch of salt into a pan.
2 Bring the water to the boil then allow it to simmer (just below boiling point).
3 Gently crack an egg into the water. Leave it to poach in the water for three to five minutes.
4 Use a perforated spoon to gently remove the cooked egg.
5 Trim, drain and serve immediately.

Poached eggs can be used as an accompaniment, or eaten on their own as a breakfast meal or as a starter dish to a main meal.

Poached eggs can be drained, cooled in iced water and stored in a refrigerator for later use. To reheat the poached egg, put it into very hot – but not boiling – salted water. When the egg starts to float, turn it once and leave it for one minute. Then remove it from the water using a perforated spoon. Drain then serve.

Healthy eating
Low-fat or unsaturated margarines and oils can be used instead of plain cooking oil for a healthier option.

Chef's tip
Use a lower heat if using margarine, as it will heat and burn more quickly than oil.

Eggs benedict

slice toast, evenly buttered	1
fine slice of ham or cooked tongue	1
poached egg	1
hollandaise sauce	20ml
Oven temperature	100°C
Cooking time	5 minutes

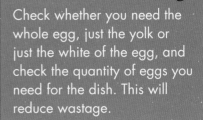

Preparation	2
Cooking skills	1
Finishing	1

Method

1 Cut a 7.5cm circle from the toast.
2 Cover the circle of toast with the slice of ham or cooked tongue and heat through in a warm oven.
3 Place a hot poached egg on to the toast and cover with hollandaise sauce.

Remember!
Check whether you need the whole egg, just the yolk or just the white of the egg, and check the quantity of eggs you need for the dish. This will reduce wastage.

Griddling

To cook eggs using a griddle, follow the method for shallow-frying, but use less oil. The egg will cook very evenly on a griddle and can be turned to cook the yolk. The cooking times are very similar to the frying method. Make sure you have any equipment you need to hand before you begin cooking. See page 125 for more information.

Baking

When eggs are baked in a dish with other ingredients, they are usually used as the agent which binds the other ingredients together as it bakes in the oven.

Quiche lorraine (cheese and bacon flan) is a good example of using eggs in a baked dish. Another good example is baked egg custard. This dish can be cooked in a baking dish on its own or baked inside a sweet paste case to make a custard tart. The eggs are whisked together with sugar and milk and flavoured with vanilla.

Some sweet egg dishes, e.g. crème brûlée or crème caramel are baked in a bain-marie. Savoury baked egg dishes, e.g. eggs en cocotte (poached egg, placed in a cocotte dish and baked in a sauce) are also popular, especially as a starter dish. For more information on baking see page 125.

Figure 12.18 A cocotte dish

Quiche lorraine

For one flan case of 15cm:

short crust pastry	120g
oil	splash
onions, finely chopped	15g
cheese, grated	45g
ham, finely diced	30g
egg	1
milk	190ml
salt	pinch
cayenne pepper	pinch
Oven temperature	190°C
Cooking time	20 minutes
Serves	6

Method

1 Roll out the pastry to 5mm thick and evenly line a 15cm flan ring.
2 Heat the oil in a pan. Add the onions. Sweat the onions.
3 Put the cheese, ham and onions into the pastry base.
4 Put the egg, milk, salt and cayenne pepper into a bowl. Beat together.
5 Pour the egg mix into the pastry base.
6 Bake in the oven until cooked.
7 Remove from the oven. Carefully remove the quiche from the flan ring. Cut into evenly sized wedges.

Scrambling

Scrambling is a style of cooking eggs rather than a cooking method. The finished dish should be light and fluffy with a creamy texture. Scrambled eggs are most commonly used as a breakfast dish but are also used in recipes such as Scotch woodcock (anchovy fillets on toast covered by scrambled eggs topped with cheese).

Chef's tip
Use a small sharp 3-inch vegetable knife to help remove the pastry from the ring. Run the tip of the blade towards you slowly along the inside edge of the flan ring.

How to scramble eggs

1 Beat or whisk the eggs using a fork or whisk.
2 Lightly season with salt and pepper.
3 Melt some butter or margarine in a pan. Add the eggs.
4 Put over a gentle heat and stir with a spatula until just cooked.

Scrambled eggs can be cooked using a microwave. Put the beaten or whisked eggs into a heatproof dish and put into the microwave. Cook for 30–40 seconds at a time and whisk until a light and fluffy texture is achieved.

Omelettes

Omelettes can best be described as lightly scrambled eggs allowed to set and wrapped over a filling. However, Spanish omelettes are thick and served flat. Omelettes are a very quick dish to prepare and can be made more substantial by adding one more egg or a little more filling.

> **Chef's tip**
> A little cream or milk can be added to the egg at the whisking stage to make the dish even lighter and creamier.

> **Remember!**
> Scrambled eggs continue to cook for a short while after they have been served, so it is important to serve them as soon as they have set.

Cheese omelette

Preparation	1
Cooking skills	2
Finishing	1

For one omelette:

eggs	2–3
salt	pinch
pepper	pinch
butter	15g
Cheddar or Parmesan cheese	30g
Cooking time	3–4 minutes
serves	1

Method

1 Break the eggs into a small bowl. Add salt and pepper. Whisk with a fork.
2 Heat the butter in a small steel omelette pan until the butter stops bubbling.
3 Add the eggs. Stir with a fork until the eggs becomes creamy in consistency.
4 Allow the eggs to set for a few moments.
5 Add the grated cheese.
6 Fold the omelette in half with a fork and shape to a tidy 'D' shape.
7 Colour the omelette slightly.
8 Turn out onto a serving dish or plate and serve immediately.

Spanish omelette

butter	15g
onions, finely diced	30g
pimento, diced	15g
tomato **concassée**	60g
eggs	2
salt and pepper	to season

Preparation	1
Cooking skills	1
Finishing	1

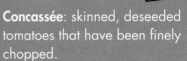

Definition

Concassée: skinned, deseeded tomatoes that have been finely chopped.

Method

1 Heat the butter in an omelette pan. Add the diced onions and cook until lightly coloured.
2 Add the diced pimento and tomato concasse and heat gently.
3 Put the eggs into a bowl and beat them with a fork.
4 Add the eggs to the pan and mix lightly. Allow to cook.
5 Serve flat, unfolded.

Safe use and storage of egg dishes

Safe service and storage of egg dishes is very important to keep the risk of food poisoning to a minimum. As eggs have a short shelf life after cooking, it is recommended that refrigerated cooked eggs are not used if they are more than two days old (check the date on the label). See page 339 for more information.

Try this! Worksheet 39

What are the five rules you must follow to reduce the risk of food poisioning caused by eggs?

List as many egg dishes as you can. Then describe the dish, including whether it's served hot or cold and whether it's sweet or savory.

Test yourself!

1 Name three methods of cooking eggs.

2 What should you do if you notice that eggs are cracked before you use them?

3 Why would you add vinegar to the water for poaching eggs?

4 Which egg dishes might be baked in a bain-marie?

5 Why should you serve scrambled eggs as soon as they are set?

13 The pastry kitchen

This chapter covers skills and knowledge in the following units:

- ○ 7132 Unit 244 (2FPC9) Prepare, cook and finish basic bread and dough products
- ○ 7132 Unit 245 (2FPC10) Prepare, cook and finish basic pastry products
- ○ 7132 Unit 246 (2FPC11) Prepare, cook and finish basic cakes, sponges, biscuits and scones

Working through this chapter could also provide the opportunity to practise the following Functional Skills at Level 2:
Functional Maths Analysing – recognise and use 2D representations of 3D objects; find area, perimeter and volume of common shapes

In this chapter you will:

Understand how and be able to prepare basic bread and dough products	7132 – 244.1,2
Understand how and be able to cook basic bread and dough products	7132 – 244.3,4
Understand how and be able to finish basic bread and dough products	7132 – 244.5,6
Understand how and be able to prepare basic pastry products	7132 – 245.1,2
Understand how and be able to cook basic pastry products	7132 – 245.3,4
Understand how and be able to finish basic pastry products	7132 – 245.5,6
Understand how and be able to prepare basic cakes, sponges, biscuits and scones	7132 – 246.1,2
Understand how and be able to cook basic cakes, sponges, biscuits and scones	7132 – 246.3,4
Understand how and be able to finish basic cakes, sponges, biscuits and scones	7132 – 246.5,6

Ingredients

Working in the pastry department can be a very rewarding experience. It is very different to working in the hot kitchen. The pastry department is more artistic and more scientific. Pastry items will not work correctly unless the balance of ingredients is right and they are handled well.

The key ingredients which are used in all pastry departments are:

- flour
- raising agents such as yeast
- sugar
- dairy products.

To get the best out of these ingredients you need to understand their characteristics and what to look for when things go wrong.

Flour

Flour is usually made from wheat. The wheat grains are crushed to remove the husks. The wheat germ, bran and endosperm are then used to make different types of flour.

- **Wholemeal** flour contains 100 per cent of the wheat grain – all the wheat germ, bran and endosperm.
- **Brown** flour contains 85 per cent of the original grain; some of the wheat germ and bran are removed.
- **White** flour contains 75 per cent of the wheat germ – the endosperm only.

Gluten

There are many important types of protein in flour. Two insoluble proteins called gliadin and glutamine are important in baking. When these are mixed with liquid a substance called **gluten** is formed. Gluten determines the strength of the flour and its best use. Gluten also develops if pastry is handled excessively.

Gluten is vital in baking because it is elastic enough to hold pockets of air in the mixture and strong enough to support the structure and stop the air escaping.

Marcus says

There are so many factors affecting the pastry kitchen and therefore results. Beware of the age of the ingredients, the humidity conditions in the kitchen that can vary with the weather and varying ovens. It is not enough to just follow a recipe – pastry also requires common sense.

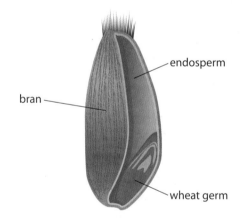

Figure 13.1 A wheat grain

Did you know?

Flour can cause fires and explosions in flour mills because of its fine particles and its heat-retaining properties.

Figure 13.2 shows the gluten contents of different types of flour.

Soft flour, also known as plain flour, can be white or brown. It can be used for a variety of tasks, e.g. sponges, cakes, biscuits, sauces and batters. It should be used within six to nine months.

Medium flour is for general use.

Strong flour is used to make bread and bun dough.

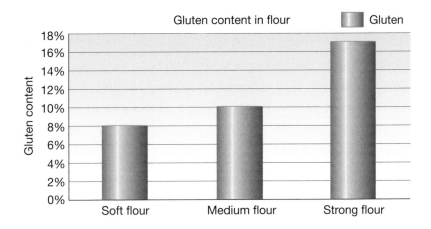

Figure 13.2 Gluten content in flour

Brown and wholemeal flour

Brown and wholemeal flour have a higher fat content than white flour and this can make the finished product heavy. White flour can be added to the brown or wholemeal flour to help make the final product lighter in texture. Brown and wholemeal flour turns rancid quicker than white flour because of its high fat content. Brown flour is best used within two to three months.

Self-raising flour

Self-raising flour is a mixture of plain flour and baking powder in a ratio of 480g flour:10g baking powder. It does not produce a consistent product, as some recipes need more baking powder. Self-raising flour is best used within six to nine months.

Gluten-free flour

Some people are intolerant of gluten. They need a gluten-free diet. Gluten-free flour can be made from maize, rice, buckwheat, potato, tapioca or chickpeas.

Storage of flour

Flour is normally supplied in 16kg bags and should be transferred into mobile storage bins, with lids. Flour must be kept dry and cool. Always wash and dry the containers before storing new flour and never put new flour on top of old flour.

For more information on flour and bread, you can visit www.heinemann.co.uk/hotlinks and enter the express code 9257P.

> **Definition**
> **Gluten:** a protein found in flour which gives it its strength. The strength of the gluten is determined by the type of wheat and when and where it is grown.

Raising agents

Yeast

Yeast is a type of fungus and is a living micro-organism similar to a bacterium. Yeast is mainly used in breadmaking but may also be used in a variety of yeast batters, e.g. for fritters or blinis.

Like bacteria, yeast requires food, warmth, moisture and time in order to grow. Under the right conditions it produces carbon dioxide. This is what makes the dough rise.

Adding sugar to yeast will feed the yeast, but too much sugar will kill the yeast and prevent it producing carbon dioxide.

Adding tepid liquids like milk and water provides moisture and some warmth. A warm temperature during mixing and proving provides the warmth needed for yeast to generate carbon dioxide.

Salt improves the flavour and colour and stops the cooked products being sticky. Take care with the amount, as too much salt can kill yeast.

Warmth encourages the growth of carbon dioxide. Yeast starts to produce carbon dioxide at temperatures of 24–29°C. However, temperatures in excess of 49°C will kill yeast.

Yeast dough is usually left to prove in a warm, moist place, such as a prover. See page 360 for more information on provers.

Using cold ingredients to slow down the growth of carbon dioxide can be an advantage, as it can produce different textures for different dough products, e.g. enriched dough products like croissants and Danish pastries.

Fresh yeast is normally supplied in 1kg blocks. When open it should have a pleasant smell and the surface should have a grey plastic look. As yeast gets older the surface colour changes to brown and looks dry and cracked. Yeast in this condition should not be used. Yeast should be kept covered in cool, moist conditions, ideally in a fridge at a temperature of 4–5°C.

There are two types of dried yeast, commonly known as baker's yeast and dried active yeast. Baker's yeast has large particles of dried yeast and has to be reconstituted in liquid and then treated as fresh yeast.

Dried active yeast is powdered and can be added directly to the flour according to the manufacturer's instructions. Dried yeast is used in smaller amounts to fresh yeast. Check the manufacturer's instructions prior to use for the exact amount to use. Dried yeast also needs food, warmth, moisture and time.

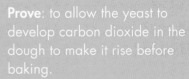

Definition

Prove: to allow the yeast to develop carbon dioxide in the dough to make it rise before baking.

Prover: a cabinet that creates heat and moisture, helping dough products to rise evenly and assists in preventing products from drying out and skinning.

Skinning: when dough is left uncovered and the surface of the dough starts to dry out and oxidise.

Try this!   **Worksheet 40**

Write down seven points you need to remember about fresh yeast.

Baking powder

Baking power is a chemical raising agent that is made from one part bicarbonate of soda to two parts cream of tartar. When liquid is added, carbon dioxide is given off which makes products rise. Too much baking powder can have an adverse effect and cakes and sponges will collapse.

Bicarbonate of soda is an alkaline raising agent and needs acidic ingredients to work as a raising agent. Apart from bicarbonate of soda and egg white, all ingredients are acidic to various degrees, making bicarbonate of soda a good raising agent.

Cream of tartar is found in the juice of grapes, after they have been fermented in winemaking. It is classified as an acid and available in powder form. It cannot be used on its own as a raising agent.

Sugar

Sugar occurs naturally in all plants, in the fruit, the leaves and the stems. However, sugar for commercial use is obtained from two major sources, sugar cane and sugar beet. The sugar extracted from these sources is refined and cleaned to produce white sugar. It is then crystallised and sieved. The largest-holed sieve produces granulated sugar, the next size down produces caster sugar, and fine linen sieves are used to produce icing sugar. Loaf or cubed sugar is obtained by pressing the crystals together when slightly damp, drying them in blocks and then cutting them into squares. Sugar that has not been refined is coated in **molasses** and produces different types of brown sugar such as light brown sugar, soft brown and demerara sugar.

Sugar is used to add sweetness and texture to pastry products. Care needs to be taken to select the correct type of sugar for the dish you are making. Using the wrong type of sugar can affect the finished product. For more information you can visit www.heinemann.co.uk/hotlinks and enter the express code 7162P.

Granulated sugar is a white medium crystalline sugar that is best used in products that require the sugar to be dissolved prior to use, e.g. when making caramel. If granulated sugar is used in pastry products it will not dissolve during cooking and will leave tiny crystals on the surface of the finished item.

Caster sugar is a white fine crystalline sugar that is best used in cakes, pastry and meringues. This type of sugar dissolves during the cooking process and gives these products the sweetness and texture they require.

> **Definition**
> **Molasses**: a dark, thick brown liquid obtained from raw sugar during the refining process. It is used to make syrup, e.g. golden syrup and black treacle.

Icing sugar is a white powdered sugar that is mixed with an anti-caking ingredient. This type of sugar is best used for decoration and icing, but there are a few other occasions when this very fine product is required as granulated or caster sugar will not dissolve sufficiently, e.g. when making tuille biscuits.

Nibbed sugar is not widely available and is normally only used in specialist confectionery shops. Nibbed sugar is sometimes used as a topping, e.g. on bath buns and rock cakes.

Cubed sugar can either be white or brown, and is the purest form of sugar you can buy. White sugar cubes do not allow any impurities to penetrate them and this make them very suitable for boiled sugar work. Brown sugar cubes are generally used to sweeten coffee.

Dark soft brown sugar is a very dark sugar with an intense flavour, and soft in texture. It is used in sticky toffee pudding and various cakes and sponges. If it is not stored tightly wrapped up, it will go hard and lumpy.

Muscovado sugar is similar to dark soft brown sugar, but lighter in colour. If a recipe suggests using this type of sugar but it is not available, use dark soft brown sugar instead.

Light brown sugar is similar in texture to dark soft brown sugar, but much lighter in colour, and milder in flavour.

Demerara sugar is a light-brown coarse sugar used for caramelising crème brûlée or in coffee.

Golden syrup is made from molasses that has been clarified. You should weigh it into a greased bowl to make it easier to use.

Black treacle is a thick, sticky dark syrup made from unrefined molasses.

Fats

Fats give pastry products taste and improve the texture. The fat coats the flour and prevents moisture activating the protein found in flour. Fats and oils contain essential fatty acids that provide the body with energy.

Unsaturated fats are derived from plants and are considered to be good fat. Saturated fats are made from animal fats and are considered to be bad fat because of their association with heart disease.

Butter is a fat made from cow's milk and is available unsalted or salted. Butter gives the final product a nicer taste than margarine, but it costs more. Butter has a fat content of 80 per cent.

Margarine is made from water and vegetable oils. Water and oil do not mix, so a stabilising agent is used to bond them together and this is known as an emulsion. It is often used as a cheaper alternative to butter. The fat content of margarine is 80–85 per cent, and it is a good source of vitamin D. Margarine has better creaming qualities than butter, but has less flavour.

Lard was originally made from pig fat. In order to promote healthier eating, lard is now usually made with vegetable oil.

Vegetable oil is available as a liquid or in solid form and is made from a variety of vegetables and seeds, each with their own taste.

Suet was originally made from the fat surrounding cow and sheep kidneys, which is then shredded. These days, shredded, hardened vegetable oil is used instead, and this is suitable for vegetarians. It is also lower in fat than the animal-based product.

Ghee is a type of clarified butter used for frying or brushing on Indian flat breads.

Trans-fats

When trans-fats occur naturally in meat and milk products they are not generally considered to be harmful.

However, artificial trans-fats (also known as hydrogenated vegetable oils) should be avoided. They are made from oils by a process called **hydrogenation**. They are used as bulking agents in cheap ice cream and to prolong the shelf life of cakes, biscuits and chocolates. They are also often found in convenience cake mixes and vegetable spreads.

> **Definition**
>
> **Hydrogenation**: an industrial process in which oil is heated to a high temperature (260–270°C) to combine it with hydrogen. The liquid oil is converted to solid or semi-solid fat.

Because of the health risks, the use of trans-fats has been reduced in recent years.

For more information on trans-fats, visit www.heinemann.co.uk/hotlinks and enter the express code 7162P.

Eggs

Eggs are one of the most important and versatile foods used in cooking. They have been eaten since the beginning of civilisation. Eggs are an important product in the pastry department. For more information on eggs, see Chapter 12.

Milk

Milk is a near-perfect food, as it provides all the five nutrients required by the body:

- carbohydrates
- vitamins
- minerals
- protein
- fats.

There are various types of fresh milk which are defined by the amount of fat they contain. Fresh milk is almost always **pasteurised** before it is consumed.

The different types of fresh milk:

- **Full fat milk**, which has a fat content of 3.5 per cent. The fat often separates and appears as a layer at the top of the milk.
- **Semi-skimmed milk**, which has half the fat of full-fat milk, i.e. 1.5 per cent.
- **Skimmed milk** has only 0.5 per cent fat as virtually all the cream or fat has been removed.

Homogenised milk is milk which has been treated to give it a uniform composition. The milk is heated to about 60°C, then forced through a very small tube at high pressure. This breaks up the globules of fat into very small droplets. The droplets remain suspended in the milk and do not float to the top forming cream.

Definition

Pasteurisation: a method of heat-treating milk to a high temperature for a short period of time to kill any pathogenic bacteria. This makes it safe for humans to consume without spoiling its taste or appearance.

The 'UHT' in **UHT milk** stands for ultra-heat treated. This milk is first homogenised and then subjected to a temperature of 135°C–150°C for at least one second. The shelf life of UHT milk can be extended to several months. UHT is normally supplied in cartons.

Evaporated milk is sweetened concentrated milk. It is produced by pasteurising the milk, then evaporating it under reduced pressure in steam-heated vacuum pans until the volume is reduced to 60 per cent. It is then homogenised, cooled and canned.

Dried milk is made by forcing the milk through very fine jets. It is then dried or heated and pressed through rollers and skimmed off. Dried milk is not a high-risk food until it comes into contact with moisture. As soon as it gets wet, it becomes a high-risk food and must be stored in the same way as fresh milk. To reconstitute dried milk, add a small amount of cold water to the powder and whisk to remove any lumps. Add this to the required amount of liquid and allow it to stand.

Figure 13.3 Milk products are often supplied in cartons

Storage of milk

Milk is a high-risk food and it must be kept under controlled conditions:

○ Fresh milk should be kept in the containers it is delivered in and used by the 'use by' date.
○ It must be stored in the fridge at 5°C or below.
○ Milk should be kept covered, as it absorbs strong smells from other foods, e.g. onions and fish.

The sugar in cow's milk is called lactose. Some people are allergic to lactose and are referred to as 'lactose intolerant'. Alternatives are soya milk (which is made from soya beans) and rice milk (which is made from rice). These are also used in a **vegan** diet.

Definition

Vegan: a person who does not eat or use products that come from animals.

Cream

Cream is the fat that rises to the surface of fresh milk when milk is left to stand.

It has different uses depending on its fat content:
○ **Single cream** is made with 18–27 per cent of milk fat. It is used mainly for cooking or as pouring cream. It cannot be used for whipping because the fat content is under 30 per cent.

- ○ **Whipping cream** is made with 33–36 per cent of milk fat. It is thicker than single cream and used mainly for whipping and in ice cream.
- ○ **Double cream** is made with 40–48 per cent of milk fat. It is thick cream which is rich in flavour and easily whipped. It is used in mousses, cream cakes or as pouring cream.
- ○ **Clotted cream** has a fat content of about 55 per cent and is very thick and rich in flavour. It is made by separating the cream from fresh milk, gently warming it over a low heat, then cooling it. It is traditionally served with scones.

Sour cream is a single cream that is soured with lactic acid fermenting bacteria. The bacteria also set the cream.

Crème fraîche is similar to sour cream, but double cream is used so it has a higher fat content.

Find out!

Why do milk products taste better in summer than in winter?

For more information on milk, visit www.heinemann.co.uk/hotlinks and enter the express code 7162P.

Preparation methods

There are many different ways to produce patisserie items. Having an understanding of the basic methods, how they affect the product and what can go wrong will help you make the products well.

Rubbing in

This method is used in making dough and pastry. It is done by placing the fat (usually butter or margarine) in the flour and rubbing the flour and fat together with the tips of your fingers. The tips of the fingers are the coolest part of the hand and mixture should not pass above the knuckle, otherwise the fat could start melting. Continue rubbing the fat into the flour until the fat is evenly distributed through the flour and the mixture looks like breadcrumbs

Figure 13.4 A chef rubbing in fat to flour

or has a sandy texture. Do not overwork the flour and fat once it gets to this stage, otherwise they will bind together into an unusable lump which will have to be thrown away.

Rubbing the fat into the flour causes the fat to coat the flour particles. This prevents moisture developing the gluten in the flour, which ensures the product is not dry and tough. The ratio of fat to flour will affect the final product.

A low fat to flour ratio is used only for taste, e.g. bread rolls. The amount of fat to flour for bread rolls does not affect the gluten development so fat is used to improve the taste and lengthen the amount of time the product will keep. Bread can be made without using fat.

A high fat to flour ratio will make the product shorter and more difficult to use, e.g. sweet paste. Sweet paste should melt in the mouth and the high fat to flour ratio softens the gluten strands making the pastry more crumbly.

Creaming

In this method the fat (usually butter or margarine) and sugar (normally castor sugar) are placed into a bowl and beaten together until a light and fluffy mixture is achieved. The finished mixture should be almost white. It turns white because of the amount of air that has been added to the butter during beating.

Over-beating this mixture can affect the final product – see page 358.

The air bubbles produced during creaming are used to trap liquid and bind the product during cooking. Without the bubbles, the mixture would curdle when liquid is added (normally eggs). The egg should be added slowly and beaten in well between each addition.

Adding the liquid to the sugar/butter mixture too quickly will make the mixture curdle, as the bubbles need time to absorb the liquid.

> **Try this!** **Worksheet 41**
>
> What does butter do to the flour in the rubbing in method?
> When using the rubbing in method why should you use the tips of your fingers? Why must you not overwork the fat and flour?
> What effect does the fat to flour ratio have on your dough?

Folding

Folding is a method of gently mixing ingredients into a mixture which has already been beaten or whisked to incorporate air. The idea is to mix in the new ingredients without losing air. Folding is normally done with a spoon which you use to cut through the mixture and turn over the remaining ingredients gently working around the bowl until all the mixture is bound together. It is sometimes called the 'cut and fold' method.

How to cut and fold flour into cake mixture

1

Make 3 cuts with your spoon in a downwards direction.

2

Make 3 cuts across to form a grid.

3

Gently draw the spoon down and turn to fold in the flour.

The term 'folding' is also used during the lamination process when making puff pastry (see Chapter 15 for more information).

Beating

Beating is mixing ingredients vigorously in a bowl with a spatula until the required consistency is achieved, e.g. when making batter for pancakes.

Whisking

Whisking is mixing the ingredients using a whisk to incorporate air into the mix. A balloon whisk is the best item to use, as its shape will assist in producing air, e.g. when making a fatless sponge or meringues. To use a balloon whisk correctly, use a round clean bowl, turn it slightly on its edge and use the whisk in either a figure of eight motion or in a circular motion from the wrist.

Equipment

Sieves

The best type of sieve for flour is a drum sieve. Flour should always be sifted before use in order to:

○ remove any lumps in the flour and to ensure an even distribution of flour particles throughout the final product

○ remove any impurities in the flour

○ start introducing air into the flour. This is the first stage in producing a light texture in the final product.

Weighing and measuring equipment

Weighing and measuring ingredients correctly is an important part of preparation for any recipe, but it is essential in patisserie, because the balance of ingredients has to be correct or the recipe will not work well.

Digital scales must be reset to zero before use. It is a good idea to test the scales before each use. Reset the scales to zero, then place a 1kg bag of sugar onto them and check the reading.

Measuring jugs are normally used for measuring liquids. If you do not have a measuring jug, then the liquid can be weighed: 1ml of liquid weighs 1g.

Some measuring jugs are designed to measure dry ingredients as well, so check to make sure you are using the right measurement.

> **Try this!**
> Measure 500ml of water then weigh it. Record your findings.

Mixers

Planetary mixer: this is commonly called a Hobart machine, however Hobart is a manufacturer's name and not a type of machine. A planetary mixer has many different uses.

When using a planetary mixer, always follow the rules below:
○ Make sure the guard is fitted before use.
○ Do not insert anything into the bowl while the machine is turned on.
○ Check the speed setting is low before turning the machine on.
○ Do not leave the machine unattended during use.
○ Switch off and unplug the machine before cleaning.

The guard is fitted to prevent fingers, arms etc. being inserted into the bowl during operation. The guard is fitted with a safety device which will turn off the machine if the guard is moved during use. The safety device is normally controlled by a series of magnets placed around the guard; these magnets have to line up otherwise the machine cannot be turned on.

Planetary mixers come with many different attachments, e.g. a stainless steel bowl, dough hook, whisk and paddle. Some also have mincing machine parts.

Each attachment has a specific role:
○ The **whisk** can be used to whisk egg whites for meringues or eggs for sponges. It can also be used to make batters to break down any lumps.
○ The **dough hook** can be used to mix dough products, scones and even pastry.
  fat into flour. It can also be used to mix pastry.

Figure 13.5 A planetary food mixer with attachments

Provers

Provers are used to control yeast dough during the proving stage; they can be used to slowly develop the carbon dioxide or to speed the process up. They use warm moisture or air to produce the warmth needed to prove yeast products.

The humidity can be controlled, which also prevents the dough forming a skin and ensures even proving.

Proving can be extended to develop flavour and produce a different texture in the yeast goods, e.g. Scottish morning rolls or ciabatta. Scottish morning rolls are proved slowly overnight, whereas dinner rolls can be proved for as little as 40 minutes.

Ovens

Deck ovens are normally found in bakeries because they are made specifically for bread and pastry products. Deck ovens are heated from the top and bottom, which bakes bread evenly and provides an extra lift to pastry and bread products.

Some deck ovens can introduce steam into the baking chamber; this stops the bread from drying out during baking or produces a crusty top if injected at the end of baking, e.g. French sticks.

Combination ovens can be used as a steamer, a dry oven or a mixture of both. With some you can control the humidity in the oven, which can be useful when cooking puff pastry products, as the extra moisture in the oven helps lift the pastry.

Combination ovens are fan-assisted and with some ovens you can control the speed of the fan, which is useful when baking soufflés as fans can cause the soufflé to rise in an uneven way.

Figure 13.6 A deck oven

Reduce the temperature by 10°C to 20°C for all fan-assisted ovens, as the heat is distributed more evenly than in normal ovens.

Convector ovens are similar to combination ovens, but they are not as versatile. Convector ovens are fan-assisted but do not have a steam facility. The heat is distributed evenly so the positioning of cooking trays is not as important.

Gas ovens are not fan-assisted and it is important to position the food correctly to achieve even cooking. If the heat source is at the back of the oven the tray should be placed in the middle of the shelf and parallel to the flames. The top of the oven is the hottest. During cooking the products may need to be turned.

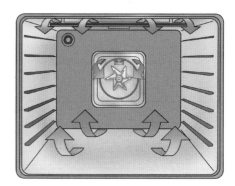

Figure 13.7 Direction of the heat flow in a fan-assisted oven

Electric ovens may or may not be fan-assisted. If they are not fan-assisted, it is important to position the food correctly to ensure even cooking. The top of the oven is the hottest. During cooking the products may need to be turned.

The position of the heat source inside the oven determines which way round a tray goes into the oven. If the heat source is at each side (normally electric ovens) then the tray should be placed in the middle of the shelf and parallel to the heat source.

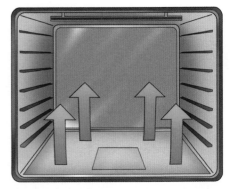

Figure 13.8 Direction of the heat flow in a conventional gas or electric oven

Test yourself!

1   What are the four key ingredients which are used in all pastry departments?

2   What is the minimum amount of fat in cream so it can be whipped?

3   What percentage of the wheat germ does white flour contain?
    a   60%
    b   75%
    c   80%
    d   55%

4   Name the two insoluble proteins that form gluten when mixed with a liquid.

5   At what temperature should you keep yeast?
    a   3–4°C
    b   4–5°C
    c   5–6°C
    d   6–7°C

6   What is baking powder made from?

7   Complete the sentence:
    The rubbing in method is done by placing the _____ in the _____ and rubbing the and together with the _____ of your _____ .

8   There are three reasons why flour should always be sifted before use. What are they?

14

Bread and dough products

This chapter covers skills and knowledge in the following unit:

o 7132 Unit 244 (2FPC9) Prepare, cook and finish basic bread and dough products

Working through this chapter could also provide the opportunity to practise the following Functional Skills at Level 2:
Functional Maths Representing – understand, use and calculate ratio and proportion, including problems involving scale

In this chapter you will:

Understand how and be able to prepare basic bread and dough products	7132 – 244.1,2
Understand how and be able to cook basic bread and dough products	7132 – 244.3,4
Understand how and be able to finish basic bread and dough products	7132 – 244.5,6

You will learn to make basic dough products, including:

o buns
o bread
o soda bread
o focaccia bread
o pizza dough
o pitta bread.

Kneading

Once all the ingredients have been combined, dough is **kneaded** by working it with the ball of the hand or by machine. This helps to develop the gluten in the dough. Strong gluten results in a better structure to hold the carbon dioxide produced by the yeast.

How to knead dough

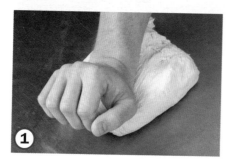

① Use the heel of your hand to push the dough down and out.

② Lift the dough back with your fingertips.

Proving

Proving allows the gluten in the flour to relax after it has been stretched by the kneading process. Insufficient proving will make the dough difficult to shape and it will contract during rolling, leading to a close, heavy texture.

There are several stages when proving dough:

- **First prove**: after sponging, cover and prove in a warm place until the yeast mixture starts to bubble and looks like honeycomb.
- **Second prove**: after the kneading process, cover and prove the dough in a warm place until double in size.
- **Final prove**: after scaling and moulding but before baking, dough products are proved, usually in a prover, until they double in size.

Dough products can be proved without a **prover** by lightly sprinkling the surface of the dough products with water and covering them with oiled plastic and then placing them somewhere warm. A new plant spray bottle with a fine spray will help to give a light and even coating of water.

It is important to cover dough products when they are proving to prevent **skinning**.

Definition

Kneading: the process of preparing dough by pressing it to assist the development of the gluten and to ensure the yeast is distributed throughout the dough.

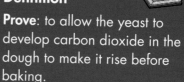

Definition

Prove: to allow the yeast to develop carbon dioxide in the dough to make it rise before baking.

Prover: a cabinet that creates heat and moisture, helping dough products to rise evenly, and assists in preventing products from drying out and skinning.

Skinning: when dough is left uncovered and the surface of the dough starts to dry out and oxidise. If this is then mixed into the dough it will leave dry pieces of dough in the finished product.

Remember!

Sponging method uses first prove, second prove and a final prove. BFT method uses second prove and final prove.

Definition

Oxidise: a chemical reaction when oxygen causes the surface of the dough to dry out.

14

Bread and dough products

This chapter covers skills and knowledge in the following unit:

○ 7132 Unit 244 (2FPC9) Prepare, cook and finish basic bread and dough products

Working through this chapter could also provide the opportunity to practise the following Functional Skills at Level 2:
Functional Maths Representing – understand, use and calculate ratio and proportion, including problems involving scale

In this chapter you will:

Understand how and be able to prepare basic bread and dough products	7132 – 244.1,2
Understand how and be able to cook basic bread and dough products	7132 – 244.3,4
Understand how and be able to finish basic bread and dough products	7132 – 244.5,6

You will learn to make basic dough products, including:

○ buns
○ bread
○ soda bread
○ focaccia bread
○ pizza dough
○ pitta bread.

Bread and dough products

People have been eating bread for thousands of years. In every culture in all parts of the world bread is a staple part of the diet. Whether it is Arabian flat bread or tiger bread the fundamental ingredients of flour, yeast, salt, and water do not change, even if different flavours and production methods are introduced.

These are some examples of bread and dough products:

- **Bread dough**: unsweetened yeast dough. Suitable for bread rolls, bread loaves and speciality breads such as focaccia bread.
- **Bun dough**: sweetened yeast dough that is enriched with butter, sugar and eggs. Suitable for Chelsea buns, hot cross buns, Bath buns, Swiss buns, jam doughnuts and ring doughnuts.
- **Soda bread**: bread made using bicarbonate of soda as the raising agent rather than yeast. Bicarbonate of soda is a chemical. Adding liquid causes a chemical reaction which means that the bread does not need time to prove before cooking. Bicarbonate of soda will start working as soon as it's mixed into the bread, so it does not need to be left to prove. The texture of the bread is firmer. Examples are white soda bread, wholemeal soda bread and soda farls (flat soda bread).
- **Naan bread**: can be made with yeast, bicarbonate of soda, baking powder or self-raising flour. It is classified as Indian flat bread and is traditionally cooked in a very hot clay oven called a tandoor oven. Traditionally, a tandoor oven is made from clay and heated by charcoal. Naan bread is only proved once. It is not proved again before cooking, unlike traditional bread.
- **Pizza dough**: unsweetened yeast dough made with olive oil which originates from Italy.
- **Pitta bread**: unsweetened yeast dough. It is classified as flat bread and is traditionally baked in a hot clay oven and the heat gives it a pocket. Best known in Turkey and Greece but served all over the Middle East. It is often stuffed with vegetables and meats.

Chef's tip
Some organisations buy in ready-made bread dough.

Figure 14.1 Bread baking in a modern tandoor oven

Try this!   Worksheet 42
Draw a picture of the following loaves: sandwich, farmhouse, plait, cob, cottage and bloomer. Then find examples of ethnic and speciality breads. Say what type of bread they are and give their country of origin, e.g. naan, lightly leavened, India.

 Find out!
Find out what types of bread your establishment uses.

Preparation methods

Mixing the dough

First, carefully weigh and measure the ingredients and sift the flour. Next, prepare the yeast. There are two main ways that yeast is used to produce carbon dioxide in bread and bun products:

○ sponging
○ bulk fermentation time.

Sponging

Sponging is a method where the yeast is allowed to produce carbon dioxide before it is added to the bulk of the flour. Sponging is the fastest method for making bun and bread products and will result in a light and open dough texture.

Put the tepid liquid into a bowl. Dissolve the yeast and add the sugar. Add enough flour from the recipe to mix to a batter (the consistency of paint). This mixture is then allowed to ferment for 10–15 minutes before being added to the rest of the ingredients.

Bulk fermentation time

In this method, the yeast liquid is mixed with all of the flour at once.

Bulk fermentation time (BFT) describes the length of time that the dough proves from the end of the mixing time until the **scaling** time. It can take 1–18 hours, depending on the recipe and the dough temperature. The end product will have a tighter texture with an improved flavour.

Put the tepid liquid into a bowl. Dissolve the yeast and add the sugar. Mix. Add this mixture to all of the flour and mix to form a dough. Then allow to prove.

For both methods, the water used to mix the dough should be at body temperature (37°C). If the temperature is too high (above 49°C) it will kill the yeast.

The amount of liquid suggested in the recipes is only approximate. The actual amount of liquid needed will vary, depending on the quality of the flour. For example, the gluten content can result in more or less liquid being needed.

Remember!
All types of flour must be sifted. The ideal type of sieve is a drum sieve. Sieving ensures that flour lumps are broken up, leading to a better leavened product. It also identifies physical contamination.

Figure 14.2 A drum sieve

Definition
Scaling: cutting and weighing the dough into the required size, e.g. for bread rolls scale dough into 60g pieces.

Chef's tip
To test the temperature of the water, place a finger into the water. If the water feels warm or cold, the water is not at the correct temperature.

Kneading

Once all the ingredients have been combined, dough is **kneaded** by working it with the ball of the hand or by machine. This helps to develop the gluten in the dough. Strong gluten results in a better structure to hold the carbon dioxide produced by the yeast.

How to knead dough

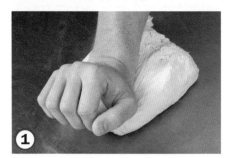

① Use the heel of your hand to push the dough down and out.

② Lift the dough back with your fingertips.

Proving

Proving allows the gluten in the flour to relax after it has been stretched by the kneading process. Insufficient proving will make the dough difficult to shape and it will contract during rolling, leading to a close, heavy texture.

There are several stages when proving dough:

○ **First prove**: after sponging, cover and prove in a warm place until the yeast mixture starts to bubble and looks like honeycomb.

○ **Second prove**: after the kneading process, cover and prove the dough in a warm place until double in size.

○ **Final prove**: after scaling and moulding but before baking, dough products are proved, usually in a prover, until they double in size.

Dough products can be proved without a **prover** by lightly sprinkling the surface of the dough products with water and covering them with oiled plastic and then placing them somewhere warm. A new plant spray bottle with a fine spray will help to give a light and even coating of water.

It is important to cover dough products when they are proving to prevent **skinning**.

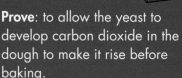

Definition

Kneading: the process of preparing dough by pressing it to assist the development of the gluten and to ensure the yeast is distributed throughout the dough.

Definition

Prove: to allow the yeast to develop carbon dioxide in the dough to make it rise before baking.

Prover: a cabinet that creates heat and moisture, helping dough products to rise evenly, and assists in preventing products from drying out and skinning.

Skinning: when dough is left uncovered and the surface of the dough starts to dry out and oxidise. If this is then mixed into the dough it will leave dry pieces of dough in the finished product.

Remember!

Sponging method uses first prove, second prove and a final prove. BFT method uses second prove and final prove.

Definition

Oxidise: a chemical reaction when oxygen causes the surface of the dough to dry out.

Knocking back and scaling the dough

Knocking back means removing the air produced during proving. It is done by kneading the dough again. This ensures the yeast is working before shaping and provides an even texture during baking. Removing all the air also assists in shaping the dough after scaling. The dough is now ready to be scaled, or cut and weighed, into pieces of the required size.

> **Marcus says**
>
> When making bread and dough – don't rush it. If you have not set aside enough time for each stage then don't even start!

Hand shaping

Shaping the dough is also known as 'moulding'. Hand shaping does take some practice but with time many different shapes can be achieved. The first two shapes to master are rounds and fingers.

How to shape rounds or balls

Mastering this shape will help you to make other shapes correctly.

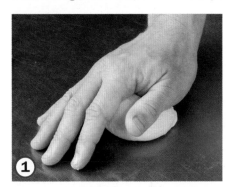

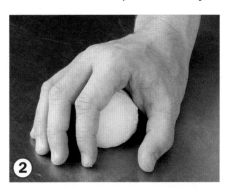

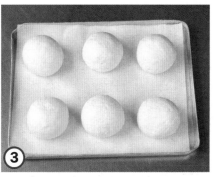

Take a scaled piece of dough and knead it briefly to remove any air. Then put the dough onto the work surface and cover it with the palm of your hand. Start to slowly rotate your hand while pressing down quite hard.

As the ball forms, slowly cup your hand until a nice smooth ball is achieved. The surface of the dough must be smooth with no cracks otherwise the roll will crack during proving and cooking.

Once the shape has been achieved, transfer the completed roll to a baking tray, lined with silicone paper, and repeat the process with the other pieces of dough. Allow them to prove until double their size. Unless you are using a steam prover, cover with oiled plastic to prevent skinning.

How to shape fingers

1 Shape as for rounds until the smooth ball has been achieved.
2 Roll the piece backwards and forwards until a finger shape has been made.
3 Transfer onto a baking tray and allow to prove.

Once the shaping of rounds and fingers has been mastered, there are many different shapes that can be achieved, including knots, double knots, three-strand plaits, five-strand plaits, twists, ropes, brioche shapes.

Cooking and finishing methods

Finishing methods applied before cooking

Before baking a product you may wish to apply a finish to the dough.

○ **Egg wash**: Use an egg wash to glaze dough products. Beat an egg well. Thin it down with a little milk or water if necessary. Brush onto the surface of products to give them a shine and a golden brown colour during baking. Dough products which can be egg-washed before baking include bread rolls, bread loaves, Bath buns. Dough products should be egg-washed before the final prove because they are fragile once proved and can collapse if touched.
○ **Toppings**: to give dough products an attractive finish, sprinkle them with different seeds, e.g. sesame, poppy, sunflower or pumpkin seeds, or oats.
For a more rustic look, dust bread dough products with flour.
○ **Cutting**: to achieve a different effect, make small cuts in the surface of the rolls or bread. Make the cuts before the final prove using a small sharp knife or a pair of scissors. Cutting the surface allows the cuts to expand prior to baking and gives the products an attractive finish.

Remember!
Do not allow the rolls to over-prove (no more than double their size) or they will collapse.

Figure 14.3 Bread rolls can be made in many attractive styles

Try this!
Cut an attractive pattern into bread roll dough using a pair of scissors or a small knife.

Baking

Dough products are baked after the final prove. Times and oven temperatures are as follows:

○ Bread rolls:
- 230°C for 20–25 minutes
- should be golden brown and when tapped on the bottom sound hollow.

○ Bread loaves:
- 230°C for 10 minutes or until a crust has developed, then reduce to 200°C for 25–45 minutes, depending on size
- should be golden brown and when tapped at the bottom sound hollow.

○ Bun dough:
- 200°C for 20–25 minutes (a lower temperature is required due to the higher, sugar, fat and egg content in bun dough)
- should be golden brown.

Cooling baked dough products

To cool bread rolls or bun dough:

○ Remove from the oven, and allow to cool for a few minutes.
○ Transfer them onto a cooling wire or rack. If products are left on the tray to cool down, the base of the rolls will go soggy as they cool down and create steam.

To cool bread loaves or tin bread:

○ Once cooked allow to cool for a few minutes. As the bread cools it will shrink slightly and allow the bread to be removed from the tin more easily. Do not leave the bread to cool down in the tins or it will create steam and go soggy.
○ To remove the bread, gently tap the side of the tin to loosen it and tip onto cooling wires.
○ If bread loaves are baked open on trays cool in a similar way to bread rolls.

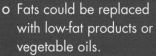

Healthy eating
○ Fats could be replaced with low-fat products or vegetable oils.
○ Sugars could be replaced with natural sweeteners like honey.
○ Salt could be replaced with a low-sodium salt.

Remember!
If there are any problems with the ingredients, the dough, or the final products, tell your supervisor immediately. Any products not suitable for service will have to be replaced or remade. The supervisor will need time to make the decision before service starts.

Quality points for baked dough products

The finished bread should:

- be golden brown
- have even colour
- have a fresh smell
- not be greasy
- have a light, even, open texture when cut into
- have no uncooked dough inside.

Frying

Fried dough products include ring doughnuts, jam doughnuts and finger doughnuts. When frying:

- do not prove any dough products in a prover
- fry in hot clean oil at 180°C until golden brown
- turn them over during frying.

Deep-frying

Doughnuts are cooked by deep-frying in hot oil. Heat the oil to 180°C before frying the doughnuts.

The following equipment should be ready before cooking the doughnuts:

- A colander placed on a metal tray, to drain the cooked doughnuts to remove excess oil.
- A spider for turning the doughnuts and lifting them from the deep fat fryer.
- A cooling wire to transfer the doughnuts to cool, and to be coated in cinnamon sugar.

You should also prepare the cinnamon sugar before cooking.

Finishing methods after cooking

Finishing methods after cooking include bun wash (sugar glaze), water icing, chocolate icing, fondant icing and coating in flavoured sugar. Dough products include Chelsea buns, hot cross buns, currant buns, Swiss buns and doughnuts.

Remember!
Dough products that will be fried, e.g. doughnuts, should not be proved in a prover because the moisture on the dough will react with the hot oil and could cause burns and be a fire risk.

Did you know?
Wholemeal flour absorbs more liquid than white flour and produces a softer dough which needs more time to prove. A **dough improver** can be added to the recipe to enhance the texture and reduce the amount of time taken for the bread to prove.

Definition
Dough improver: adding ascorbic acid (vitamin C) assists the gluten development and can speed up the process of fermentation.

Healthy eating
Add a percentage of wholemeal flour to white flour. Add seeds or nuts into the flour before mixing. Add vegetables, e.g. capsicums, carrots, onions, when making bread products.

Faults and problems with bread and dough products

Fault	Cause	Remedy
Dough will not prove	Insufficient yeast	Start again and double-check recipe. Weigh out correctly
	Yeast old	Start again and use fresh yeast
	Dough cold	Move to warmer area
	Dough too tight	Remake and check liquid content
	Too much salt/sugar	Start again and double-check recipe. Weigh out correctly
Dough collapses during cooking	Dough over-proved	Make again and reduce proving time
Products split during cooking	Dough not proved sufficiently before cooking	Prove longer next time
Dough will not hold its shape when shaping	Too much liquid	Bake in tins
Lack of volume	Not proved long enough	Prove longer next time
	Yeast old	Make again with fresh yeast
	Oven too hot	Make again and reduce oven temperature
	Liquid used to start yeast was too hot	Make again and check temperature of the liquid

Figure 14.4 Faults and problems and how they can be remedied

Storage

Cooked dough products are best kept at room temperature. Keep them covered to prevent contamination and to stop them drying out.

Dough products with high-risk foods (e.g. fresh cream) should be stored in the fridge until ready for service and consumed within 24 hours.

Rolls can be warmed prior to service. Put them on a tray, cover them with foil – shiny side down – and put them in an oven at 180°C for ten minutes. Serve immediately.

To store unused dough: this can be stored in the fridge covered in oiled plastic. It will still prove, but very slowly. The dough must be used within 24 hours. If the dough smells sour it should be thrown away, as this means that the yeast has turned sour.

Recipes

White bread dough

strong flour	600g
salt	10g
milk powder	15g
caster sugar	15g
butter, cold	30g
fresh yeast	25g
tepid water	350ml
Makes	20 rolls or 1 loaf

Preparation	2
Cooking skills	2
Finishing	2

Wholemeal bread dough

Preparation	2
Cooking skills	2
Finishing	2

wholemeal flour	400g
strong flour	200g
salt	10g
milk powder	15g
caster sugar	15g
butter cold	30g
fresh yeast	25g
tepid water	350ml
Makes	20 rolls or 1 loaf

Sponging method

1 Sift the flour, salt, milk powder and half the sugar into a bowl.
2 Rub in the butter.
3 Put the yeast into a smaller bowl. Dissolve it in half the water using a whisk.
4 Add the remaining half of the sugar to the diluted yeast.
5 Make a well in the centre of the flour and butter mixture. Add the diluted yeast mixture. With a wooden spoon, draw some of the flour from the sides to combine with the yeast mixture. The mixture should resemble a thick pancake batter.
6 Dust the mixture with some flour from the sides of the bowl and cover with a cloth or a tray.
7 Put in a warm place until the yeast starts to bubble. This will take approximately 10–15 minutes.
8 Grease baking trays or tins, prepare the egg wash and any seeds for decoration.

Did you know?
Baking bread in tins allows a lower protein flour to be used, as the dough is prevented from spreading outwards and ensures that it rises upwards as the dough proves. The tin also protects the dough from the heat and stops the crust being too hard. If bread loaves are baked open (on trays without a tin) the dough will spread.

9   Once the yeast has bubbled, add the remaining water and mix in the rest of the ingredients using your hands until the dough forms a ball.

10 Place onto the table and start kneading. Use a little flour if the dough feels too sticky.

11 Once kneaded into a clear dough, put the dough back into the bowl and cover it up so the dough can relax and prove.

12 Once proved until double in size knock back the dough and use as required.

13 To make bread rolls, scale the dough into 60g pieces.

14 Once scaled and shaped, brush with egg wash, decorate with seeds and prove until double in size. Use a prover, or if no prover is available sprinkle a little water onto the tray, cover with oiled cling film and prove in a warm place.

BFT method

1   Sift the flour, salt and milk powder into a large bowl.

2   Put the yeast into a smaller bowl and add the water. Dissolve the yeast in the water, then add the sugar.

3   Add the butter to the flour and rub in.

4   Make a well. Add all the yeast mixture and half the remaining water. Mix and gradually draw in the flour and butter mixture from the edge of the bowl. Make it into soft and pliable dough, adding more water as required. The dough should come away from the edge of the bowl cleanly.

5   Place the dough onto a lightly floured worksurface and knead until it is smooth.

6   Place the dough back into its bowl, cover and allow to prove.

The finished dough – testing the dough

The completed dough should feel soft and smooth – a bit like an inflated balloon. If the dough feels tight and dry the yeast will not be able to develop the carbon dioxide required to make the dough rise. Bread made with a tight and heavy dough will be dry with a very hard exterior and a heavy texture.

While the dough is proving, prepare the trays to bake the rolls on. Lightly oil the tray and dust the surface with flour, ground rice or semolina. If the establishment has silicone mats, use those.

Once the dough has doubled in size remove the cover and knock back.

Focaccia bread

Preparation	3
Cooking skills	2
Finishing	2

Part one

strong flour	500g
fresh yeast	75g
sugar	10g
tepid water	680ml

Mix to form a batter and allow to sponge.

Part two

strong flour	500g
salt	10g
olive oil	30ml

1 Add all the part two ingredients to the sponge mixture and mix well. Cover with oiled plastic and prove.
2 Place on a greased baking tray and press down to flatten. Push finger marks all over to make indentations on the surface.
3 Brush with olive oil and allow to prove.
4 Repeat indentations. Sprinkle the surface with rock salt.
5 Bake for 20 minutes at a temperature of 230°C. Once baked test by tapping the surface to see if it sounds hollow. The surface should be a golden brown.
6 Brush the surface with some more olive oil while it is still warm. The oil will be absorbed into the bread.
7 Turn out of the baking tray on to cooling wires to prevent the base going soggy. Once cooled, wrap in cling film, to stop the bread from drying.

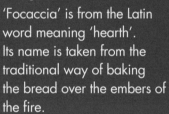

Did you know?

'Focaccia' is from the Latin word meaning 'hearth'. Its name is taken from the traditional way of baking the bread over the embers of the fire.

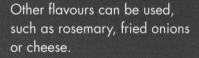

Chef's tip

Other flavours can be used, such as rosemary, fried onions or cheese.

Pizza

strong flour	500g
salt	10g
fresh yeast	25g
water	250ml
olive oil	50ml
Oven temperature	230°C
Cooking time	approx. 15 minutes
Serves	6–8

Preparation	3
Cooking skills	2
Finishing	2

Method

1 Sift the flour and salt together into a bowl.
2 Make a well in the centre.
3 Put the yeast into a smaller bowl. Add the water. Dissolve the yeast in the water. Pour the yeast mixture and olive oil into the well.
4 Mix and draw the flour from the edge of the bowl. Continue mixing until all the flour has been absorbed.
5 Knead and allow to prove.
6 Knock back and pin out with a rolling pin to the desired thickness, then place onto a baking tray.
7 Top with ingredients as required. To ensure the base is fully cooked, it can be pre-cooked. Follow steps 8 to 11.
8 Make holes in the dough with a fork or a **docker**.
9 Cover and prove in a warm place until double in size.
10 Bake until golden brown.
11 Place topping and cheese onto the pre-baked base.
12 Bake for a further 15 minutes or until the cheese has melted and is golden brown.

Did you know?

Pizzas are traditionally baked in a stone oven at 600°C. Normal kitchen ovens do not reach that temperature.

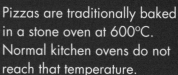

Definition

Docker: a tool that has spikes that can be used to add decoration to products before cooking and to put holes into flan cases and puff pastry goods to prevent them rising during baking.

Flat breads

Naan and pitta bread are classed as flat breads. These types of bread do not require proving for a second time before cooking as they are generally thin and cooked at a high temperature.

Pitta bread

strong white flour	500g
sugar	30g
salt	10g
fresh yeast	25g
olive oil	10ml
tepid water	250ml
Oven temperature	240°C
Cooking time	20 minutes
Makes	8

Preparation	3
Cooking skills	2
Finishing	1

Method

1 Sift flour, sugar and salt into a bowl, and mix.
2 Dissolve the yeast in a small amout of the water.
3 Add the oil and enough water to make a soft pliable dough.
4 Knead for ten minutes until smooth. Wrap in cling film and rest for 30 minutes.
5 Preheat the oven to 240°C.
6 Divide the dough into 100g balls and pin these out into flat oval shapes.
7 Place on baking sheets. Bake until the dough puffs up.
8 Remove from the oven and leave to cool a little. After ten minutes the bread will slowly collapse.

Naan bread

plain flour	250g
yoghurt	5 tbsp
sugar	1 tsp
butter	25g
salt	¼ tsp
bicarbonate of soda	½ tsp
eggs	2
dried yeast	1 tbsp
or fresh yeast	15g
milk	5 tbsp
sesame or poppy seeds	2 tbsp
Oven temperature	200°C
Cooking time	10–12 minutes
Makes	4

Preparation	2
Cooking skills	2
Finishing	3

Method

1 Beat the yoghurt, gradually add milk, pour into a pan and heat until tepid.
2 Remove from heat and add the lightly beaten eggs, the bicarbonate of soda and melted butter.
3 Sieve the flour. Add salt and sugar.
4 Gradually work the yoghurt mixture into the flour.
5 If using fresh yeast, make a well in the centre of the flour and add warm yoghurt mixture to blend the yeast and yoghurt. Gently incorporate the flour to form a soft dough.
6 If using dried yeast, mix the yeast with a little of the yoghurt mixture to form a paste. Gradually incorporate the remaining yoghurt mixture into the yeast and add to flour to form a soft dough.
7 Knead until smooth.
8 Place somewhere warm until the dough has doubled in size (approximately 4 hours).
9 Break off large pieces of dough and flatten into tear shaped pancakes.
10 Brush with melted butter and milk.
11 Sprinkle seeds on top and bake in a hot oven for 10–12 minutes.

Chemically raised bread

Bread made without yeast but with a chemical raising agent is a good alternative when time is short.

Soda bread

plain flour	340g
salt	5g
bicarbonate of soda	5g
buttermilk	290ml
Oven temperature	200°C
Cooking time	30 minutes

Preparation	1
Cooking skills	1
Finishing	–

Method

1 Preheat the oven to 200°C.
2 Sift the flour, salt and bicarbonate of soda into a large bowl and stir.
3 Make a well. Pour in the buttermilk and mix quickly to form a soft dough.
4 Turn onto a lightly floured surface and knead briefly.
5 Form into a round and flatten the dough slightly before placing it on a lightly floured baking sheet.
6 Cut a cross on the top and bake for about 30 minutes or until the loaf sounds hollow when tapped. Cool on a wire rack.

Bun dough

Bun dough can be made using either the sponging method or the BFT method (see page 365).

Basic bun dough – sponging method

strong flour	600g
milk powder	15g
salt	5g
fresh yeast	40g
tepid water	approx. 300ml
caster sugar	75g
soft butter	60g
egg	1 medium

Preparation	3
Cooking skills	–
Finishing	–

Video presentation

Prepare bun dough shows you an alternative method of making this product. Which do you prefer?

Method

1 Sift the flour, milk powder and salt into a bowl.
2 Put the yeast into a smaller bowl. Dissolve the yeast with half the amount of tepid water and half the amount of sugar.
3 Make a well in the centre of the flour and pour in the diluted yeast mixture. Use a wooden spoon to draw some of the flour from the sides and mix it with the yeast water. The mixture should resemble a thick pancake batter.
4 Dust the surface with some flour from the sides of the bowl and cover with a cloth or a tray.
5 Put in a warm place until the yeast starts to bubble. This will take approximately 10–15 minutes.
6 Add the egg, soft butter, remaining sugar and water and mix. Gradually draw in all the rest of the flour, until a soft pliable dough is achieved.
7 Place onto a lightly floured surface and knead until smooth and free from stickiness.
8 Cover and prove, then knock back and use as required.

Basic bun dough – BFT method

Preparation	3
Cooking skills	–
Finishing	–

strong flour	600g
salt	5g
soft butter	60g
milk	300ml
caster sugar	75g
egg	1 medium
fresh yeast	40g

Method

1 Sift the flour and salt into a bowl.
2 Rub the butter into the flour.
3 Place the milk in a pan, warm to blood temperature. Add the yeast and dissolve it. Add half the sugar to this mixture.
4 Make a well in the centre of the flour. Add the remaining sugar. Crack the egg onto the sugar and mix to dissolve the sugar.
5 Add the yeast mixture and mix, making sure the sugar has dissolved. Mix in the flour from the sides until a soft pliable dough is achieved.
6 Knead and prove. Use as required.

Did you know?

The egg used in these recipes has two functions. First to help moisten and enrich the dough, secondly to give the dough a slight yellow colour. This colour helps to turn the dough to a nice golden brown during cooking.

Chelsea buns

Preparation 3
Cooking skills 2
Finishing 2

basic bun dough recipe	
butter, melted	to brush dough
dark soft brown sugar	30g
mixed spice	4g
sultanas	120g
currants	120g
mixed peel	30g
Oven temperature	200°C
Makes	10

Method

1 Follow the basic bun dough recipe.
2 Roll into a rectangle approximately 30cm × 20cm.
3 Brush with melted butter.
4 Sprinkle with the sugar.
5 Sprinkle with the mixed spice.
6 Sprinkle with sultanas, currants and mixed peel.
7 Roll up along the short end like a swiss roll. Brush with melted butter on the outside.
8 Cut into 10cm × 3cm pieces.
9 Turn the cut pieces so you can see the filling when put onto the table. Put into individual moulds which have been buttered and floured or a large cake ring, allowing space in between to prove.
10 Prove until doubled in size.
11 Bake until golden brown.
12 Allow to cool slightly before turning out the moulds onto a cooling rack.
13 While still warm glaze with bun wash.

Bun wash

Preparation 1
Cooking skills 1
Finishing –

caster sugar	100g
milk or water	100ml

Method

1 Put the ingredients in a pan and boil for about five minutes on a medium heat.
2 Glaze the warm buns with the hot bun wash.

Swiss buns

basic bun dough

Oven temperature	200°C
Makes	20

Preparation 3
Cooking skills 1
Finishing 2

Method

1. Follow the recipe for the basic bun dough.
2. Scale the dough into 60g pieces and roll into finger shapes.
3. Place onto a greased baking tray.
4. Prove in a warm place until doubled in size.
5. Bake until golden brown.
6. Allow to cool slightly before placing onto a cooling rack.
7. When cooled, glaze with fondant icing or water icing.

Water icing

icing sugar	200g
water	30ml

Preparation 1
Cooking skills –
Finishing –

Method

1. Sift the icing sugar into a bowl.
2. Add the water and beat using a wooden spoon.

Jam doughnuts

basic bun dough

caster sugar	to roll
red jam	

Preparation 3
Cooking skills 3
Finishing 2

Method

1. Prepare the basic bun dough.
2. Scale 60g pieces and roll into round rolls.
3. Place on an oiled tray.
4. Prove in a warm place until doubled in size.
5. To deep-fry the doughnuts, heat the oil to 180°C.
6. Coat a wide spatula in the hot oil. Then place the oiled spatula under the doughnuts and carefully lift them into the oil.
7. Turn over with a spider. Remove with the spider when golden brown on both sides.
8. Place onto a cooling rack and allow excess oil to drip off.
9. Roll in sugar.
10. Pipe red jam into the centre once cooled down.

Did you know?

Swiss buns can be filled with fresh whipped cream and/or fruit to make cream buns.

Video presentation

Follow these goodies being made step-by-step and learn more about fondant in *Make iced Swiss buns*.

Chef's tip

Add 20g cocoa powder to make chocolate icing.

Chef's tip

As an alternative, you can glaze doughnuts with water icing or chocolate icing and fill them with whipped cream.

A machine can be used to inject doughnuts with jam. The machine has a hopper that contains the jam and two injection points that insert the jam into the centre of the doughnut. The cooled doughnuts are pushed onto these points and a set amount of jam is inserted into the doughnut.

If no machine is available use a piping bag. Fill the piping bag with softened jam and make a hole into the doughnut with something like the end of a spatula. Give the spatula a wiggle to open the inside of the doughnut a little. Remove the spatula and push the piping bag into the space. Squeeze the jam using an even pressure to fill the gap. Remove the piping bag slowly.

Healthy eating
Replace the sugar coating on doughnuts with icing sugar.

Healthy eating
Use a vegetable-based cream instead of double cream.

Test yourself!

1   Why should strong flour be used to make bread and bun products?

2   What gives flour its strength?

3   Describe the sponging method used for proving.

4   What chemical is used to make soda bread rise?

5   List three different bun dough products that are deep-fried.

6   What are bread rolls glazed with before cooking?

7   What temperature should the liquid be to enable the yeast to start producing carbon dioxide?
   a   37°C
   b   39°C
   c   47°C
   d   49°C

8   How many proving steps are there when using the BFT proving method?

9   List three toppings that could be used to give bread loaves a pleasing look.

10   What is meant by the term 'scaling'?

11   What could be the cause of these bread-making problems?
   a   Dough collapses during cooling.
   b   Products split during cooling.
   c   Lack of volume.

12   What is the common name for ascorbic acid?

15

Pastry

This chapter covers skills and knowledge in the following unit:

○ 7132 Unit 245 (2FPC10) Prepare, cook and finish basic pastry products

Working through this chapter could also provide the opportunity to practise the following Functional Skills at Level 2:
Functional Maths Representing – understand, use and calculate ratio and proportion, including problems involving scale

In this chapter you will:

Understand how and be able to prepare basic pastry products	7132 – 245.1,2
Understand how and be able to cook basic pastry products	7132 – 245.3,4
Understand how and be able to finish basic pastry products	7132 – 245.5,6

You will learn to cook basic pastry products, including:

○ short pastry
○ sweet pastry
○ suet pastry
○ choux pastry
○ puff pastry
○ convenience pastry.

Types of pastry

Pastry has many different uses from savoury starters to delicious desserts. The ingredients and proportion of fat to flour affects the pastry and what it can be used for. Generally, a soft flour with a low gluten content should be used. The exceptions are choux pastry and puff pastry. For these, flour with a high gluten content produces a better-quality final product.

There are three different ways to give pastry a lighter texture:
○ Mechanical: whisking, creaming, beating, sifting.
○ Chemical: baking powder, bicarbonate of soda.
○ Lamination: layers of fat and pastry.

With the exception of suet paste, which is normally steamed, and some choux pastry goods which are deep-fried, pastry items are normally baked. The cooked product should be an even golden brown with a crumbly melt-in-the-mouth texture.

Pastry products include:
○ **Short pastry**, commonly called short paste. This is an unsweetened paste that is normally used to make savoury dishes. When baked, short paste should be tender, easily broken and melt-in-the-mouth. Products that can be made with short paste include savory flans (quiches), pasties and meat pies.
○ **Sweet pastry**, commonly called sweet paste. It is a sweetened paste used to make sweet dishes, e.g. lemon tart and fruit tartlets.
○ **Suet pastry**, commonly called suet paste. This is an unsweetened paste that is used for sweet and savoury dishes. These dishes are normally steamed. Products include: jam roly-poly, dumplings, meat puddings, steamed fruit puddings and steamed syrup pudding.
○ **Choux pastry**, commonly called choux paste. This is a cooked mixture of fat, flour and water with a little sugar and salt in which eggs are beaten. It is used to make éclairs and profiteroles.
○ **Puff pastry**, commonly called puff paste. This is a **laminated** paste where fat has been sandwiched between layers of dough through folding. Puff paste is versatile and used for sweet and savoury dishes. It is one of the most complicated pastries and it requires a lot of patience to make puff paste well. Savoury products using puff paste include sausage rolls, vol-au-vents,

Healthy eating
Lard is a saturated animal fat, but provides additional flavour to the pastry; however it is not very healthy. It is not suitable for vegetarians or vegans. Lard can be replaced with butter or vegetable lard for vegetarians or margarine or vegetable lard for vegans.

Marcus says
There is a risk of overworking pastry when the gluten in the flour develops, making it chewy rather than crisp.

Definition
Lamination: forming layers of fat in pastry to create texture and lift as the pastry cooks.

bouches, cheese straws, beef Wellington and tops for pies. Sweet products made with puff paste include cream horns, Eccles cakes and apple turnovers.

o **Convenience pastry**: this is any bought pre-prepared pastry. It could be a powder that water is added to or pre-made pastry. Types of convenience pastry include:
  – filo pastry, which is used to make baklava and strudels
  – spring roll pastry, which is used to make spring rolls
  – won ton pastry, which is used to make won ton and dim sum
  – puff pastry
  – short crust pastry.

Preparation and cooking methods

Short pastry

Short pastry

soft flour	500g
cornflour	25g
salt	5g
butter	125g
lard	125g
cold water	200ml

Preparation	3
Cooking skills	–
Finishing	–

Rubbing-in method

1 Sift the flour, cornflour and salt into a bowl.
2 Rub the butter and lard into the flour and salt.
3 Make a well. Add 160ml (80 per cent) water and mix to form a soft dough. Add more water if required.
4 Do not over-mix the pastry once it has been made.
5 Wrap the pastry in cling film and allow it to rest in the fridge for at least 30 minutes.

Chef's tip

Paste that has not been used before will produce a better-eating product. Paste that has been rolled and used more than once will be tougher.

Chef's tip

When making short paste make sure all the ingredients are cold, especially the water. The cold butter stops the water developing the gluten in the flour and makes the pastry crispier once cooked.

Did you know?

In short paste the proportion of fat to flour is 50 per cent. Recipes for other pastries will have higher proportions of fat. These pastries have different qualities and require different methods of preparation.

Chef's tip

Adding cornflour to the recipe softens the flour to help to produce a better-quality pastry.

Sweet pastry

There are three methods that can be used to make sweet paste. Each produces a slightly different sweet paste with its own properties and benefits. The choice of method depends on the product being made. The rubbing-in method will give a sweet paste with a close, firm texture that is easy to handle. It is generally used for apple pies, etc. Creaming method 1 will give a sweet paste with a light and loose texture. It can be difficult to handle. It is generally used for fruit flans, e.g. lemon tart and fruit tartlets. Creaming method 2 will give a sweet paste with a medium to soft texture, similar to creaming method 1, but easier to handle. It is used for similar products to creaming method 1.

Video presentation

Watch *Prepare sweet paste (rubbing in method)* to see how to make this working directly onto the work surface without using a bowl.

Sweet paste

Preparation	3
Cooking skills	–
Finishing	–

soft flour	500g
salt	pinch
butter	125g
caster sugar	300g
medium eggs	2

Rubbing-in method

1 Sift the flour and salt.
2 Rub the butter into the flour and salt.
3 Make a well. Break the egg into the well.
4 Add the sugar. Mix the sugar until it has dissolved.
5 Draw the flour into the egg and sugar mixture until a soft dough is achieved.

Creaming method 1

1 Make sure the butter is soft and not chilled.
2 Sift the flour and salt into a bowl.
3 Put the sugar and butter into another bowl and beat to a light and fluffy texture.
4 Crack the eggs into a smaller bowl and whisk to break the eggs down.
5 Add the egg to the butter and sugar mixture a little at a time and beat well. Too much egg will make the mixture curdle. If the mixture looks like little specks of butter it is starting to curdle. To stop this add a spoonful of the flour to the mixture and gently mix in. It is better not to add any flour if possible, though, as this starts the gluten development early.

Did you know?

One reason why pastry is chilled is that the gluten in the flour has been stretched and needs time to relax and spring back to its original size. If the paste is used straight away it will shrink during cooking. Chilling also makes the pastry easier to handle.

Chef's tip

The creaming method is a very good one for making sweet paste, but the paste is harder to use so it takes practice.

Chef's tip

When using a creaming method make sure the eggs are used at room temperature, as this reduces the risk of curdling.

6   When all the egg has been added, add the flour and gently mix it in until a soft dough is achieved. Do not over-mix.

7   Cover the pastry with cling film and allow it to rest in the fridge for at least 30 minutes.

Creaming method 2

1   Make sure the butter is soft and not chilled.
2   Sift the flour and salt into a bowl.
3   Crack the eggs into a smaller bowl and whisk to break the eggs down.
4   Dissolve the sugar into the eggs.
5   Cream the soft butter with half the flour until combined well.
6   Add the sugar and egg mixture.
7   Fold in the remaining half of the flour. If the pastry seems too soft, do not add any additional flour. Once the pastry has been chilled the fat will set and the pastry will be easier to handle.
8   Wrap the pastry in cling film and allow it to rest in the fridge for 30 minutes.

Try this!   **Worksheet 43**

Using the three recipes above make three sweet pastries and compare them.

Lining a flan ring with pastry

Sweet paste is often used to make flans which are filled to make desserts. You should only roll out the required amount of pastry for one flan at a time and keep the remaining pastry chilled. Before you start lightly grease the inside of a flan ring and the tray that it is being cooked on.

Chef's tip

Do not use too much extra flour when pinning the paste as this will change the balance of the ingredients and make the paste tough and harder to use.

Healthy eating

To make pastry healthier, you could:
o   replace butter with margarine
o   replace some of the plain flour with wholemeal flour, or
o   use wholemeal flour instead of white flour.

Chef's tip

To give a nutty flavour seeds can be added to the flour before making the pastry.

Chef's tip

Slide a palette knife under the pastry during pinning out to prevent the paste sticking to the table.

How to line and finish a flan ring

1

Pin out the paste until it is approximately 3mm thick. Dust the surface of the paste with flour to prevent it from sticking to itself and roll up the paste with the rolling pin inside. This helps to prevent stretching the paste.

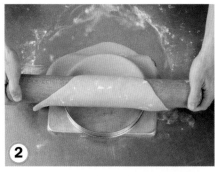

2

Transfer the paste over the flan ring. Remove the rolling pin.

3

Lift the edge of the paste and gently ease the pastry into the flan ring. Do not tear the paste. Use your fingers to press the paste into the flan ring. Make sure the paste touches all of the ring and tray.

4

Roll the rolling pin over the flan ring to trim off the excess.

5

Pinch the paste around the flan ring.

6

Crimp the paste.

Video presentation
Line a flan ring takes you through this procedure.

Definitions
Crimping: to give a decorative edge to pastry using forefinger and thumb or specialist tools.

Blind baking process

1 Dock the base of the pastry by using a fork or **docker** to make little holes. These will prevent air bubbles building up under the pastry during baking.
2 Line the flan with a **cartouche** and fill it with baking beans.
3 Chill the flan for 15 minutes.
4 Bake it in the oven. The oven temperature and cooking time will depend on the type of pastry, but should be roughly 200°C for 10–15 minutes.
5 When the sides are golden brown, remove it from the oven and allow to cool slightly. Then remove the beans and cartouche.
6 Brush the inside of the flan with egg white to close the holes. Return it to the oven until the base is golden brown.

Suet pastry

Suet paste

flour	500g
salt	10g
baking powder	25g
vegetable suet	250g
water	330ml

Preparation	2
Cooking skills	–
Finishing	–

Method

1 Sift the flour, salt and baking powder into a bowl.
2 Add the suet and mix it in.
3 Make a well and add the water. Mix until combined well.
4 You can use the pastry straight away.

Steaming

Suet paste products are normally steamed. This is a long, slow method of cookery. It does not have any negative effects on the other ingredients. The suet paste needs to be covered well to prevent water getting into the paste and making it soggy.

Modern steamers are self-contained and form part of a combination oven with a steam mode. Combination ovens can be adjusted to increase the amount of humidity inside the oven and this can provide an effective lift to the pastry, as the steam assists the layer to rise. Make sure the oven is switched to steam mode.

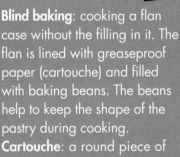

Video presentation

Watch *Bake blind* where a professional chef will take you through this process and show you how to make a cartouche. *Finish a flan* will give you ideas for, and skills to make, tasty fillings.

Definitions

Blind baking: cooking a flan case without the filling in it. The flan is lined with greaseproof paper (cartouche) and filled with baking beans. The beans help to keep the shape of the pastry during cooking.
Cartouche: a round piece of greaseproof paper used to line or cover.
Docker: a spiked tool used to put holes in flan cases to prevent them rising during baking.

Did you know?

The egg white will seal the holes so the flan case can be later filled with liquid fillings such as lemon tart or quiche mix.

Use caution. Before opening the door to any steamer, make sure no one else is close. Turn off the oven, slowly open the door and allow the steam to escape. Then open the door fully and place the item inside. Close the door and restart the cooking process.

Jam roly poly

Preparation	2
Cooking skills	–
Finishing	–

suet pastry	1 quantity – see above
jam (strawberry, raspberry etc.)	200g
Serves	8

Method

1 Roll out the suet pastry into a rectangle approximately 30cm × 15cm and place onto a piece of greased baking paper.
2 Spread the jam onto the pastry leaving a 1cm gap on all edges.
3 Fold the two shorter ends inwards about 1cm and then roll the suet pastry from the longer side down towards you, ensuring that the sides do not unfold. Moisten the bottom edges to seal the jam roll.
4 Roll the jam roll tightly into the greased baking paper and then roll in tin foil or a pudding cloth. Seal both ends with a piece of string.
5 Steam for 1½–2 hours in the steamer.

Low pressure steaming

Place a cooling rack into a rectangular basin of water and fill the basin with enough water so that the cooling rack is just about covered in water. Bring to the boil and place the jam roll onto the cooling rack and close the basin with tin foil. Turn the stove down enough so that the water just about keeps boiling. Keep an eye on the water; you may have to top up the water as it evaporates.

Choux pastry

Choux paste

butter	65g
water	185ml
salt	5g
caster sugar	7g
eggs	3
strong flour, sifted	130g
Oven temperature	200°C
Cooking time	30–40 minutes, depending on product

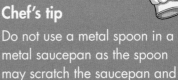

Preparation	3
Cooking skills	3
Finishing	–

Method

1. Dice the butter and place it into a saucepan with the water, salt and sugar.
2. Cook until the butter melts, then bring to the boil.
3. Crack the eggs into a bowl and whisk them.
4. As soon as the mixture boils add all the flour. Mix with a spatula until all the flour has been absorbed.
5. Cook out the flour or the mixture will not absorb the correct amount of egg to make the final product rise sufficiently. To do this, cook until the mixture comes away from the sides of the saucepan. Then cook for a further minute.
6. Place the mixture (**panade**) into a clean bowl to cool. Do not start adding the egg while the mixture is hot, otherwise the egg will cook before the mixture goes into the oven.
7. When the panade has cooled, place it back into the saucepan and slowly add the egg. Beat well between each addition until the paste is smooth. The eggs give the finished cases the light and open texture.
8. Continue adding the egg until a dropping consistency has been achieved. Lift up the paste on the spatula and slowly count to seven. The mixture should drop off. Add more egg if required.
9. Shape the paste as required (see below).
10. Cooking times are shown below.

Chef's tip

Do not use a metal spoon in a metal saucepan as the spoon may scratch the saucepan and this will turn the paste grey.

Did you know?

The main raising agent in choux paste is water. The water in the pastry gets hot during baking and turns into steam which reacts with the flour and eggs causing the choux product to rise. Keep the oven door closed for at least 10–15 minutes, otherwise the steam will escape and will not be able to react with the eggs and flour. This will result in a flat end product.

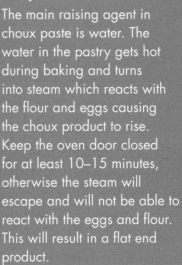

Definition

Panade: a paste of flour, butter and a little liquid.

Products you can make with choux paste

Éclairs

These are 3cm- to 12cm-long pastries filled with cream and decorated with chocolate or fondant. Pipe the mixture onto lightly greased trays with a medium tube and savoy bag, about 7cm long. Keep the tube at 90° to the tray.

Figure 15.1 Eclairs

To make sure the éclair is completely round do not let the tube touch the tray or the top of the mixture coming out of the tube. To pipe the éclair straight, only move the tube as fast as the mixture is coming out of the bag. Apply consistent pressure.

Apply an egg wash to give an even colour during cooking. Cook for approximately 15 minutes.

Paris Brests

These are choux rings filled with hazelnut cream. The rings represent the car rally route between the cities of Paris and Brest. Pipe with a medium tube. Use the same piping technique as for éclairs. Cook for approximately 15–20 minutes.

Figure 15.2 Paris Brests

Profiteroles

These are small cases filled with chantilly or pastry cream (crème pâtissière) and served with chocolate sauce. Pipe downwards onto lightly greased trays, to about the size of a ten pence piece. The tips will burn if they are allowed to remain proud; dampen a finger and press the mixture down to level it off. Cook for approximately 15–20 minutes.

Figure 15.3 Profiteroles

Choux pastry ring

Pipe in a large ring and decorate with flaked almonds. Bake for 20–30 minutes. Cut the ring in half. Fill with cream and dust with icing sugar.

Figure 15.4 Choux pastry ring

Swans

1 Pipe a teardrop shape. This will form the body and the wings.
2 Pipe the neck with a small nozzle in the shape of a number 2.
3 Bake for approximately 15–20 minutes.
4 Cut the teardrop shape in half. Use one half for the body.
5 Cut the other half in half again lengthways for the wings. Dip the top in chocolate.
6 Fill the body with whipped cream and insert the wings into the cream.
7 Push the neck in between the wings to complete the swan.
8 You can decorate the body with fruit and dust with icing sugar.

Figure 15.5 Swans

Choux paste fritters (*Beignets soufflés*)

These are small, walnut-sized pieces of choux paste, deep-fried in hot oil and served with apricot sauce.

1 Heat the oil to 190°C–200°C.
2 With two spoons, take uncooked choux paste about the size of a walnut and carefully drop into the hot oil.
3 Cook for approximately 10–15 minutes until brown.
4 Remove from the oil and drain well, sprinkle with caster sugar (it may be flavoured with cinnamon).
5 Serve fritters and apricot sauce separately.

How to check if choux pastry is cooked

1 Check the products are golden brown.
2 Open the oven door carefully and remove one piece from the tray, then close the door gently, leaving the rest in the oven.
3 Break open the product and touch the inside. It should feel slightly damp.
4 If it feels wet and sticky leave the products in the oven and check again in a few minutes.
5 Once cooked, cool on a cooling wire.

Storage of choux products

Filled choux cases must be stored in the fridge, unless they have been glazed with fondant icing; fondant icing will sweat in the fridge and fall off the case.

Unfilled cooked cases should be stored in airtight conditions to prevent them going soft and used within three days.

> **Chef's tip**
> If unfilled, cooked choux pastry cases go soft. Place them in an oven at 180°C (convection), 200°C or gas mark 6 (normal oven) for a few minutes to crisp up.

Puff pastry

This is one of the most complicated pastes used in patisserie. Few establishments make their own, because of the length of time needed to make it. Understanding how puff paste is made and works will help you when working with either commercial puff pastry or puff pastry made from scratch.

The proportion of fat to flour in puff pastry can be:
- 1kg strong flour to 1kg of fat – full puff.
- 1kg strong flour to 750g of fat – three-quarter puff.
- 1kg strong flour to 500g of fat – half puff.

Between 80 and 90 per cent of the fat used in puff pastry is pastry margarine. Pastry margarine has a higher melting temperature than normal margarine. This creates steam during cooking, which gives the pastry its light crispy texture.

Puff pastry is made using a lamination method which gives the pastry its distinctive layered effect when cooked.

Methods of making puff paste

There are three different methods of making puff paste:

1 **French method**: a ball of paste rolled out to a shape similar to an opened-out envelope; the pastry margarine is placed into the centre. The folds are then used to seal in the margarine. Then the paste is pinned and folded.

2 **Scotch method**: this is a quick way to make puff pastry but its quality is not as good as the French or English methods. It can also be messy. All the fat is cut into small pieces and added to the flour. Then the liquid is added and mixed to form a dough, with the fat pieces whole. The paste is then pinned out and folded.

3 **English method**: three-quarters of a rectangle of paste is covered with pastry margarine and folded in thirds to seal in the margarine. The paste is then pinned and folded as described below. This is the most popular method.

Remember!
A high cooking temperature is needed to create steam to make the pastry rise as the layers of margarine melt during cooking.

Puff paste

lemon juice	5ml
salt	5g
cold water	315ml
strong flour	500g
margarine (block)	60g
pastry margarine	440g

Preparation	4
Cooking skills	–
Finishing	–

Method

1. Add the lemon juice and salt to the ice cold water. Stir to dissolve the salt.
2. Sift the flour into a bowl.
3. Cut the block of margarine into smaller pieces and rub it into the flour.
4. Make a well in the flour. Add the **acidulated water** and mix to make a soft, pliable dough – similar to short paste.
5. Gently knead the dough to a smooth paste.
6. Cut a cross in the top of the dough and cover it with an upturned bowl.
7. Allow the paste to rest in the fridge for 30 minutes. This allows the gluten to relax.
8. Follow the instructions on the next page to fold in the paste.

Video presentation

Did you know you can prepare puff paste by mixing it on the work surface rather than into a bowl? Watch *Prepare puff paste* to see how this is done. Then watch *Make puff paste (English method)*.

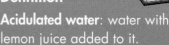

Definition

Acidulated water: water with lemon juice added to it.

Did you know?

The lemon juice helps to strengthen the gluten.

How to fold puff pastry – English method

1 Take a clean plastic bag about the size of an A4 sheet and open it out. Put it on the work surface. Cover two-thirds of one half of the plastic in sliced pastry margarine.

2 Fold the other half of the plastic over the butter. Pin out to flatten the butter so that it fills the rest of the plastic and is of an even thickness. Put it to one side.

3 Lightly flour the work surface and place the prepared puff pastry dough onto it. Open out the corners of the cross in the top of the dough to make a square.

4 Pin out the dough into a rectangle a third longer and slightly wider that the pastry margarine.

5 Take the pinned out pastry margarine. Open up one side of the plastic. Put the margarine onto one end of the pastry and peel off the plastic. It should cover two-thirds of the pastry.

6 Fold the uncovered third of the pastry over to create 3 layers (2 pastry, 1 fat).

7 Use the pastry brush to remove any excess flour and fold over again creating 5 layers.

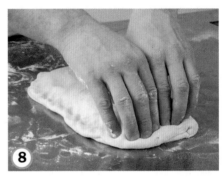

8 Seal the edges by pressing with your fingers.

9 Pin out the pastry again until it is just over 1cm thick.

10 Fold one third down. Brush away any excess flour as you go.

11 Fold the other third up and seal.

12

Turn the pastry and margarine envelope through 90° so the sealed edge is on the left. Wrap it in silicone paper and allow it to rest in the fridge for 20 minutes. This is one turn.

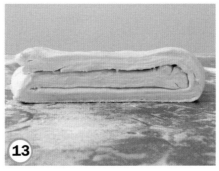

13

Repeat steps 9–12 until you have made 6 turns.

Cutting and cooking puff paste

When cutting puff paste use a guillotine method to prevent the layers of pastry causing distortion during cooking.

Do not twist pastry cutters when making vol-au-vents and bouchées, as this will cause the pastry cases to rise unevenly.

Cooked puff pastry should be golden brown in colour, well but evenly risen, and have crisp texture. The bases should be cooked – turn them over and check.

Storage of puff paste

Uncooked puff paste should be covered in plastic to prevent skinning and stored in the fridge. All cooked puff pastry products not containing high-risk foods can be stored in airtight conditions to prevent them going soft. All products containing high-risk foods must be stored in the fridge.

Find out! Worksheet 44

What does salt and lemon juice do for puff pastry? Use the Internet to find five sweet and five savoury pastry recipes.

Tart Tartin

granulated sugar	200g
apples (golden delicious) or pears or bananas	3
light brown sugar	50g
cinnamon	pinch
puff pastry	15cm disc
melted butter	25g
Oven temperature	180°C
Cooking time	30 minutes
Serves	4

Preparation	2
Cooking skills	3
Finishing	1

Method

1 Brush a cake tin (15cm round by 5cm deep) with melted butter.
2 Heat up a small saucepan. When hot, add 50g of the granulated sugar, stirring gently with a wooden spoon. As soon as the sugar has melted, add the remaining granulated sugar gradually until it has all caramelised.
3 Remove from the heat and pour the caramel into the buttered cake tin.
4 Allow the caramel to set, sprinkle the light brown sugar and cinnamon onto the set caramel.
5 Peel apples or pears, cut each fruit into 4 wedges and remove the core. Place into the prepared cake tin.
6 If using bananas, peel and cut in half lengthways, then each half into three.
7 Cover the fruits with a puff pastry disc.
8 Bake at 180°C for about 30 minutes or until the pastry is golden brown.
9 Allow to cool slightly before turning over onto a plate.

Chef's tip

Keep the fruits chunky, as otherwise they are cooked before the pastry is baked.

Lemon tart

For the sweet pastry:

soft flour	125g
cold butter	75g
caster sugar	35g
egg (beat one whole egg and then use half)	½
Oven temperature	180°C
Cooking time	15 minutes

For the filling:

eggs	3
caster sugar	140g
lemon, grated zest	1
lemon juice	70ml
double cream	90ml
Oven temperature	120°C
Cooking time	30 minutes
Serves	4

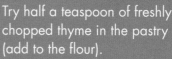

Preparation	3
Cooking skills	3
Finishing	2

Chef's tip

Try half a teaspoon of freshly chopped thyme in the pastry (add to the flour).

Method

Blind bake a 15cm sweet pastry flan case:

1 Mix together the egg and the sugar.
2 Sieve the flour.
3 Cut the butter into small pieces and rub into the flour until it resembles fine crumbs.
4 Add the egg/sugar mixture and stir together using a wooden spoon or hands.
5 Ensure that all ingredients are combined well but do not overwork the pastry.
6 Wrap in cling film and refrigerate for at least 30 minutes.
7 When cool, line the flan case with the pastry and blind bake at 180°C.
8 Seal the base (not the sides) with egg white and finish baking the pastry case.

For the filling:

1 Whisk the eggs with the caster sugar and strain.
2 Add lemon zest, lemon juice, and the cream. Continue to whisk until all the ingredients are thoroughly combined. Skim any froth from the top.
3 Pour the filling into the prepared tart case and bake at 120°C for about 30 minutes or until fully set.
4 Chill for at least 1 hour before serving.

Bakewell tart

For the sweet pastry:

soft flour	125g
cold butter	75g
caster sugar	35g
egg (beat one whole egg and then use half)	½

For the filling:

raspberry jam	50g
flaked almonds	30g
soft butter	60g
caster sugar	60g
egg	1
ground almonds	60g
plain flour, sieved	20g
icing sugar	20g
Oven temperature	175°C
Cooking time	25–30 minutes
Serves	4

Preparation	3
Cooking skills	2
Finishing	2

Method

1 Mix together the egg and the sugar.
2 Sieve the flour.
3 Cut the butter into small pieces and rub into the flour until it resembles fine crumbs.
4 Add the egg/sugar mixture and stir together using a wooden spoon or hands.
5 Ensure that all ingredients are combined well but do not overwork the pastry.
6 Wrap in cling film and refrigerate for at least 30 minutes.
7 When cool, line the flan case with the pastry and chill.
8 Beat together the butter, caster sugar, egg, ground almonds and flour until well combined.
9 Remove the prepared sweet pastry case from the fridge and spread the jam on the bottom of the sweet pastry.
10 Spread the almond butter onto the jam and decorate the top with flaked almonds.
11 Bake at 175°C for about 25–30 minutes or until golden brown.
12 Allow to cool slightly, remove from the flan case and lightly dust with icing sugar.

Convenience pastry

Any pastry that is available commercially, including pre-made pastry and pre-mixed pastry mixes, is called convenience pastry.

Puff pastry and filo pastry are the most commonly used commercial pre-made pastes. Puff pastry can be purchased either frozen, chilled or in a pre-mixed mix. Filo pastry is available chilled or frozen and is made up of very thin sheets of pastry, which are very crispy when cooked.

Filo pastry is made by rolling and pulling the dough until extremely thin sheets of the paste are produced. Filo is made in a similar way to strudel dough. It is often bought because the commercial product is of a high and consistent quality.

Because it is extremely thin, filo pastry needs to be kept moist or it dries and cannot be used. Melted butter is used to stick the sheets together and to keep the sheets moist until cooking. Any sheets not being used immediately should be covered with a damp cloth.

Dry pre-mixed mixes normally only require liquid. The method of production should be in accordance with the manufacturer's instructions. They should be stored in airtight conditions to prevent moisture and pest infestation.

> **Remember!**
> The manufacturer's storage instructions and 'use by' dates should be followed.

Test yourself!

1 When making short paste, what does the butter do to the flour?

2 Describe the creaming method for short paste.

3 When making short paste using creaming method 1, why should you not add all the egg in one go?

4 List five sweet and five savoury puff pastry products.

5 There are three ways to give pastry a lighter texture. What are they?

6 How is suet paste cooked normally?
   a Baked
   b Deep-fried
   c Steamed
   d Microwaved.

16 Cakes, sponges and scones

This chapter covers skills and knowledge in the following unit:

- 7132 Unit 246 (2FPC11) Prepare, cook and finish basic cakes, sponges, biscuits and scones

Working through this chapter could also provide the opportunity to practise the following Functional Skills at Level 2:
Functional English Writing – use a range of writing styles for different purposes

In this chapter you will:

Understand how and be able to prepare basic cakes, sponges, biscuits and scones	7132 – 246.1,2
Understand how and be able to cook basic cakes, sponges, biscuits and scones	7132 – 246.3,4
Understand how and be able to finish basic cakes, sponges, biscuits and scones	7132 – 246.5,6

You will learn to cook basic cakes, sponges and scones including:

- Victoria sponge
- Genoise sponge
- Swiss roll
- Madeira cakes
- scones: plain, fruit, cheese, potato, drop
- steamed sponge.

Preparation, cooking and finishing methods

Cakes, sponges and scones are very popular either as a snack or for a formal afternoon tea. Unlike dough, the flour used for cakes, sponges and scones is soft flour and it should not be over-mixed. Over-mixing will cause a tighter crumb and make the product dry. It is important to weigh and measure the ingredients correctly and to sieve the flour before use.

Sponges, cakes and scones are available in a vast range of different textures, flavours, shapes, sizes and fillings. The texture of a cake or sponge will vary in accordance to the type and recipe used. However, they all should display the following qualities:

o a good even volume and uniform shape.
o a thin and even crust.
o not dry to the palate.
o a good flavour and aroma.

Texture and lightness are provided by different methods, which include:

o mechanical
o chemical
o physical.

Ready mixes

In some establishments ready mixes are used to save time and money or because the establishment does not have the skill base to produce cakes and sponges from scratch.

There is a huge variety of pre-mixes on the market. Most pre-mixes require the addition of liquid such as milk, water and sometimes eggs. The manufacturer's instructions must be followed.

Pre-mixes can be an excellent choice for producing cakes and sponges for those customers with special dietary needs, e.g. diabetic or gluten-free.

Weighing and measuring

o Check all ingredients are of the right quantity and quality.
o Dry ingredients should be sieved before use.
o Ensure scales are working correctly.

Methods of making cakes, sponges and scones

The different methods of making cakes and sponges:
o creaming/beating
o whisking
o rubbing-in.

Creaming/beating

The creaming/beating method is also known as the sugar batter method. It is suitable for Victoria sponges, Madeira cake, steamed sponges and slab cakes.

Cream the softened butter and sugar by mixing them together until light and fluffy. Next add the eggs a little at a time, beating well between each addition. Finally, fold in the dry ingredients.

Creaming the butter and sugar together brings air into the butter which traps the liquid. Curdling occurs when the egg is added too quickly, causing the fat and liquid to separate.

Whisking

The whisking method is used to make Swiss rolls, Genoise sponge and sponge fingers/drops.

Cold whisking: whisk together the eggs and sugar until the mixture increases three times in size. Use a mixing machine on the highest setting with the whisk attachment to speed up the process. Gently fold in the dry ingredients. The end product will have a closer texture than with the warm whisking method.

Marcus says
Try to get all ingredients at the same temperature, unless specified, to ensure a smooth and even cake mix.

Chef's tip
When using the creaming method make sure the eggs are at room temperature to help prevent the mixture curdling.

Chef's tip
If the mixture starts to curdle before all the eggs have been added, mix in a little flour and then continue adding the rest of the egg.

Warm whisking, method 1: put the eggs into a mixing bowl. Warm the sugar on a tray in the oven until warm (do not melt the sugar). Pour the warmed sugar onto the eggs and quickly whisk together, and continue whisking until the mixture increases three times in size. Gently fold in the dry ingredients. This method can be used to save time. A mixer with the whisk attachment will also speed up the process.

Warm whisking, method 2: put the eggs and sugar into a mixing bowl and whisk over a bain-marie. Whisk until the mixture is three times the size. To test the consistency, lift the whisk and allow the mixture to fall. If the mixture sits on top of the main mixture without collapsing, then it is ready. This is known as 'ribboning'. Gently fold in the dry ingredients. This method produces a very light and airy texture.

Folding refers to ingredients being added gently and in stages, without knocking out air. The folding process usually occurs as the last stage in preparation. The following points should be remembered:
- Flour, raising agents and the other dry ingredients should be sifted before folding in.
- If adding butter it should be melted but not too hot.
- Butter should be folded into the egg at the same time as the flour.

Rubbing-in

This method involves rubbing the fat into the flour using your fingertips until the mixture has a sandy texture. Liquid and eggs are added at the end. This method is suitable for scones, rock cakes, and steamed sponges.

Chef's tip
Melted butter may be added to enrich the sponge and make it taste even better.

Other preparation and finishing techniques

Glazing: in cake making this means brushing the surface of the product with egg wash before baking in order to enhance its appearance and flavour, e.g. scones.

Greasing and dusting: this refers mainly to trays and cake tins that have been greased with melted butter and sometimes also dusted with a thin coating of flour to prevent the cake or sponge sticking to the tin. Grease tins or trays before starting to make the cake or sponge.

Lining: greasing a cake tin or baking tray and then lining with greaseproof or baking parchment, that has been cut to size.

Drumming when using a cake ring without a base this means adding a piece of greaseproof paper to the cake ring to prevent the cake mixture seeping out. The greaseproof paper looks like the skin of a drum.

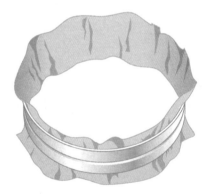

Figure 16.1 How to drum and line a flan ring

Mixing: combining different ingredients together.

Portioning: can mean dividing a cake or sponge mixture before baking. Portioning after baking refers to dividing the finished product into equal portions.

Piping: this is mainly used when shaping sponge fingers or drops before baking to fill or decorate baked products.

Rolling: often referred to as pinning out, used, for example, in making scones.

Shaping: this means cutting or shaping out scones or sponge fingers or drops.

Baking: all cakes and sponge products must be baked as soon as they have been prepared. The longer they sit around the more air will escape and a denser end product will be produced.

Dusting: a finishing method used to decorate cooled cake and sponge products. Icing sugar or cocoa powder are used for dusting. A variety of stencils can be used to create different effects.

Filling: layering or rolling baked cakes and sponges with different creams, icing and/or jam.

Icing refers to covering the top and or sides of a cake or sponge with icing as a decoration.

Spreading and smoothing: methods used when filling or icing a cake or sponge product. A palette knife can be used to achieve a smooth, even coating or filling.

Trimming: cutting small amounts from the sides or top of a cake or sponge to create a cleaner, neater finish.

Sponges

Different methods can be used to make sponges but the balance of ingredients must always be correct.

Sponges can be either baked or steamed depending on the product. If baked, they should be light in texture and a golden brown colour. The amount of sugar in the recipe will determine the temperature of the oven.

Victoria sponge

Victoria sponge is made using the creaming method. When used for making sponges this method is also known as the sugar batter method.

Chef's tip

Set the oven temperature and prepare the cake tins or trays before starting to make the cake or sponge.

Did you know?

A special sugar called 'neige décor' can be used to dust onto warm cakes or sponges. It does not melt when used on warm cakes or sponges.

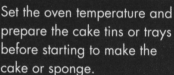

Video presentation

Prepare a sponge cake mix shows you how to make a Victoria sponge mix for a sandwich cake. For the skills to make an excellent sponge you should also watch *Correct a sponge cake mix* and *Finish a Victoria sponge cake.*

Did you know?

The Victoria sponge was supposedly introduced by the Duchess of Bedford in the 1880s. She was one of Queen Victoria's ladies-in-waiting. Queen Victoria was so fond of this cake it was named after her and became a sensation at royal events.

Victoria sponge cake is as popular now as it was then.

Victoria sponge sandwich

Preparation	3
Cooking skills	3
Finishing	2

butter	120g
caster sugar	120g
eggs	3 medium eggs
flour	120g
baking powder	5g
Oven temperature	180°C
Cooking time	25 minutes
Serves	6–8 portions

Method

1 Cream the butter and sugar in a bowl until the mixture is light and creamy.
2 Beat the eggs together in a smaller bowl and slowly add to the creamed butter mixture. Mix well between each addition.
3 Sift the baking powder and flour together in another bowl. Fold them into the sugar/butter mix. Do not over-mix.
4 Grease and flour two 15cm sponge sandwich pans.
5 Portion the mixture between the two sandwich pans and smooth with a palette knife.
6 Bake. To test if the sponge is cooked, gently press down the centre of the cake. If the cake is cooked it will pop back up again.
7 Once cooked, allow to cool slightly before turning out of the pans. Cooling will cause the sponge to shrink slightly, making it easier to remove from the pan. Turn out onto a cooling wire and allow to cool.
8 Using a palette knife, spread raspberry jam onto one of the Victoria sponge bases.
9 Pipe Chantilly cream over the jam or spread it using a palette knife.
10 Put the other Victoria sponge onto the cream and press gently.
11 Dust the surface of the cake with icing sugar.

Chef's tip

Cut the top sponge before assembling to avoid the cream being squashed out when portioning.

Chef's tip

Use a doily or a cooling wire to decorate the top of the sponge. Put the doily or cooling wire on top of the sponge and then dust with icing sugar. When you remove the doily/cooling wire, it will leave a pattern.

Chantilly cream is lightly whipped double cream, sweetened with caster sugar and flavoured with vanilla.

Chantilly cream

Preparation	1
Cooking skills	-
Finishing	-

fresh double cream	564ml
caster sugar	60g
vanilla extract or vanilla pod	to taste

Method

1 Put the cream in a bowl. Add the sugar and vanilla seeds to the cream.
2 Whisk together keeping the cream cold (whisk straight from the fridge, or over ice). Keep whisking until the desired consistency is achieved.
3 If using a vanilla pod, split the pod and remove the seeds, then add the seeds to the cream.

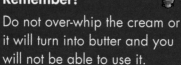

Remember!
Do not over-whip the cream or it will turn into butter and you will not be able to use it.

Basic slab cake

Basic slab cake uses a general sponge mix. Different flavours and fruit can be added to make different cakes.

Basic slab cake

Preparation	3
Cooking skills	1
Finishing	-

flour	500g
baking powder	20g
caster sugar	500g
butter	500g
eggs	13 medium
Oven temperature	180°C
Cooking time	25–50 minutes, depending on size
Makes	35–40 pieces

Method

1 Make the sponge cake using the creaming method.
2 Grease and flour 20cm tins as required.
3 Bake in the oven.

Different types of slab cake can be made by following the ideas below.

For **Madeira cakes**, add the **zest** of four lemons. Adding the lemon at the creaming stage will enhance the lemon flavour but it can also be added with the flour.

For **cherry cakes**, add 250g of glacé cherries. To prepare the cherries, wash the sugar off them and dry them. Cut them in half and cover them with flour. Add the cherries to the cake mix at the same time as the flour. Do not over-mix as the cherries can sink to the bottom.

For **sultana cakes**, add 180g of washed and dried sultanas. Add the sultanas with the flour.

For **chocolate slab cakes**, exchange 30g of flour for 30g of cocoa powder. Sift the flour, baking powder and cocoa powder together.

Definition

Zest: the outer coloured part of the peel of the lemon or other citrus fruit. It is often used as a flavouring.

Did you know?

Covering the cherries in flour helps to prevent them sinking.

Steamed sponge

Steamed sponge can be made using the creaming method or the rubbing-in method. The rubbing-in method will produce a heavier sponge and the keeping qualities will be affected.

Steamed sponge (rubbing-in method)

Preparation	2
Cooking skills	1
Finishing	–

flour	340g
baking powder	20g
butter	170g
sugar	170g
eggs	1
milk	125ml
Cooking time	Steam for 40 minutes–2½ hours, depending on the size

Method

1 Sift the flour and baking powder together into a bowl, rub in the butter.
2 Make a well in the flour and add the sugar. Break the egg and add it to the well, then add the milk.
3 Dissolve the sugar and draw in the flour, gradually bringing in the flour from the sides into the main mixture.
4 Continue mixing until a smooth texture has been achieved.
5 Pipe into prepared moulds.
6 Steam.

Steamed sponge pudding (creaming method)

Preparation	3
Cooking skills	1
Finishing	–

butter	250g
caster sugar	250g
eggs	4 medium
plain flour	250g
baking powder	5g
Cooking time	steam for 40 minutes–2½ hours, depending on the size
Serves	10

Method

1 Use the creaming method to achieve the desired mixture.
2 Pipe into pre-prepared moulds.
3 Steam.

Different types of slab cake can be made by following the ideas below:

Blackcap pudding has currants on the top.

Golden sponge pudding has golden syrup on top.

Chocolate sponge pudding is chocolate flavoured sponge. Replace 50g of flour with 50g of coca powder. It is usually served with chocolate flavoured sauce.

Jam or **Marmalade sponge pudding** has jam or marmalade on the top.

Frangipane

Frangipane is an almond sponge made using ground almonds instead of flour. The ground almonds provide texture and flavour to the sponge. Some of the almonds may be replaced with plain flour to achieve a lighter sponge. To make a lighter almond sponge, up to 50 per cent can be replaced with plain flour. Frangipane has lots of different uses, from desserts to cakes.

Frangipane

ground almonds	250g
almond essence	few drops, if needed
butter	250g
caster sugar	250g
eggs	6 medium

Preparation	2
Cooking skills	–
Finishing	–

Method

1 Sieve the ground almonds. Almond essence can be used to enhance the flavour.
2 Follow the creaming method.

Cup cakes

The cup cake recipe can be used for small sponge cakes, fairy cakes, butterfly cake and castle cakes.

Cup cake mixture

butter	120g
caster sugar	120g
eggs	4 medium
flour	180g
Oven temperature	200°C
Cooking time	15–20 minutes
Makes	18

Preparation	3
Cooking skills	2
Finishing	–

Method

1 Follow the creaming method.
2 Transfer the mixture into a savoy bag with a medium tube and pipe the mixture into paper cases.
3 Bake in the oven.

Cup cake mixture can be used to make the following small cakes:

o **Fairy cakes**: wash and dry some currants. Pipe the mixture into paper cases. Put the currants on top and bake.

o **Butterfly cakes**: cook and cool the cakes. Cut the tops off, cut them in half. Pipe butter cream onto the cake and push the two halves of the top into the butter cream to make a butterfly.

o **Castle cakes**: pipe the mixture into greased and floured **dariole moulds**. Bake and cool them. Dip them in boiling raspberry jam and then coat them with desiccated coconut.

Definition
Dariole mould: a small mould shaped like a flower pot.

Genoese

Genoese sponges can be used for many different types of desserts and cakes.

Genoese

flour	125g
caster sugar	125g
eggs	3 medium
melted butter	30g
Oven temperature	185°C
Cooking time	35–40 minutes
Makes	1 × 20cm ring

Preparation	4
Cooking skills	4
Finishing	–

Method

1 Sift the flour.
2 Whisk together the sugar and eggs over a bain-marie until the mixture is thick and light. To test the consistency, lift the whisk and allow the mixture to fall. If the mixture sits on top of the main mixture without collapsing, then it is ready. This is known as 'ribboning'.
3 Once the mixture ribbons, remove it from the bain-marie and whisk gently until it cools.
4 Fold in the flour in three different stages.
5 Add the melted butter with the third flour stage. Be careful not to over-mix, otherwise the air will be knocked out and the sponge will be heavy.
6 Put the mixture into the prepared cake ring. Do not press the mixture down or smooth it, as the air will be knocked out and the surface will be damaged.
7 Bake until the sponge is well risen and springy when touched. Do not slam the oven door as this can cause a vacuum and this will cause the cake to sink.
8 When it is cooked, leave the sponge in the cake ring to cool slightly.
9 Remove the cake ring and transfer the sponge onto a cooling wire.

For best results allow the sponges to rest for a few hours before use.

To make chocolate genoese, replace 25g flour with 25g cocoa powder and sift them together.

Fresh cream gateau

Preparation	3
Cooking skills	–
Finishing	4

| genoise sponge | 1 quantity (as above) |
| jam (strawberry, raspberry or apricot) | 50g |

For the fresh cream filling:

double cream	500ml
caster sugar	80g
vanilla essence	

For the brushing syrup:

sugar	50g
water	50ml
Serves	10

Method

1 Cut the sponge into three horizontally.
2 Place the bottom slice of the sponge onto a cake board.
3 Boil water and sugar and flavour as required.
4 Brush bottom slice of sponge with syrup.
5 Spread a little jam onto the brushed sponge disc.
6 Spread whipped cream onto the jam.
7 Press some fruits if required into the cream.
8 Repeat for the middle layer.
9 Place the top layer of the sponge onto the cream but skin side down.
10 Brush with required syrup.
11 Cover the top and side of the gateau with the remaining cream.
12 Mark the gateau into 10 portions and decorated as required.

Add 100g of fruit puree into the whipped cream for fruit creams.

Add 100g melted chocolate into the whipped cream for chocolate cream.

Flavour options for syrup:

almond essence

vanilla essence

coffee essence

any type of alcohol such as brandy, rum etc.

any type of fruit juice such as passion fruit, orange, lemon.

Fruit options:

mandarins, strawberry, raspberry, mango, kiwi, pineapple, cherry.

Other options include: almonds or any other type of nut.

Decoration:
chocolate shavings
roasted ground or flaked almond and hazelnuts
cream rosettes on top
fresh fruit on top

Swiss roll

Swiss roll

soft flour	75g
cornflour	25g
eggs	4 medium
caster sugar	125g
extra caster sugar for dusting	
jam for filling	
Oven temperature	230°C
Cooking time	10–12 minutes
Makes	1 Swiss roll, suitable for 10–12 portions

Preparation	4
Cooking skills	4
Finishing	3

Method

1 Grease, line and flour a swiss roll tin.
2 Sift the flour.
3 Whisk the sugar and eggs together until they reach the ribboning stage.
4 Gently whisk until cold.
5 Fold in the dry ingredients in three stages, as for Genoese.
6 Bake in the oven.
7 Lightly dust a cloth or greaseproof paper with caster sugar.
8 Once cooked, turn the roll out onto the sugared cloth or greaseproof paper.
9 Remove the back paper.
10 Spread the Swiss roll thinly with beaten jam. Use a palette knife.
11 Start the rolling process with the hands and then pull the Swiss roll towards you with the aid of the cloth or paper.
12 Leave the Swiss roll wrapped in the cloth or paper as this prevents it unwrapping. Transfer to a cooling wire.
13 Once it is cool, remove the cloth or paper. Dust with caster sugar. Slice with a serrated knife to portion and serve.

To make chocolate Swiss roll, use 50g soft flour and 25g cocoa powder.

Sponge fingers or drops

The mixture is piped onto silicone paper in the shape of fingers or small discs, sprinkled liberally with caster sugar and baked.

Sponge fingers or drops

Preparation	3
Cooking skills	2
Finishing	2

flour	150g
eggs	3 medium
egg yolks	35g (3–4)
castor sugar	150g
Oven temperature	200°C
Cooking time	5–10 minutes
Makes	48 fingers or drops

Method

1. Follow steps 1 to 5 of the recipe for Swiss rolls.
2. Put the mixture into a savoy bag with a medium plain tube. Pipe into fingers approximately 8cm in length onto silicone paper or 4cm diameter circles.
3. Sprinkle liberally with caster sugar.
4. Bake until light brown. Once cooked transfer onto a cooling wire.
5. Sandwich together with whipped cream and jam or butter cream.
6. A **dredger** may be used to ensure the sugar coating is even. Place a finger onto the top when using to prevent the lid coming off.

Chef's tip

Butter cream is a creamed mixture of 380g icing sugar and 500g butter which can be flavoured and coloured as required.

Definition

Dredge: to sprinkle or coat food with flour and sugar to enhance presentation.

Scones

Scones are very popular. Some scones are baked, other cooked on a griddle, and some are even fried and eaten for breakfast.

The recipe for plain scones can be adapted to different types of scone with the addition or removal of different items.

Kneading is a technique used in the preparation of scones to combine ingredients after rubbing-in. Unlike the kneading of bread dough, it must be carried out in a gentle manner. Scones are made with soft flour so a full kneading process would ruin the final product. See Chapter 14 to compare techniques used with bread and dough products.

Plain scones

Preparation		2
Cooking skills		2
Finishing		1

plain flour	500g
baking powder	30g
salt	good pinch
butter	100g
caster sugar	100g
egg	1 medium
milk	230ml
Oven temperature	225°C
Baking time	15–20 minutes
Makes	16 scones using a 5–6cm pastry cutter

Method

1. Sift the flour, salt and baking powder together into a bowl.
2. Rub in the butter.
3. Make a well. Add the sugar to the well.
4. Break egg into a jug. Add the milk.
5. Add the egg and milk mixture to the well and dissolve the sugar.
6. Draw in the flour and butter and continue mixing until a soft dough is achieved. Do not over-mix at this stage, but gently knead to smooth off the dough.
7. Pin out on a lightly dusted floured surface to a thickness of approximately 2cm.
8. Cut out using a scone cutter. Transfer onto lightly greased trays.
9. Knead the trimmings into a ball, pin it out and cut out as before.
10. Egg wash the tops and allow the items to relax for 15 minutes.
11. Put into the oven. To test if they are cooked, tap the bottom of the scone – it should sound hollow.
12. Allow to rest for ten minutes and transfer onto cooling wires.

Use these suggestions to make different types of scones:

- **Sultana scones**: add 125g washed and dried sultanas. Add them at the same time as the flour, before the liquid.
- **Cheese scones:** use 125g of grated cheddar cheese instead of sugar. Add a teaspoon of English mustard powder and a teaspoon of cayenne pepper. The spices bring out the flavour of the cheese.
- **Treacle scones**: replace 50g of the sugar with 50g of black treacle. Add the treacle with the milk.

417

○ **Wholemeal scones**: replace 375g of flour with 375g of wholemeal flour. A little more milk may be required.

○ **Potato scones**: replace up to 50 per cent of the flour with cold mashed potato and omit the sugar. Pin out to a thickness of 0.5cm and cook on a lightly oiled griddle.

Drop scones

Drop scones are more like a pancake and in some places they are known as Scotch pancakes. Traditionally they are cooked on a griddle.

Drop scones

plain flour	250g
baking powder	5g
caster sugar	10g
eggs	2 medium
milk	200ml
Makes	12–18

Preparation	3
Cooking skills	2
Finishing	–

Chef's tip

As an alternative, add 75g soaked sultanas to the drop scone batter.

Method

1 Sift the flour and baking powder together.
2 Make a well and add the sugar, milk and eggs.
3 Whisk to a thick batter.
4 Heat a lightly oiled griddle or a heavy-based frying pan.
5 Drop sufficient batter onto the griddle to make a circle approximately 5cm in diameter.
6 As the scone cooks, the surface will dry out. Once this has been achieved turn the scone over using a palette knife.
7 Once cooked remove from griddle and serve hot. The scones should be a golden brown colour.

Drop scones can be served with butter and jam.

Try this!   Worksheet 45

What methods are used to produce:
○ **victoria sponge**
○ **swiss roll**
○ **steamed sponge**
○ **sponge fingers**
○ **genoise sponge**
○ **frangipane**
○ **plain scones**
○ **rock cakes?**

Rock cakes

Rock cakes are similar to scones but are more rustic.

Rock cakes

plain flour	500g
baking powder	30g
salt	3g
butter	125g
currants, washed and dried	60g
mixed peel, washed and dried	25g
caster sugar	60g
egg	1
milk	225ml
eggs for egg wash	2
granulated sugar	25g
Oven temperature	225°C
Baking time	15 minutes
Makes	16 cakes

Preparation	2
Cooking skills	2
Finishing	–

Method

1. Sift the flour, salt and baking powder together.
2. Rub in the butter until a sandy texture is achieved.
3. Add the dried fruit and mix.
4. Make a well in the centre and add the sugar. Add the egg and milk and dissolve the sugar.
5. Draw in the flour and make a soft dough. Do not over-mix.
6. Break off evenly sized pieces and place onto a lightly greased tray. Do not make them too uniform.
7. Brush the rock cakes with egg wash and sprinkle them with granulated sugar.
8. Bake until golden brown. Once cooked remove from the oven and allow to cool slightly. Then transfer them to a cooling wire.

Raspberry buns are similar to rock cakes but are more formal.

Raspberry buns

		Preparation	2
		Cooking skills	2
		Finishing	–

plain flour	500g
baking powder	30g
salt	3g
butter	125g
caster sugar	125g
egg	1
milk	240ml
raspberry jam	100g
Oven temperature	220°C
Cooking time	15–20 minutes
Makes	16 buns

Method

1 Follow steps 1–5 for rock cakes.
2 Roll out the dough on a lightly floured surface and make it into a sausage shape.
3 Cut the dough into 16 pieces and shape each piece into a ball.
4 Dip the top of each ball into caster sugar and place them onto lightly greased baking trays.
5 Make an indentation on the top of each bun. Fill each indentation with raspberry jam.
6 Allow the items to rest for 15 minutes. Put them in the oven and bake to a golden brown colour.
7 Once cooked let the buns rest for a few minutes and then transfer them to a cooling wire.

Test yourself!

1 How many grams are there in one kilogram?

2 How many millilitres are there in one litre?

3 What protein is developed in flour during kneading?

4 What effect will it have in cakes?

5 Why is baking powder used?

17

Cold and hot desserts

This chapter covers skills and knowledge in the following unit:

○ 7132 Unit 249 (2FPC14) Prepare, cook and finish basic cold and hot desserts

Working through this chapter could also provide the opportunity to practise the following Functional Skills at Level 2:
Functional Maths Analysing – recognise and use 2D representations of 3D objects; find area, perimeter and volume of common shapes

In this chapter you will:

Understand how and be able to prepare basic cold and hot desserts	7132 – 249.1,2
Understand how and be able to cook basic cold and hot desserts	7132 – 249.3,4
Understand how and be able to finish basic cold and hot desserts	7132 – 249.5,6

You will learn to make basic cold and hot desserts, including:

○ ice cream
○ mousses
○ egg-based desserts
○ batter-based desserts
○ sponge-based desserts
○ fruit-based desserts.

Types of desserts

Desserts all have one thing in common – most people love them. The art of making desserts can be learnt by everyone, but some chefs have a particular passion for creating them.

Basic cold and hot and desserts include:

○ **Ice creams**: made from milk, cream, sugar, eggs and flavouring, then churned in an ice-cream maker to achieve a smooth texture and consistency. Ice cream is available in many different flavours.

○ **Mousses**: cold desserts such as chocolate or fruit mousse, generally light and airy in texture, often held together with a setting agent such as gelatine.

○ **Egg-based desserts**: can be either served hot or cold. Cold desserts include crème brûlée, crème caramel and baked egg custard. Hot desserts include bread and butter pudding and cabinet pudding. Egg-based desserts also include meringues.

○ **Batter-based desserts**: these are usually fried, e.g. pancakes and fritters.

○ **Sponge-based desserts**: these include steamed sponges and bakewell tart.

○ **Fruit-based desserts**: these include fruit flans, Eve's pudding, fruit crumble and summer puddings.

Marcus says

When using chocolate, use the correct percentage of cocoa solids to achieve the correct flavour. With desserts, the taste is as important as how pretty it looks on the plate, often forgotten.

Ice cream

Ice cream is a very popular dessert, available in many different flavours. Ice cream is normally made using a sorbetière (ice-cream maker). It can be made using a normal household freezer, but the ice cream will not be such good quality.

A sorbetière slowly churns and freezes the ice-cream mixture. As the mixture freezes ice crystals are produced. These are kept small by the churning action. Small ice crystals mean high-quality ice cream with a smooth texture.

Freezing the ice-cream mixture in a normal freezer produces larger ice crystals so the texture is not so smooth.

Ice cream is generally made using high-risk products so it must be stored below –22°C. This temperature makes the ice cream hard to serve, so it is best to remove ice cream from the freezer and place

Remember!

Melted ice cream must not be re-frozen.

it into the fridge before service. This allows the ice cream to be served more easily.

Vanilla ice cream

milk	1 litre
vanilla pod	½
egg yolks	5
caster sugar	375g
double cream	500ml

Preparation	3
Cooking skills	–
Finishing	–

1. Put the milk into a pan and warm it.
2. Split the vanilla pod and scrape out the seeds. Put the pod into the warm milk to **infuse**.
3. Put the egg yolks and sugar into a bowl and whisk together until light and fluffy.
4. Bring the milk to the boil and add to egg mixture. Mix with a spatula.
5. Put the mixture back into the saucepan.
6. Cook the mixture over a gentle heat until the mixture coats the back of the spatula. To test, stir the mixture well, take out the spatula and draw a spoon through the mixture. The mixture should not rejoin quickly.
7. Strain the cooked mixture through a conical strainer and allow to cool.
8. When the mixture is completely cool, add the cream and freeze.

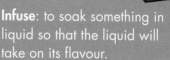

Definition

Infuse: to soak something in liquid so that the liquid will take on its flavour.

Chef's tip

If the pan has any burnt milk left on it, use a clean pan.

Chef's tip

To stop the milk burning, sprinkle some of the sugar from the recipe onto the bottom of the saucepan, then add the milk but do not stir. The sugar on the base of the pan will protect the lactose and stop the milk from burning before it boils.

To freeze in a sorbetière: transfer the mixture into the sorbetière, churn and freeze. Once the mixture has doubled in volume and is firm transfer it to a clean container, cover and store in the freezer until required for service.

To freeze in a freezer: cover and put into the freezer. Stir every 30 minutes until firm. Freeze until ready for service.

This basic recipe can be used for many different flavours, by removing the vanilla pod and substituting other ingredients:

○ **Chocolate**: added to the milk before boiling.
○ **Fruit**: puréed and added after the double cream.
○ **Dried fruits or nuts**: added just before the final freezing stage.
○ **Alcohol**: added after the double cream.

Chef's tip

Do not overcook the mixture for ice cream, Vavarois or mousse or it will curdle and will have to be thrown away. Too much heat will cause the egg to cook and separate from the milk. Small pieces of egg will be evident in the milk and it will not thicken.

Mousse

Mousse is light in texture and is normally served chilled.

Gelatine

Mousse is set using gelatine. Too little gelatine and the mousse will not set, too much gelatine and the mousse will set too hard and the texture will be tough.

Gelatine comes in either powder or leaf form. Leaf gelatine is a more expensive form of gelatine but is a superior product.

Gelatine needs to be soaked in cold water before use. The best way to soak powdered gelatine is to measure the correct amount of water and sprinkle the powder onto the water and allow it to sponge.

Leaf gelatine turns into a jellied mass when soaked in water. The remaining water is thrown away and the jellied mass squeezed to remove as much excess water as possible.

Gelatine is made from beef bones and therefore not suitable for vegetarians. A setting agent suitable for vegetarians and vegans is made from seaweed and is known as agar agar; it is usually available in flake form. It has weaker setting properties than gelatine. It must be used in accordance with manufacturer's instructions.

Figure 17.1 Gelatine – leaf and powdered

Figure 17.2 Agar agar

Egg-custard sauce based

Vanilla mousse

leaf gelatine	40g
cold water for soaking gelatine	
caster sugar	150g
egg yolks	6
milk	400ml
vanilla pod	1
double cream	700ml
granulated sugar	150g
egg whites	6
Serves	8–10

Preparation	3
Cooking skills	-
Finishing	3

Method

1. Soak the leaf gelatine in cold water.
2. Cream together the caster sugar, egg yolks and a little milk.
3. Put the remaining milk into a pan. Split the vanilla pod and remove the seeds. Put the pod into the remaining milk.
4. Bring the milk to the boil and infuse the vanilla pod.
5. Bring the milk to the boil again and add to egg mixture. Mix with a spatula.
6. Put the mixture back into the saucepan.
7. Cook the mixture over a gentle heat until the mixture coats the back of the spatula. To test, stir the mixture well, take out the spatula and draw a spoon through the mixture. The mixture should not rejoin quickly.
8. Squeeze the water out of the soaked gelatine and add the gelatine to the hot mix. Dissolve the gelatine completely.
9. Strain the mixture through a fine-meshed conical strainer and allow to cool.
10. Whisk the double cream until it just peaks and put it into the fridge.
11. Put the granulated sugar into a pan and just cover with water. Bring to the boil and skim to remove any impurities. Cook the sugar until it reaches 120°C.
12. While the sugar is cooking, whisk the egg whites until they peak and slowly pour in the hot sugar. Continue whisking until the meringue is firm.
13. Fold the whipped cream into the cold mousse base and then fold in the meringue.
14. Pour the mix into serving dishes or moulds and place into the fridge to set.
15. When set, decorate with rosettes of whipped cream and any other garnish as directed by the establishment.

This type of mousse can be flavoured with coffee and/or chocolate.

To make coffee mousse, replace the vanilla pod with instant coffee to taste and colour. To make chocolate mousse, replace the vanilla pod with 100g grated chocolate. Add it to the milk before boiling.

How to create rosettes

1 Whip cream until stiff.
2 Transfer into a savoury piping bag with a medium five-star piping tube.
3 Pipe the rosettes directly onto the mousse.
4 Keep the piping bag upright when piping.

Bavarois

Vanilla bavarois

gelatine	3 leaves
caster sugar	50g
eggs	2
milk	250ml
vanilla essence	to taste
double cream	240ml
Makes	6 × 6cm mousse ring

Preparation	4
Cooking skills	–
Finishing	2

Figure 17.3 Creating a rosette

Method

1 Put the gelatine in a bowl and soak it in cold water.
2 Separate the egg yolks and egg whites.
3 Put the sugar and egg yolks into another bowl. Whisk them together.
4 Put the milk and vanilla essence into a pan and boil them.
5 Pour the hot milk over the sugar and egg mixture and mix.
6 Get a clean bowl and a conical strainer.
7 Pour the mixture into a clean saucepan.
8 Return to the heat and stir gently using a wooden spoon.
9 Once the mixture starts to thicken remove from the heat and pour through the strainer into the clean bowl. Do not boil.
10 Take the soaked gelatine out of the water and squeeze out the excess water.
11 Gently stir it into the warm mixture until fully dissolved.
12 Allow the mixture to cool down.
13 While the mixture is cooling, half whip the double cream until it starts to thicken.
14 Once the egg mixture starts to set, gently fold in the whipped cream.
15 Whip the egg whites to a stiff snow (until the egg white peaks and the peaks do not drop to one side) and gently fold in.
16 Fill moulds as required and store in the fridge until ready for service.

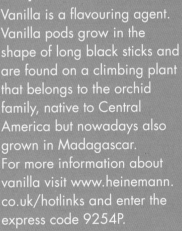

Did you know?

Vanilla is a flavouring agent. Vanilla pods grow in the shape of long black sticks and are found on a climbing plant that belongs to the orchid family, native to Central America but nowadays also grown in Madagascar.
For more information about vanilla visit www.heinemann.co.uk/hotlinks and enter the express code 9254P.

To make chocolate bavarois, add 50g dark chocolate to the milk before boiling.

To make coffee bavarois, add 10g instant coffee powder to the milk before boiling.

To make fruit bavarois, make the base recipe with only 125ml milk and add 125g fruit purée after the gelatine has been added. Serve with fruit coulis (see page 305).

Panna cotta

Panna cotta is an Italian vanilla mousse made without eggs, that has the consistency of jelly. 'Panna cotta' means 'cooked cream'.

Panna cotta

		Preparation	3
gelatine	2 leaves	Cooking skills	–
vanilla pod	½	Finishing	–
double cream	380ml		
milk	130ml		
caster sugar	60g		
Serves	8		

Method

1 Soak the gelatine in cold water.
2 Cut the vanilla pod lengthways and scrape out the seeds with the back of a knife.
3 Boil the cream, milk, vanilla seeds and vanilla skin.
4 Put the sugar into a clean bowl. Pour the hot vanilla cream through a strainer over the sugar.
5 Mix together using a whisk.
6 Cool down over a bowl of ice and fill eight small dariole moulds just before setting.
7 Serve with fresh fruits, fruit compote or fruit sauces.

Did you know?

Panna cotta only needs to be cooled on ice before filling the moulds if vanilla pods have been used. Vanilla seeds are heavier than cream and milk. If the panna cotta is put into the moulds while still hot, the vanilla seeds will sink to the bottom and the flavour will be concentrated at the base. Cooling the panna cotta on ice will distribute the vanilla seeds evenly.

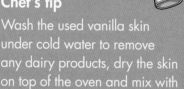

Chef's tip

Wash the used vanilla skin under cold water to remove any dairy products, dry the skin on top of the oven and mix with caster sugar to produce vanilla-flavoured sugar.

Fruit mousse

Fruit mousse

gelatine	4 leaves
fruit purée	250g
juice of a lemon	1
caster sugar	80g
double cream	250ml
egg whites	2
Serves	6

Preparation	3
Cooking skills	–
Finishing	2

Method

1 Soak the gelatine in cold water.
2 Put the fruit purée, lemon juice and sugar into a bowl and whisk together.
3 Put the double cream into another bowl and half whip it until it thickens slightly.
4 Take the soaked gelatine out of the water, squeeze out the excess water and put the gelatine into a clean saucepan.
5 Add 3 tbsp of the fruit purée and dissolve the gelatine over a moderate heat.
6 Put the rest of the fruit purée into a bowl. Whisk the gelatine mixture into the fruit purée.
7 Whip the egg whites until stiff.
8 Just before the fruit mixture starts to set, fold in the whipped cream and egg white.
9 Fill 6cm mousse rings and chill until set.
10 Store in the fridge until ready for service.

Chef's tip
The lemon juice will enhance the flavour of the fruit purée.

Egg-based desserts

Many egg-based desserts combine milk or cream, eggs, sugar and flavouring. The egg mix cooks and sets the liquid content. Examples of egg desserts:

○ Baked egg custard
○ Baked egg custard tart
○ Bread and butter pudding
○ Queen of puddings
○ Cabinet pudding
○ Crème caramel
○ Crème brûlée
○ Small pots of chocolate.

Any egg custard mixture needs enough eggs to set the liquid (milk or cream). Cream gives a much richer texture, but costs more.

Excess heat while cooking egg custard dishes will result in the egg and liquid separating – known as 'curdling'. Overcooking the custard mix will leave a clear liquid on the surface of the cooked product.

Too much heat will also lead the sugar in the custard mix to produce bubbles throughout the mixture.

To reduce the risk of overheating the custard mix, most egg custard-based desserts are cooked in a bain-marie.

Other egg-based desserts:

○ Sweet omelettes
○ Floating islands
○ Meringues
○ Pavlova.

Try this!　　　　　　　　　　　　　**Worksheet 46**

How many desserts do you know which are part made from egg custard?

What are the main ingredients of egg custard? Why is a bain-marie used?

Egg custard

Egg custard

eggs	6	Preparation	1
granulated sugar	150g	Cooking skills	2
milk	565ml	Finishing	–
vanilla pod	1		
nutmeg, grated	to taste		
Serves	6–8		

Method

1 Put the eggs and sugar into a bowl. Whisk to mix, but do not incorporate air as this will affect the final product.
2 Put the milk into a saucepan. Split the vanilla pod and put the seeds into the milk. Warm the milk to infuse the flavour. Do not boil.
3 Pour the hot milk onto the egg and sugar mixture. Whisk to mix but do not make frothy.
4 Strain through a conical strainer.
5 Transfer to a buttered dish and grate nutmeg onto the surface.
6 Cook in a bain-marie for approximately 30 to 35 minutes at 200°C.
7 Once cooked allow to cool. Store in the fridge until required for service.

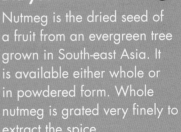

Did you know?

Nutmeg is the dried seed of a fruit from an evergreen tree grown in South-east Asia. It is available either whole or in powdered form. Whole nutmeg is grated very finely to extract the spice.

Did you know?

This mixture can also be cooked inside a blind baked sweet pastry case. See Chapter 15.

Queen of puddings is another egg custard-based dessert with added raspberry jam and cake crumbs. It is finished with crossed meringue and then each space is filled alternately with apricot and raspberry jam.

It is a very sweet, very decorative dessert. The egg custard mix can also be flavoured with lemon zest.

Cabinet pudding is egg custard with mixed dried fruits and sponge, served with sauce anglaise.

Diplomat pudding is a Cabinet pudding served cold, turned out of its cooking dish and decorated with whipped cream.

Marcus says

With a hot dessert such as an egg custard tart, use fresh free range eggs for optimum colour, flavour and silkiness. When making egg custard tart, remember to pour the egg mixture into the tart whilst it is still in the oven – this allows you to fill right to the top without having to carry it!

Bread and butter pudding

With the addition of sliced bread, sultanas and butter another very popular dessert can be made.

Bread and butter pudding

Preparation		2
Cooking skills		2
Finishing		2

eggs	6 medium
granulated sugar	150g
milk	500ml
vanilla pod	1
sultanas	100g
white bread	250g (approx 7 slices)
butter	100g
Cooking time	30–35 minutes
Oven temperature	190°C
Serves	6

Method

1 Make the egg custard as normal.
2 Butter and sugar a pie dish.
3 Wash and dry the sultanas.
4 Butter the bread and cut each slice into four triangles. (The crusts can be removed if required.)
5 Layer the pie dish with alternate layers of buttered bread and sultanas. Finish with a layer of buttered bread. Do not use any sultanas on the top layer as they will burn during cooking and taste bitter.
6 Pass the egg custard through a conical strainer onto the bread. Allow the bread to soak up the egg custard mixture for at least 30 minutes.
7 Place the dish into a deep tray. Half fill the tray to make a bain-marie.
8 Bake the pudding until set and golden brown. Serve hot.

A modern twist on this classic dessert is to replace the milk with cream and glaze the top with sugar after cooking to give a crisp sweet topping. Another twist is to use **brioche** instead of normal sandwich bread. By adding melted chocolate or chocolate powder to the egg custard mixture you can create a Chocolate bread and butter pudding.

Definition

Brioche: yeast dough that has been enriched with eggs and butter. It is similar to croissants.

Crème caramel

Crème caramel

Preparation   2
Cooking skills   2
Finishing   1

For the egg custard:

milk	850ml
sugar	90g
eggs	6
vanilla essence	to taste

For the caramel:

sugar	180g
water	90ml and 20ml
Oven temperature	180°C
Cooking time	30–40 minutes
Serves	6

Method

1. Make the egg custard as normal.
2. Make a caramel by mixing the sugar and 90ml of water in a heavy-bottomed saucepan.
3. Dissolve the sugar and bring it to the boil. Skim.
4. With a clean pastry brush and some clean water, wash down the inside of the saucepan to remove any sugar crystals from the edge. Continue washing down throughout the boiling process.
5. Cook the sugar until an amber colour has been achieved, approx. 15–20 minutes.
6. Add the 20ml of water. This will stop the cooking process and thin down the sugar to produce a caramel sauce.
7. Pour the caramel into some greased moulds and allow to set. The caramel will set more quickly if the moulds are put into cold water.
8. Strain the egg custard mix onto the caramel.
9. Transfer the moulds into a bain-marie.
10. Cook in the oven until the custard is set.
11. When cooked remove from the bain-marie and allow to cool.
12. When completely cold remove from the moulds and serve.

Did you know?

The reason for washing down the side of the pan when boiling sugar is to stop the liquid sugar from crystallising.

Chef's tip

Put a clean unused cleaning cloth into the bottom of the bain-marie before you put the moulds in. This prevents the base of the moulds getting too hot.

How to remove the Crème caramel from the moulds

1 Tilt the mould onto its side at 90° and loosen the edge of the custard from the mould. Continue all the way round.
2 Turn the mould upside down onto a serving plate, hold the plate and the mould and shake to loosen.
3 Remove the mould.
4 Any remaining caramel should be poured over the custard.

Crème brûlée

Crème brûlée translates as burnt cream, which indicates how the dessert is finished prior to service. Crème brûlée can be served hot or cold.

Crème brûlée

egg yolks	10
eggs	2
caster sugar	150g
double cream	1000ml
vanilla pod	1
demerara sugar	for topping
Oven temperature	180°C
Cooking time	30–40 minutes
Serves	8–10

Preparation	2
Cooking skills	2
Finishing	2

Method

1 Make the custard as for egg custard. Then poach the custard in a bain-marie as for crème caramels.
2 Once set, sprinkle an even coating of demerara sugar onto the surface.
3 Glaze the sugar to a light brown colour under a salamander.
4 Once glazed, serve.

Meringues

A meringue is a mixture of whipped egg whites and sugar. Usually, caster sugar is used as the grains are much smaller and more easily suspended in the bubbles of the whipped egg white.

> **Remember!**
> The caramel should be rich and amber in colour, the surface of the cream should be smooth and not full of bubbles. The cream should stand proud and not dipped in the middle.

> **Chef's tip**
> Make sure the salamander has been pre-heated or the sugar will take a long time to brown and cause the custard mix to overheat and curdle.

When making hot or cold meringue, there are a few basic rules that must be followed:

○ All whipping equipment must be free from grease. Plastic bowls are not recommended; use either stainless steel or glass, as these can be scalded with very hot water to remove the grease. If you dry the bowl, use clean disposable tissue, not a cloth. A cloth could transfer grease to the surface of the equipment.

○ The easiest way to make meringue is by machine. However, if making by hand use a stainless steel balloon whisk. This type of whisk allows more air to be incorporated quickly.

○ Egg yolks consist mainly of fat and if any traces of yolk are present in the egg white, it will prevent the egg white whipping to a **stiff peak**.

○ Once made, the meringue mixture must be used straight away or the egg and sugar will start to separate and the egg white will start to turn back into liquid as the air escapes.

There are three different types of meringue:

1 **Cold meringue** (French meringue), used for cakes, sponges and pavlovas.
2 **Hot meringue** (Swiss meringue), used for piping shells and nests.
3 **Boiled meringue** (Italian meringue), used for mousses, ice parfaits and lemon meringue.

Definition

Stiff peak: when the peaks of the whipped egg white stand up without falling to one side. The final test is to turn the bowl upside down to see if the white drops out.

Chef's tip

A pinch of salt in the egg white helps the whipping process.

Cold meringue

Preparation	3
Cooking skills	–
Finishing	–

1 part of egg white to 2 parts of caster sugar

For example:

| egg white | 100g |
| caster sugar | 200g |

Method

1 Whisk the egg white in a clean bowl on the highest setting of a mixing machine.
2 Whisk until tripled in size.
3 Slowly add the sugar in small amounts while the machine is still running on full speed.
4 Turn the machine off once all the sugar has been incorporated and use as required.

Hot meringue

1 part of egg white to 2 parts of caster sugar

Preparation	3
Cooking skills	–
Finishing	–

Method

1 Put the sugar and egg white into a clean mixing bowl that will fit onto a machine. Combine using a hand whisk.
2 Put the bowl onto a bain-marie and whisk until the sugar has dissolved. To check this, remove the bowl from the heat and dip in a wooden spoon. Remove the wooden spoon and rub a finger over the spoon. If the mixture feels gritty return it to the heat and whisk until the sugar has dissolved.
3 Fit the bowl onto the machine, attach the whisk and whisk on the highest setting until the mixture is cold and in a stiff peak.
4 Use as required.

Video presentation

Watch *Finishing a flan* for an alternative method of making hot meringue. Try out both methods and see which you prefer.

Boiled meringue

granulated sugar	300g
water	90ml
cream of tartar	pinch
egg white	150g

Preparation	3
Cooking skills	–
Finishing	–

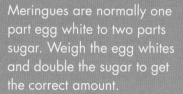

Chef's tip

Meringues are normally one part egg white to two parts sugar. Weigh the egg whites and double the sugar to get the correct amount.

Method

1 Put the sugar, water and cream of tartar in a clean saucepan. Combine with metal spoon.
2 Put the pan on a low heat. Wash the sides of the pan down with water and a clean brush (as for caramel for crème caramel).
3 Bring to the boil.
4 Boil the sugar mixture to 118°C. Test using a sugar thermometer. Do not stir the sugar, just let it boil.
5 In the meantime whisk the egg white to a stiff snow using a machine on the highest setting.
6 Once 118°C is reached remove from the heat and pour slowly into the whipped egg white while the machine is still running on full speed. Take care not to burn yourself.
7 Continue whipping until the mixture is cold and stiff peak.
8 Use as required.

Granulated sugar is used in this type of meringue because it is a cleaner type of sugar with fewer impurities than caster sugar. In this method the sugar has to be boiled with the water and therefore the granulated sugar is more suitable.

Cream of tartar is found in the juice of grapes, after they have been fermented in winemaking. It is classified as an acid, available in the form of a powder and used in baking powder. It helps to stabilise meringue once it has been whisked.

Pavlova

Pavlova is a meringue dish that is soft and chewy inside with a crunchy outside. Cornflour and vinegar are added to the meringue.

Pavlova

egg whites	100g	
caster sugar	200g	
vinegar	5ml	
cornflour	5g	
Serves	6–8	

Preparation	3
Cooking skills	2
Finishing	–

Method

1 Make meringue as previously described (cold meringue, steps 1–4).
2 Fold in the cornflour and vinegar.
3 Transfer onto silicone paper and bake at a temperature of 140°C for approximately two hours.
4 Cool and decorate with fruits and **Chantilly cream**.

Meringue shells, cases, nests and vacherins

These are all made with Swiss meringue and piped with star or plain piping tubes.

They can be dried on top of the oven overnight or dried in an oven on a low heat of about 90°C. This could take four to eight hours. Make sure that meringue products are not dried at too hot a temperature as they may discolour and lose their characteristic white colour.

Vacherins can either be large or individual round gateau-type meringues filled with fruit and cream and then decorated.

> **Did you know?**
> Pavlova was named after Anna Pavlova, a Russian ballerina.

> **Definition**
> **Chantilly cream**: cream that has been sweetened, flavoured and lightly whipped (see Chapter 16 for recipe).

Batter-based desserts

Batter-based desserts can be as simple as a lemon pancake or a more classic dish like crêpes suzette. Batter can also be used as a light crispy coating used to protect fruit during cooking.

Pancakes

Pancakes should be cooked in **crêpe** pans, which are small flat pans which make tossing the pancakes easier. They can also be cooked in frying pans but tossing them is a little more difficult.

Definition

Crêpes: the French term for pancakes. Crêpes need to be as thin as possible.

Basic pancake batter

soft flour	240g
salt	a pinch
milk	565ml
eggs	2
melted butter	30g

Preparation	1
Cooking skills	2
Finishing	1

Figure 17.4 Crêpe pan

Method

1 Sift the flour and salt together into a bowl.
2 Add the milk and eggs and whisk together until smooth.
3 Whisk in the melted butter.
4 Allow to rest for at least 60 minutes or the pancakes will be tough and rubbery. Whisk after resting.
5 Heat the crêpe pan, add a little vegetable oil (butter will burn and make the pancake taste burnt and bitter).
6 Coat the base of the pan with the hot oil and pour off any excess. (Too much oil will not only make the pancake greasy, it will also splash back and cause a serious burn.)
7 Fill a small ladle with pancake batter and pour the batter into the centre of the pan. Lift the pan and coat the base of the pan with the batter ensuring a thin even coat.
8 Put the pan back onto the heat, and cook the batter. When all the liquid has cooked, the pancake is ready to be turned over. Lift one edge of the pancake off the pan to check the colour; it should be a light golden brown.
9 To turn the pancake over, use a palette knife to run around the edge of the pancake to loosen it and make sure it has not stuck to the pan. Slide the palette knife under the pancake and turn it over to cook on the other side.
10 Once cooked turn onto an overturned plate if the pancake is to be served later, or onto a serving dish if being served straight away.

Ideas for service:

- **Lemon pancakes**: prepare and cook pancakes as described, turn out onto a plate, sprinkle with caster sugar and fold into four. Serve with lemon quarters.
- **Jam pancakes**: prepare and cook pancakes as described, turn out onto a plate and spread a spoon of red jam on each and roll up, sprinkle with caster sugar and serve.
- **Apple pancakes**: apple pancakes are the same as jam pancakes, but with apple purée instead of jam. Refer to fruit-based desserts (page 442) for making apple purée.

> **Try this!**   **Worksheet 47**
>
> Find out what faults there might be in pancake batters and the problems these can cause. Find out some possible recipes for yeast and pancake batters.

American-style pancakes

American-style pancakes are made using a slightly thicker batter that has a raising agent added, normally baking powder. Due to their thickness the batter needs sweetening, unlike normal pancakes that have jam, lemon and sugar etc.

American-style pancakes

soft flour	135g
salt	3g
milk	140ml
egg	1 large
baking powder	10g
caster sugar	50g

Preparation	1
Cooking skills	2
Finishing	1

Method

1. Follow steps 1–4 for basic pancake batter.
2. Add the baking powder just before cooking the pancakes, otherwise the effectiveness of the baking powder will be destroyed.
3. Cook the pancakes on a griddle. Pour the batter onto the hot surface about the size of a saucer. Cook and turn the pancakes.
4. Serve with maple syrup, fruit, ice cream, whipped cream or any sweet flavourings and accompaniments specified by the establishment.

Find out!

What else could be used to make the pancake lighter in texture?

Fritters

Fritters can be either sweet or savoury. Examples of sweet fritters:

o **Apple fritters**: peel and core apples, slice into four rings and keep covered in acidulated water (water with a squeeze of lemon juice). Drain well and dip the apple rings into flour and then into batter (see recipes below). Place into the deep fat fryer and cook on both sides until golden brown. Remove from fryer, drain well and coat in either plain or cinnamon sugar.

o **Banana fritters**: do not prepare the bananas until required as they will turn black. Peel and cut the bananas into approximately 5cm pieces, place into the batter and cook as for apple fritters. Can be served with apricot sauce.

o **Pineapple fritters**: remove the skin from the pineapple, slice into rings approximately 1cm thick, remove the core, and proceed as for apple fritters.

The frying batter is used to protect the items being fried, and gives them a crunchy texture.

A raising agent is needed for a frying batter to be light and fluffy. It could be whipped egg white, baking powder or yeast. The type of fritter and the establishment will determine the type of frying batter used.

After frying, transfer the cooked product to a colander and allow to drain. Serve as per menu requirements. Fritters are best served straight after cooking. Leaving them to cool will cause the batter to turn soggy.

Healthy eating

To encourage healthy eating, do not coat the fritters in sugar. They could be sweetened with honey as an alternative.

Frying batters

Egg white batter

soft flour	240g
salt	a pinch
cold water	300ml
egg whites	2

Preparation	1
Cooking skills	–
Finishing	–

Method

1 Sift the flour and salt together into a bowl.
2 Gradually add the cold water, whisking well to a smooth batter.
3 Allow to rest for a minimum of 20 minutes before using.
4 Whisk the egg whites until they are stiff.
5 Fold the egg whites into the batter.
6 Use straight away.

Baking powder batter

soft flour	240g
salt	a pinch
vinegar	30ml
yellow colouring	4 drops
water	280ml
baking powder	20g

Preparation	1
Cooking skills	–
Finishing	–

Method

1 Sift the flour and salt together in a bowl. Add the vinegar and colouring.
2 Gradually add the cold water, whisking well to form a smooth batter.
3 Add the baking powder just before cooking and whisk well.

Did you know?

The vinegar in the batter helps to make the batter crispy and reacts with the baking powder to create carbon dioxide.
The yellow colouring helps to make the batter turn golden brown during cooking.

Yeast batter

strong flour	240g
salt	a pinch
fresh yeast	30g
yellow colouring	4 drops
water	300ml

Preparation	1
Cooking skills	–
Finishing	–

Method

1 Sift the flour and salt into a bowl. Add the yeast and colouring.
2 Gradually add the cold water, whisking well to form a smooth batter.
3 Prove for 30–40 minutes before using.

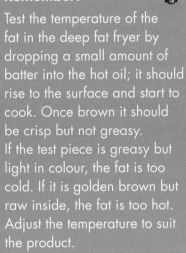

Remember!

Test the temperature of the fat in the deep fat fryer by dropping a small amount of batter into the hot oil; it should rise to the surface and start to cook. Once brown it should be crisp but not greasy.
If the test piece is greasy but light in colour, the fat is too cold. If it is golden brown but raw inside, the fat is too hot. Adjust the temperature to suit the product.

Sponge-based desserts

Sponge-based desserts can be a combination of different products or a simple steamed sponge pudding. For more information about making sponges, see Chapter 16.

Bakewell tart

To make Bakewell tart, coat the base of a sweet paste case with raspberry jam. Fill the case with frangipane (see page 400). Decorate it with lattice pastry strips then bake it and finish it with apricot glaze and water icing.

Steamed sponge pudding

Steamed sponge pudding is a sponge that is cooked in a steamer; it can be served with a variety of toppings and sauces:

- **Blackcap pudding** has currants on the top.
- **Golden sponge pudding** has golden syrup on the top.
- **Chocolate sponge pudding** has chocolate-flavoured sponge and is normally served with chocolate sauce. To make it, replace 50g flour with 50g cocoa powder.
- **Jam/marmalade sponge pudding** has jam or marmalade on the top.

Basic sponge pudding

Preparation	3
Cooking skills	1
Finishing	–

soft flour	250g
baking powder	5g
butter	250g
caster sugar	250g
eggs	4 medium
Serves	10

Method

1 Sift the flour and baking powder together into a bowl.
2 Flour and butter ten individual moulds.
3 Cream together the butter and sugar until light and fluffy.
4 Beat in the egg a little at a time.
5 Add the sifted flour and baking powder. Lightly mix until incorporated. Do not over mix.
6 Use as required.

All the sponges can be prepared individually or for portioning.

Did you know?

Apricot glaze is made with apricot jam, sugar and water. It is used to make the surface of sweet products shine. Apricot jam is used because apricots are very low in **pectin**. The glaze does not stain or change the colour of the final product and does not affect the taste. However, if the apricot glaze burns it will darken and taste bitter.

Definition

Pectin: a natural setting agent found in fruit.

Find out! **Worksheet 48**

Find examples of 10 steamed puddings using different types of mix and an appropriate sauce for each.

Use **dariole moulds** or pudding bowls. The insides of these must be buttered and floured. Once they are prepared, do not touch the inside as this could cause the cooked pudding to stick to the mould.

Put the topping at the bottom of the dish and the sponge mixture on top.

Do not over-fill the mould as the sponge will expand during cooking. Cover the top of the mould with a piece of greased greaseproof paper to prevent the steam penetrating the sponge.

Cooking times will depend on the size of the mould, but individual sponges can take up to 40 minutes, whereas large ones can take up to two hours.

Another popular sponge pudding is **Sticky toffee pudding**, which has soaked dates and is a soft sponge. Some recipes also have nuts and customers need to be informed in case one of them has a nut allergy.

Eve's pudding is a sponge and apple dessert. The apple is placed into a baking dish and covered with a basic sponge. It is then baked and normally served with fresh egg custard.

See page 443 for how to prepare the apples.

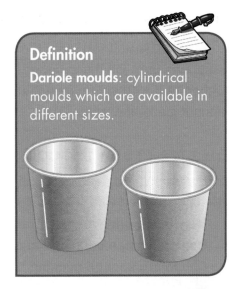

Definition

Dariole moulds: cylindrical moulds which are available in different sizes.

Did you know?

Eve's pudding is so called because of the story from the Bible about Eve eating an apple in the garden of Eden.

Fruit-based desserts

Fruit-based desserts can be as simple as a Fresh fruit salad or even a Rhubarb crumble. All fruit-based desserts have flexibility which can be adjusted to suit every establishment.

Syrup

When making fresh fruit salad, keep the pieces of fruit roughly the same size.

Fresh fruit salads normally have a base syrup to stop the fruit discolouring after being prepared. Fruit has a natural sugar called fructose, so the base syrup does not need to be too sweet, however this does depend on the type of fruit being used.

Place all the fruit together and add sufficient stock syrup to cover the fruit. Just before service, peel and slice the bananas and add them. Gently stir to mix the fruit and syrup and serve.

The syrup could be a simple stock syrup or even an unsweetened fruit juice. Stock syrup is a mixture of sugar and water, dissolved and boiled together.

Stock syrup

sugar	720g
water	565ml

Preparation	1
Cooking skills	1
Finishing	–

Method

1. Put the sugar and water into a saucepan.
2. Boil them and skim off any impurities.
3. Cool and use as required.

Stock syrup can also be flavoured with:

- cinnamon sticks
- lemons
- oranges
- coriander seeds.

Preparation of fruit

All fruit should be washed and dried before preparing or eating.

Apples need to be peeled, cored and quartered. Apples tend to turn brown very quickly once peeled. To prevent this, peeled apples should be kept in acidulated water. There are hundreds of varieties of apples, from the common Granny Smith to pink lady. Each apple has its own level of sweetness and crispness.

Bramley apples are normally used for cooking but eating apples can also be cooked. They require less cooking time and less sugar.

For fruit salad the quarters should be sliced into small pieces.

Healthy eating

The vitamins and nutrients found in apples are just under the skin, so use a vegetable peeler to remove the peel. To increase roughage in people's diets leave the peel on.

Cooking apples should be peeled, cored, quartered and kept in acidulated water until ready for cooking. The time of year and the variety of apple used will determine whether the apple needs additional water and sugar added during cooking. As a rough guide only, 1kg of cooking apples needs 125g sugar. After cooking, taste the apples and add extra sugar if required, or if too sweet add some lemon juice.

> **Remember!**
> Acidulated water is water with lemon juice added to it.

How to cook apples

1 Put sugar into a saucepan, add the drained apple slices and squeeze half a lemon over the top.
2 Put a tight-fitting lid on and place on the heat to cook. The steam created should provide enough liquid to cook the apples. Water can be added if necessary.
3 Test to see if the apple is cooked by tasting a small piece. If using the fruit in pieces it should be soft but still firm. For purée, cook slightly longer until there is no bite left.
4 Remove the fruit from the pan and allow to cool.
5 To purée the fruit, use a food processor. Purée can also be made using a potato masher, but it will not be so smooth.

Oranges should be peeled and segmented, but the most important part is to make sure there is no pith left on the segments.

How to peel an orange

1 To peel the orange, top and tail it first, so that you can see how thick the skin is.
2 Run a vegetable knife from the top of the fruit to the bottom, judging the correct thickness to remove all the pith and skin.
3 Once the first slice has been removed it will allow the next piece to be removed more easily, as you can then see how much skin to remove each time to remove all the pith and skin. Continue removing slices round the orange until all the skin and pith has been removed. Try to keep the round shape of the orange.

How to segment an orange

The orange is then ready to cut into segments which should be free from pith, pips or the membrane which divides up the inside of the orange. There are two different methods to achieve this:

Method 1

1

2

3

Place a container underneath the orange. Hold the peeled fruit in one hand and run a paring knife down towards the centre of the fruit just inside the segment membrane.

Once the centre is reached push the segment away from the centre.

The segment should come away from the membrane on the other side. Continue until all the segments have been removed. Squeeze the remaining pulp to remove any juice that remains.

Method 2 This is similar to method 1, but instead of pushing the segment away from the centre, cut the other side of the segment away from the membrane too. Method 2 is slightly easier but can cause more waste.

Bananas should not be prepared until required for service. Bananas turn brown very quickly and in fruit salad they will go black and spoil the presentation of the fruit. Bananas can be coated in lemon juice to slow down but not stop the browning process.

Peel the banana and cut slices about 3mm thick. If using bananas for fritters, cut them into three or four depending on the size of the fruit.

Grapes should be halved and the seed removed.

Kiwi fruit should be topped and tailed and peeled in the same way as oranges. Once peeled, slice and use as required.

Pears are either red or green and are also available in many varieties. Some are suitable for cooking. The normal method of cooking pears is poaching.

Pears can be peeled with a vegetable peeler and cored, then cut into quarters and then into smaller pieces to go into fruit salad.

Find out!

Worksheet 49

Find the names of four types of pears suitable for cooking and a suitable recipe for each.

To poach pears, do not core them until after poaching as this will help stop them falling apart. Pears can be poached in stock syrup, red wine or even sweet dessert wine. It depends on the dessert being produced, but the method of poaching is the same.

How to poach pears

1 Peel the pears and keep them covered in acidulated water.
2 Bring the poaching liquid to the boil and remove from the heat.
3 Put the pears into the liquid and cover with a cartouche.
4 Put back onto the heat and simmer gently for 10–25 minutes depending on the type of pear and the liquid being used.
5 The pears will change colour slightly to a translucent pale colour.

For more general information on fruits, visit www.heinemann.co.uk/hotlinks and enter the express code 7162P.

Fruit compote

Fruit compote is a mixture of stewed fruit which can be made with soft fruit, hard fruit and dried fruit.

Soft fruit should be chosen, washed and covered in hot stock syrup. Cool and serve as required.

Dried fruit should be washed and soaked overnight in cold water. Then sugar is added and the fruit is gently cooked in its juice. It is cooled and served as required.

Hard fruit should be washed, prepared, put in a shallow dish and covered in stock syrup. Put a cartouche on top and place in the oven to stew until the fruit is tender. Allow to cool in the syrup and serve as required.

Fruit compotes can be served at breakfast or with sweet sauces and ice cream. They can also be flavoured with alcohol. The fruit should retain its original colour, so the correct preparation method is important.

Fruit crumbles

Crumbles are a very popular but simple baked dessert. A crumble has fruit on the bottom and a topping of butter, flour and sugar.

Sometimes the fruit is cooked before the crumble topping is placed on top. This depends on the type of fruit used. For example, apples, rhubarb and gooseberries should be cooked, whereas raspberries, blackberries and peaches can be used raw.

Crumble

flour	450g
butter	200g
sugar	200g
fruit	1.5kg
Serves	8–10

Preparation	1
Cooking skills	1
Finishing	–

Method

1. Rub all the ingredients together until you achieve a sandy texture.
2. Put approx 1.5kg of prepared fruit in an ovenproof dish.
3. Sprinkle the crumble mixture on top of the fruit. Do not press the topping mixture down as this compacts the topping and makes it soggy.
4. Bake in a moderate oven until the fruit is cooked and the crumble topping is golden brown.

Find out!   **Worksheet 50**

Find five ingredients that could be used to make the crumble topping healthier to eat.

Fruit flans

Apple meringue flan is a simple dessert, but care is still needed to produce it well. An apple meringue is a blind-baked sweet paste flan (see Chapter 15), three-quarters filled with apple purée and with meringue piped on top.

To finish the flan, sprinkle caster sugar on top and bake in a moderate oven until the top is golden brown and the apple is hot.

When piping the meringue, keep it even and level as any peaks will burn during cooking.

Lemon meringue flan is prepared exactly the same as apple meringue; just replace the apple with lemon filling. Lemon filling is available pre-made or in powdered form, or it can be made from fresh ingredients.

> **Video presentation**
>
> Watch *Finish a flan* to see this being produced. You may also find *Prepare sweet paste (rubbing in method)*; *Line a flan ring*; and *Bake blind* useful.

Lemon filling for lemon meringue flan

Preparation	2
Cooking skills	2
Finishing	–

sugar	120g
water	150ml
lemon juice	60g
cornflour	25g
butter	30g
egg yolks	2

Method

1 Put the sugar and half the water into a pan over a low heat.
2 Dissolve the sugar. Add the lemon juice. Bring to the boil.
3 Dissolve the cornflour in the remaining water to make a **slake**. Add to the water and lemon juice and cook until the mixture thickens.
4 Add the melted butter.
5 Whisk in the egg yolks.
6 Remove from the heat. Pour into a cooked flan case and allow to cool.

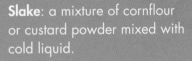

> **Definition**
>
> **Slake:** a mixture of cornflour or custard powder mixed with cold liquid.

Apple flan is a blind-baked sweet paste flan, three-quarters filled with apple purée, topped off with sliced raw apple. Sprinkle with sugar and cook in a moderate oven until the apple slices are cooked and browned. Coat with apricot glaze.

Fruit flans are completed differently from apple flans. First the case is filled with pastry cream and then fruit is overlapped on top to completely cover the pastry cream. It is then coated in apricot glaze to protect the fruit from discoloration.

Pastry cream

Preparation	2
Cooking skills	2
Finishing	–

milk	850ml
vanilla pod	1 (can be replaced with essence or extract)
egg yolks	8
sugar	240g
plain flour	120g

Method

1 Put the milk into a saucepan. Split the vanilla pod and put seeds into the milk, add the pod and infuse over a low heat.
2 Put the egg yolks and sugar into a bowl and whisk together until light.
3 Sift the flour and add to the egg mixture. Mix to a smooth paste.
4 Bring the milk to the boil and remove the pod.
5 Gradually add the milk to the sugar mix and stir well.
6 Put the mixture into a clean pan and bring it back to the boil, stirring continuously.
7 Pour into a clean bowl and cover with a cartouche to prevent skinning. Allow to cool.

These desserts are only a small sample of the vast selection available, but mastering them is the first step to understanding how to produce fantastic hot and cold desserts.

Figure 17.5 Dessert service

Test yourself!

1 What setting agent is used in mousse?

2 What is a sorbetière?

3 True or false? It is safe to re-freeze melted ice cream.

4 Why does milk boil over?

5 How would you prepare the following for a fruit salad:
   a bananas
   b kiwi
   c grapes
   d apples.

6 How can you reduce the risk of overheating the custard mix when making an egg custard-based dessert?

7 What ingredients do you need to make rhubarb crumble?

8 At what temperature should you store ice cream?

18

Prepare and present food for cold presentation

This chapter covers skills and knowledge in the following unit:

- 7132 Unit 250 (2FPC15) Prepare and present food for cold presentation

Working through this chapter could also provide the opportunity to practise the following Functional Skills at Level 2:
Functional ICT – finding and selecting information
Functional Maths Representing – understand, use and calculate ratio and proportion

In this chapter you will:

| Understand how and be able to prepare and present food for cold presentation | 7132 – 250.1,2 |

Cold presentation of food

Cold presentation of food can be as simple as a display of bread for breakfast or as complicated as a plated starter for a banquet. Each is just as important. If food is presented well, it will attract people to eat it.

There is a fine line between making food look appetising and over-garnishing. Garnishing should be used to complement the dish and not to overwhelm it.

Pre-prepared food for cold presentation is generally high-risk food. It must be stored and held for service at the correct temperature otherwise the potential to cause food poisoning is huge.

If the establishment does not have a chilled service area, it is recommended that only products to be served immediately should be on display. Replace with new chilled food items as required.

This will help you to meet the current HACCP guidelines.

The storage temperature should be below 8°C, ideally 5°C. The food should be served at 5°C or below and food should not be on display for longer than four hours. Any high-risk product that has been kept on display for longer than four hours should be disposed of.

Remember!
If you are unsure of the quality of any product, do not use it. Ask your supervisor for advice.

Marcus says
Ensure you are following the food safety guidelines!

Bread products

See Chapter 14 for instructions on how to prepare and bake bread products. Bread displays should have a variety of bread shapes, toppings and types to appeal to the customer.

When displaying different types of bread for cold presentation in the service container, try and achieve different heights and ensure the bread products are the correct way up.

Bread loaves and French sticks can be sliced before being displayed in a service container. To make the slices look more appealing, slice them at a 45° angle using a serrated knife. Make sure the slices are kept even both for portion control and to ensure the most attractive presentation. A serrated knife will cut through the crust without damaging the bread and will help to produce an even slice.

Sandwiches

Sandwiches are a very popular and nutritious cold food. They are enjoyed by lots of people every day, either as a snack or as part of a lunchtime meal. There are hot and cold varieties of sandwiches.

The types of sandwiches include:

o Closed sandwiches
o Open sandwiches
o Wraps and pittas

All of these can be served hot or cold.

Closed sandwiches

A closed sandwich is two slices of bread with a filling between – e.g. meat, vegetables, cheese or jam, together with condiments, sauces or other accompaniments to enhance the flavour and texture. The bread can be used plain, but it is usually spread with butter, oil, mayonnaise or mustard.

It can be sliced bread, or it can be a roll. There are various speciality types of rolls which are used in sandwich making. For example, panini is a small Italian white bread roll, usually long and thin in shape. It would have been traditionally served with dry cured ham, and these days many panini still contain Italian style fillings such as mozzarella cheese and sun dried tomatoes, but the variety of fillings is almost endless. Another example might be a French baguette. Panini and baguettes tend to be reheated rather than toasted. Reheating can be in a microwave or between two griddles or grill bars. Panini are often reheated in this way.

Open sandwiches and toasted products

Open sandwiches use a single piece of bread, traditionally rye bread, with a hot or cold topping. They are usually garnished with various items to enhance their appearance. As with closed sandwiches, the choice of toppings is virtually endless. It is up to the chef to use his or her creative flair to make them appetizing and appealing to customers.

Popular toasted bread products which are not technically open sandwiches but are based on the same principle include cheese on toast, beans on toast, welsh rarebit.

Wraps and pittas

Wraps are becoming very popular these days and can provide a good alternative to filled rolls or sandwiches. The filling is placed inside a wrap such as a tortilla which is then rolled up. Depending on the filling in the wrap, sometimes these are reheated, for example, a chicken or a meat filling.

Pitta bread is a flat bread usually oval in shape. Pittas are cut lengthways down the side and then filled. Fillings can be as numerous and diverse as for sandwiches.

Pittas can be served warm, in which case they are usually split first, filled and then reheated, although they can be reheated first and then filled. Care should be taken when reheating pitta bread as it is very thin and can easily dry out.

Presenting sandwiches

If sandwiches are being presented as part of a finger buffet or an afternoon tea menu, they may have the crusts cut off the bread and be cut into small shaped portions such as triangles, squares, fingers and circles. This makes them more appealing to the eye and also easier to eat. In a buffet you would normally allow one and a half rounds of bread per person, so you need to calculate how many fingers or triangles this is equal to.

Egg mayonnaise	Cream cheese
Ham and tomato	Cucumber
Beef and horseradish	Roast beef and tomato
Smoked salmon	Scrambled egg and bacon
Cheese and pickle	Bacon, lettuce and tomato (BLT)
Tuna and sweetcorn	Curried chicken mayonnaise (Coronation chicken)

Figure 18.3 Some suggested sandwich fillings or toppings for canapes

Figure 18.2 A selection of sandwiches

Did you know?

Open sandwiches are popular in Scandinavian countries such as Denmark, Norway and Sweden, where they are a big feature of the traditional buffets – called 'smorgasbord'.

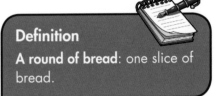

Definition

A round of bread: one slice of bread.

Salads

Salads can be classified as simple or compound salads. Compound salads are any salad containing a mixture of ingredients bound together with a dressing or a sauce, e.g. a **vinaigrette** or **mayonnaise**.

Salads are only limited by your imagination and the ingredients available. They can be served as accompaniments to dishes, the main part of the dish, or as a selection of starters known as **hors d'oeuvres**.

Simple salads (one salad ingredient)

Cucumber salad

1 Check the quality points for cucumbers on page 143.
2 Wash the cucumber, then peel with a vegetable peeler.
3 Next top and tail the cucumber and slice it very thinly and evenly. Use a mandolin to slice it more quickly and easily.
4 Put the slices into a serving dish and decorate the top of the salad with slices of cucumber overlapping each other.
5 Wrap the bowl in cling film and store in the fridge until 15 minutes before service.
6 To serve, dress the salad with vinaigrette dressing and garnish with chopped parsley.

Tomato salad

1 Check the quality points for tomatoes on page 143.
2 Wash the tomatoes and remove the stem.
3 Blanch the tomatoes (see page 150).
4 Peel the skins off.
5 Put the tomato with the stem at 90° to the chopping board and slice thinly with a very sharp knife. Keep the slices in the order you cut them, to enable you to put them back into the tomato shape.
6 Transfer the tomato into a serving dish and fan out slightly but evenly.
7 Dress the sliced tomatoes with vinaigrette then place a fine line of finely chopped shallot onto each tomato. Complete with chopped parsley.

Definition
Vinaigrette: a simple dressing made from mustard, oil and either vinegar or lemon juice.
Mayonnaise: a cold egg-based sauce made from eggs and oil.
Hors d'oeuvre: a savoury appetiser that does not form part of the main meal. They can be served hot or cold.

Chef's tip
If you add the dressing too early the water to come out of the cucumber making it go soggy.

Remember!
A mandolin is a very sharp cutter. The blades can cause serious cuts so the guard must be used to prevent injury.

Capsicum (pepper) and onion salad

This can be made with any single colour capsicum or a mixture.

1 Remove the top of the capsicum and pull out the stalk. Remove the seeds and white pith from inside the capsicum.
2 Cut into quarters. Carefully split each piece into two giving eight pieces, then cut into julienne.
3 Finely shred some onion and mix with the julienne of pepper.
4 Dress with vinaigrette and transfer into a service dish. Sprinkle with chopped parsley.

Beetroot salad

This can be made with pre-cooked pickled beetroot, pre-cooked beetroot or fresh beetroot, which will need cooking.

1 Check the quality of the beetroot.
2 To cook fresh, raw beetroot, wash the beetroot well and put it into a pan of cold salted water. Bring to the boil and simmer until the beetroot is cooked. Test the same as for cooking potatoes.
3 Remove the beetroot from the water and allow it to cool slightly.
4 Peel the beetroot while it is still warm.
5 Slice the beetroot approximately 5mm thick, place into a serving dish and dress with vinaigrette. The beetroot will absorb the flavours from the vinaigrette while it is still warm.
6 Once cool, cover and place into the fridge.
7 To serve, place onion rings onto the top of the salad and garnish with chopped parsley.

Chef's tip
Keep the tops of the capsicums to make stir frys.

French salad

Simple salads can be combined to make this classic salad.

French salad

lettuce, round	3
tomatoes	500g
eggs, boiled	3
cucumber	1
Serves	10

Preparation	1
Cooking skills	1
Finishing	–

Method

1 Check the quality points for the ingredients on pages 143.
2 Prepare the ingredients as follows:
   - lettuce: remove any bruised leaves and discard. Place the lettuce upside down in iced water (this will help crisp the lettuce)
   - tomatoes: blanch, skin and quarter
   - eggs: hard-boil, cool, shell and cut into quarters
   - cucumber: peel and slice.
3 Remove the lettuce from the water and drain well. Put any large outer leaves to one side and remove excess stalk.
4 Cut the lettuce into quarters, and then trim away excess stalk, but keep enough to stop the leaves falling apart.
5 Once the lettuce is drained well, place the large leaves into a salad bowl. Make sure the leaves face upwards.
6 Place the quarters of lettuce around the bowl evenly, and then place slices of cucumber in the centre of the dish.
7 Place tomato quarters next to the lettuce and quartered hard-boiled egg opposite.
8 Once complete, cover and place in the fridge.
9 For service, dress with vinaigrette and chopped parsley.

Compound salads

Coleslaw salad

This is a mixture of white cabbage, onions and carrots bound together with mayonnaise.

Coleslaw

white cabbage	1kg
carrots	150g
onions	75g
mayonnaise	150ml

Preparation	1
Cooking skills	–
Finishing	–

Method

1. Wash the cabbage; remove any bruised outer leaves and discard.
2. Quarter the cabbage and remove the stalk.
3. Finely shred the cabbage.
4. Wash, peel and rewash the carrots. Grate using a medium grater.
5. Peel and shred (or finely chop) the onions.
6. Mix all the ingredients together and season with salt and white pepper.
7. Bind together with mayonnaise just before service. See page 468 for a recipe for mayonnaise.
8. Place into a salad bowl, ready for service.

Russian salad

This is a mixture of different vegetables cut into macedoine or even smaller pieces. They are cooked, cooled and bound with mayonnaise.

Potato salad

This is made of diced potatoes flavoured with finely diced onions. It can be flavoured and garnished with either parsley or chives and bound with mayonnaise.

Chef's tip

Adding salt to the cabbage will soften it and draw out the water, so do not add the seasoning or mayonnaise until ready for service.

Potato salad

Preparation	1
Cooking skills	1
Finishing	1

potatoes	1kg
vinaigrette	100ml
onions, finely diced	75g
mayonnaise	450ml
parsley or chives	to garnish

Method

1 Boil or steam the potatoes in their jackets. Do not overcook. Allow them to cool slightly.
2 Peel and cut the potatoes into 12mm dice.
3 Sprinkle the warm diced potatoes with vinaigrette. Adding the vinaigrette allows the potatoes to absorb the dressing.
4 Add finely diced onion.
5 Bind together with mayonnaise. Do not over-mix or the potatoes will break down.
6 Transfer into a serving dish and garnish with chopped parsley or chives.

Waldorf salad

This is a classic salad. Unlike the other compound salads it is bound with sour cream rather than mayonnaise.

Waldorf salad

Preparation	1
Cooking skills	–
Finishing	–

walnuts	50g
celery	500g
apples (russet)	500g
lemon	½
double cream	125ml

Did you know?
Adding lemon juice to double cream will cause it to thicken. This is called 'acidulated cream'.

Method

1 Chop the walnuts and put them in a small bowl.
2 Wash and peel the celery and then cut into 5mm dice. Put into another bowl.
3 Wash, peel and core the apples, then cut into 5mm dice. Add the apples to the celery. Mix together.
4 Squeeze the lemon juice onto the apple and celery mixture.
5 Add the double cream and the walnuts.
6 Mix to bind together. Season to taste.
7 Put into a serving dish, cover and put into the fridge until ready for service.

Grain salads

Grain salads are extremely easy to make and can be very healthy.
They are also very popular.

Tabbouleh

This is made using bulgar wheat. Bulgar wheat is also known as
cracked wheat and it is made by boiling and drying the wheat grains.
It is used extensively in Middle Eastern cookery. See page 333.

Tabbouleh

Preparation	2
Cooking skills	-
Finishing	2

bulgar wheat	125g
water to cover	250ml
tomatoes, diced	250g
onion, finely diced	125g
mint, finely chopped	1 tbs
fresh parsley, chopped	1 tbs
salt and pepper	to taste
olive oil	50ml
juice of lemons	2
salad onions	4, to garnish
fresh mint leaves	to garnish

Method

1 Cover the bulgar wheat in cold water and soak for
   20 minutes. Drain thoroughly.
2 Add the tomatoes, onion, mint and parsley.
3 Season with salt and pepper, add olive oil and lemon juice,
   and allow to stand to develop the flavours.
4 Garnish with salad onions and fresh mint leaves.

This recipe is very basic and the addition of different herbs and
vegetables can introduce different flavours.

Couscous salad

Couscous is a cereal processed from semolina, rolled into small balls. Couscous does not need to be cooked; it does however need to be soaked. Couscous will absorb its own weight in liquid and the liquid can be used to help flavour it. See page 333 for more information on couscous.

Couscous salad

		Preparation	1
		Cooking skills	1
		Finishing	–

water or stock	300ml
garlic cloves	2
onion, finely diced	125g
couscous	250g
fresh coriander, chopped	a bunch
red capsicum, diced	60g
olive oil	15ml
salt and pepper	to season

Method

1 Put the stock or water into a saucepan and add the garlic cloves and finely diced onion.
2 Warm the stock until it just comes to the boil.
3 Put the couscous into a bowl and cover with the warmed stock/water. Cover and leave to absorb the liquid. (This should take about three minutes.)
4 Add chopped coriander, diced capsicum and olive oil and mix gently.
5 Season with salt and pepper to taste.
6 Allow flavours to infuse. Add more olive oil if required.

This salad can have other ingredients introduced to enhance and offer alternative flavours, e.g. dried fruits such as apricots.

Find out!

Worksheet 51

Find eight different salads from books, the Internet or your local restaurant. Record where the recipes are located and explain why you selected them.

Pre-prepared pies

Pies are a common commodity on buffets. They can vary from a chilled home-made chicken and ham pie or game pie to a simple bought pork pie.

These products are high-risk and must be stored in the fridge at a temperature below 8°C, ideally 5°C before service.

Pies are available in many different flavours and shapes; the garnish should complement the product inside. Your establishment will choose the most appropriate garnish, e.g. vegetables, fruit or herbs.

To serve, portion the pie according to the establishment's requirements. Place only sufficient portions on the service dish to meet the immediate service period.

Cooked red and white meat

Cooked meats can be sliced by hand or by machine.

When slicing meats, keep each slice in the order it is removed. This way the meat can be fanned and the shape of the meat will be uniform and will look more appetising on display.

Meat that is to be used for cold service is normally cooked the day before to allow it to cool and relax. This makes it easier to slice. Chicken, however, is normally cooked on the day, as this helps to retain moisture in the cooked bird.

Examples of meat that can be used for display:

○ **Gammon**: boil, cool, remove the fat, then glaze. The glaze is used to give flavour to the outside of the meat and to make it look more appetising. A popular glaze is brown sugar, honey, cloves and mustard. Gammon is normally served whole with the chef slicing the meat as required. To allow the customer to see the cooked meat, a slice is normally removed and placed onto the tray with the whole gammon. If the surface of the meat dries out, remove another slice and discard the dried piece. This ensures the best-looking meat is displayed to the customer.

> **Remember!**
> If slicing by machine you must be 18 or over and trained to use the equipment. Slicing machines are extremely dangerous.

- **Beef**: this is normally roasted, and can be served whole or pre-sliced.
- **Pork**: this is roasted and served whole or pre-sliced.
- **Chicken**: whole chickens can be roasted and served whole, ready to be carved, or pre-carved to speed up service. Breasts can be poached or even fried.
- **Turkey**: normally served whole and carved in front of the customer. Some establishments will only use the **crown** of the turkey, as most people prefer breast meat.

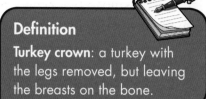

Definition

Turkey crown: a turkey with the legs removed, but leaving the breasts on the bone.

Pre-sliced meat can be displayed on trays. Keep the slices at an equal distance and allow enough space for the customer or serving staff to lift up the edge of one slice of meat for service.

The meat can be sparingly garnished with different things to complement the display. Some examples of garnishes:

- Parsley – chopped, picked.
- Tomatoes – rose, whole, wedges, slices, swans.
- Cucumber – slices, wedges, fans.
- Lettuce – leaves, chiffonade – very finely shredded.
- Fruit – carved, wedges, fans.

Each establishment will have its own preferred garnishes.

A selection of cold sauces can also be served as accompaniments. These are often bought ready-made. Some examples:

- Beef: horseradish sauce, English mustard.
- Pork: apple sauce.
- Chicken: satay, lemon, black bean, barbecue.
- Lamb: mint sauce, redcurrant jelly, cumberland sauce.
- Turkey: cranberry sauce.
- Duck: plum sauce, orange sauce.

Some of these sauces are the classic sauces normally served with hot cooked meat. However, with new tastes and modern trends the number of accompaniments is vast.

Figure 18.4 Cooked meats on display for a buffet

Fish

Fish can be smoked, poached or even fried before being served cold. Smoked trout and herrings are served with horseradish sauce and lemon wedges. Other cold fish can be served with dressings as determined by the establishment. They can be portions of fish or even whole fish, poached and decorated for display.

The skin can be removed to expose the flesh and make the fish look more attractive to the customer.

Examples of fish that can be served cold:
- Salmon: poached whole, darnes, demi-darnes, smoked, normally sliced.
- Trout: smoked or poached.
- Tuna: seared.
- Mackerel: smoked.

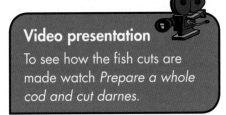

Video presentation
To see how the fish cuts are made watch *Prepare a whole cod and cut darnes.*

 **Find out!**   **Worksheet 52**

Find three more sauces that can be served as an accompaniment to meat and fish.

Pre-prepared terrines

A terrine is made up of different textures of meat, fish or vegetables layered inside a mould, poached, chilled and turned out. During chilling it should set. It can then be sliced and served as a starter or as part of a cold buffet.

A terrine can be served with a sauce to enhance the dish or with salad items to enhance the presentation.

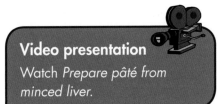

Video presentation
Watch *Prepare pâté from minced liver.*

Figure 18.5 A terrine for buffet service

Pre-prepared pâtés

These are prepared and cooked in the same manner as terrines but are normally smoother. They should be sliced and covered, then stored in the fridge until ready for service.

Pâtés and terrines discolour very quickly, so keep them covered until ready for service.

Cured meats

Cured meats are normally meats that have been salted to preserve the meat or processed to extend the use-by date and introduce different flavours into the meat.

The most well-known type of cured meat is Parma ham, which is cured at Langhirano, near Parma. Only ham cured and processed in this region can be called Parma ham.

Parma ham can be supplied whole, but it is normally supplied in pre-sliced packets with each slice separated by a piece of plastic. This allows the slices to be picked up without tearing the meat.

Some other types of cured hams:
- Bayonne – France
- Bradenham – England
- Seager – England
- Westphalia – Germany
- Serrano – Spain.

These are only a small selection of the hams available. They are all are sliced extremely thin. Because they are sliced very thinly they will dry out very quickly and must be kept covered until service.

Other regions produce cured meats, and a popular one at the moment is chorizo, which is a spicy Spanish sausage made with pork and hot pepper. Some are fresh, but mostly they are dried and smoked. They can be served in cold slices or may be added to cooked dishes.

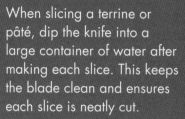

Chef's tip

When slicing a terrine or pâté, dip the knife into a large container of water after making each slice. This keeps the blade clean and ensures each slice is neatly cut.

Shellfish

Some shellfish will be supplied pre-cooked and frozen and will need to be defrosted thoroughly under controlled conditions to prevent food poisoning. Ideally, they should be defrosted in a defrosting cabinet or a fridge. For more information on shellfish, see Chapter 9.

Figure 18.6 Seafood must be kept at the correct temperatures to be safe

Ideally, shellfish should be served on crushed ice to keep them cool. Some will be covered in a sauce, but all must be kept under 8°C until ready for service.

Vinaigrette and cold sauces

Vinaigrette

Vinaigrette is a basic mixture of oil, vinegar and seasoning often called 'French dressing'. It is very easy to make and is used extensively in the cold kitchen.

Basic vinaigrette is one part vinegar to two parts oil, but this ratio can be changed depending on the flavours used.

Video presentation

Make basic vinaigrette shows you just how easy this is to make.

Vinaigrette

		Preparation	1
		Cooking skills	–
		Finishing	–

vinegar	200ml
salt	5g
pepper	pinch
dijon mustard	1tsp
vegetable oil	400ml

Method

1. Put all the ingredients except the oil into a bowl.
2. Add the oil gradually and mix vigourously between each addition.
3. Taste and correct seasoning.
4. Transfer to a bottle for storage.
5. Keep cool and use as required. Shake before use.

Other flavours can be introduced into the basic dressing, e.g. fresh herbs, garlic, mustard and spices.

To change the colour and flavour of the vinaigrette, a proportion of balsamic vinegar can be used or the vinegar can be replaced with red wine vinegar, herb vinegars, white wine vinegar or lemon juice.

The oil can be replaced with olive oil, groundnut oil or even a mixture of vegetable oils.

The range of flavours that can be introduced into the dressing is vast. Make vinaigrette dressings in advance to improve the flavour. They will separate, but shaking them will mix the oil and vinegar again.

Cold sauces

Mayonnaise

Mayonnaise is used a lot in the cold kitchen. It can be mixed with other ingredients to make different sauces. It is unlikely that mayonnaise will be made freshly in many establishments because eggs can be problematic.

However, having an understanding of how mayonnaise is made will make sure the sauce is kept and used correctly.

For a successful mayonnaise all the ingredients should be at the same temperature. If the oil is slightly warm it will be clear rather than cloudy. This means the mayonnaise will be less likely to **curdle**.

> **Definition**
> **Curdle**: when food particles separate into curds or lumps.

> **Video presentation**
> Watch *Make mayonnaise* and then *Recover curdled mayonnaise* to see what to do if it goes wrong.

> **Chef's tip**
> To recover curdled mayonnaise, put a tablespoon of warm water into a bowl and slowly add the curdled mixture and whisk well. Alternatively, you can add another egg yolk, but this will make the sauce thicker and it will taste more of egg.

Mayonnaise

salt	pinch
pepper	pinch
mustard	1tsp
egg yolks	3
vinegar	1tbsp
vegetable oil	300ml

Preparation	3
Cooking skills	–
Finishing	–

Method

1 Put the salt, pepper, mustard, egg yolk and vinegar into a glass or stainless steel bowl.
2 Whisk together until light and the egg yolks are slightly thickened.
3 Very slowly add the oil and whisk well. The mixture will curdle if the oil is added too quickly.
4 Cover and store in the fridge.
5 Before use allow the mayonnaise to slowly come to room temperature before stirring. If you do not do this it will separate.

The diagram below shows some sauces that can be made using mayonnaise.

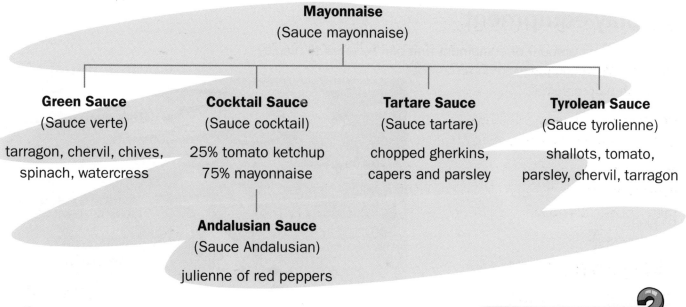

Mayonnaise
(Sauce mayonnaise)

Green Sauce
(Sauce verte)

tarragon, chervil, chives, spinach, watercress

Cocktail Sauce
(Sauce cocktail)

25% tomato ketchup 75% mayonnaise

Tartare Sauce
(Sauce tartare)

chopped gherkins, capers and parsley

Tyrolean Sauce
(Sauce tyrolienne)

shallots, tomato, parsley, chervil, tarragon

Andalusian Sauce
(Sauce Andalusian)

julienne of red peppers

Figure 18.7 Mayonnaise-based sauces

These sauces are basic and form a basis for learning about how different cold sauces can be produced.

Serve cold sauces separately – unless they are used to bind. Place the sauce close to the food item it is intended for.

Did you know?
Cocktail sauce is also called 'marie rose'.

Did you know?
If you add unwashed chopped parsley to a sauce the chlorophyll in the parsley will turn the sauce green.

Display and service

Display equipment

There is a vast amount of equipment that can be used to display cold food. This includes:

- slates
- mirrors
- tiles
- platters
- stainless steel trays
- crockery
- glass
- baskets
- chilled display cabinets.

Make sure they are clean before use.

Figure 18.8 Many different types of equipment can be used to display food

Service

When setting out a buffet for service, the following points need to be taken into consideration:

- **The type of service, waiting staff or self-service**: the type of service will affect portion control. If waiting staff are serving there is a greater level of control. If it is self-service, more food may be required as there is less control. To help with portion control when the food is being self-served, use serving spoons which are smaller than kitchen spoons and reduce the number of portions in the serving dish.
- **Number of covers**: the number of covers is very important to make sure there is sufficient food to feed all the guests. It can also determine the number of service points and how many of each item needs to be dressed ready for service.
- **Length of service**: the length of service can be important to determine how many service points and what type of service is required. For example, if 120 people are to be fed in an hour, how many service points will be needed to ensure all customers are fed?
- **Location**: the location of the buffet is important to ensure it is easy to replace any items that run out.

Find out! Worksheet 53

Choose four items that could be used to display cold food. Write about why you chose them and describe how they could be used.

- **Flow of customers**: it is important to ensure the customers can collect their plates and leave the service area in one direction. When placing food items in the direction of the customer, face the presentation side of the food item in the direction the customers are coming from.
- **Height**: when placing food items onto the service area, try to use different heights. This allows more food to be placed onto the service area and also provides a nicer-looking buffet.
- **Colour**: try not to mix too many of the same colours next to each other when placing items on the service area.
- **Texture**: try not to place the same food items next to each other. Look at the type of dressings and the type of food.
- **Type of buffet**: the type of buffet could include a hot section, uses chafing dishes to keep the food hot. You need to think about how dishes will impact on the service area and consider whether or not a separate area is needed.
- **Time of year**: the time of year will impact on the food choice customers make. In the summer more people are likely to go for the cold buffet, whereas in the winter more people are likely to choose the hot buffet.

Figure 18.9 An attractive buffet

Try this!   Worksheet 54

List five establishments where cold food is on display for consumption. Say why you chose the place and what you liked about the display.

Try this!   Worksheet 55

See how many of the salad-related words you can find in the wordsearch.

471

Test yourself!

1 What is the purpose of garnishing?

2 Name two simple salads and two combination salads.

3 What are the ingredients of a Waldorf Salad?

4 What ingredients make a popular glaze for gammon?

5 Pre-prepared pies are high-risk products. At what temperature should they be stored?

6 What is a terrine?

7 What is the difference between a pâté and a terrine?

8 Ideally, what should shellfish be served on?
   a Absorbent paper
   b Salad leaves
   c Lemon juice
   d Crushed ice.

9 Which of the following would you serve with beef?
   a Cranberry sauce
   b Apple sauce
   c English mustard
   d Mint sauce.

10 Which of the following would you serve with chicken?
   a Satay sauce
   b Cranberry sauce
   c Plum sauce
   d Redcurrant jelly.

11 Write down three sauces that can be made using mayonnaise.

12 Write down five pieces of equipment that can be used to display cold food.

13 There are ten points you must consider when setting out a buffet for service. Write down five of them and say why they are important.

Glossary

Acidulated water: water with lemon juice added to it.

Aerate: to introduce air into a mixture or liquid, making the texture lighter.

Alkaline: a chemical substance that is not acidic.

Appraisal: an assessment of performance providing feedback.

Aromatic: having a pleasant smell. Aromatic ingredients such as leaves, flowers, seeds, fruits, stems and roots are used for their fragrance to enhance flavour of stocks.

Bacterium: a single bacteria, which is a single-celled organism.

Bard: to place strips of fat onto or around a piece of meat while it cooks to slowly release juices over the meat. Mainly used for meat that has little fat.

Baste: to moisten with liquid, fat, gravy etc.

Baton: a cut of vegetable evenly sized 2.5cm long × 0.5cm × 0.5cm.

Bed of root: chopped root vegetables which act as a base to put a bird on to prevent it sticking to and burning on the tray.

Beurre manie: equal quantities of plain flour and butter mixed together to form a paste and added to a boiling liquid in small quantities as a thickening agent.

Bisque: a shellfish soup where the shellfish is puréed to add flavour.

Blend: to mix two or more ingredients together in the food processor or liquidiser.

Blind bake: to cook a flan case without the filling in it. The flan is lined with greaseproof paper (cartouche) and filled with baking beans. The beans help to keep the shape of the pastry during cooking.

Boning: to remove the bones from a joint of meat or poultry.

Borsch: a traditional Russian soup made with beetroot.

Bran: the hard outer layer of a rice seed or grain.

Brioche: yeast dough that has been enriched with eggs and butter. It is similar to croissants.

Carcass: the dead body of an animal.

Cartouche: a round piece of greaseproof paper used to line or cover.

Castrated: testes removed before sexual maturity.

Caustic: a substance that will stick to a surface and burn chemically. It is used for heavy duty cleaning.

Cavity: the hollow space left inside a bird once all the innards have been removed.

Chantilly cream: cream that has been sweetened, flavoured and lightly whipped.

Char: to use the hot bars on a griddle to darken or pattern an item of food (e.g. meat, fish or vegetables) as it is cooking.

Clarify: to purify stocks, making the cloudy liquid clear using egg whites and albumen from the minced lean shin of beef.

Concassées: finely diced skinned tomato flesh (seeds and juice removed).

Condensation: a coating of tiny drops formed on the surface by steam or vapour.

Couscousier: a tall pot where stews or vegetables are cooked in the bottom and a smaller pot sits above with the couscous in it. The couscous cooks by steaming and absorbs the flavour from the meat or vegetables below it.

Crêpes: the French term for pancakes. Crêpes need to be as thin as possible.

Crimp: To give a decorative edge to pastry using forefinger and thumb or specialist tools.

Cross-contamination: the transfer of harmful bacteria from one food source to another by the food handler using the same equipment for different tasks, not cleaning their tools properly or not washing their hands before handling another food type.

Croûtes: sliced bread flutes toasted or evenly baked in the oven to a golden brown colour.

Croutons: 1cm cubes of white bread, shallow-fried to a golden brown colour in clarified butter.

Crustaceans: soft-bodied creatures with legs (and sometimes claws), whose exterior is a hard shell, e.g. crab.

Cull: to kill an animal.

Curdle: when food particles separate into curds or lumps.

Dariole mould: a small mould shaped like a flower pot.

Deglaze: to add wine or stock to a pan used for frying in order to lift the remaining sediment to make a sauce or gravy.

Degraisse: the liquid fat which is removed from the surface of simmering stock using a ladle by the process of skimming.

Demi-glaze: a sauce which is made up of equal quantities of brown stock and brown sauce (espagnole sauce), reduced by a third until the consistency coats the back of a spoon.

Dilute: to add extra liquid (usually water) to make the solution weaker.

Docker: a tool that has spikes that can be used to add decoration to products before cooking and to put holes into flan cases and puff pastry goods to prevent them rising during baking.

Document: make a detailed record of information.

Dormant: not active or growing.

Dough improver: adding ascorbic acid (vitamin C) assists the gluten development and can speed up the process of fermentation.

Dredge: to sprinkle or coat food with flour and sugar to enhance presentation.

Dressed: birds that have been cleaned, plucked and trussed.

Dry method: a dish which is cooked using a dry method of cookery e.g. roasting, grilling.

Duchesse potatoes: mashed potato piped onto trays and then grilled before service.

Due diligence: when every possible precaution has been taken by the business to avoid a food safety problem.

Duxelle: a ravioli filling made up of very finely diced shallots, mushrooms or other vegetables, sautéed together in a little butter, cooked and dried out using breadcrumbs. It is a quick and cheap filling. Cuttings and stalks from mushrooms can be used.

Escalopes: large slices of meat cut from the leg of pork or veal, or the breast of poultry such as turkey. An escalope is batted to flatten it before cooking. Because they are very thin, escalopes cook quickly.

Excrement: solid waste matter passed out through the bowel.

External boning: to remove bones by cutting through the skin to expose the flesh and bone, and then to cut away the bone from the meat.

Faeces: solid waste matter from the body.

Fines herbes: a mixture of aromatic herbs such as chervil, tarragon, chives and parsley.

Finger stall: a plastic tube that fits over a dressing (bandage or plaster) on an injured finger to protect it. It is secured by an elastic strap around the wrist.

Flambé: a French term used to describe cooking at the table in the restaurant and setting fire to the dish using alcohol to give a few seconds of flame.

Fricassee: a light, reduced meat stew bound with a liaison of cream and egg yolks.

Garnish: to add the final touches required to enhance a dish.

Germ: the heart of the rice seed or grain.

Gluten: a protein found in flour which gives it its strength. The strength of the gluten is determined by the type of wheat and when and where it is grown.

Hazard: something which could be dangerous.

Hors d'oeuvres: savoury appetizers that can be served hot or cold.

Hydrogenation: an industrial process in which oil is heated to a high temperature (260–270°C) to combine it with hydrogen. The liquid oil is converted to solid or semi-solid fat.

Immerse: to cover something completely in liquid.

Inedible: unable to be eaten.

Infuse: to soak something in liquid so that the liquid will take on its flavour.

Jointed: cuts of poultry removed from the carcass during preparation, e.g. legs and breasts.

Knead: to prepare dough by pressing it to assist the development of the gluten and to ensure the yeast is distributed throughout the dough.

Lamination: forming layers of fat in pastry to create texture and lift the pastry as it cooks.

Liaison: this is used to bind or thicken a sauce and is often based on egg yolks and cream.

Liquidise: to mix two or more ingredients together in the food processor or liquidiser.

Lost property: an item left behind by somebody else.

Mayonnaise: a cold egg-based sauce made from eggs and oil.

Micro-organism: a very small life form which cannot be seen without a microscope.

Mise en place: having all equipment and ingredients ready prior to starting a task.

Molasses: a dark, thick brown liquid obtained from raw sugar during the refining process. It is used to make syrup, e.g. golden syrup and black treacle.

Molluscs: soft-bodied creatures contained in a hard shell.

Napper: a French term meaning to coat or mask a tray of food.

Organism: any living animal or plant.

Oxidize: a chemical reaction when oxygen causes the surface of the dough to dry out.

Panade: a paste of flour, butter and a little liquid.

Pass: to separate food from marinade, water or cooking liquor using a strainer, colander or sieve.

Pasteurisation: a method of heat-treating milk to a high temperature for a short period of time to kill any pathogenic bacteria. This makes it safe for humans to consume without spoiling its taste or appearance.

Pasteurised: has been heat treated.

Pathogen: an organism that causes diseases.

Paysanne: a small cut of vegetable in a variety of shapes such as triangles, squares, circles and oblongs.

Pectin: a natural setting agent found in fruit.

Plankton: a layer of tiny plants and animals living just below the surface of the sea.

Pluck: to remove the feathers from a game bird, either by hand or machine.

Portion: to cut meat or other food items into the correct size for it to be served. The correct size depends on the dish.

Prove: to allow the yeast to develop carbon dioxide in the dough to make it rise before baking.

Prover: a cabinet that creates heat and moisture, helping dough products to rise evenly and assists in preventing products from drying out and skinning.

Quark: a German cheese with the texture and flavour of soured cream.

Reduce: to boil a liquid rapidly until it reduces in volume.

Residue: the content left in the pan once the food, e.g. poultry, has been cooked or sealed, including liquid and solid materials which all contain intense flavours which enhance a dish.

Round of bread: one slice of bread.

Sauté: to cook meat, fish or vegetables in fat until brown using a sturdy frying pan.

Scale: to cut and weigh dough into the required size, e.g. for bread rolls scale dough into 60g pieces.

Sealing: lightly cooking meat on all sides in order to seal in the flavour and juices and add colour. It is usually done prior to putting the meat in a stew or braised dish.

Sear: to use the hot bars on a griddle to darken or pattern an item of food (e.g. meat, fish or vegetables) as it is cooking.

Skim: to remove impurities from the surface of a simmering liquid with a ladle or similar equipment.

Skin: to remove the fur or skin from an animal in preparation for use in cooking.

Skinning: when dough is left uncovered and the surface of the dough starts to dry out and oxidise, it forms a skin. If this is then mixed into the dough it will leave dry pieces of dough in the finished product.

Slake: a mixture of cornflour or custard powder mixed with cold liquid.

Slaughter: to kill an animal for food.

Smoulder: to burn slowly with a small red glow and little smoke.

Spores: cells produced by bacteria and fungi.

Stiff peak: when the peaks of the whipped egg white stand up without falling to one side. The final test is to turn the bowl upside down to see if the white drops out.

Strain: to separate food from marinade, water or cooking liquor using a strainer, colander or sieve.

Swab: a sterile piece of cotton used to take a sample for analysis.

Toxin: a poison produced by bacteria.

Truss: a method of securing a bird in an appropriate shape during the cooking process. One or two pieces of string or twine are threaded through the body of a game bird or poultry using a trussing needle, then tied.

Tunnel boning: removing the bones without breaking the skin of a bird.

Turkey crown: a turkey with the legs removed but leaving the breasts on the bone.

Unpasteurised: has not been heat treated.

Vegan: a person who does not eat or use products that come from animals.

Velouté: a stock-based white sauce that is thickened with a blond roux.

Vinaigrette: a simple dressing made from mustard, oil and either vinegar or lemon juice.

Wet method: a dish which is cooked and served in a liquid.

Wooden mushroom: a piece of equipment used to press the solid cooked food ingredients through a sieve to make a purée.

Zest: the outer coloured part of the peel of the lemon or other citrus fruit. It is often used as a flavouring.

Index

Recipe index

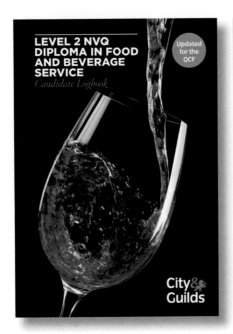
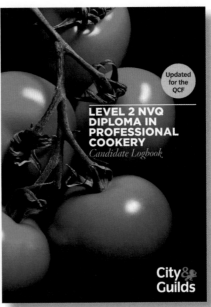